Kazunari Kakei

I want to thank everyone who's sent me fan mail! Some people send me a letter every month, and sometimes I receive fan art and homemade items. I respond to as many people as I can, but I can't cover everybody who writes to me. I want to apologize for that.

NORA: The Last Chronicle of Devildom is Kazunari Kakei's first manga series. It debuted in the April 2004 issue of *Monthly Shonen Jump* and eventually spawned a second series, *SUREBREC: NORA the 2nd*, which premiered in *Monthly Shonen Jump*'s March 2007 issue.

NORA

THE LAST CHRONICLE OF DEVILDOM

VOL. 8

SHONEN JUMP ADVANCED
Manga Edition

STORY AND ART BY
KAZUNARI KAKEI

English Adaptation/Park Cooper & Barb Lien-Cooper
Translation/Nori Minami
Touch-up Art & Lettering/Annaliese Christman
Design/Sam Elzway
Editor/Shaenon K. Garrity

VP, Production/Alvin Lu
VP, Sales & Product Marketing/Gonzalo Ferreyra
VP, Creative/Linda Espinosa
Publisher/Hyoe Narita

NORA - THE LAST CHRONICLE OF THE DEVILDOM © 2004
by Kazunari Kakei. All rights reserved.
First published in Japan in 2004 by SHUEISHA Inc., Tokyo.
English translation rights arranged by SHUEISHA Inc.

The stories, characters and incidents mentioned
in this publication are entirely fictional.

Printed in the U.S.A.

Published by VIZ Media, LLC
P.O. Box 77010
San Francisco, CA 94107

10 9 8 7 6 5 4 3 2 1
First printing, December 2009

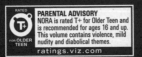

SHONEN JUMP ADVANCED
Manga Edition

NORA

THE LAST CHRONICLE OF DEVILDOM

Volume 8:
The Shout of the Soul

Kazunari Kakei

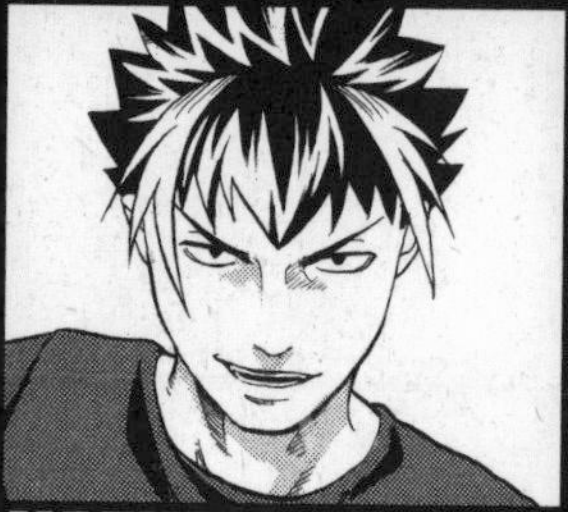

KAZUMA (KAZUMA MAGARI)

KAZUMA SEEMS TO HAVE IT ALL. HE'S THE PRESIDENT OF THE STUDENT COUNCIL AS WELL AS A CLEVER GUY WHO'S GOOD AT SPORTS. HE'S ALSO NORA'S MASTER. DESPITE SEEMING CALM AND COMPOSED, KAZUMA'S GOT QUITE A TEMPER. AS A RESULT, OTHER STUDENTS FEAR HIM. VERDICT: HE'S MORE DEVILISH THAN ANY DEMON.

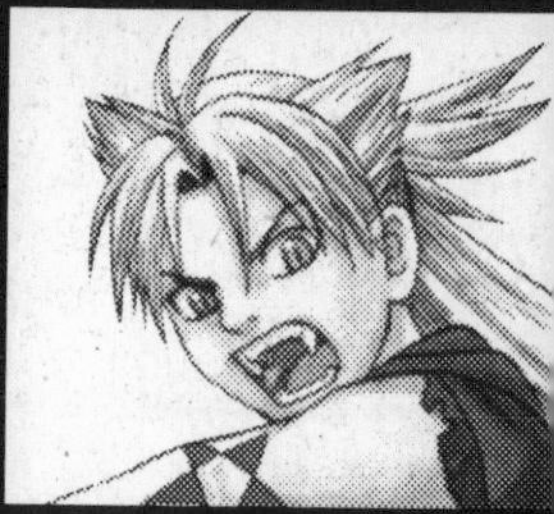

NORA

THE DEMON WORLD'S PROBLEM CHILD, NORA'S FOUL TEMPER IS SURPASSED ONLY BY HIS STUPID NORA IS BETTER KNOWN AS THE VICIOUS DOG OF DISASTER, THE LEGENDARY DEMON CERBERUS HIS POWER IS SAID TO SURPASS THAT OF THE DARK LIEGE HERS

DARK LIEGE A

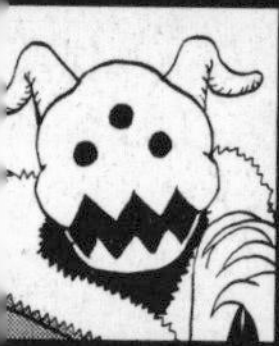

HER INFERNAL MAJESTY, THE DARK LIEGE

THE COMMANDER IN CHIEF OF THE DARK LIEGE ARMY AS WELL AS THE ONE WHO EXILED NORA TO THE HUMAN WORLD. WHEN SHE WEARS HER GLAMOUR SPELL, SHE'S ONE SMOKIN' HOTTIE.

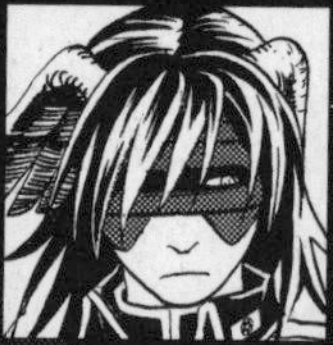

KAIN

A GOVERNOR-GE AIDE AND RIGHT- MAN TO THE DAR IN ADDITION TO B COMMANDER, HE DARK LIEGE'S MO TRUSTED CONFID

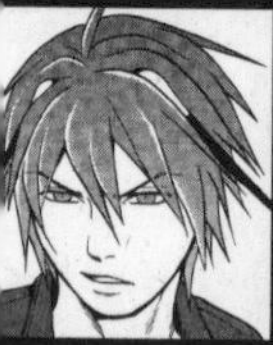

NAVAL FLEET GENERAL RIVAN

LAID BACK AND SEEMINGLY LAZY, ONCE RIVAN SNAPS, NOBODY CAN HOLD HIM DOWN. HE'S INTO FISHING.

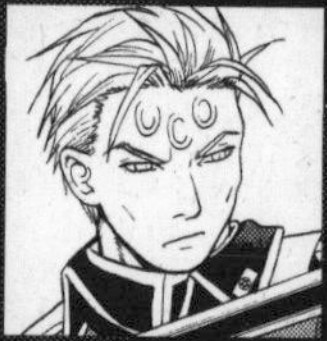

LAND CORPS GENER LEONARD

THE DEMON WO NUMBER ONE G GUY. DEDICATE SERIOUS, LEON ALWAYS WORRY LEADING TO ST RELATED MALA

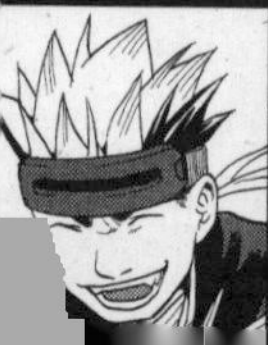

WIND DIVISION GENERAL BAJEE

THE WIND DIVISION GENERAL AND THE STRONGEST, TOUGHEST SON OF A GUN IN THE DARK LIEGE ARMY. HE COMES OFF AS A BIT OF A JERK, BUT A FUN ONE. HE'S LIKE

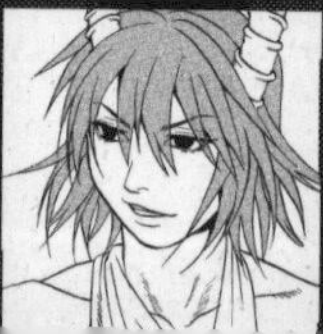

FIRE BRIGADE GENE MELFIA

DESPITE HER TO GIRL LOOKS, SHE CANNY FIGHTER W USES HER BRAINS THAN HER FISTS. TRAINED KAZUMA CONTROL HIS MA

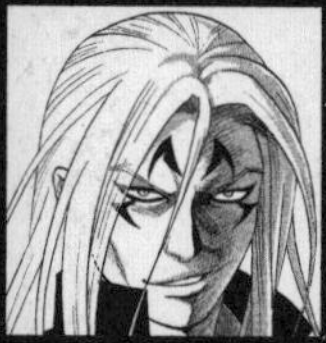

FALL

A MEMBER OF THE PREVIOUS GENERATION OF ANCIENT RACES, FALL IS THE FOUNDER AND HEAD OF THE RESISTANCE. HIS MISSION: DESTROY BOTH THE DEMON WORLD AND THE HUMAN WORLD. WHY? HE HAS... ISSUES.

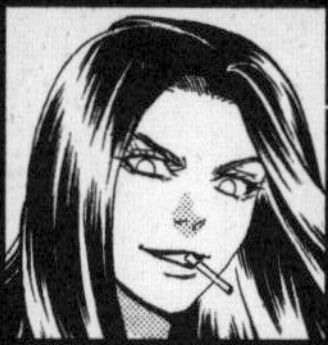

DEUCE

FALL'S CLOSEST ALLY. SHE'S OBSESSED WITH WEEDING OUT THE WEAK.

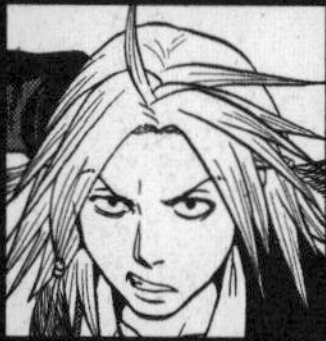

NICKS

ANOTHER BIGWIG IN THE RESISTANCE. ALTHOUGH HE POSSESSES POWERFUL ABILITIES, HE'S OFTEN HESITANT TO FIGHT.

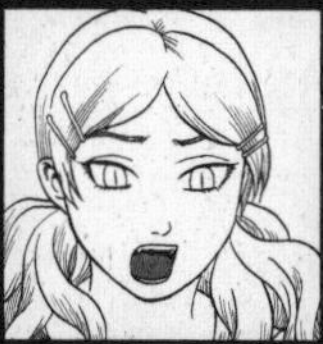

KEINI

ALTHOUGH SHE SELDOM LEAPS INTO THE FRAY, KEINI'S A TERROR WHEN SHE'S MIFFED. SHE ALSO SEEMS TO HAVE A THING FOR HER BOSS.

TENRYO ACADEMY MIDDLE SCHOOL, STUDENT COUNCIL

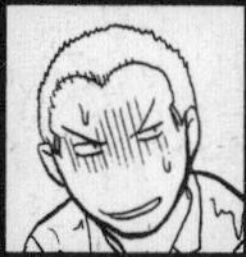

FUJIMOTO

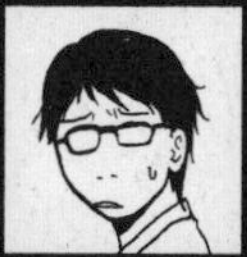

YANO

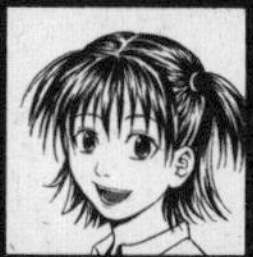

KOYUKI HIRASAKA

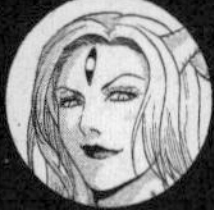

LISTEN TO TEACHER! ♥
THE DARK LIEGE EXPLAINS IT ALL

HELLO SWEETIE PIES! IT'S THE DEMON WORLD'S DARLING AGAIN: ME! ♥

FOR THOSE WHO'VE JUST ARRIVED... GOSH, MY LITTLE DEMON PUP NORA HAS BEEN A BOTHER! DON'T I HAVE ENOUGH TROUBLE WITH THE RESISTANCE AND OUTLAW DEMONS REBELLING AGAINST MY DARK LIEGE ARMY WITHOUT NORA CAUSING ME PROBLEMS?

BECAUSE I'M AS CLEVER AS I AM HOT, I SENT MY STRAY DOG TO THE HUMAN WORLD. HE WOULDN'T BE LONELY—I GAVE HIM A MASTER, AFTER ALL. I PUT THAT DEVIOUS SCHOOLBOY KAZUMA MAGARI IN CHARGE OF NORA'S OBEDIENCE TRAINING AND TOLD NORA TO TAKE CARE OF THE OUTLAW DEMONS FOR ME. IT KILLED TWO BIRDS WITH ONE STONE! AREN'T I A GENIUS??

BY ENTERING INTO A MASTER AND SERVANT CONTRACT WITH KAZUMA, NORA BECAME KAZUMA'S "FAMILIAR SPIRIT." AS SUCH, NORA CAN'T USE HIS MAGIC OR RELEASE HIS SEAL SPELL TO RETURN TO HIS TRUE FORM WITHOUT HIS MASTER'S "APPROVAL."

AFTER THE TWO LEARNED THE TRUE ORIGIN AND PURPOSE OF THE CERBERUS, THEY HIGH TAILED IT OVER TO MY HEADQUARTERS TO GET ANSWERS. MEANWHILE, THE RESISTANCE SUDDENLY ATTACKED! TALK ABOUT BAD TIMING! I WAS FORCED TO FIGHT THEIR MASTERMIND, FALL. HE SURPASSED MY POWER AS DARK LIEGE... BELIEVE IT OR NOT. OH, WELL... AT LEAST I'M CUTER! MEANWHILE, NORA AND KAZUMA ARRIVED ON THE SCENE AND FOUGHT FALL'S SIDEKICK DEUCE. WHEN NORA LET HIS GUARD DOWN, SNAKES UNLEASHED BY DEUCE PIERCED HIS BODY! WHAT NEXT? WELL, A GIRL'S GOT TO HAVE HER SECRETS...

NORA
THE LAST CHRONICLE OF DEVILDOM

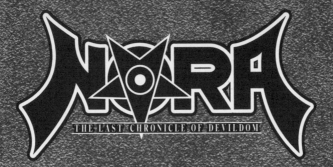

CONTENTS

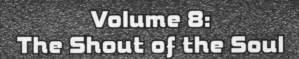

Volume 8:
The Shout of the Soul

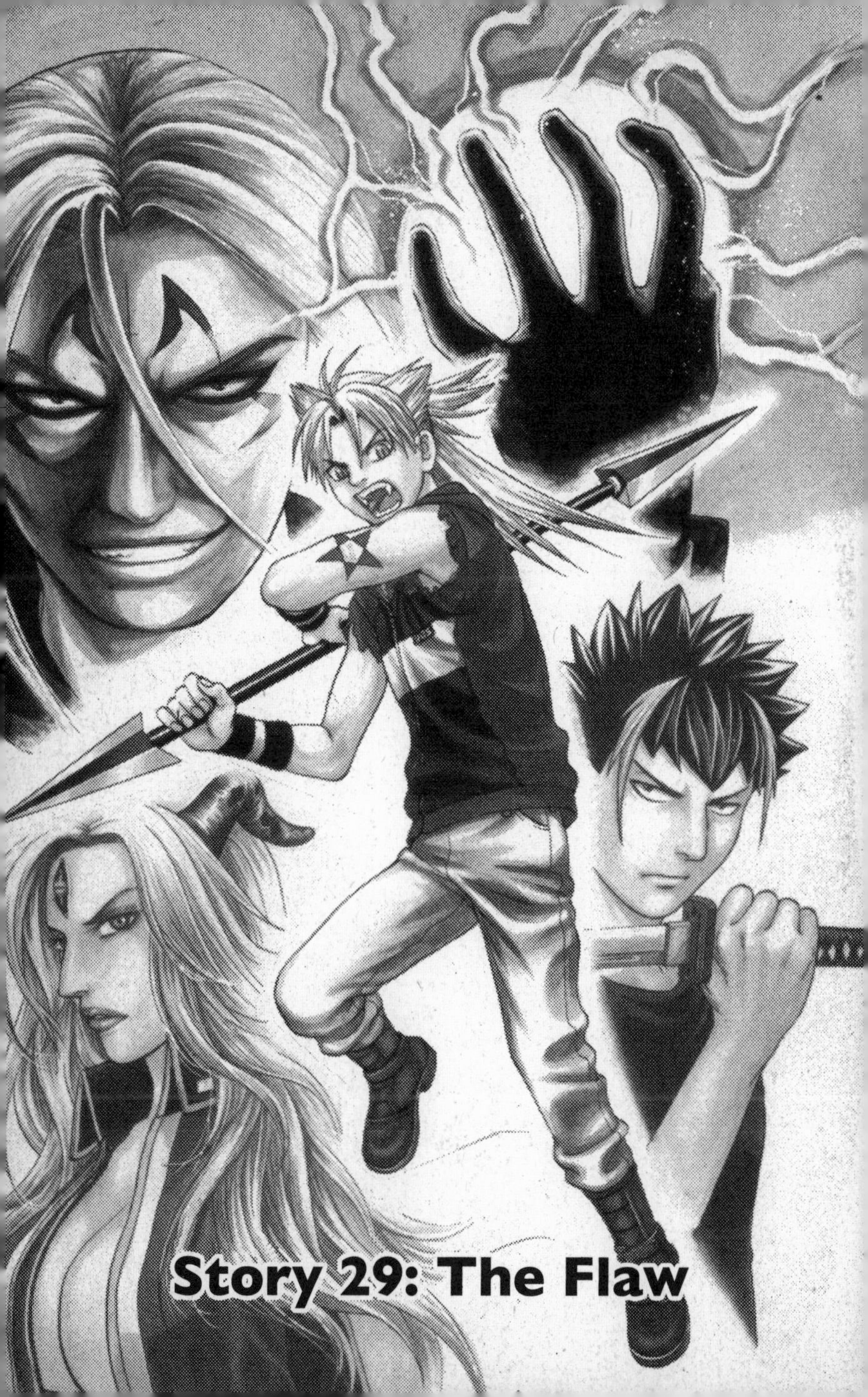
Story 29: The Flaw

READ THIS WAY

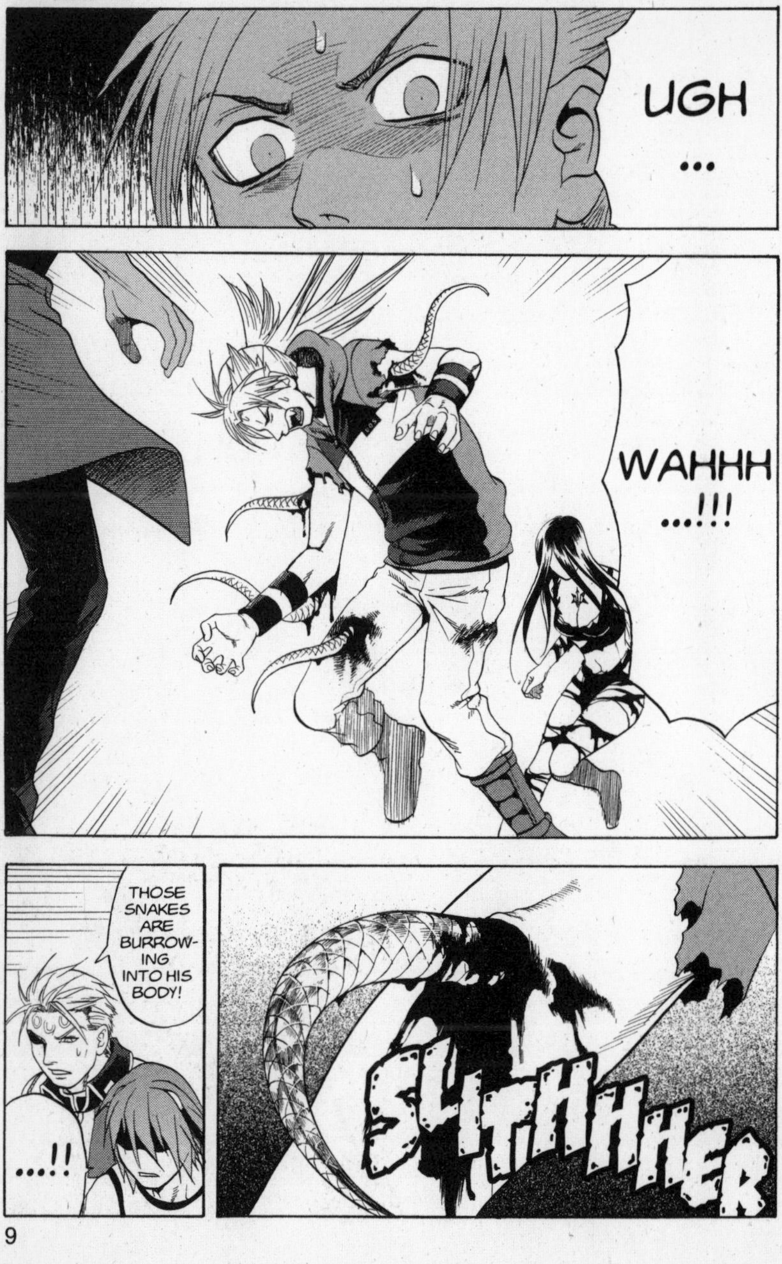
UGH ...
WAHHH ...!!!
SLITHHHER
THOSE SNAKES ARE BURROWING INTO HIS BODY!
...!!

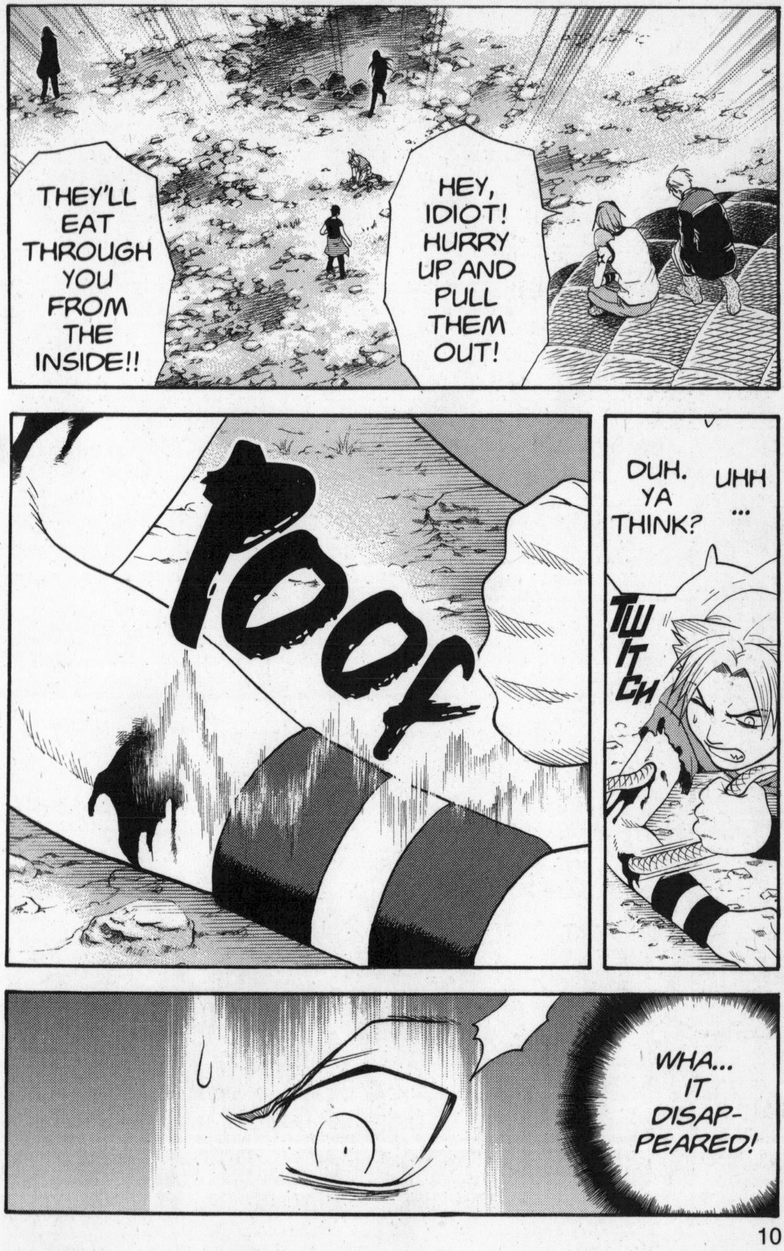
HEY, IDIOT! HURRY UP AND PULL THEM OUT!
THEY'LL EAT THROUGH YOU FROM THE INSIDE!!
UHH ...
DUH. YA THINK?
TWITCH
POOF
WHA... IT DISAP-PEARED!

READ THIS WAY

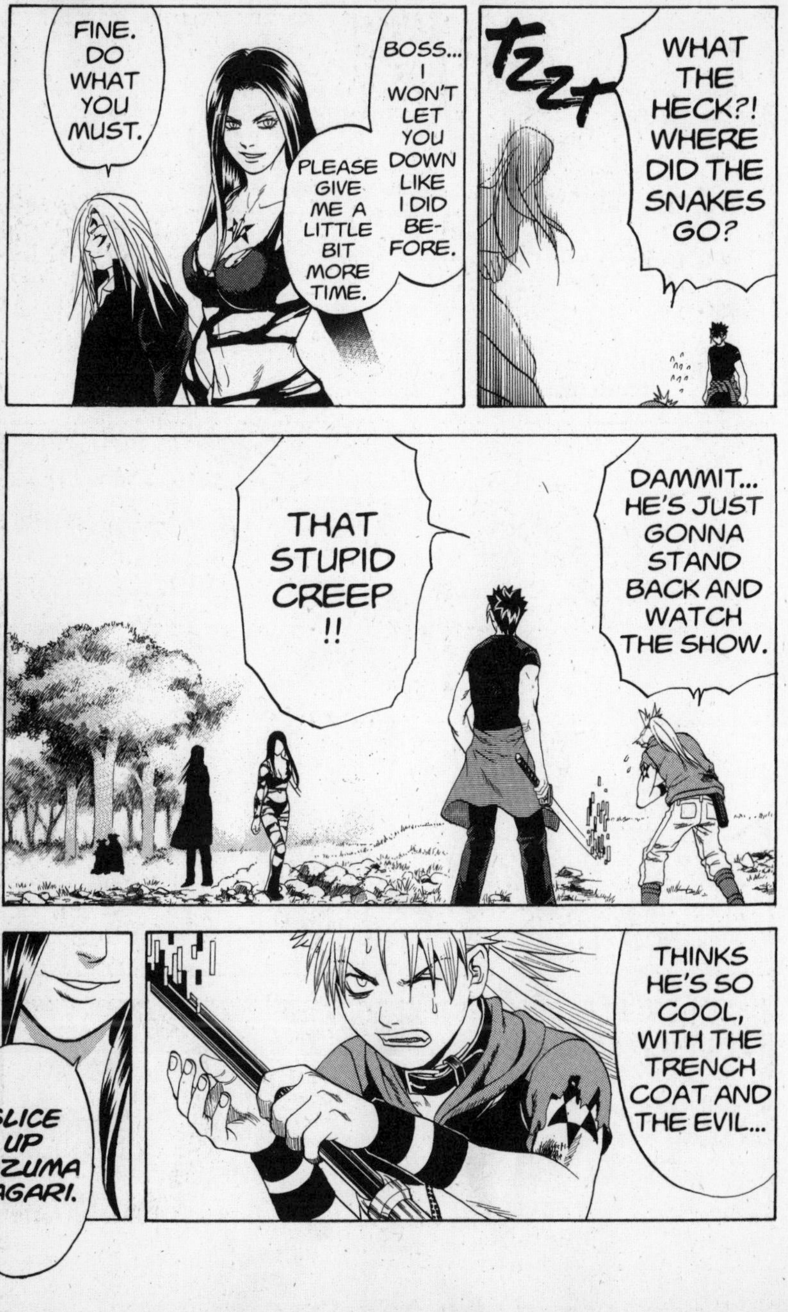
WHAT THE HECK?! WHERE DID THE SNAKES GO?
TZZT
BOSS... I WON'T LET YOU DOWN LIKE I DID BEFORE.
PLEASE GIVE ME A LITTLE BIT MORE TIME.
FINE. DO WHAT YOU MUST.
DAMMIT... HE'S JUST GONNA STAND BACK AND WATCH THE SHOW.
THAT STUPID CREEP!!
THINKS HE'S SO COOL, WITH THE TRENCH COAT AND THE EVIL...
SLICE UP KAZUMA MAGARI.

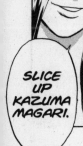

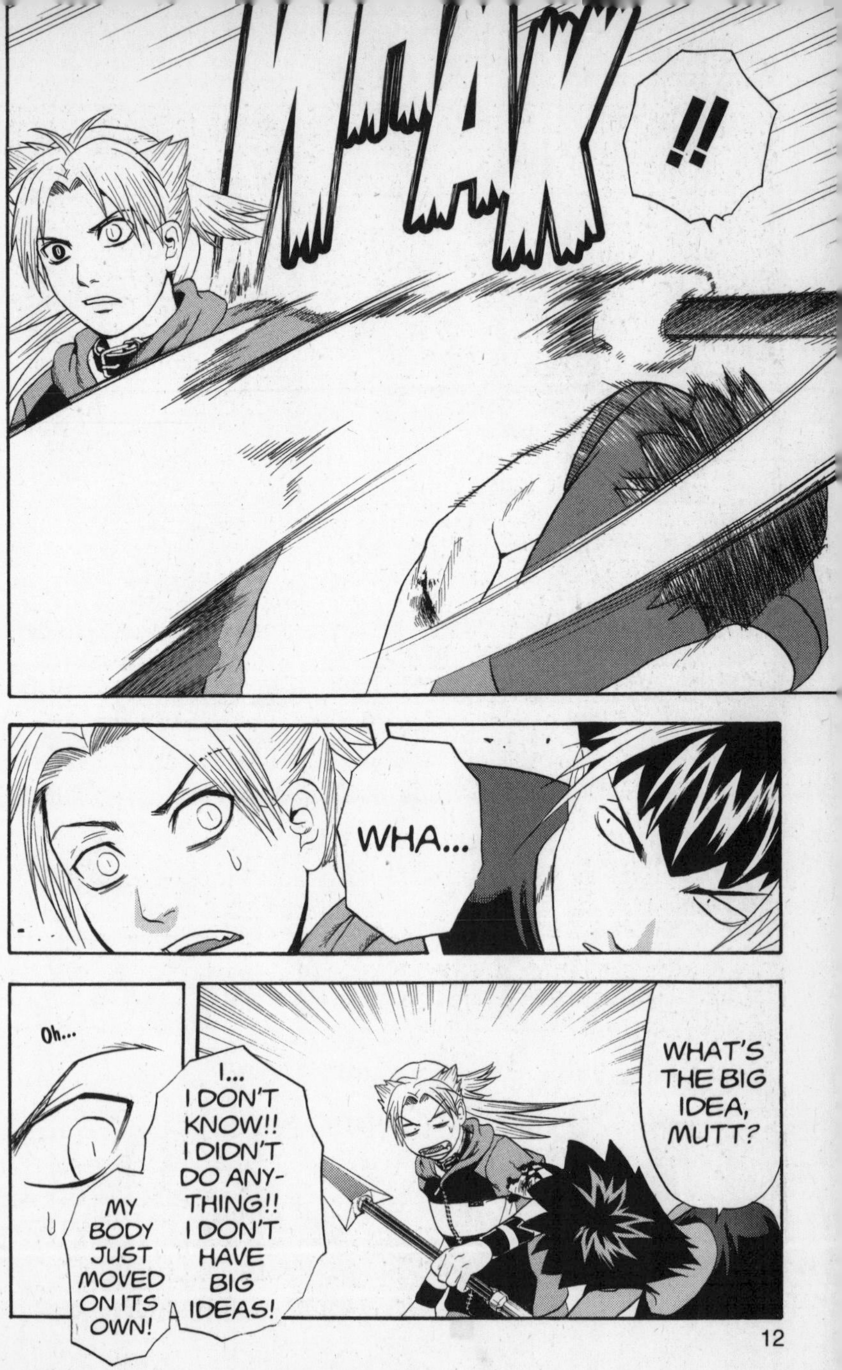
WHAK
!!
WHA...
WHAT'S THE BIG IDEA, MUTT?
I... I DON'T KNOW!! I DIDN'T DO ANY-THING!! I DON'T HAVE BIG IDEAS!
MY BODY JUST MOVED ON ITS OWN!
Oh...

READ THIS WAY

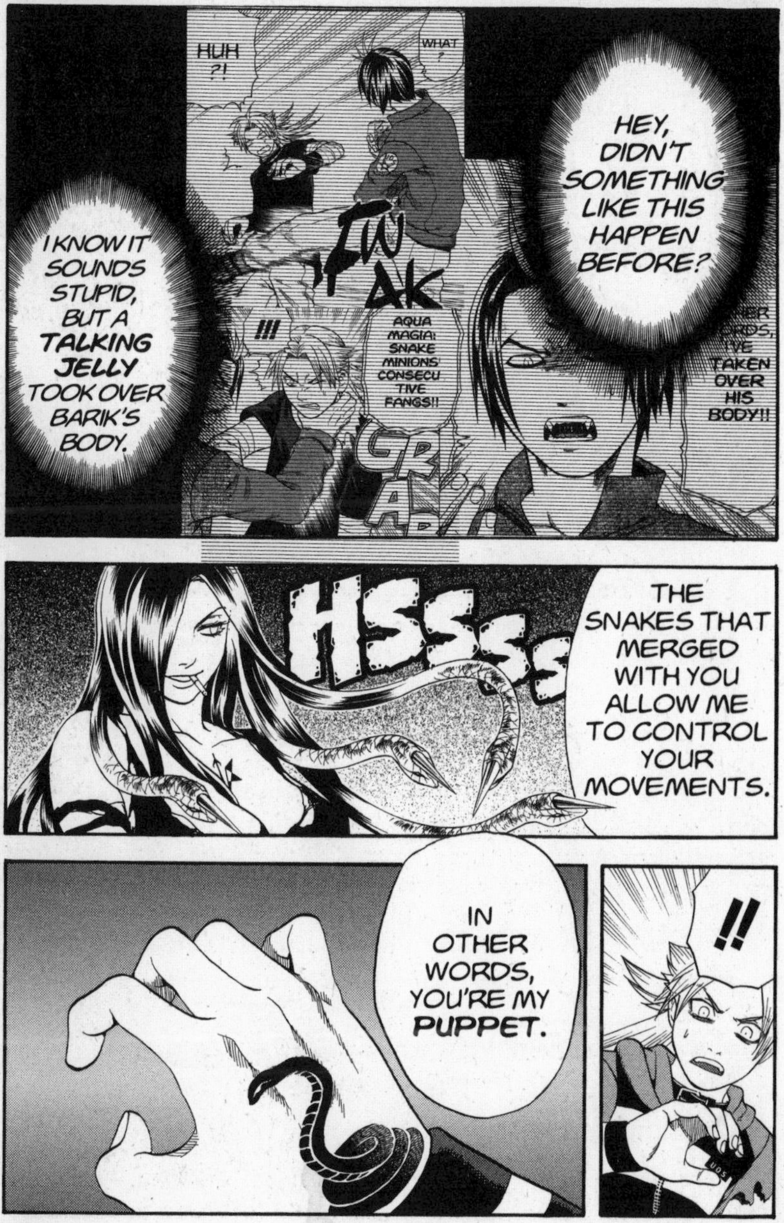
HEY, DIDN'T SOMETHING LIKE THIS HAPPEN BEFORE?
WHAT ?
HUH ?!
TWAK
I'VE TAKEN OVER HIS BODY!!
AQUA MAGIA: SNAKE MINIONS' CONSECUTIVE FANGS!!
!!!
I KNOW IT SOUNDS STUPID, BUT A **TALKING JELLY** TOOK OVER BARIK'S BODY.
THE SNAKES THAT MERGED WITH YOU ALLOW ME TO CONTROL YOUR MOVEMENTS.
HSSss
!!
IN OTHER WORDS, YOU'RE MY **PUPPET**.

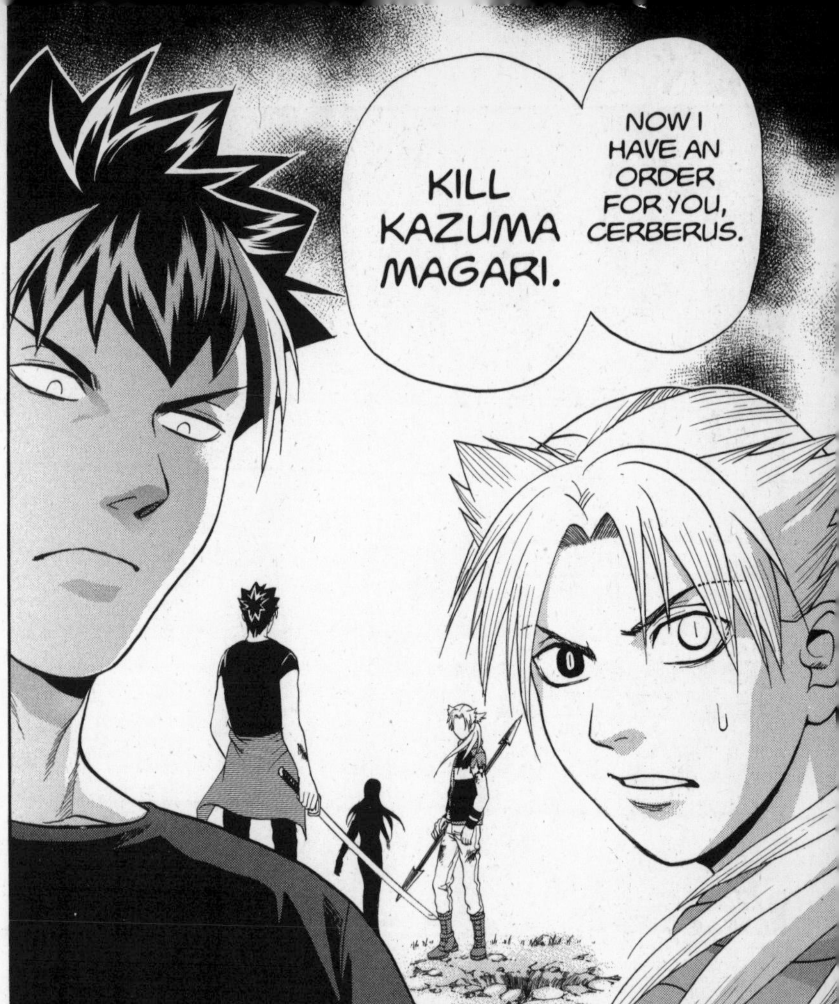
NOW I HAVE AN ORDER FOR YOU, CERBERUS.
KILL KAZUMA MAGARI.

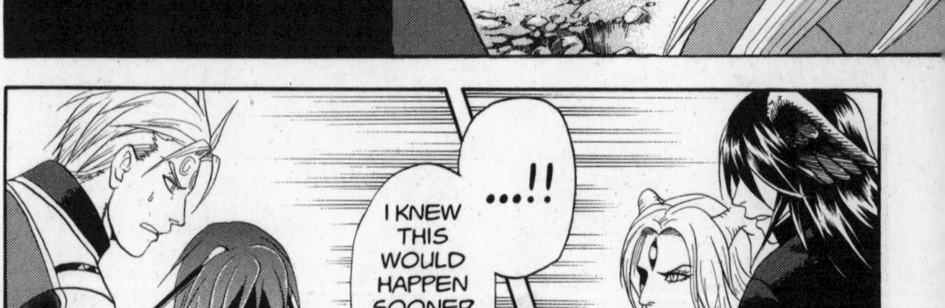
...!!
I KNEW THIS WOULD HAPPEN SOONER OR LATER...

READ THIS WAY

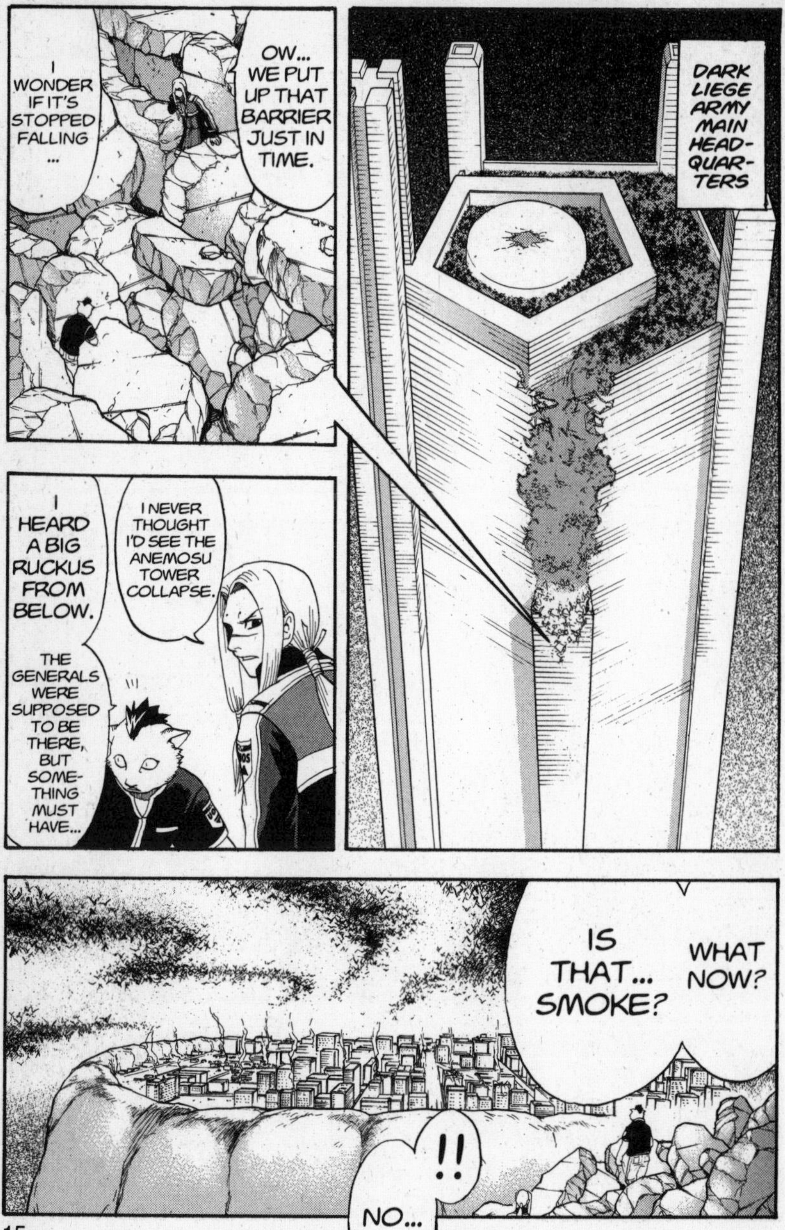

DARK LIEGE ARMY MAIN HEADQUARTERS
OW... WE PUT UP THAT BARRIER JUST IN TIME.
I WONDER IF IT'S STOPPED FALLING...
I NEVER THOUGHT I'D SEE THE ANEMOSU TOWER COLLAPSE.
I HEARD A BIG RUCKUS FROM BELOW.
THE GENERALS WERE SUPPOSED TO BE THERE, BUT SOMETHING MUST HAVE...
WHAT NOW?
IS THAT... SMOKE?
!!
NO...

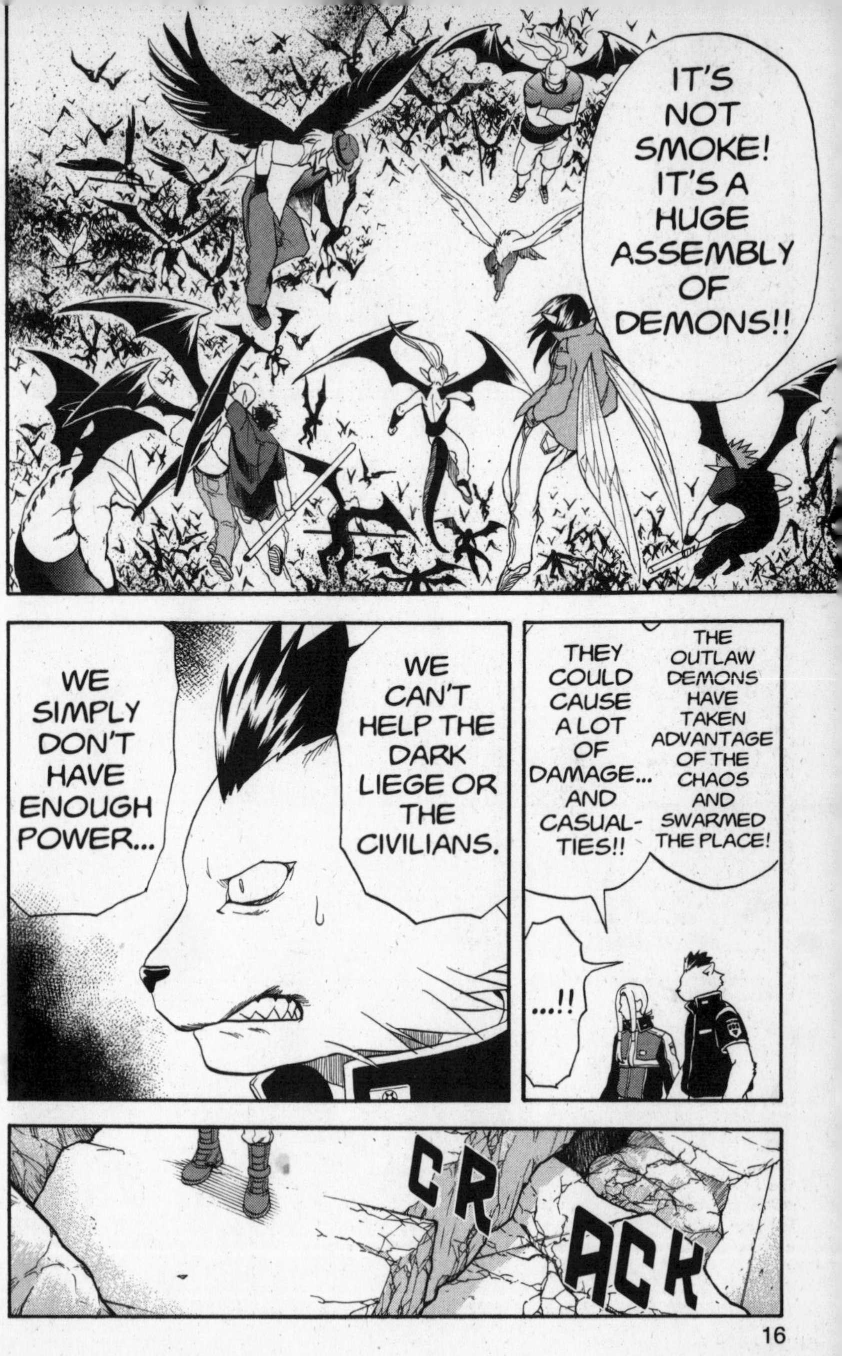
IT'S NOT SMOKE! IT'S A HUGE ASSEMBLY OF DEMONS!!
THE OUTLAW DEMONS HAVE TAKEN ADVANTAGE OF THE CHAOS AND SWARMED THE PLACE!
THEY COULD CAUSE A LOT OF DAMAGE... AND CASUAL-TIES!!
...!!
WE CAN'T HELP THE DARK LIEGE OR THE CIVILIANS.
WE SIMPLY DON'T HAVE ENOUGH POWER...
CRACK

READ THIS WAY

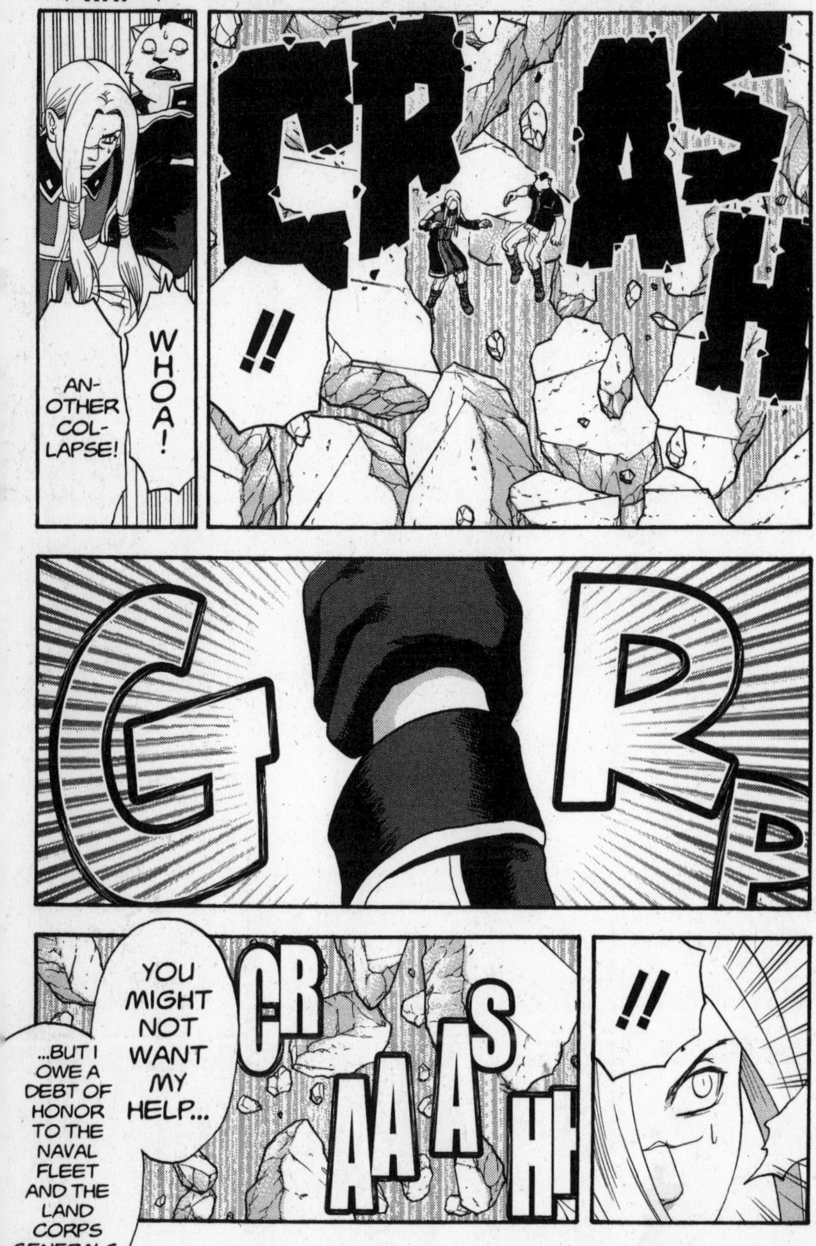
CRASH
!!
WHOA!
AN-OTHER COL-LAPSE!
GRR
!!
CRAAASH!
YOU MIGHT NOT WANT MY HELP...
...BUT I OWE A DEBT OF HONOR TO THE NAVAL FLEET AND THE LAND CORPS GENERALS.

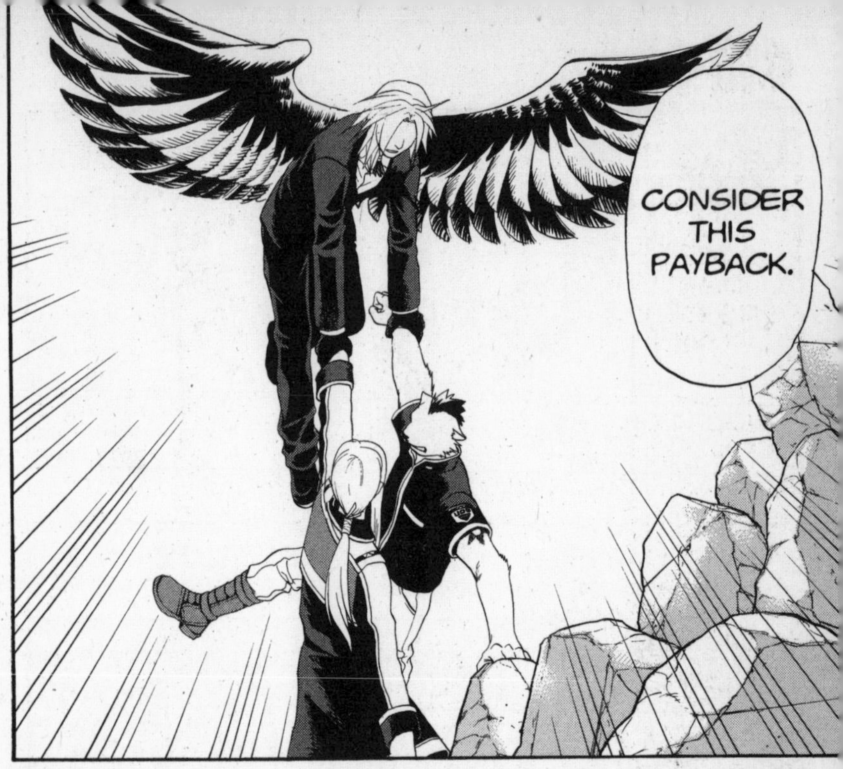
CONSIDER THIS PAYBACK.

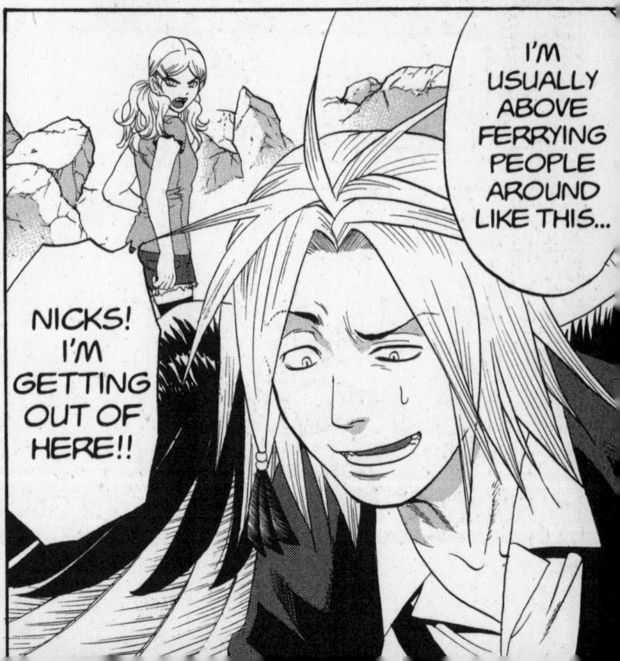
I'M USUALLY ABOVE FERRYING PEOPLE AROUND LIKE THIS...
NICKS! I'M GETTING OUT OF HERE!!

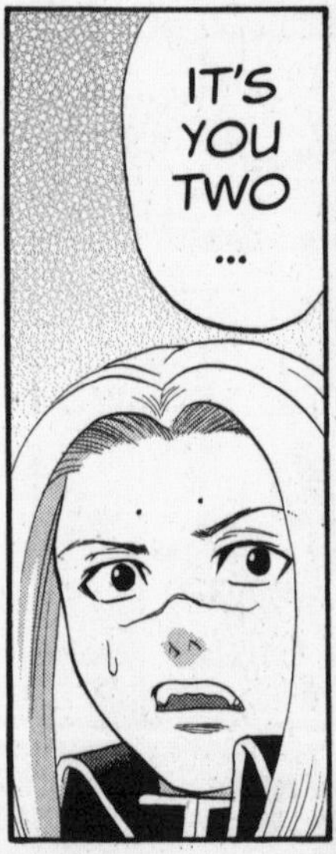
IT'S YOU TWO ...

READ THIS WAY

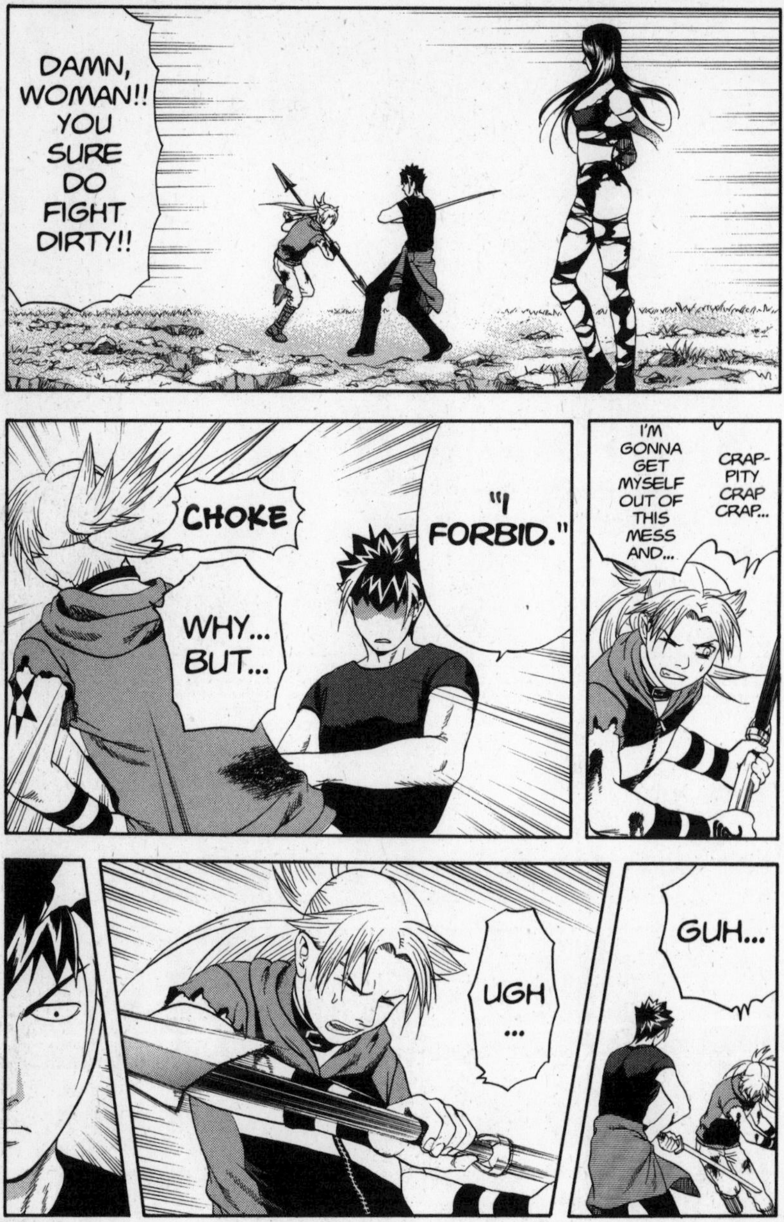
DAMN, WOMAN!! YOU SURE DO FIGHT DIRTY!!
CRAP-PITY CRAP CRAP...
I'M GONNA GET MYSELF OUT OF THIS MESS AND...
"I FORBID."
CHOKE
WHY... BUT...
GUH...
UGH ...

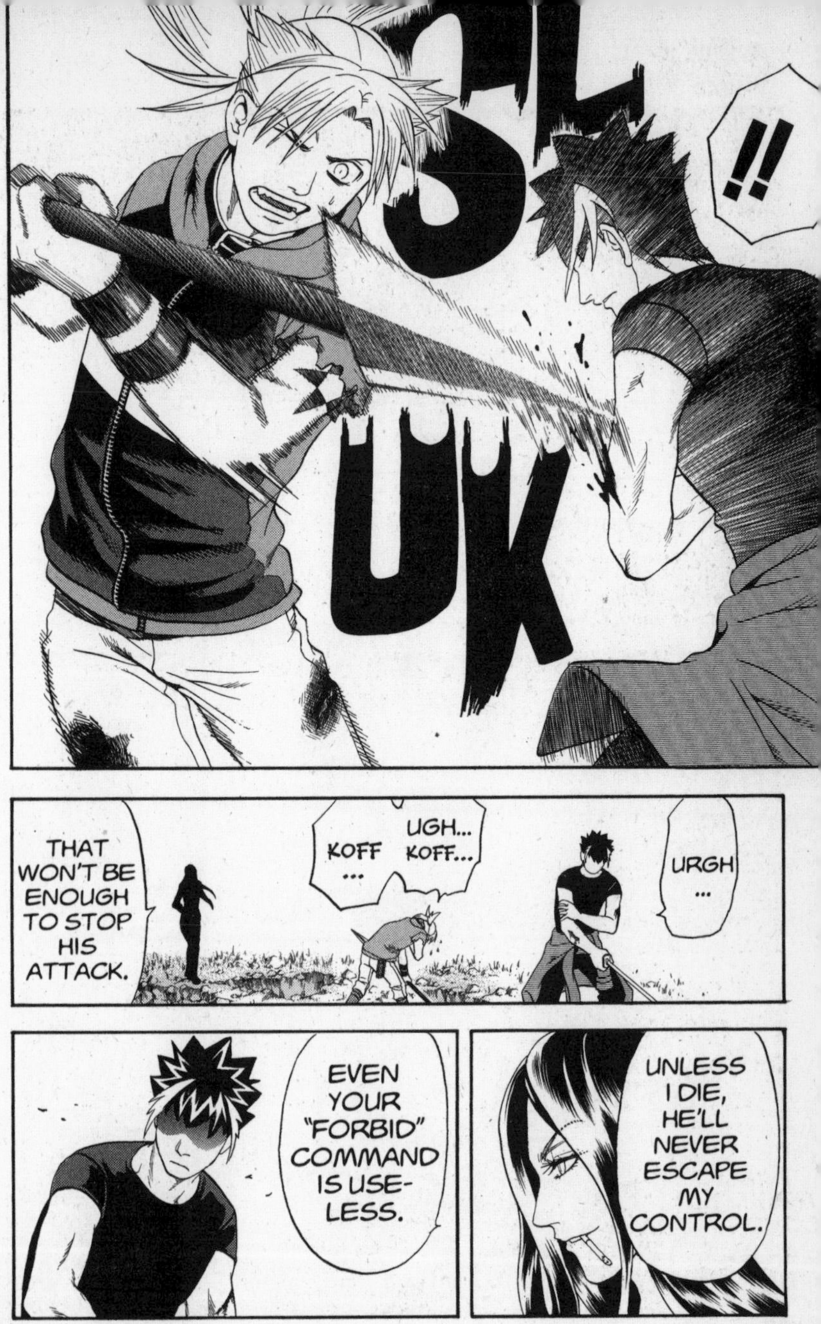
!!
URGH ...
UGH... KOFF... KOFF ...
THAT WON'T BE ENOUGH TO STOP HIS ATTACK.
UNLESS I DIE, HE'LL NEVER ESCAPE MY CONTROL.
EVEN YOUR "FORBID" COMMAND IS USE- LESS.

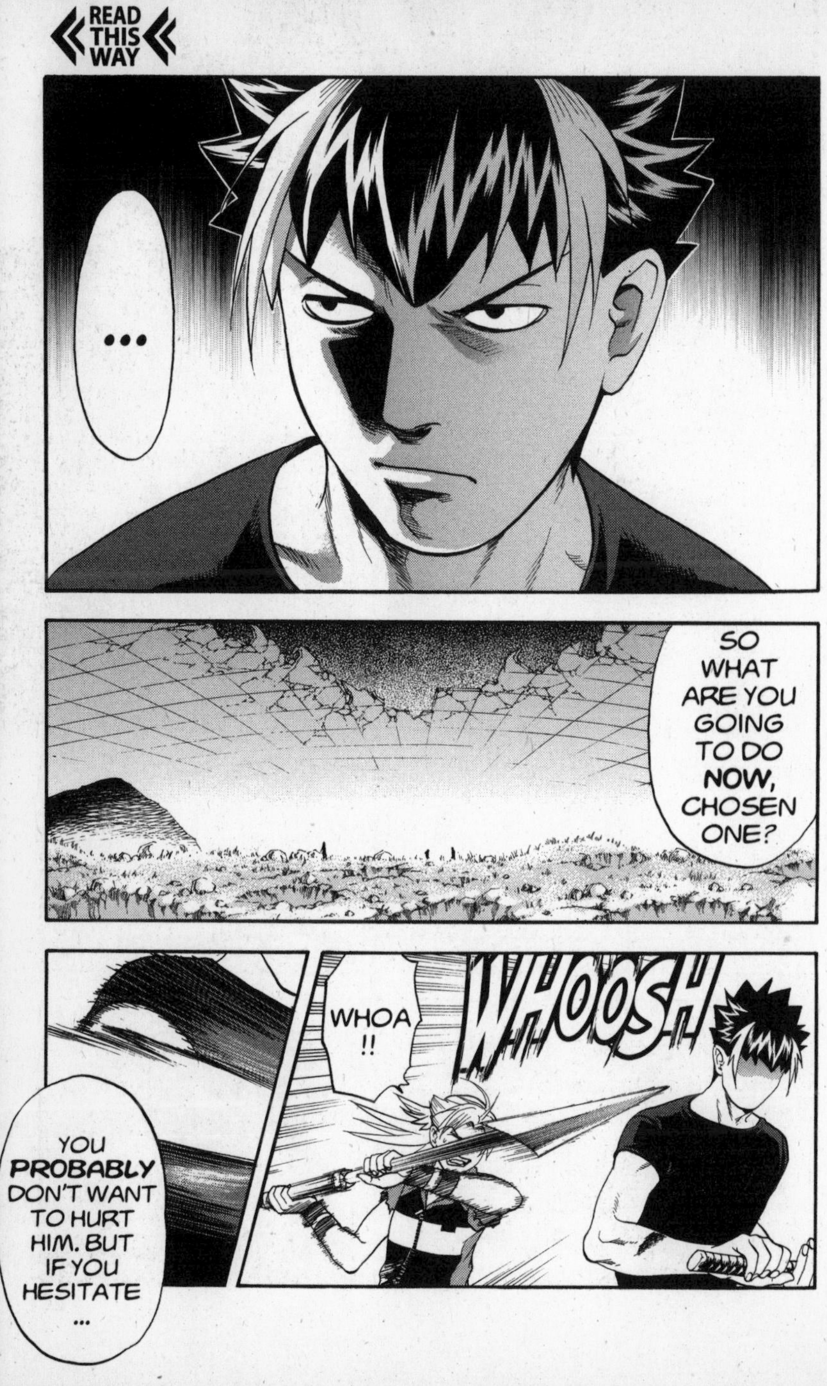
READ THIS WAY
...
SO WHAT ARE YOU GOING TO DO NOW, CHOSEN ONE?
WHOOSH
WHOA !!
YOU PROBABLY DON'T WANT TO HURT HIM. BUT IF YOU HESITATE ...

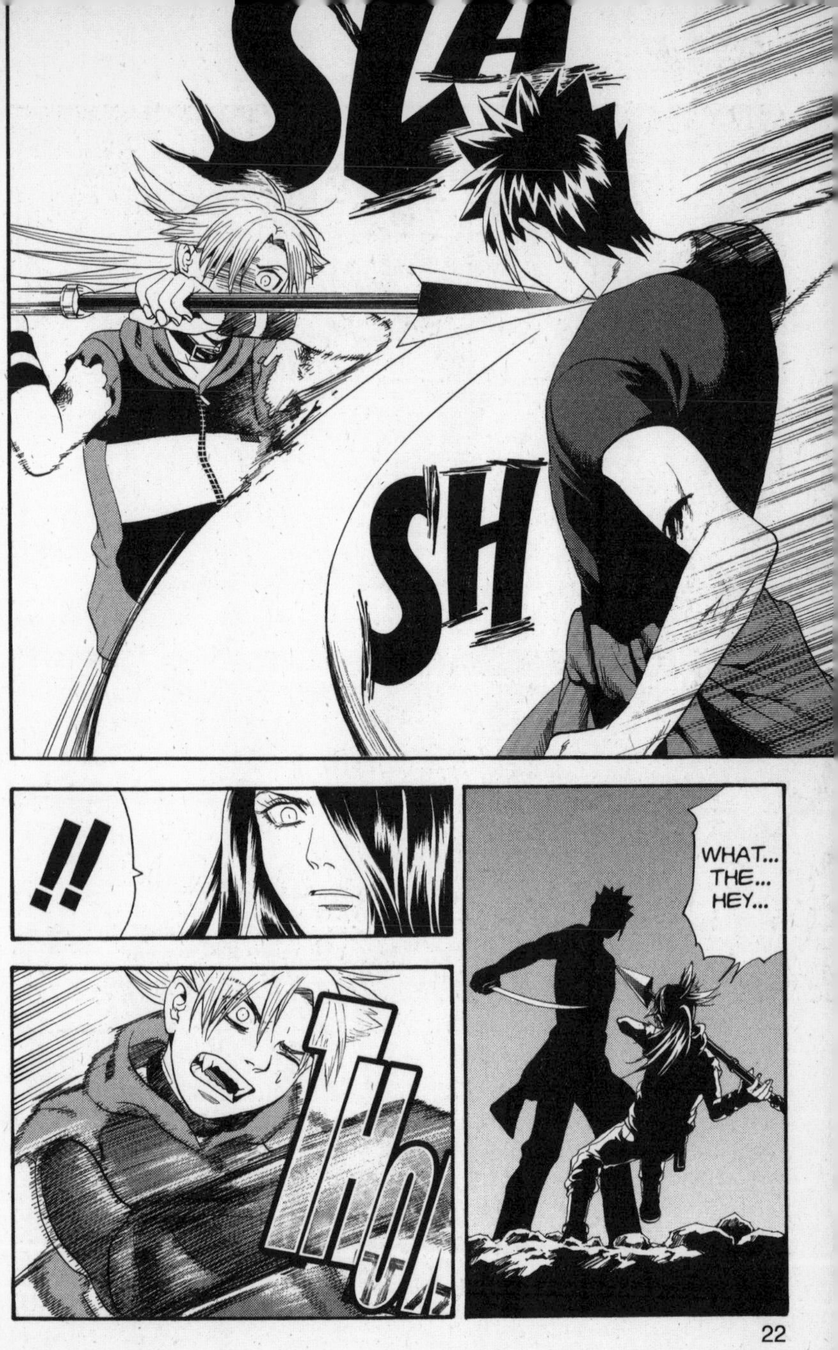
SLA
SH
WHAT... THE... HEY...
!!
THO...

READ THIS WAY

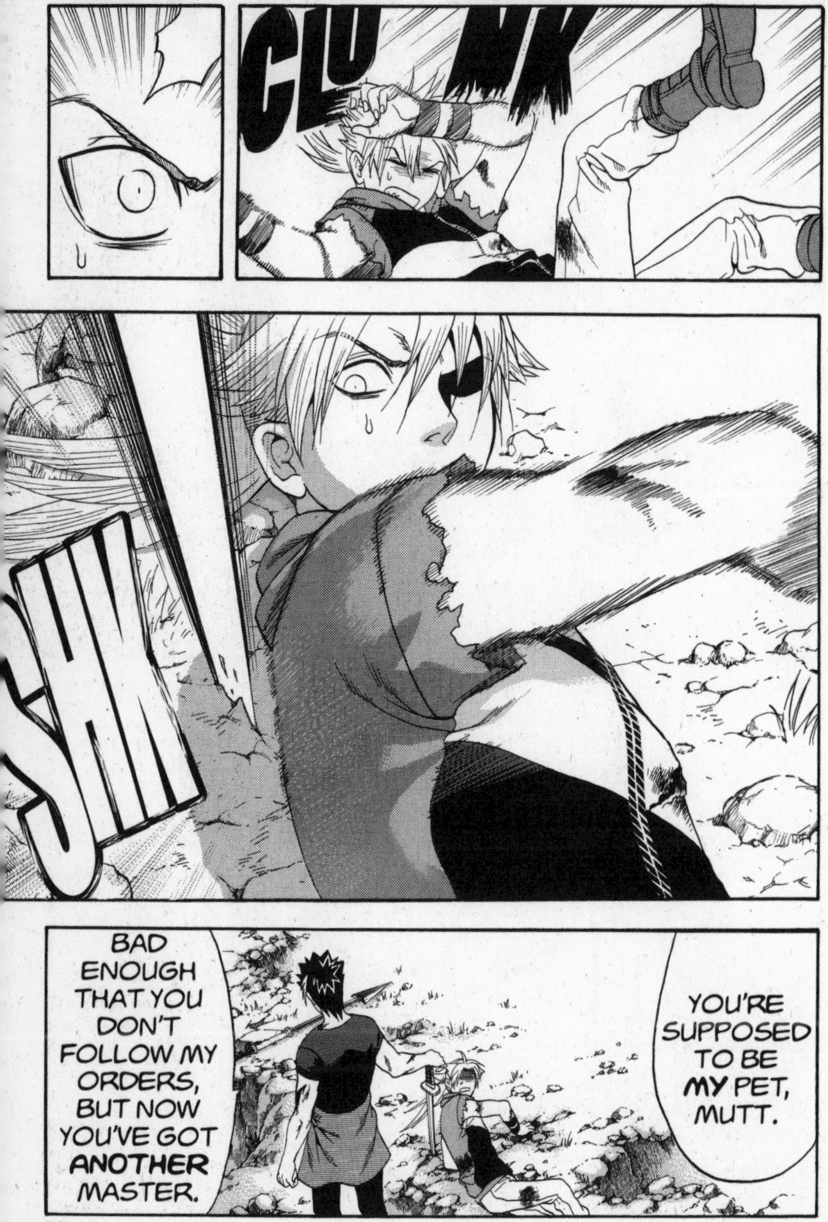

YOU'RE SUPPOSED TO BE MY PET, MUTT.
BAD ENOUGH THAT YOU DON'T FOLLOW MY ORDERS, BUT NOW YOU'VE GOT ANOTHER MASTER.

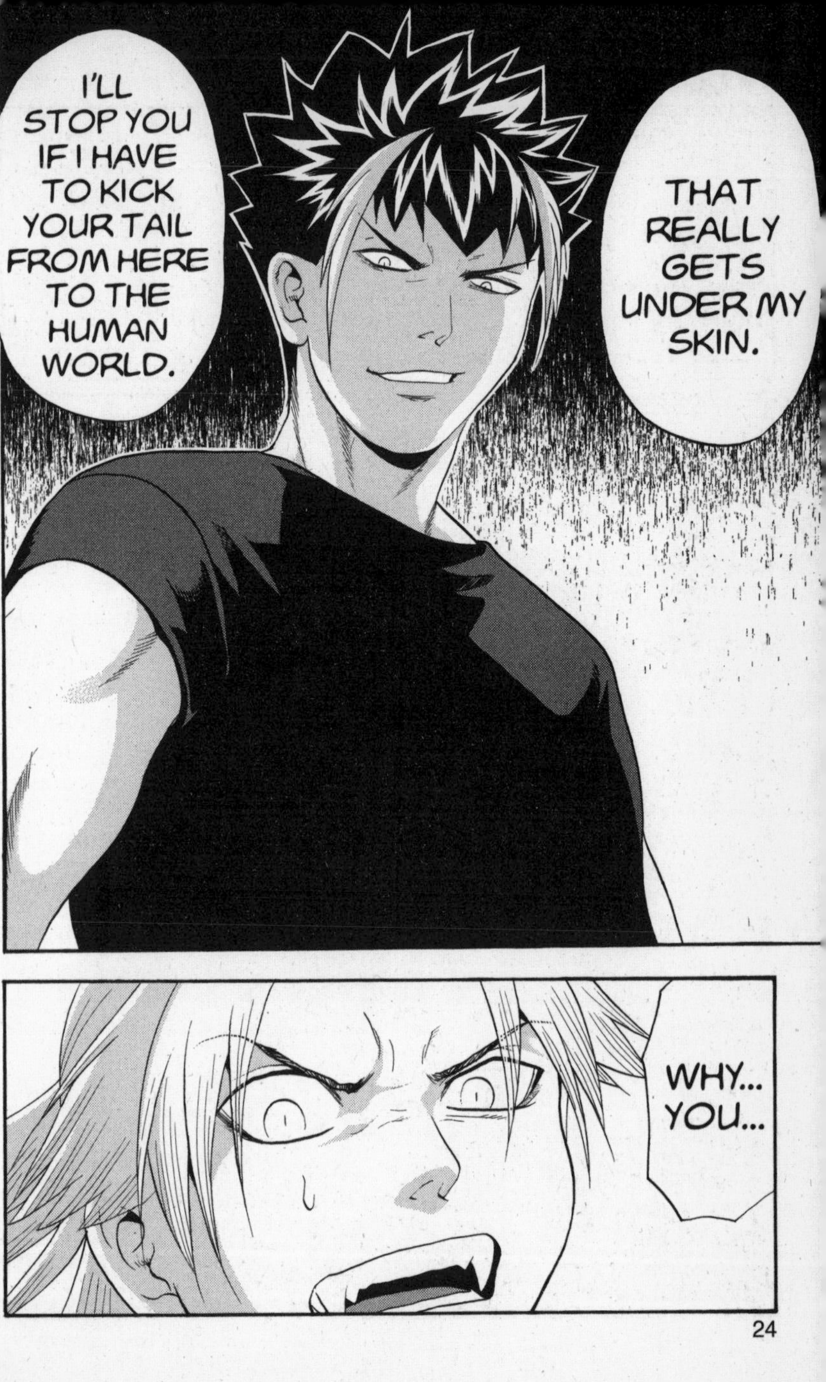
THAT REALLY GETS UNDER MY SKIN.
I'LL STOP YOU IF I HAVE TO KICK YOUR TAIL FROM HERE TO THE HUMAN WORLD.
WHY... YOU...

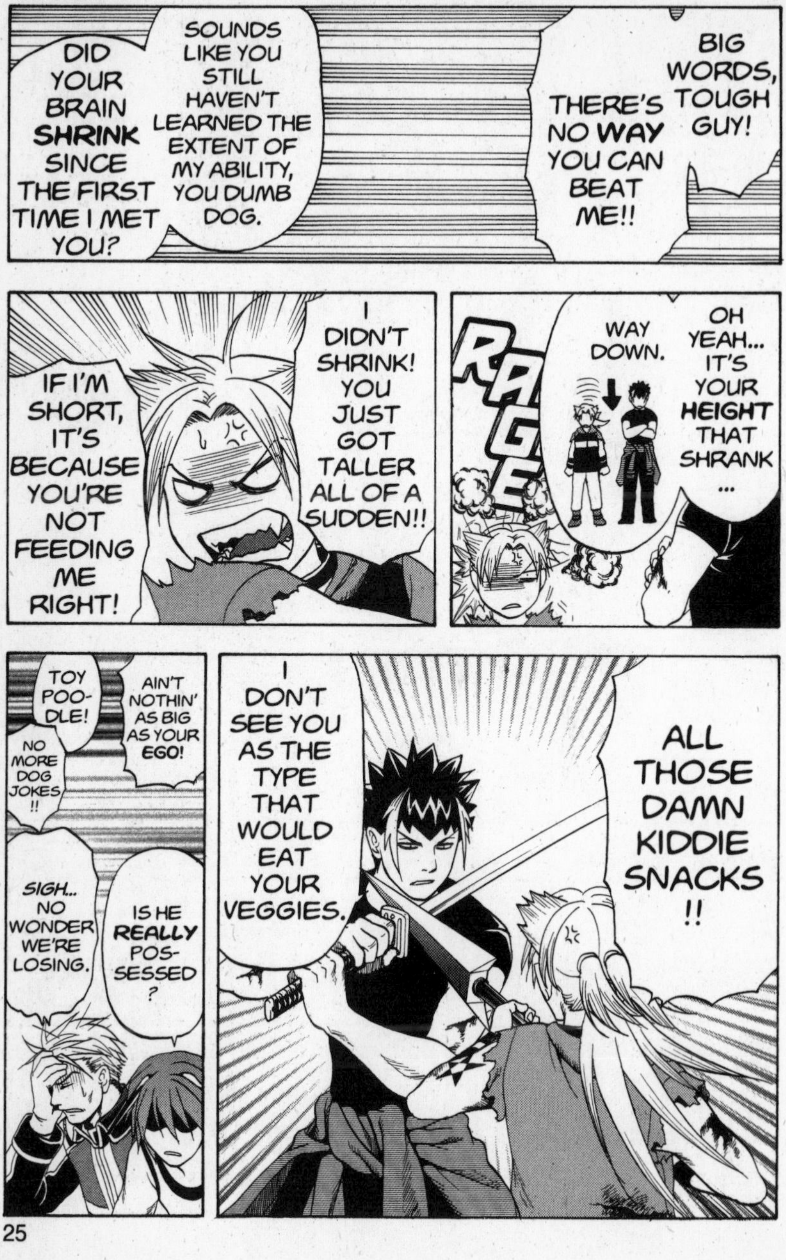
BIG WORDS, TOUGH GUY!
THERE'S NO WAY YOU CAN BEAT ME!!
SOUNDS LIKE YOU STILL HAVEN'T LEARNED THE EXTENT OF MY ABILITY, YOU DUMB DOG.
DID YOUR BRAIN SHRINK SINCE THE FIRST TIME I MET YOU?
OH YEAH... IT'S YOUR HEIGHT THAT SHRANK...
WAY DOWN.
RAGE
I DIDN'T SHRINK! YOU JUST GOT TALLER ALL OF A SUDDEN!!
IF I'M SHORT, IT'S BECAUSE YOU'RE NOT FEEDING ME RIGHT!
ALL THOSE DAMN KIDDIE SNACKS!!
I DON'T SEE YOU AS THE TYPE THAT WOULD EAT YOUR VEGGIES.
TOY POODLE!
AIN'T NOTHIN' AS BIG AS YOUR EGO!
NO MORE DOG JOKES!!
IS HE REALLY POSSESSED?
SIGH... NO WONDER WE'RE LOSING.

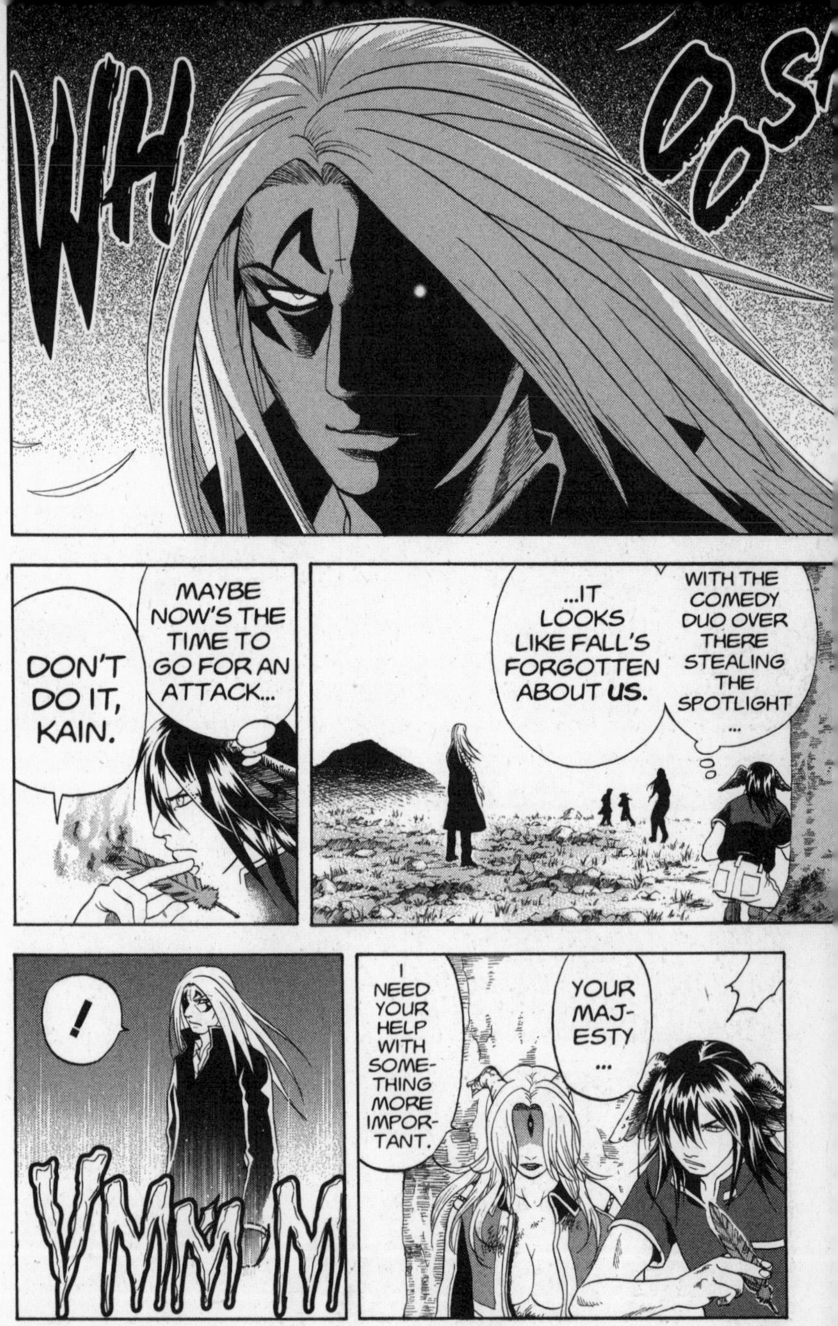
WH
OOS
WITH THE COMEDY DUO OVER THERE STEALING THE SPOTLIGHT ...
...IT LOOKS LIKE FALL'S FORGOTTEN ABOUT **US.**
MAYBE NOW'S THE TIME TO GO FOR AN ATTACK...
DON'T DO IT, KAIN.
YOUR MAJ-ESTY ...
I NEED YOUR HELP WITH SOME-THING MORE IMPOR-TANT.
!
VMMM

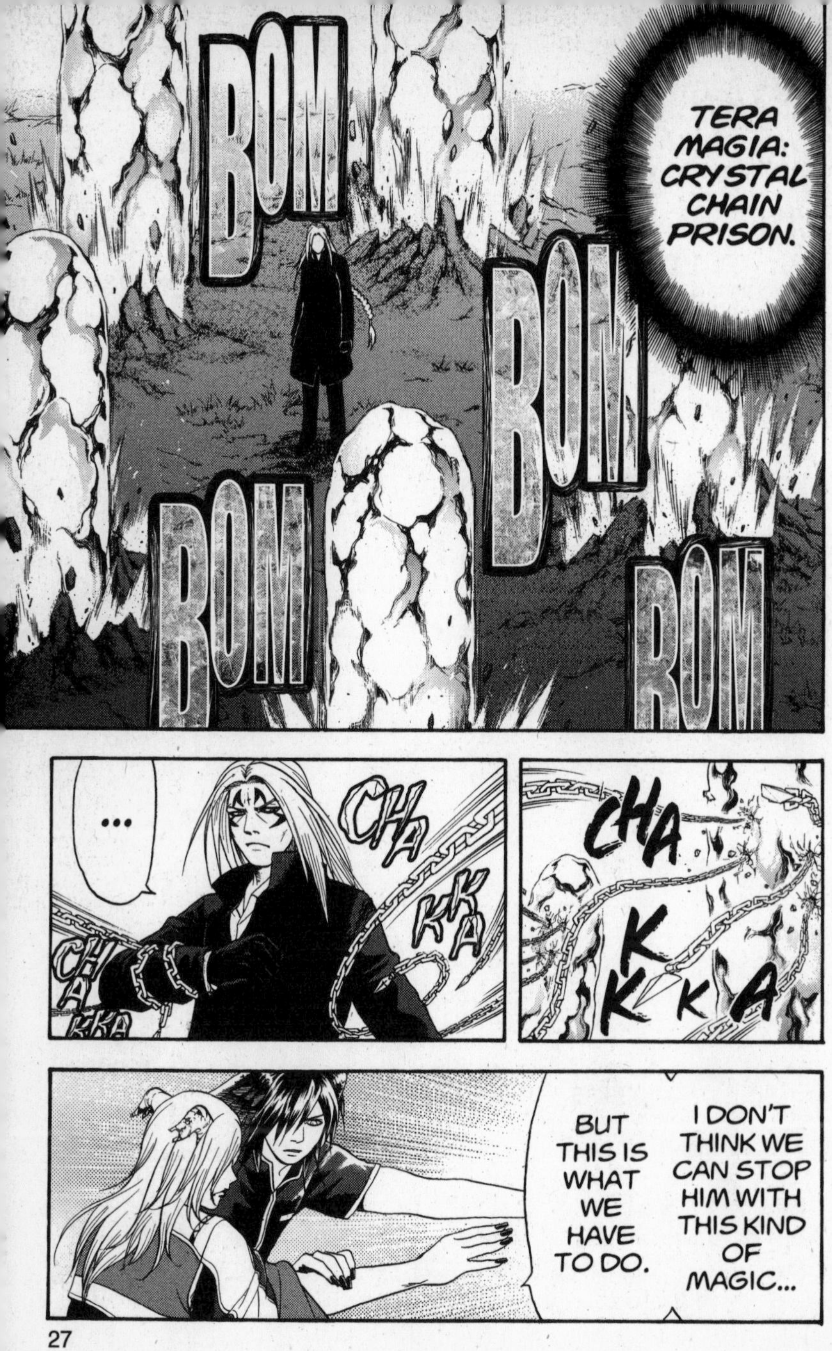
TERA MAGIA: CRYSTAL CHAIN PRISON.
BOM
BOM
BOM
ROM
CHAKKKKA
...
CHAKKA
CHAKKA
I DON'T THINK WE CAN STOP HIM WITH THIS KIND OF MAGIC...
BUT THIS IS WHAT WE HAVE TO DO.

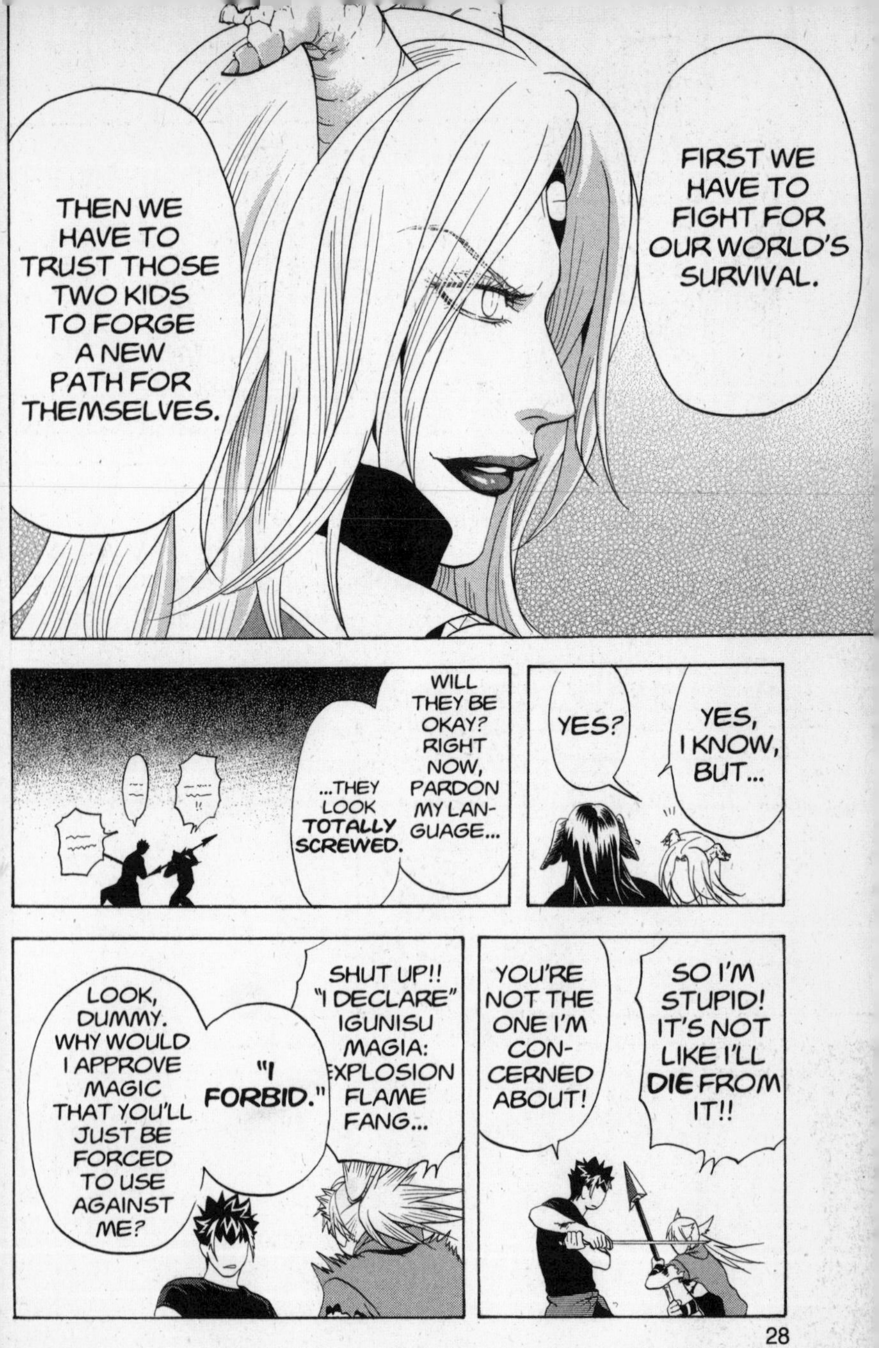
FIRST WE HAVE TO FIGHT FOR OUR WORLD'S SURVIVAL.
THEN WE HAVE TO TRUST THOSE TWO KIDS TO FORGE A NEW PATH FOR THEMSELVES.
YES, I KNOW, BUT...
YES?
WILL THEY BE OKAY? RIGHT NOW, PARDON MY LANGUAGE...
...THEY LOOK **TOTALLY** SCREWED.
SO I'M STUPID! IT'S NOT LIKE I'LL **DIE** FROM IT!!
YOU'RE NOT THE ONE I'M CONCERNED ABOUT!
SHUT UP!! "I DECLARE" IGUNISU MAGIA: EXPLOSION FLAME FANG...
"I **FORBID.**"
LOOK, DUMMY. WHY WOULD I APPROVE MAGIC THAT YOU'LL JUST BE FORCED TO USE AGAINST ME?

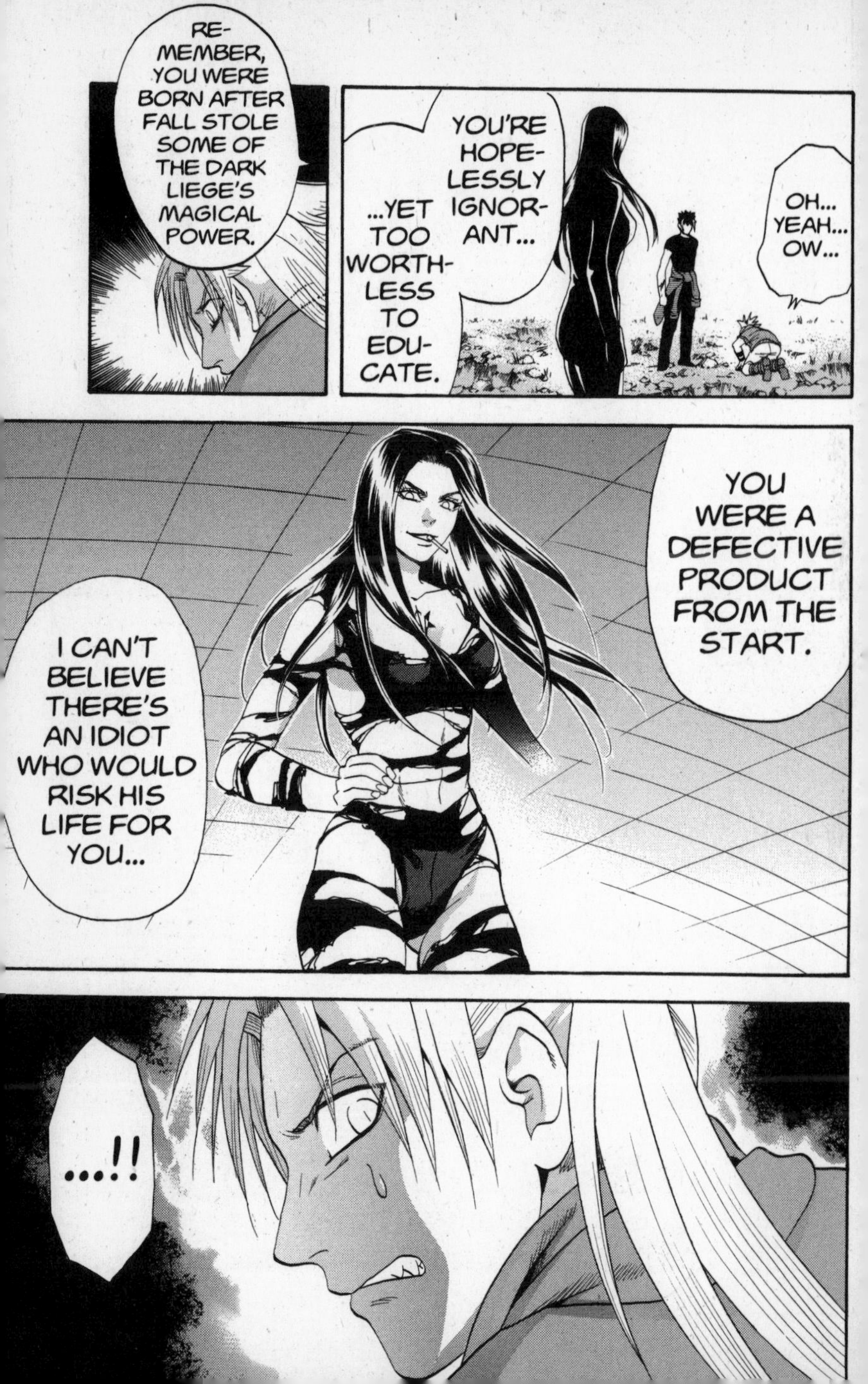
OH... YEAH... OW...
YOU'RE HOPELESSLY IGNORANT...
...YET TOO WORTHLESS TO EDUCATE.
REMEMBER, YOU WERE BORN AFTER FALL STOLE SOME OF THE DARK LIEGE'S MAGICAL POWER.
YOU WERE A DEFECTIVE PRODUCT FROM THE START.
I CAN'T BELIEVE THERE'S AN IDIOT WHO WOULD RISK HIS LIFE FOR YOU...
...!!

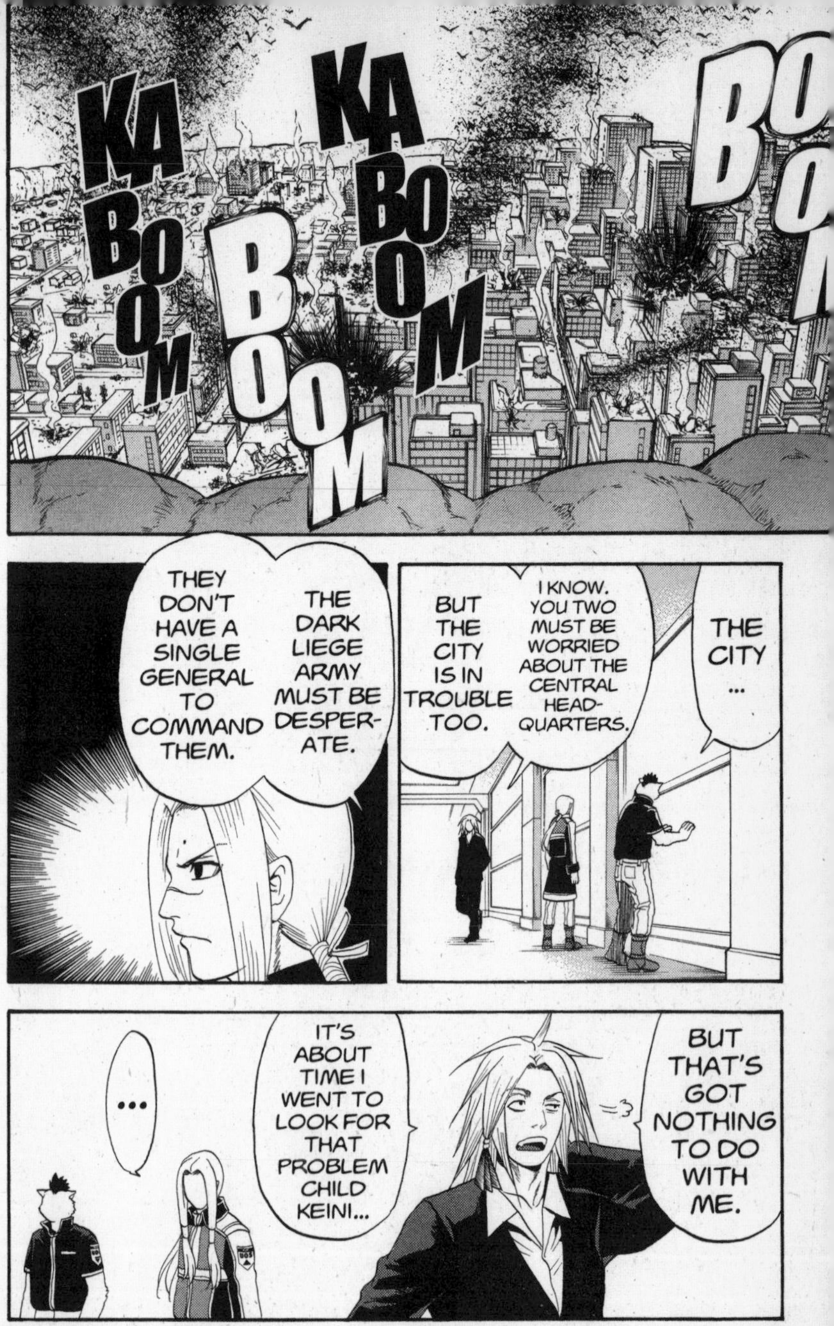
KABOOM
BOOOM
KABOOM
THE CITY ...
I KNOW. YOU TWO MUST BE WORRIED ABOUT THE CENTRAL HEAD-QUARTERS.
BUT THE CITY IS IN TROUBLE TOO.
THE DARK LIEGE ARMY MUST BE DESPER-ATE.
THEY DON'T HAVE A SINGLE GENERAL TO COMMAND THEM.
BUT THAT'S GOT NOTHING TO DO WITH ME.
IT'S ABOUT TIME I WENT TO LOOK FOR THAT PROBLEM CHILD KEINI...
...

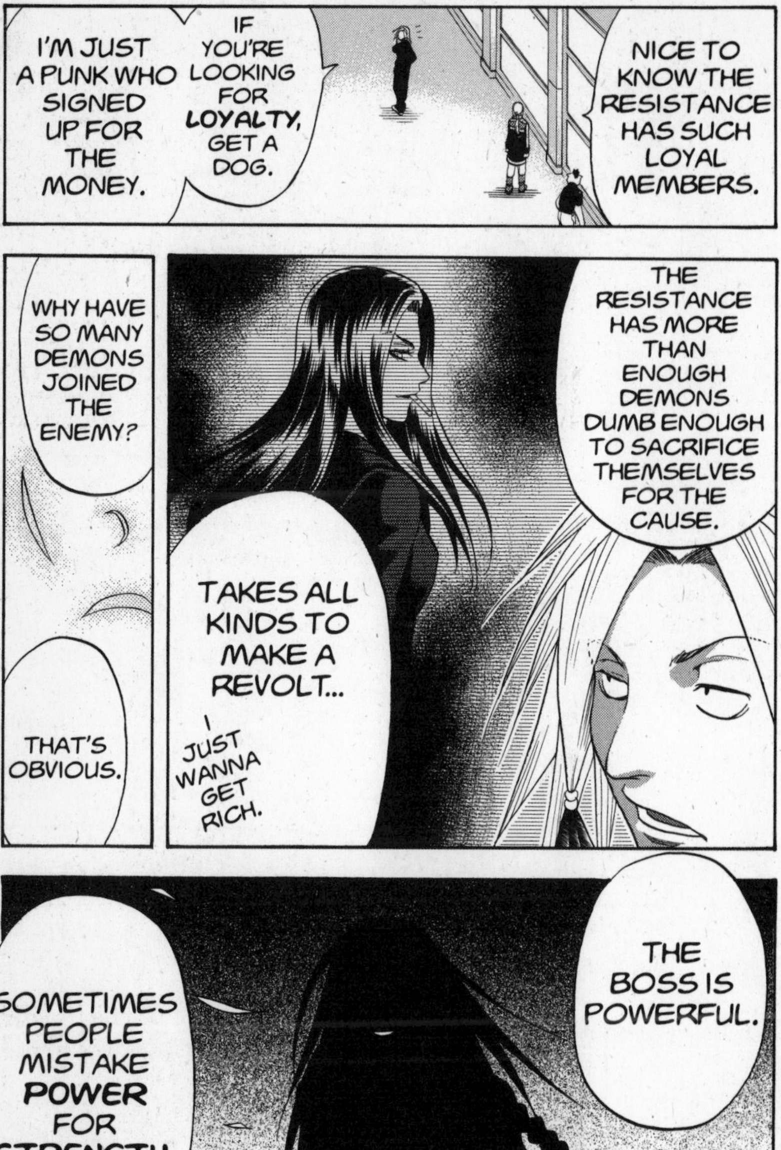
NICE TO KNOW THE RESISTANCE HAS SUCH LOYAL MEMBERS.
IF YOU'RE LOOKING FOR LOYALTY, GET A DOG.
I'M JUST A PUNK WHO SIGNED UP FOR THE MONEY.
THE RESISTANCE HAS MORE THAN ENOUGH DEMONS DUMB ENOUGH TO SACRIFICE THEMSELVES FOR THE CAUSE.
TAKES ALL KINDS TO MAKE A REVOLT...
I JUST WANNA GET RICH.
WHY HAVE SO MANY DEMONS JOINED THE ENEMY?
THAT'S OBVIOUS.
THE BOSS IS POWERFUL.
SOMETIMES PEOPLE MISTAKE POWER FOR STRENGTH.

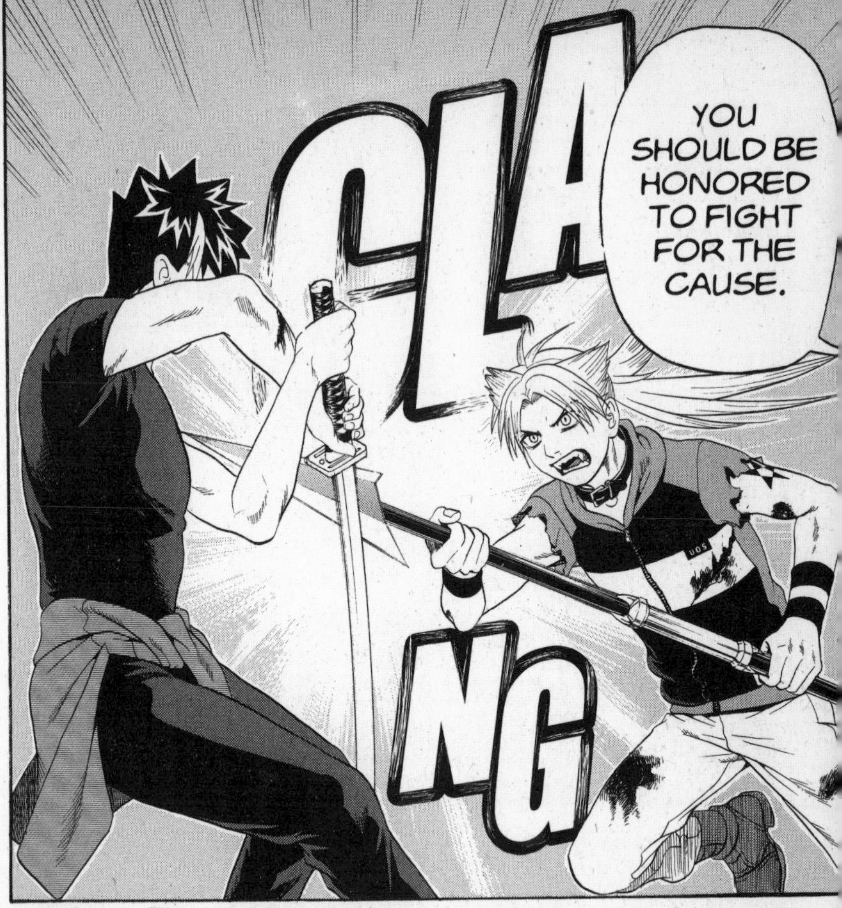
CLANG
YOU SHOULD BE HONORED TO FIGHT FOR THE CAUSE.
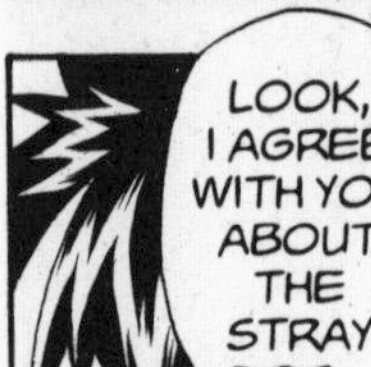
LOOK, I AGREE WITH YOU ABOUT THE STRAY DOG...
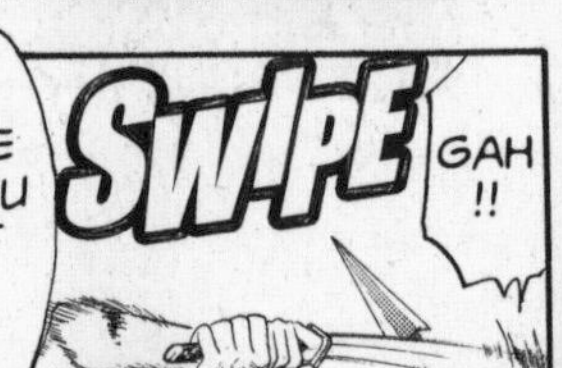
SWIPE
GAH !!
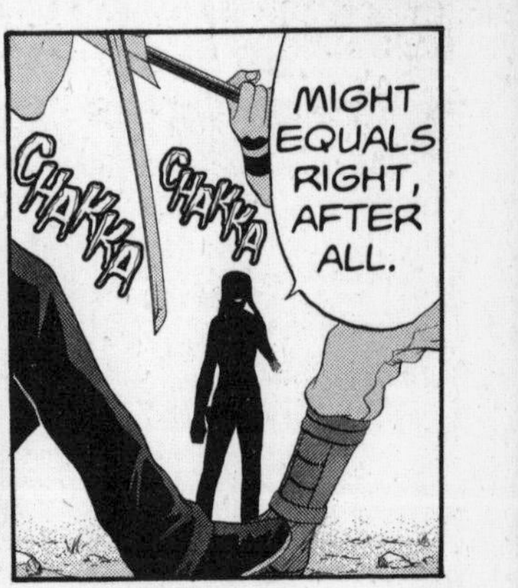
CHAKKA
CHAKKA
MIGHT EQUALS RIGHT, AFTER ALL.

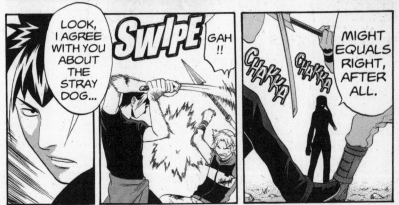

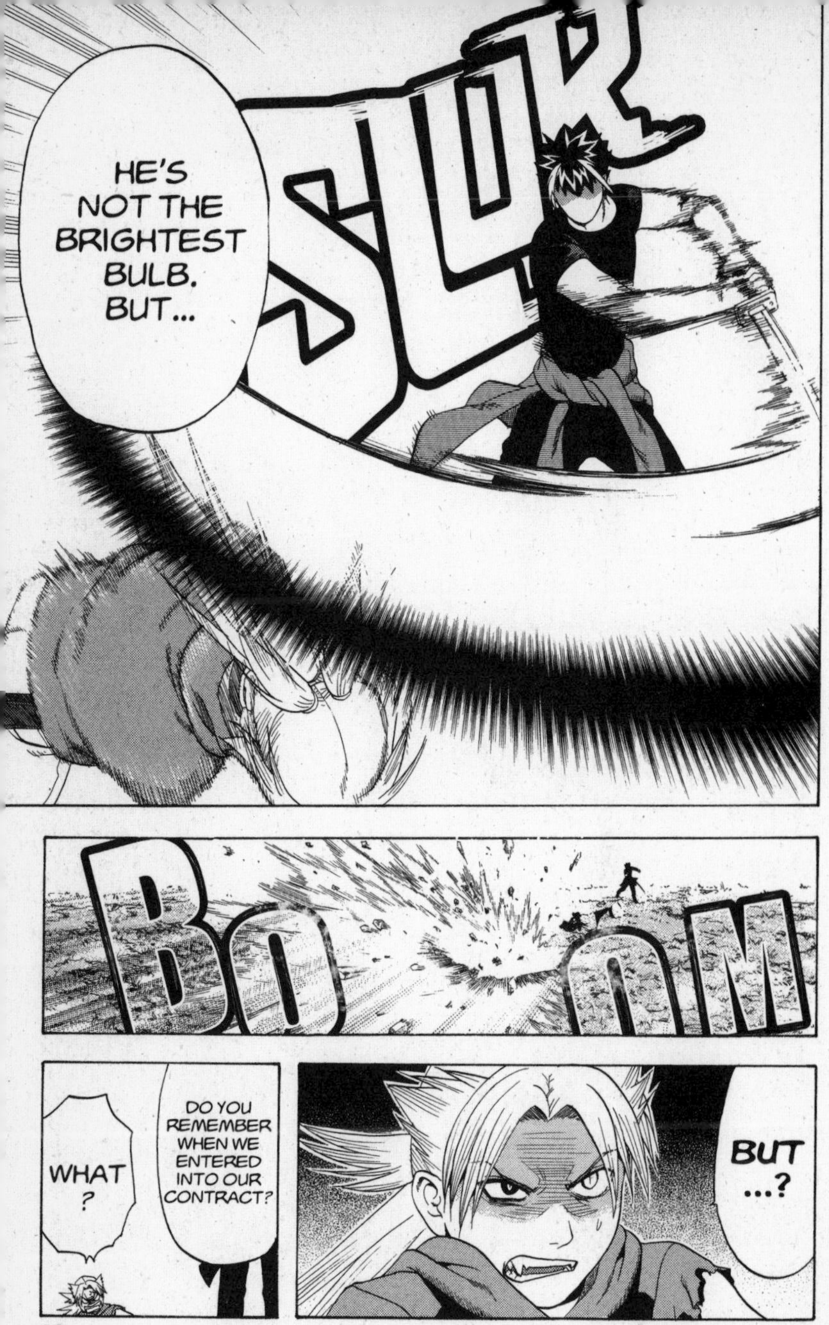

HE'S NOT THE BRIGHTEST BULB. BUT...
BOOM
BUT ...?
DO YOU REMEMBER WHEN WE ENTERED INTO OUR CONTRACT?
WHAT ?

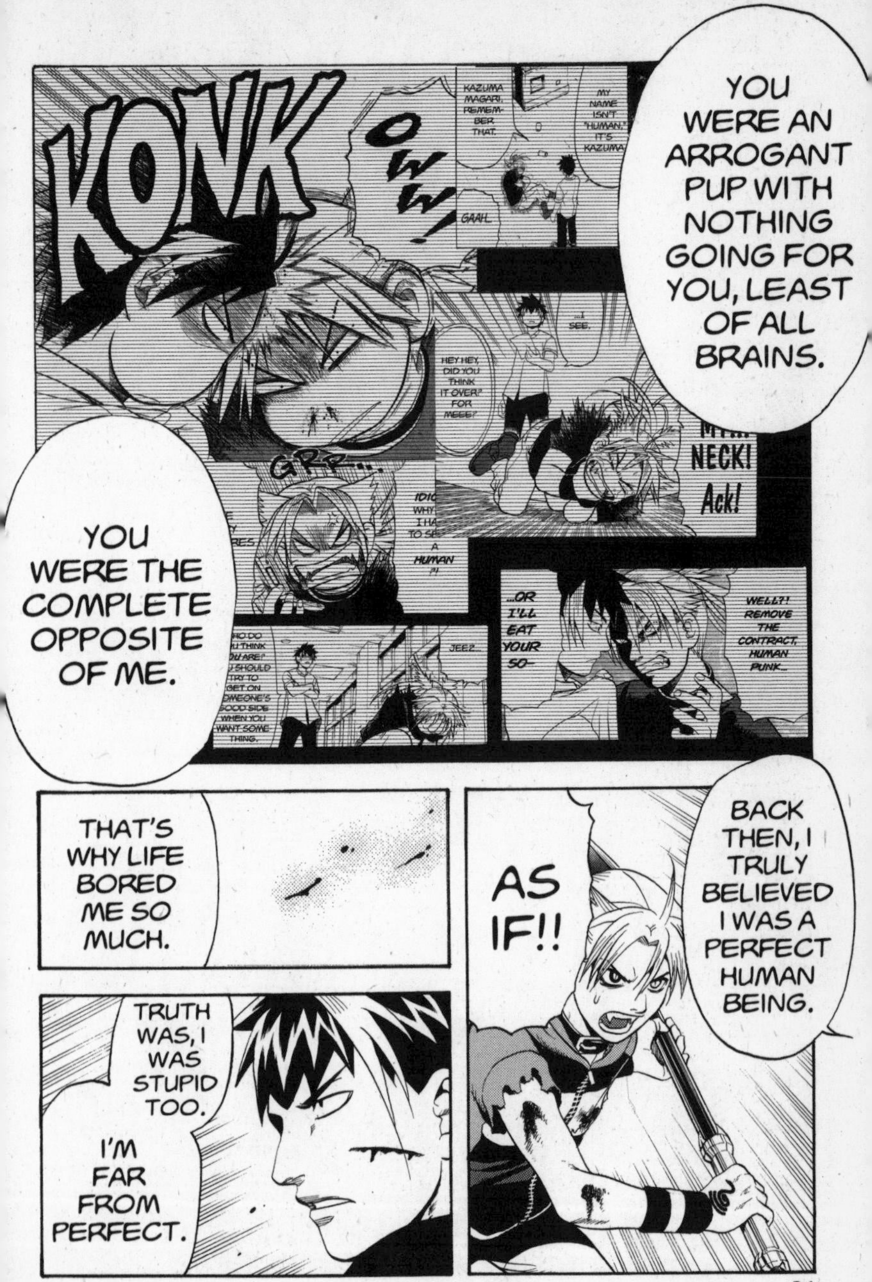
YOU WERE AN ARROGANT PUP WITH NOTHING GOING FOR YOU, LEAST OF ALL BRAINS.
MY NAME ISN'T "HUMAN," IT'S KAZUMA.
KAZUMA MAGARI. REMEMBER THAT.
GAAH.
OWW!
KONK
...I SEE.
HEY HEY, DID YOU THINK IT OVER? FOR MEEE?
NECK!
Ack!
GRR...
WELL?! REMOVE THE CONTRACT, HUMAN PUNK...
...OR I'LL EAT YOUR SO—
JEEZ.
YOU WERE THE COMPLETE OPPOSITE OF ME.
BACK THEN, I TRULY BELIEVED I WAS A PERFECT HUMAN BEING.
AS IF!!
THAT'S WHY LIFE BORED ME SO MUCH.
TRUTH WAS, I WAS STUPID TOO.
I'M FAR FROM PERFECT.

READ THIS WAY

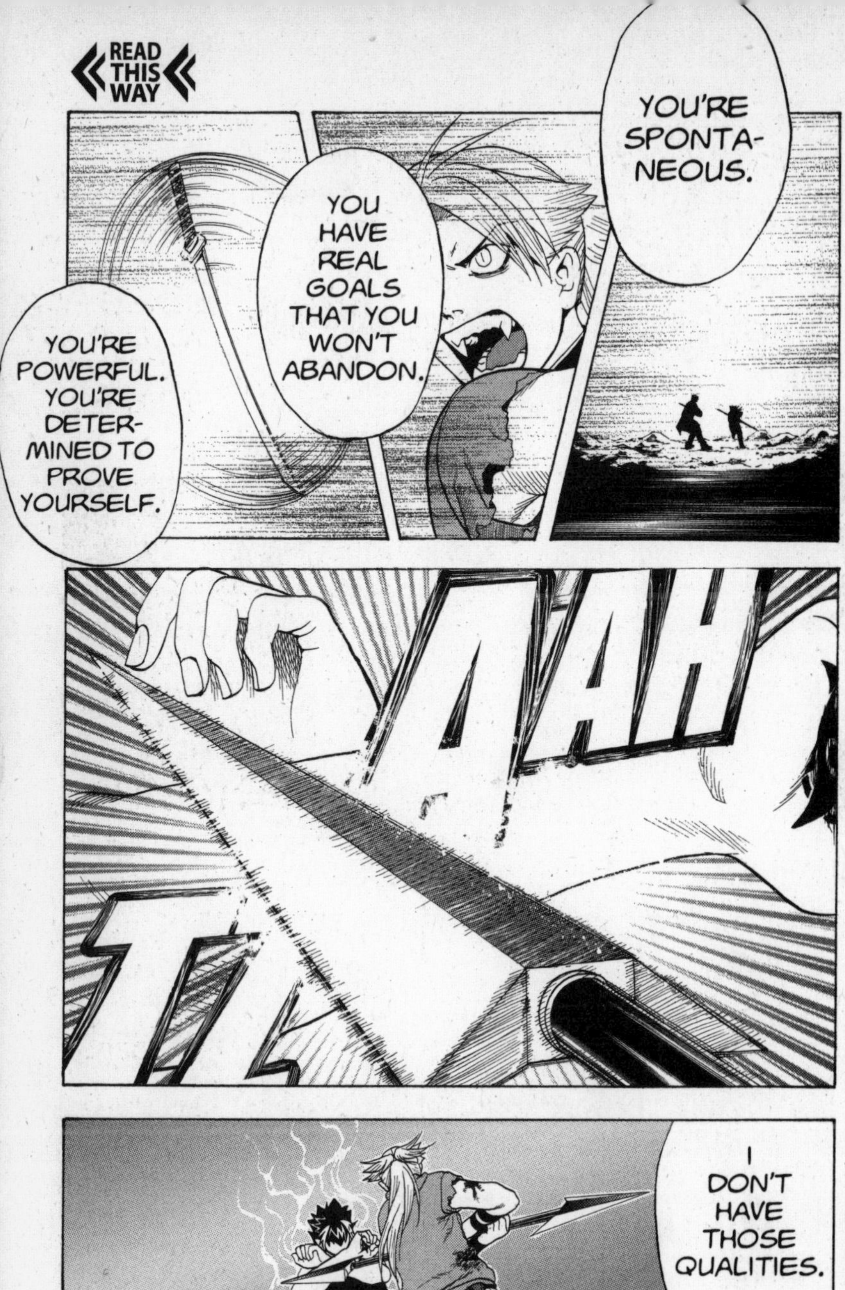

YOU'RE SPONTA- NEOUS.
YOU HAVE REAL GOALS THAT YOU WON'T ABANDON.
YOU'RE POWERFUL. YOU'RE DETER- MINED TO PROVE YOURSELF.
TAAH
I DON'T HAVE THOSE QUALITIES.

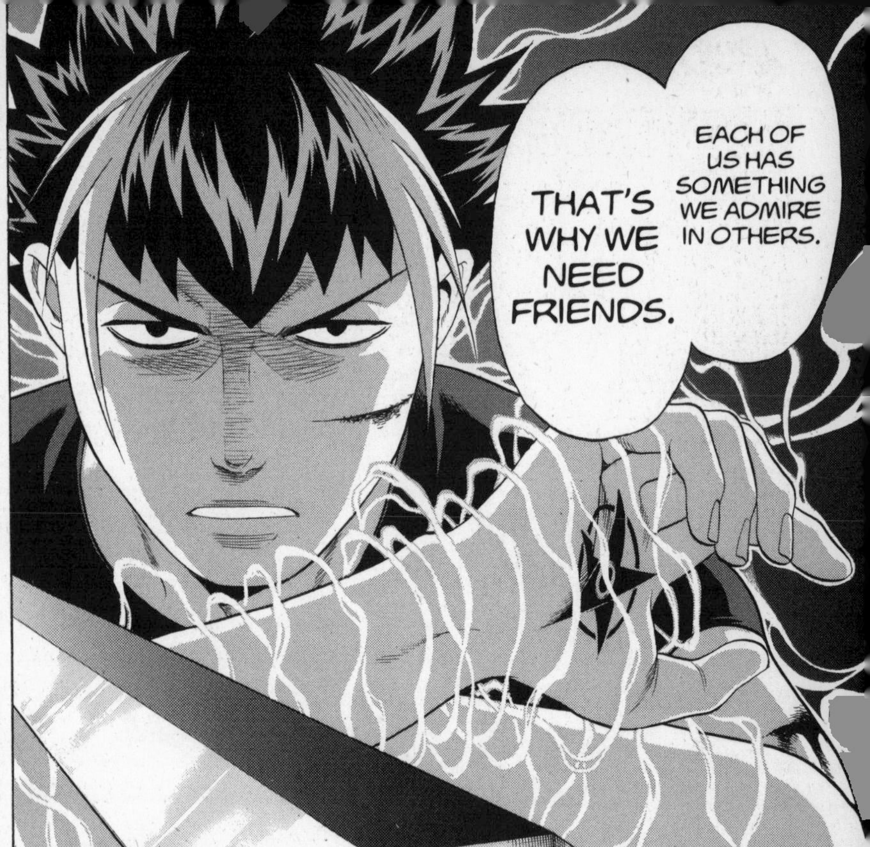
EACH OF US HAS SOMETHING WE ADMIRE IN OTHERS.
THAT'S WHY WE NEED FRIENDS.
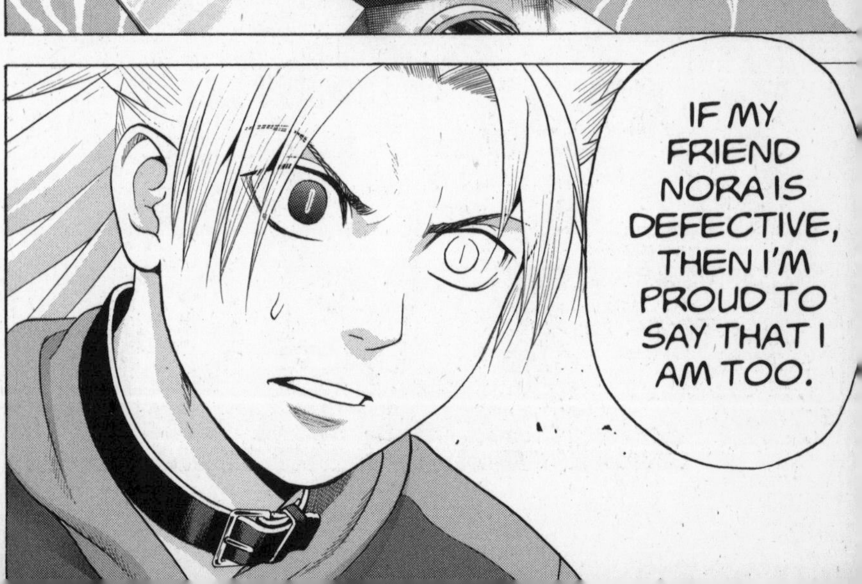
IF MY FRIEND NORA IS DEFECTIVE, THEN I'M PROUD TO SAY THAT I AM TOO.

READ THIS WAY

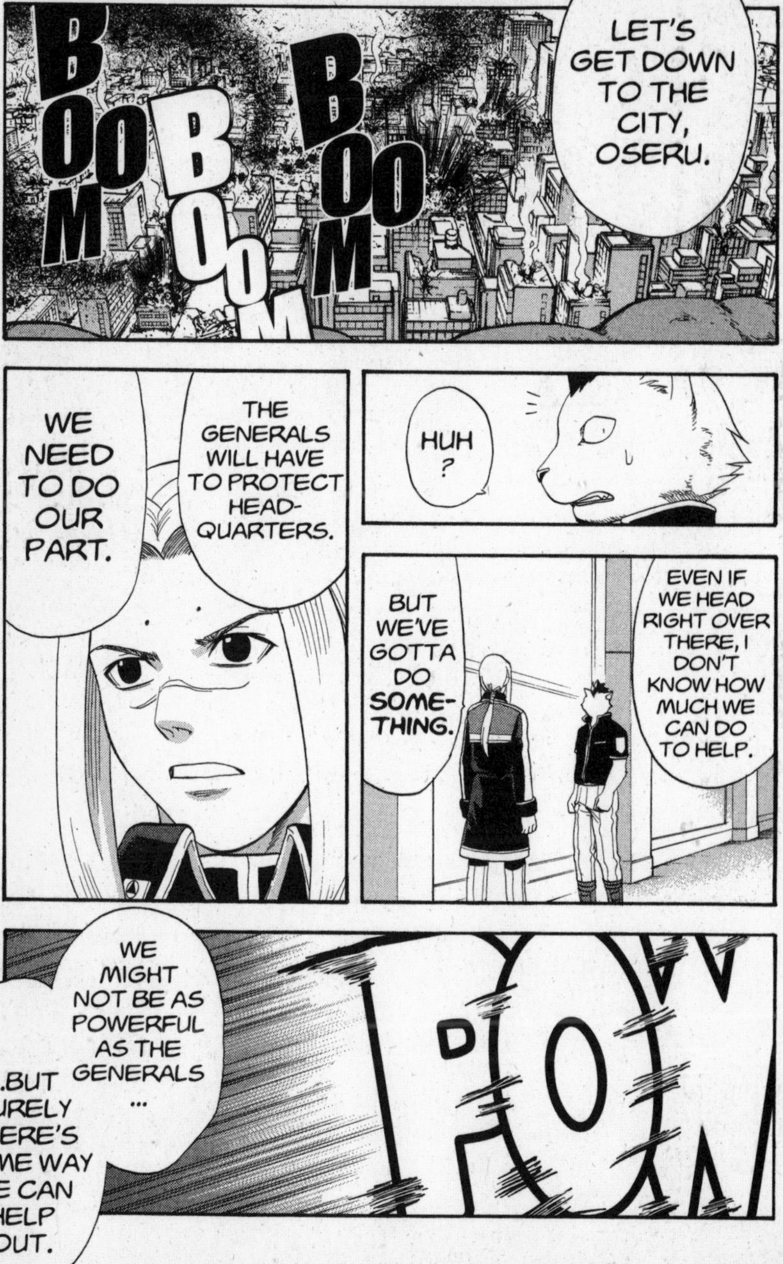
LET'S GET DOWN TO THE CITY, OSERU.
BOOOM
BOOOM
BOOM
HUH?
EVEN IF WE HEAD RIGHT OVER THERE, I DON'T KNOW HOW MUCH WE CAN DO TO HELP.
BUT WE'VE GOTTA DO SOME-THING.
THE GENERALS WILL HAVE TO PROTECT HEAD-QUARTERS.
WE NEED TO DO OUR PART.
POM
WE MIGHT NOT BE AS POWERFUL AS THE GENERALS...
...BUT SURELY THERE'S SOME WAY WE CAN HELP OUT.

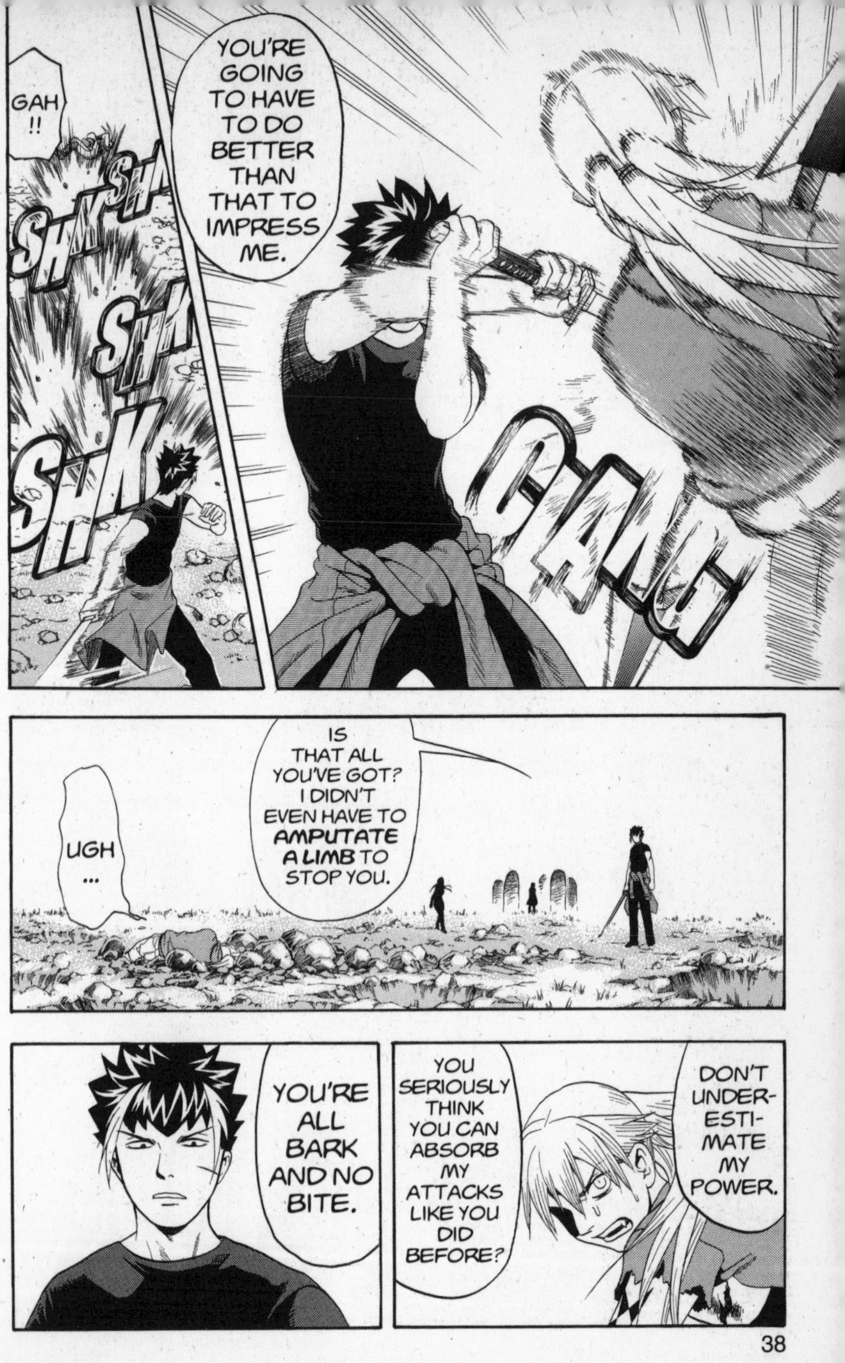
YOU'RE GOING TO HAVE TO DO BETTER THAN THAT TO IMPRESS ME.
CANG
GAH !!
SHK
IS THAT ALL YOU'VE GOT? I DIDN'T EVEN HAVE TO **AMPUTATE A LIMB** TO STOP YOU.
UGH ...
DON'T UNDER-ESTI-MATE MY POWER.
YOU SERIOUSLY THINK YOU CAN ABSORB MY ATTACKS LIKE YOU DID BEFORE?
YOU'RE ALL BARK AND NO BITE.

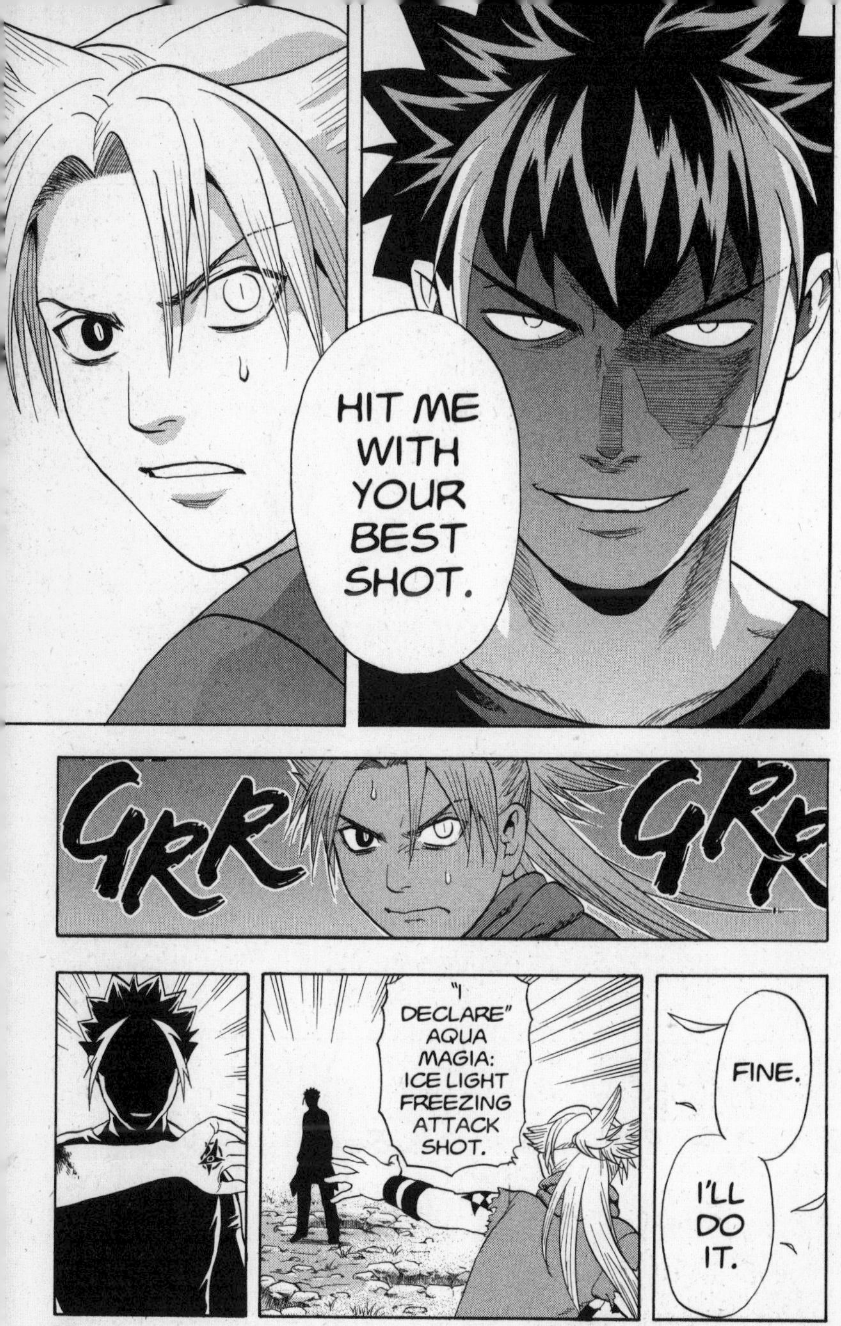
HIT ME WITH YOUR BEST SHOT.
GRR GRR
FINE.
I'LL DO IT.
"I DECLARE" AQUA MAGIA: ICE LIGHT FREEZING ATTACK SHOT.

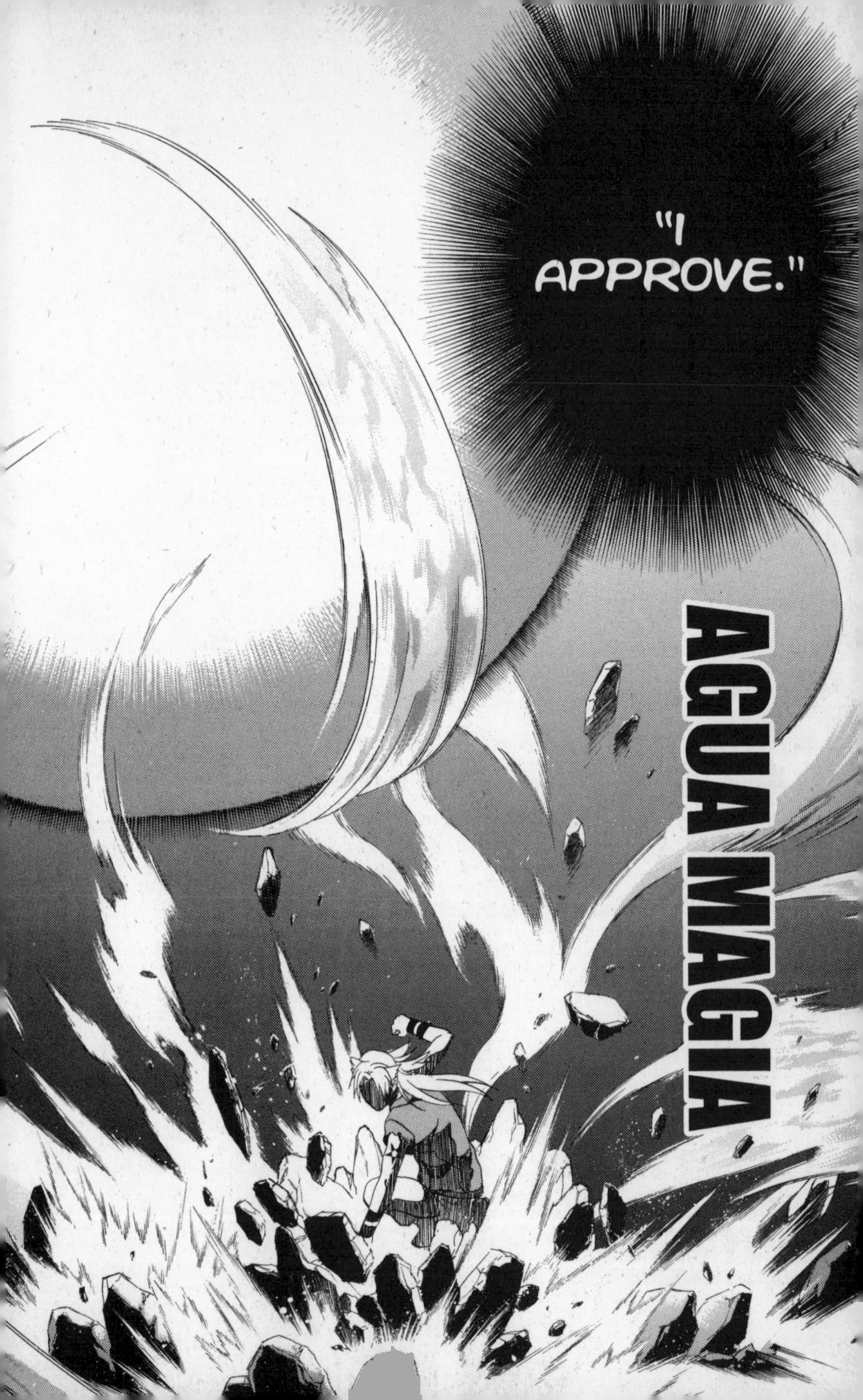
"I APPROVE."
AGUA MAGIA

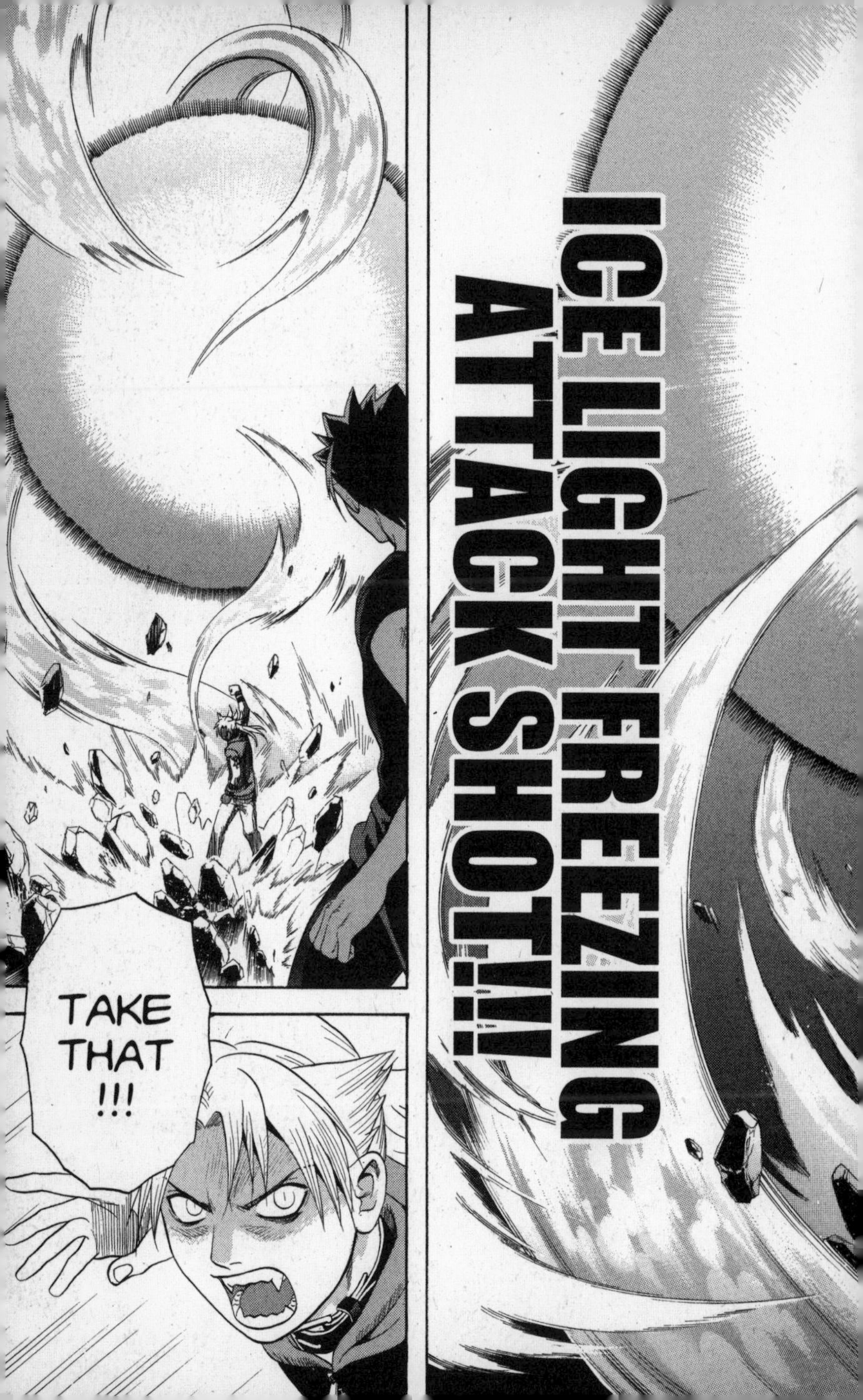
ICE LIGHT FREEZING ATTACK SHOT!!!
TAKE THAT !!!

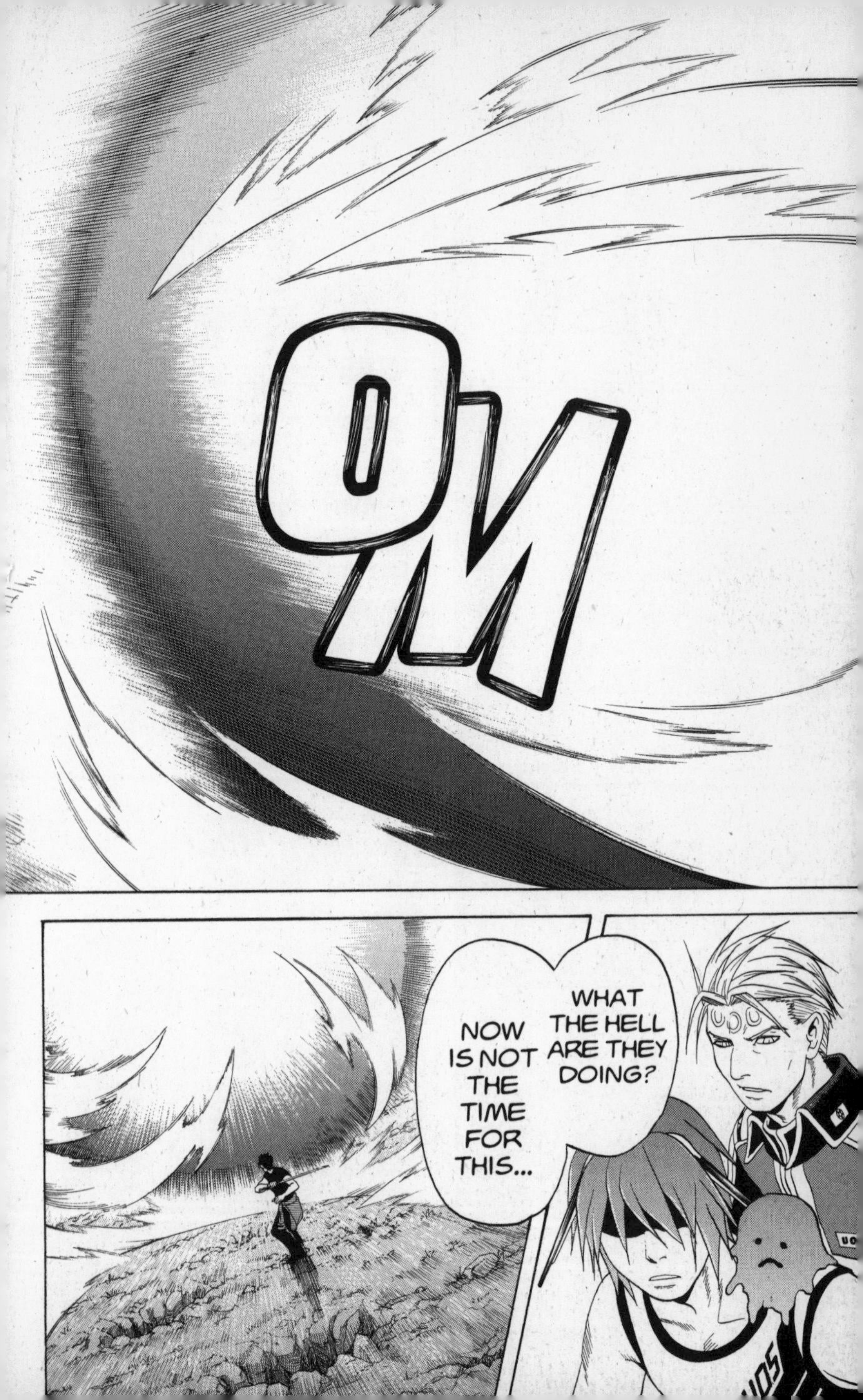
OM
WHAT THE HELL ARE THEY DOING?
NOW IS NOT THE TIME FOR THIS...

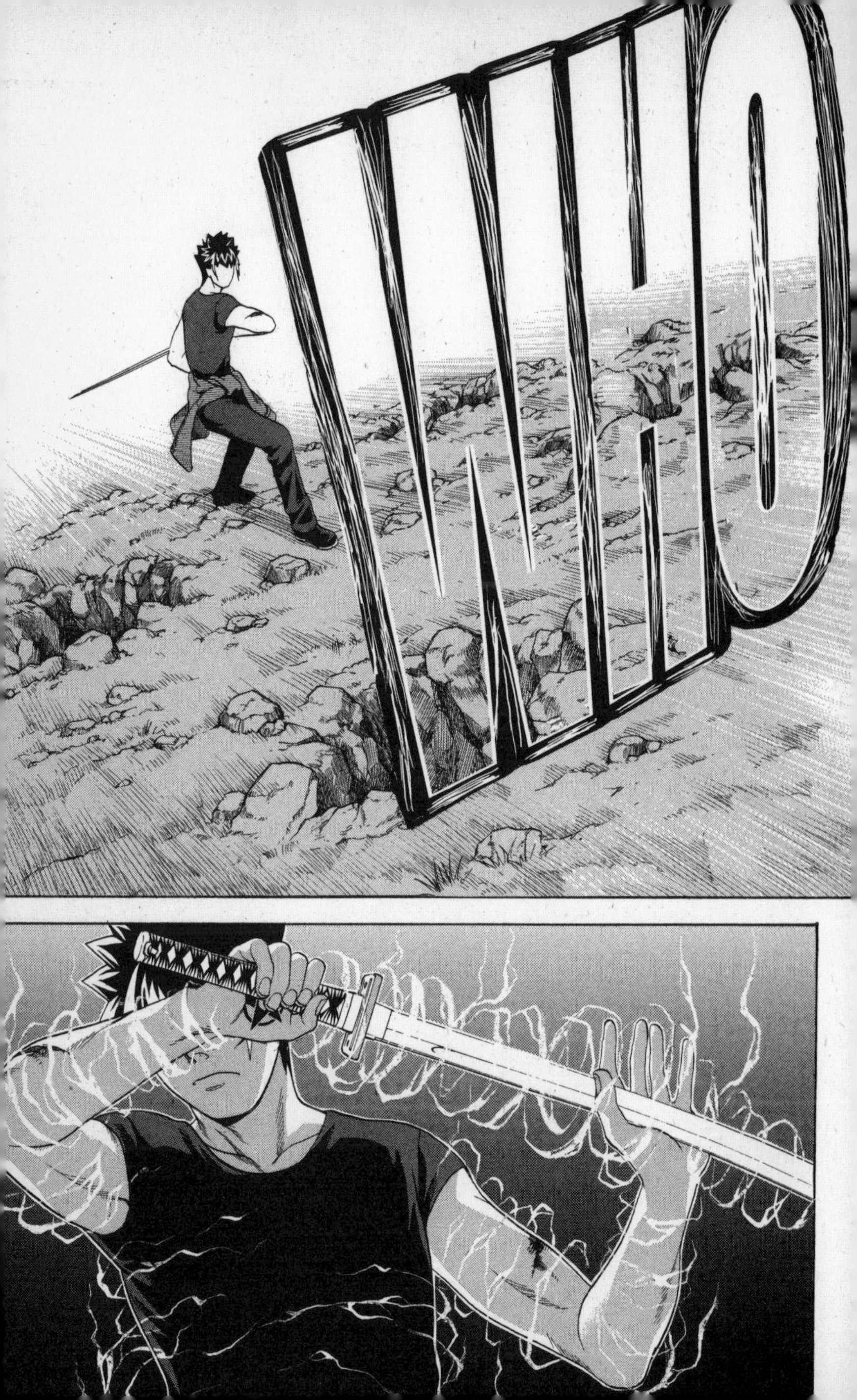
WHO

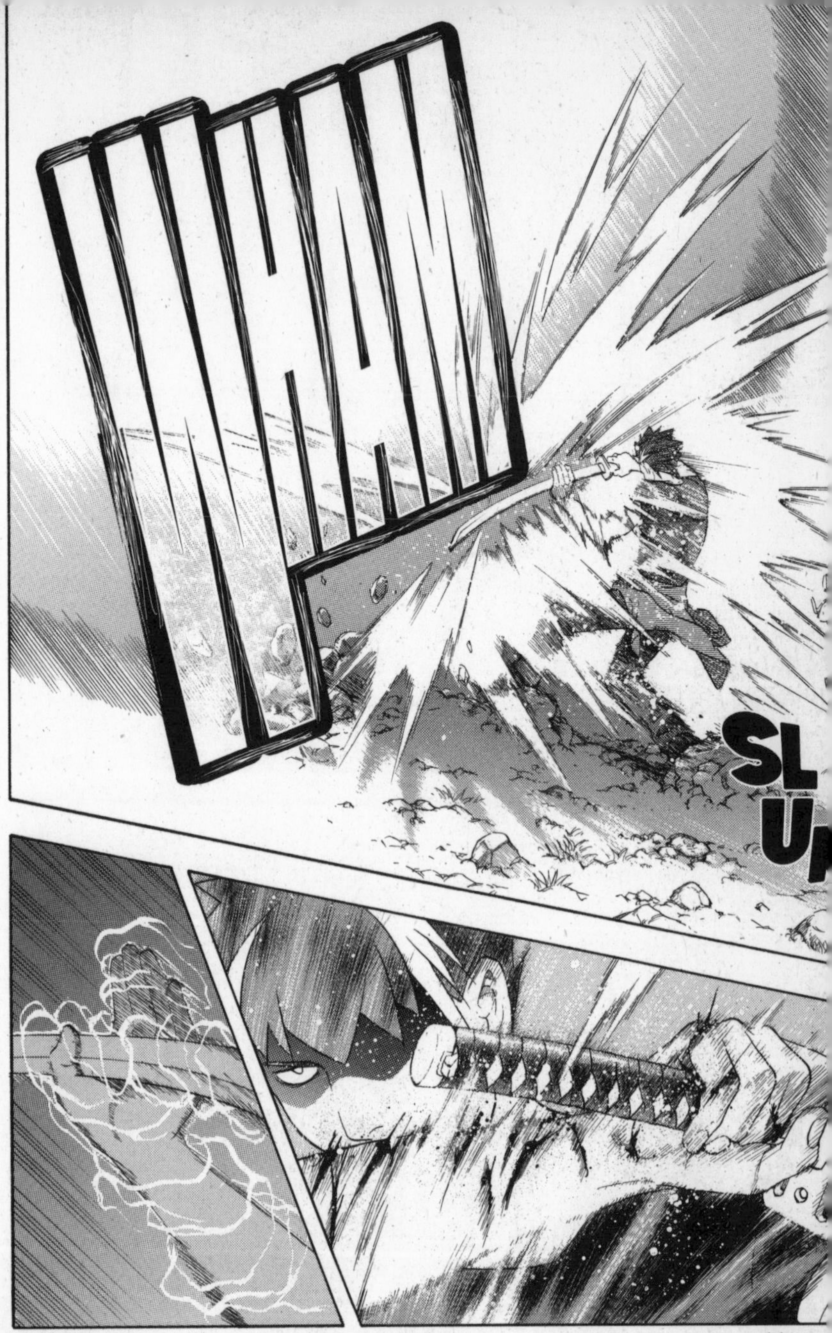
WHAM

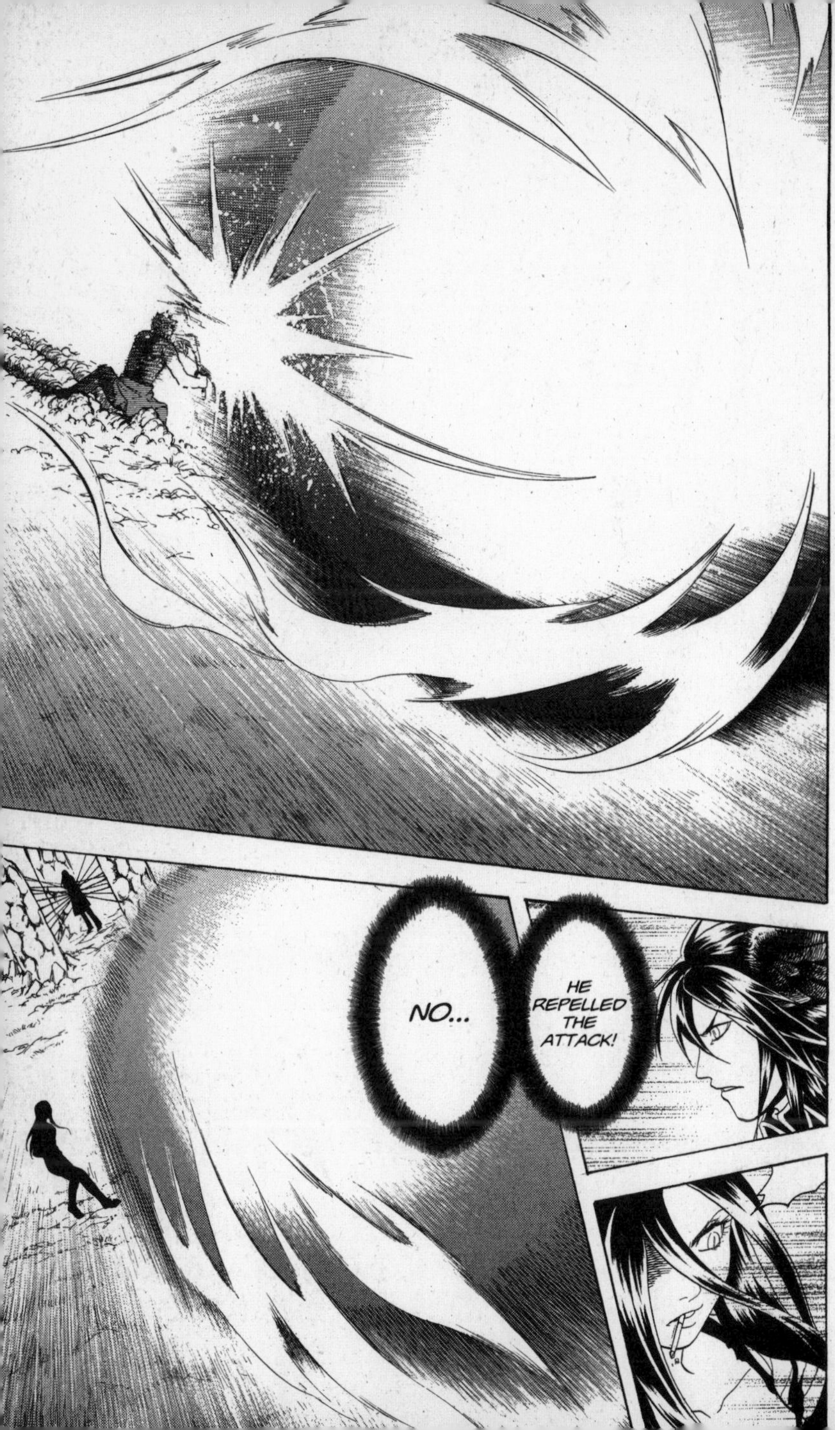
HE REPELLED THE ATTACK!
NO...

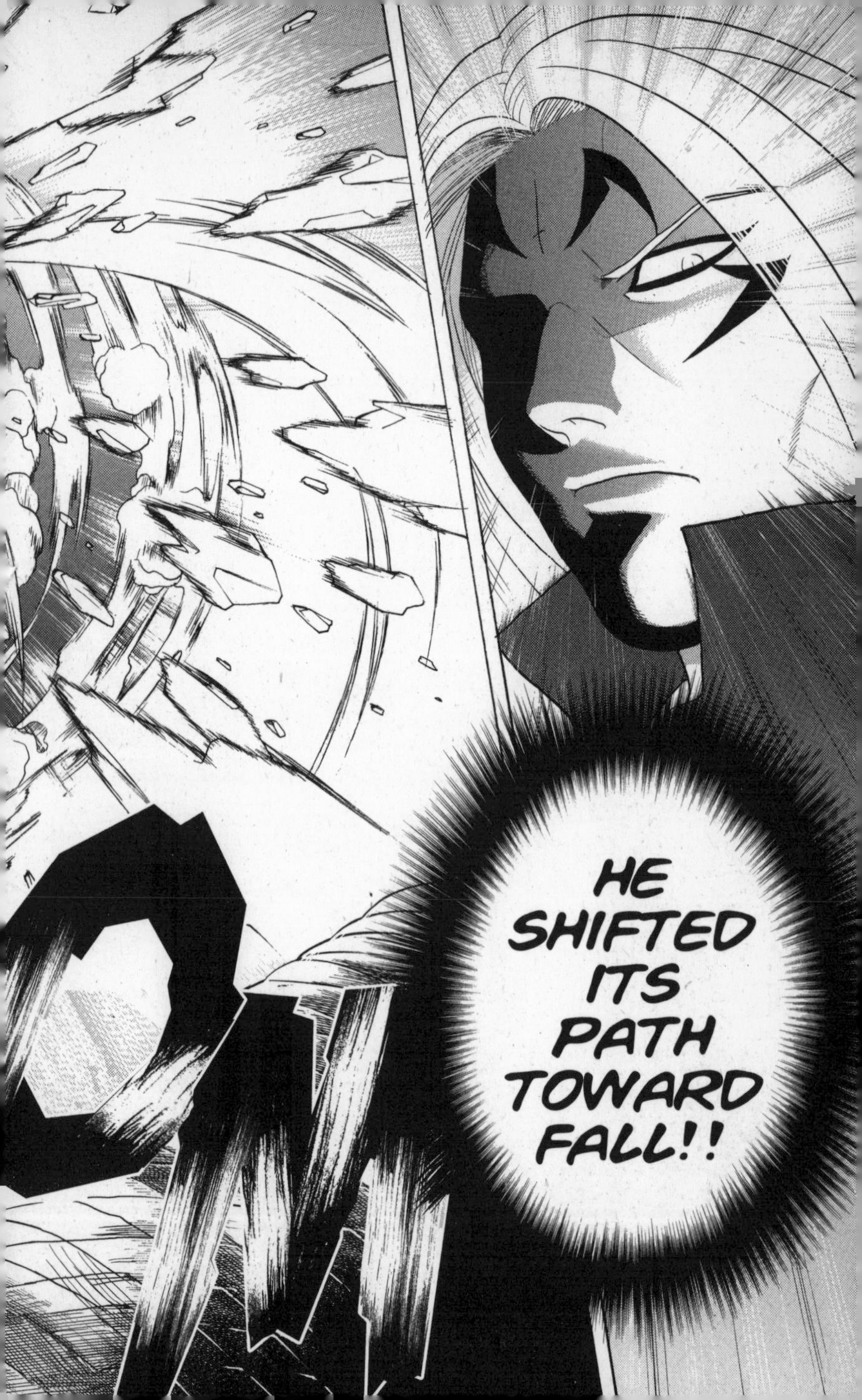
HE SHIFTED ITS PATH TOWARD FALL!!

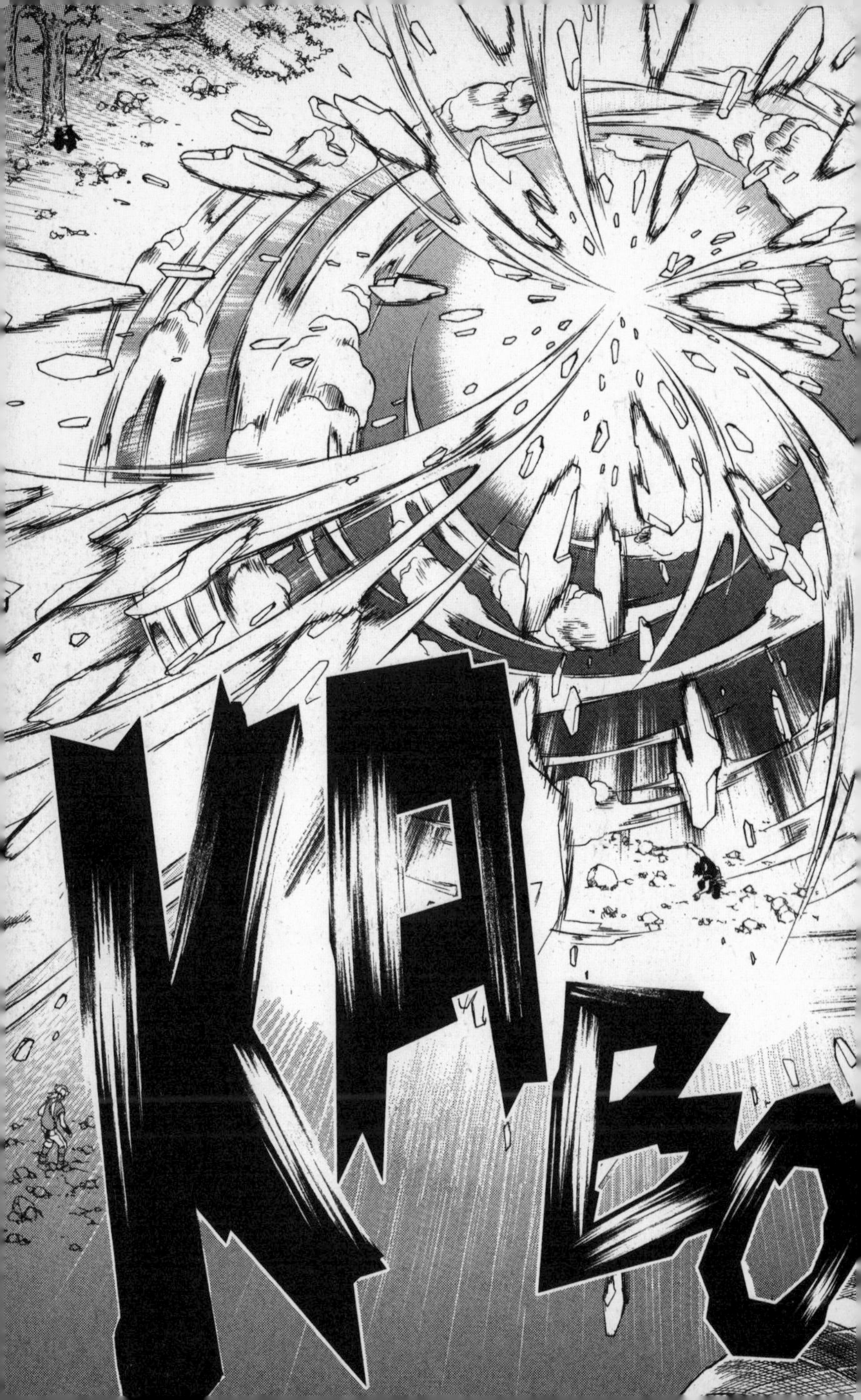
KABO

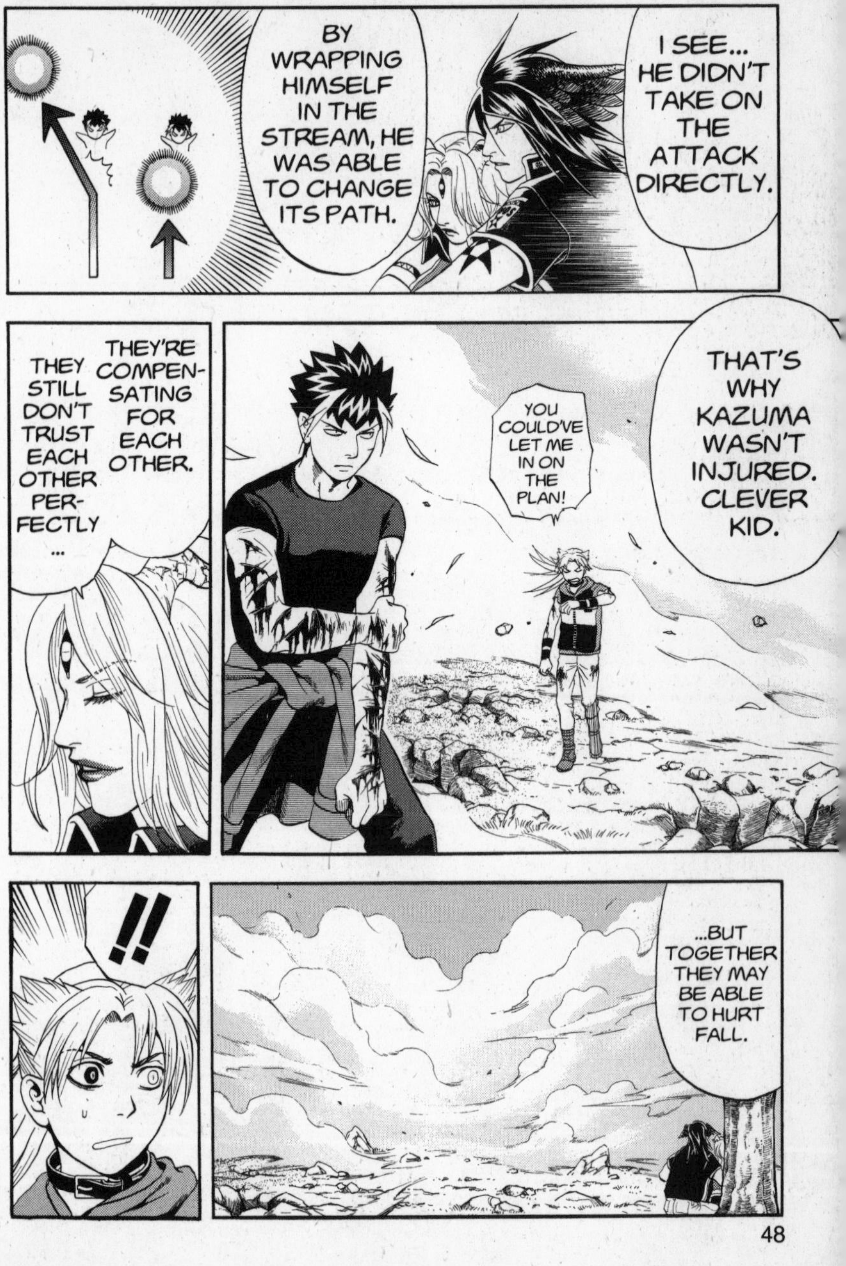
I SEE... HE DIDN'T TAKE ON THE ATTACK DIRECTLY.
BY WRAPPING HIMSELF IN THE STREAM, HE WAS ABLE TO CHANGE ITS PATH.
THAT'S WHY KAZUMA WASN'T INJURED. CLEVER KID.
YOU COULD'VE LET ME IN ON THE PLAN!
THEY'RE COMPEN-SATING FOR EACH OTHER.
THEY STILL DON'T TRUST EACH OTHER PER-FECTLY ...
...BUT TOGETHER THEY MAY BE ABLE TO HURT FALL.
!!

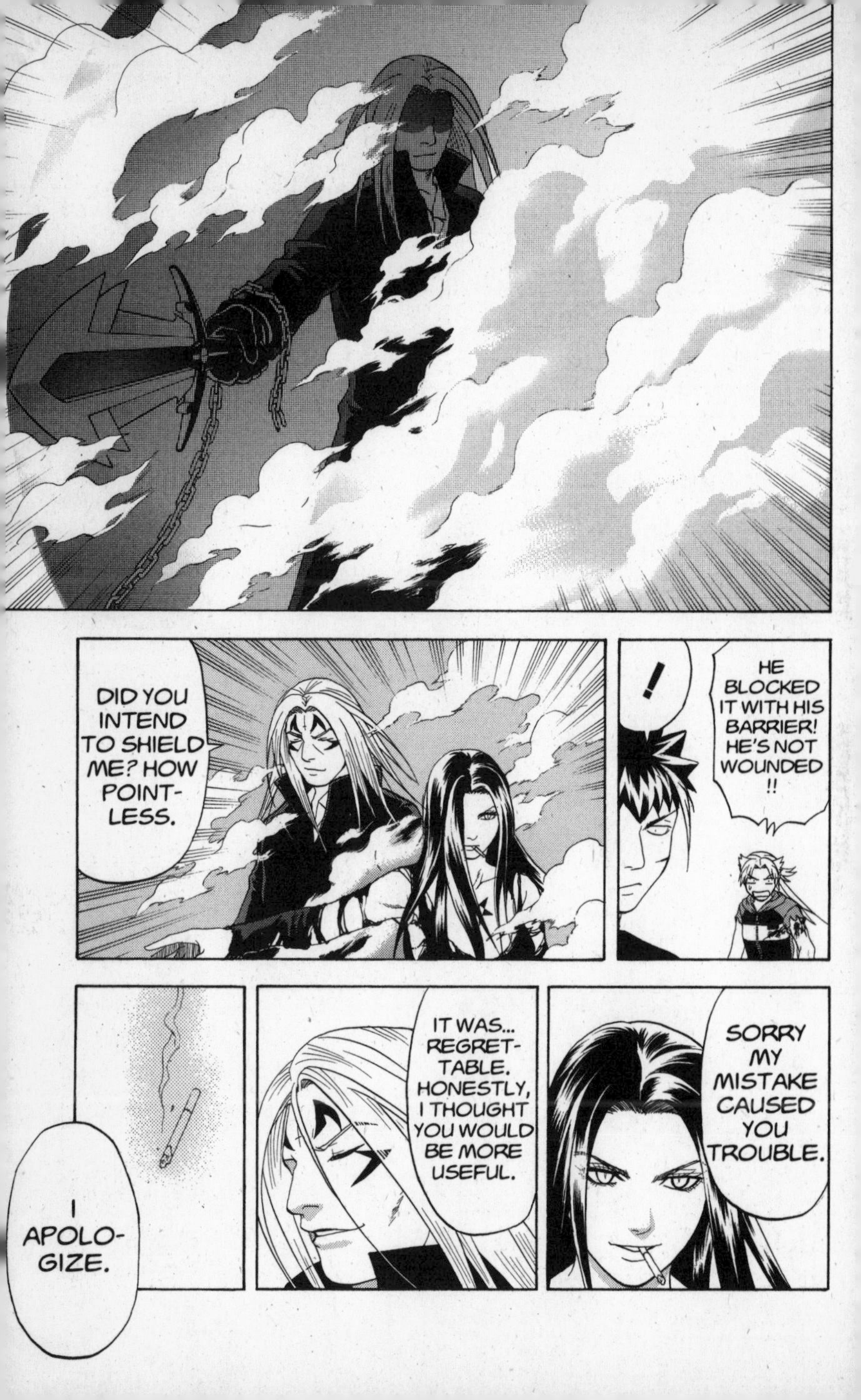
!
HE BLOCKED IT WITH HIS BARRIER! HE'S NOT WOUNDED !!
DID YOU INTEND TO SHIELD ME? HOW POINTLESS.
SORRY MY MISTAKE CAUSED YOU TROUBLE.
IT WAS... REGRETTABLE. HONESTLY, I THOUGHT YOU WOULD BE MORE USEFUL.
I APOLOGIZE.

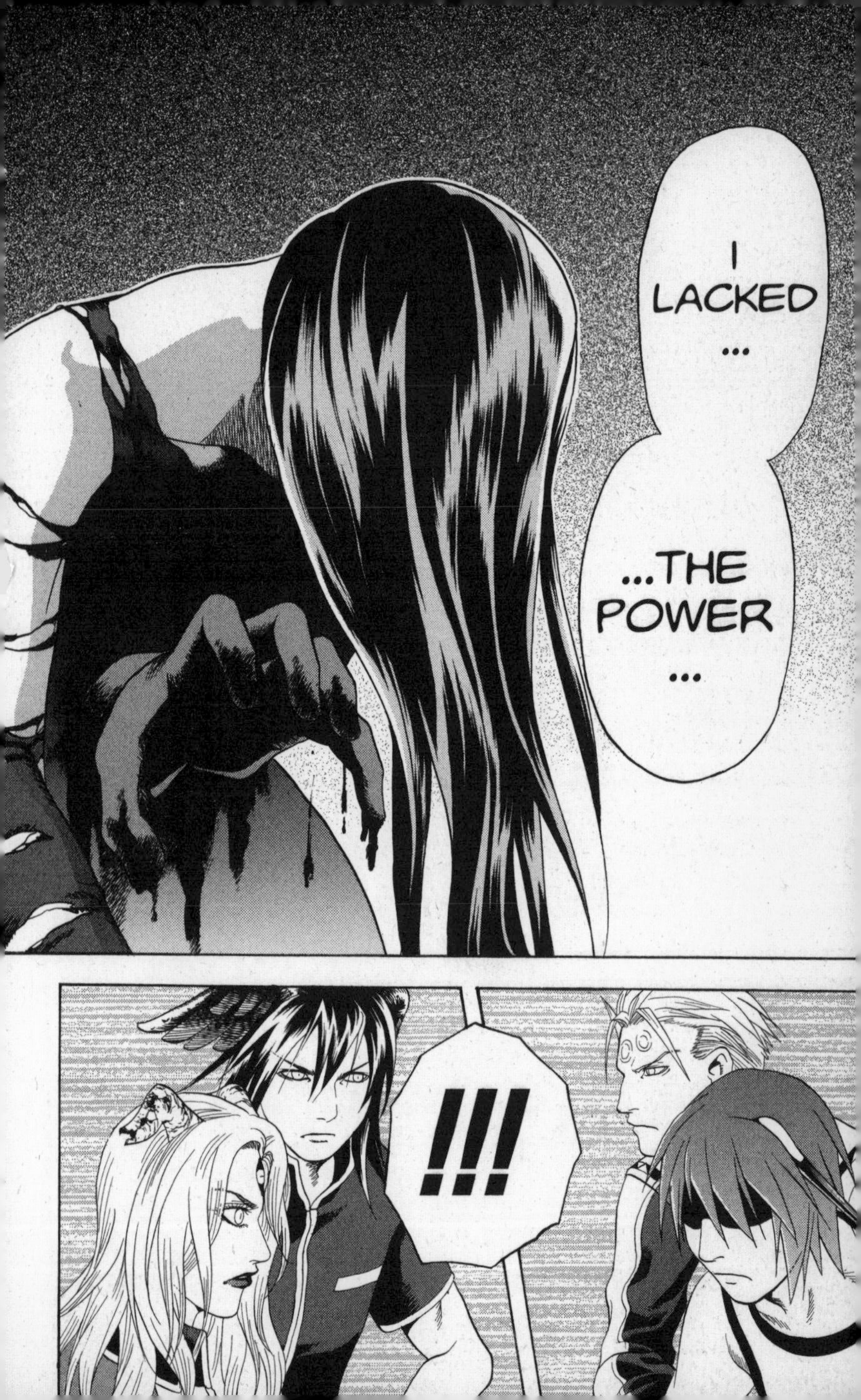
I LACKED ...
...THE POWER ...
!!!

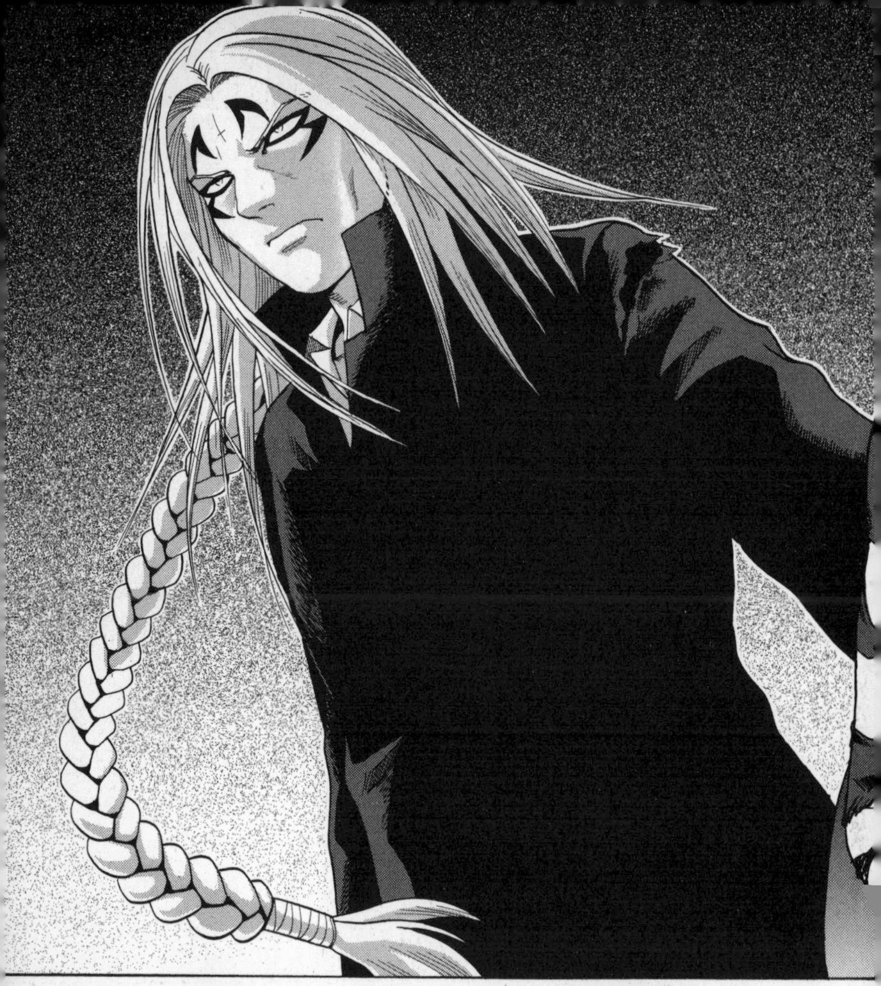

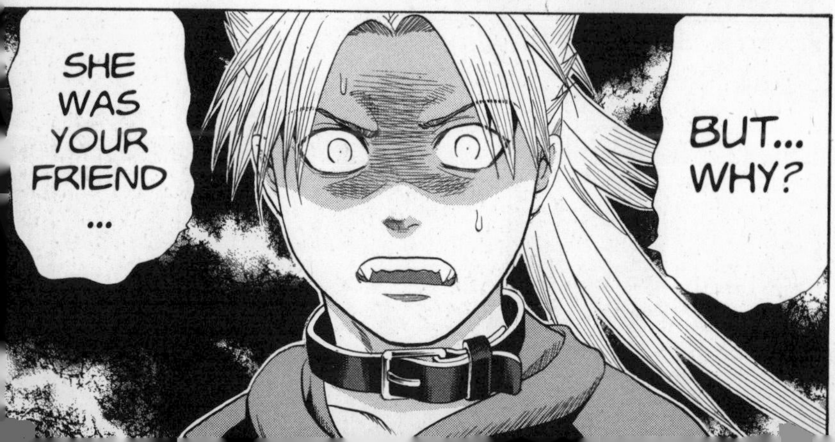
BUT... WHY?
SHE WAS YOUR FRIEND ...

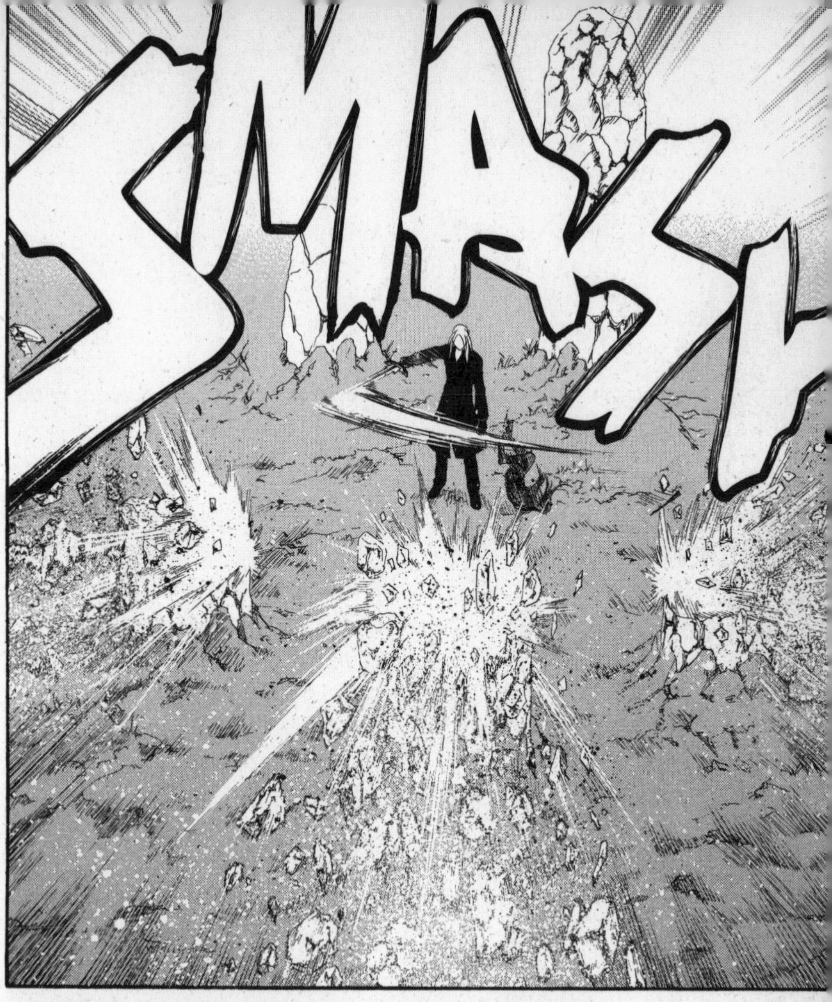
SMASH

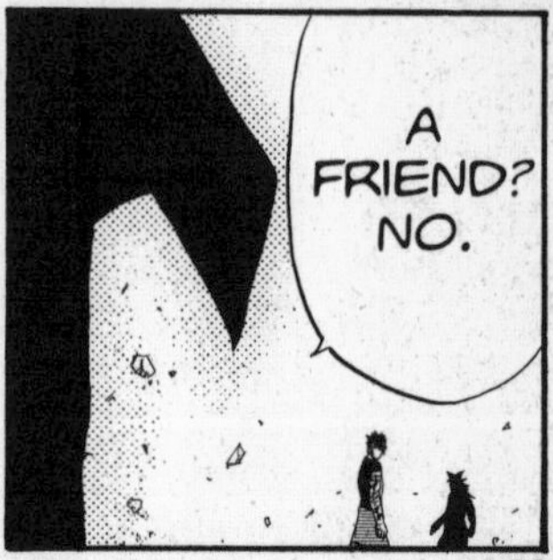
A FRIEND? NO.

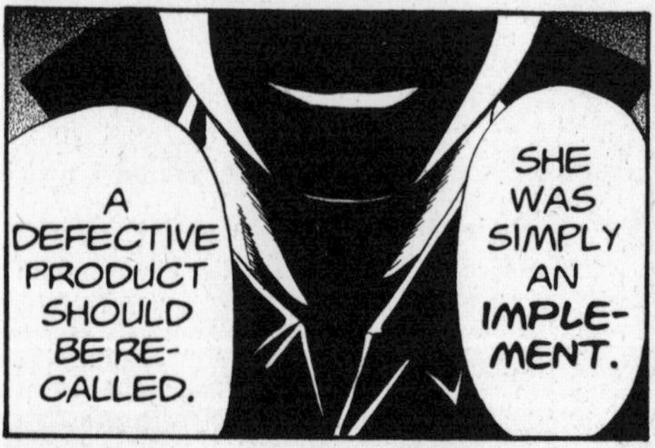
SHE WAS SIMPLY AN IMPLEMENT.
A DEFECTIVE PRODUCT SHOULD BE RECALLED.

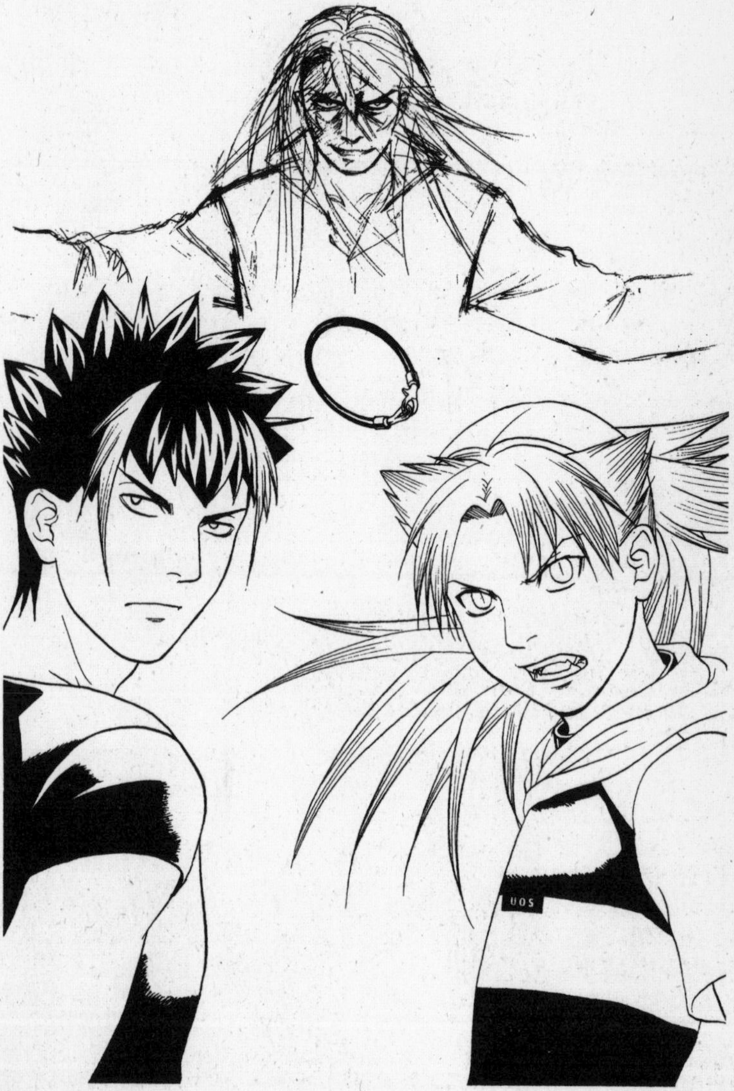
UOS

Story 30: For My Comrades

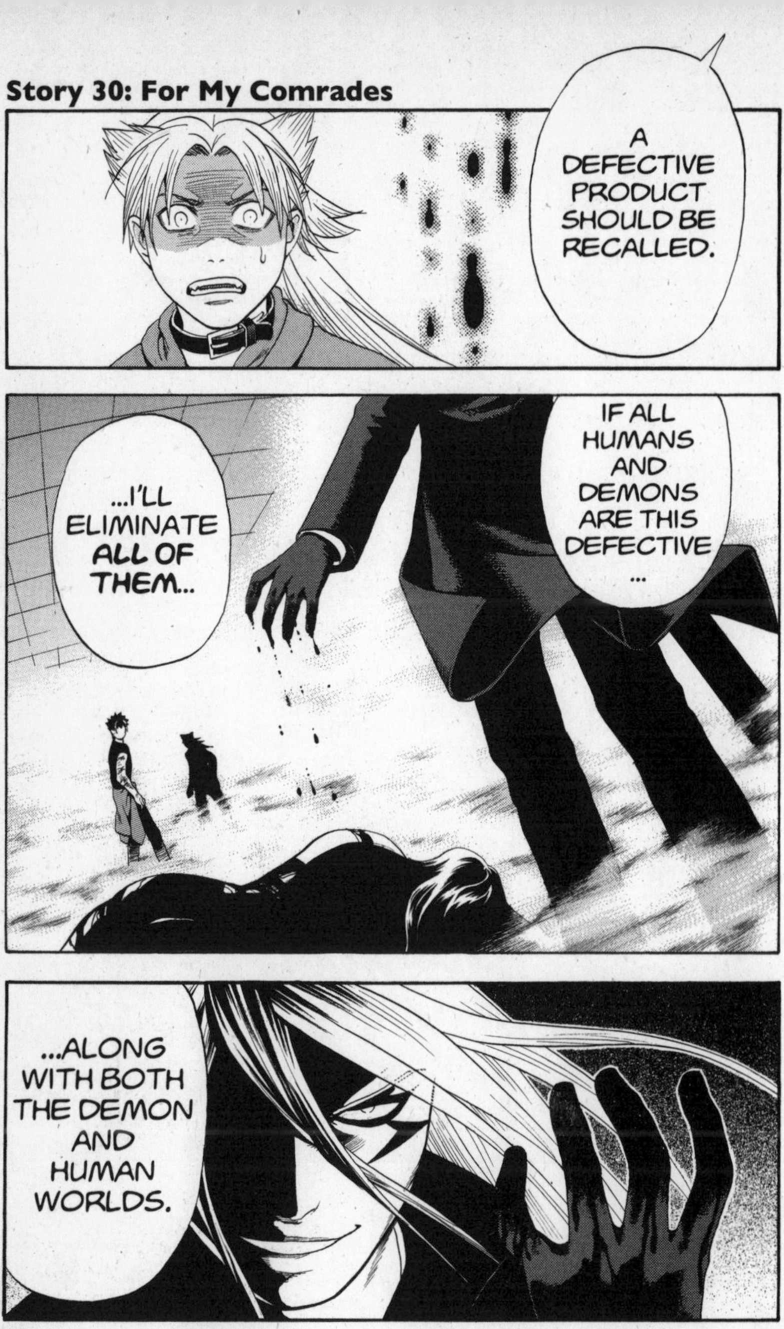
A DEFECTIVE PRODUCT SHOULD BE RECALLED.
IF ALL HUMANS AND DEMONS ARE THIS DEFECTIVE...
...I'LL ELIMINATE ALL OF THEM...
...ALONG WITH BOTH THE DEMON AND HUMAN WORLDS.

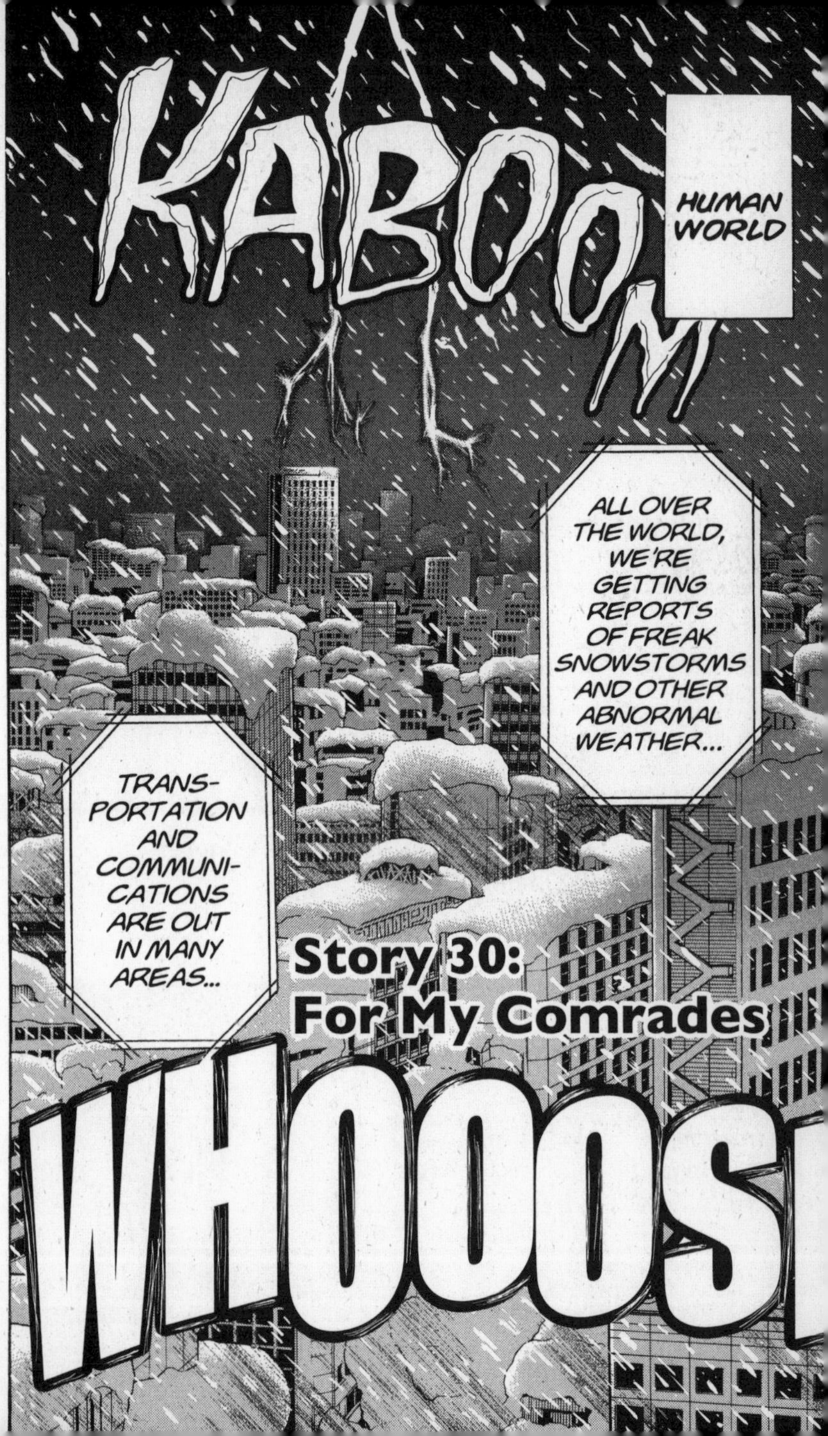

Story 30: For My Comrades

READ THIS WAY

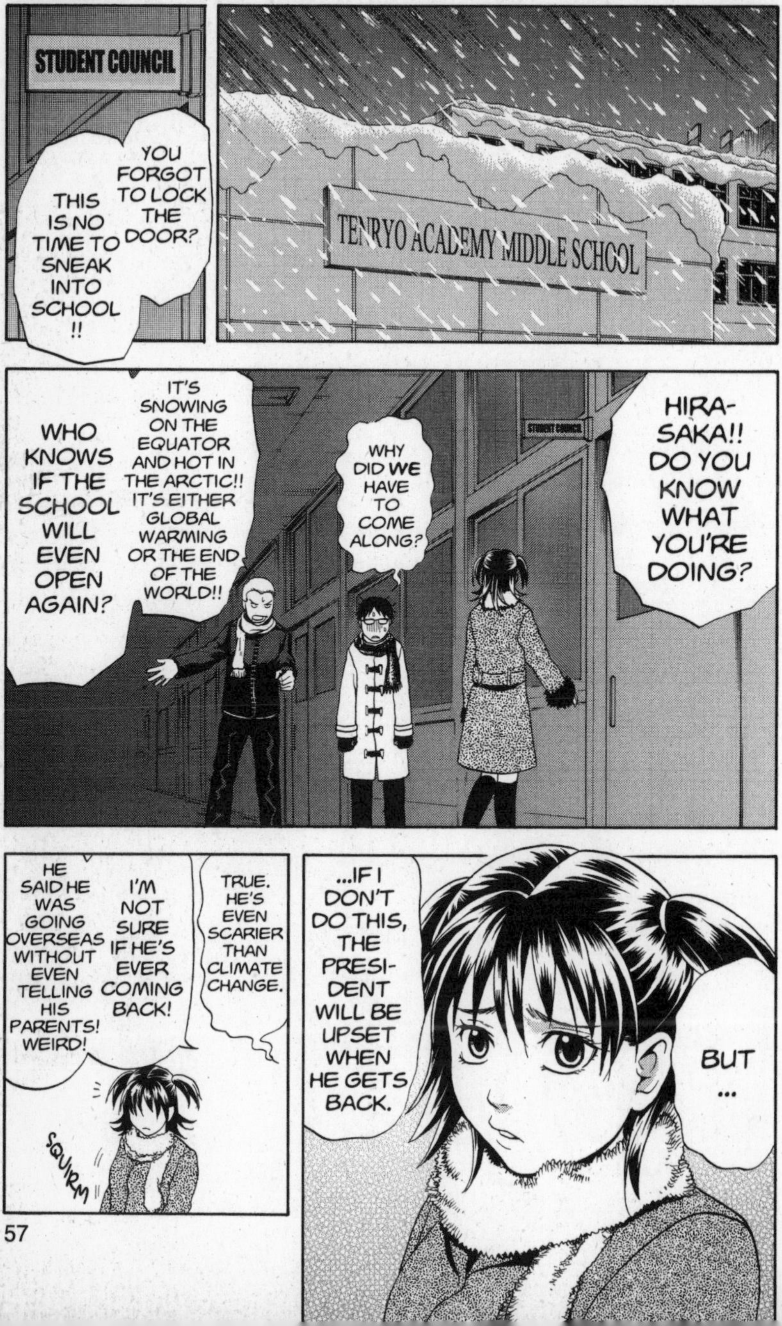
TENRYO ACADEMY MIDDLE SCHOOL
STUDENT COUNCIL
YOU FORGOT TO LOCK THE DOOR?
THIS IS NO TIME TO SNEAK INTO SCHOOL!!
HIRA-SAKA!! DO YOU KNOW WHAT YOU'RE DOING?
STUDENT COUNCIL
WHY DID WE HAVE TO COME ALONG?
IT'S SNOWING ON THE EQUATOR AND HOT IN THE ARCTIC!! IT'S EITHER GLOBAL WARMING OR THE END OF THE WORLD!!
WHO KNOWS IF THE SCHOOL WILL EVEN OPEN AGAIN?
BUT...
...IF I DON'T DO THIS, THE PRESIDENT WILL BE UPSET WHEN HE GETS BACK.
TRUE. HE'S EVEN SCARIER THAN CLIMATE CHANGE.
I'M NOT SURE IF HE'S EVER COMING BACK!
HE SAID HE WAS GOING OVERSEAS WITHOUT EVEN TELLING HIS PARENTS! WEIRD!
SQUIRM

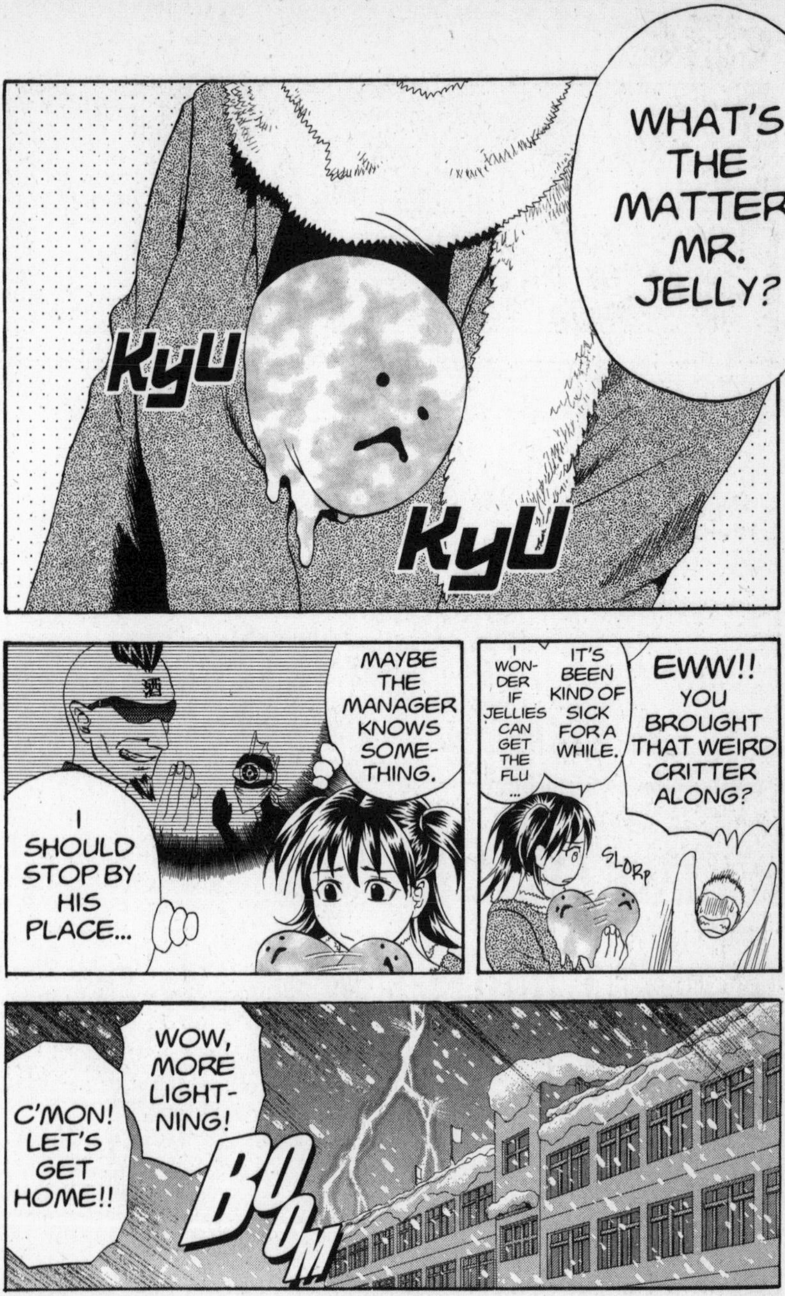
WHAT'S THE MATTER, MR. JELLY?
KYU
KYU
EWW!! YOU BROUGHT THAT WEIRD CRITTER ALONG?
IT'S BEEN KIND OF SICK FOR A WHILE.
I WONDER IF JELLIES CAN GET THE FLU...
SLORP
MAYBE THE MANAGER KNOWS SOMETHING.
I SHOULD STOP BY HIS PLACE...
WOW, MORE LIGHTNING!
C'MON! LET'S GET HOME!!
BOOM

READ THIS WAY

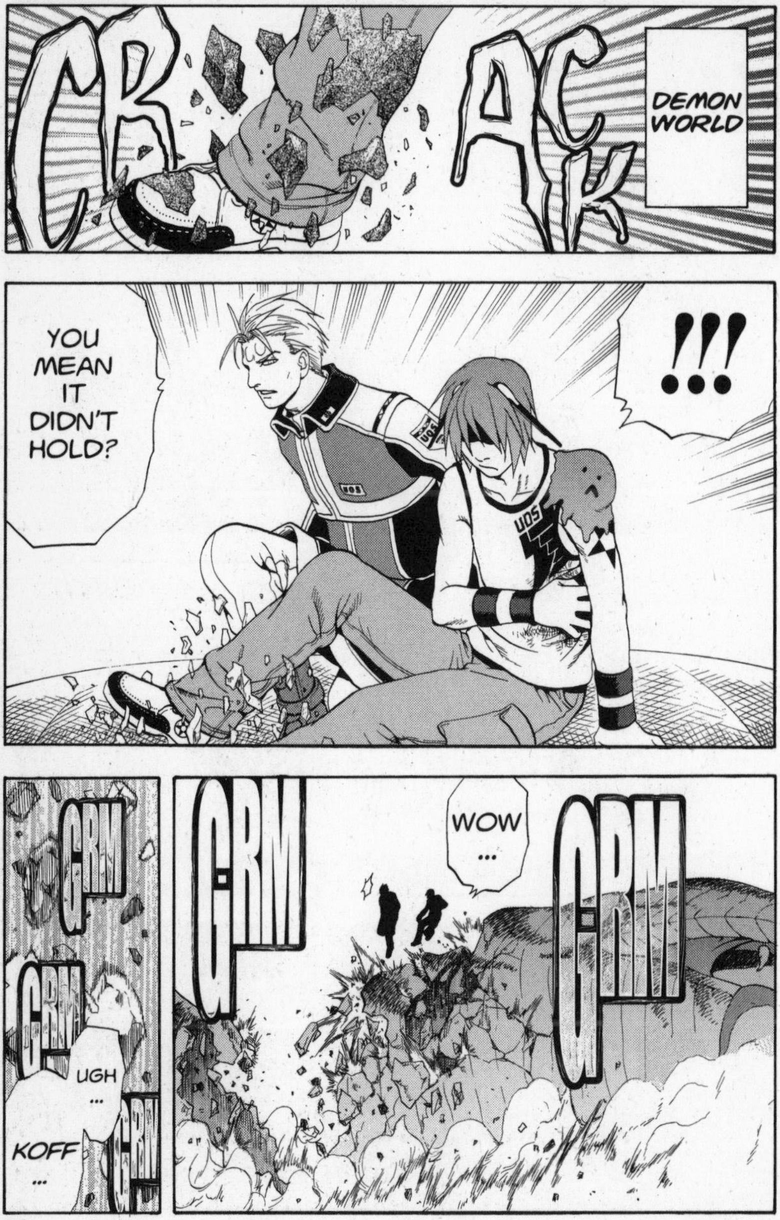
DEMON WORLD
CRACK
!!!
YOU MEAN IT DIDN'T HOLD?
GRM
WOW ...
GRM
GRM
GRM
UGH ... KOFF ...
GRM

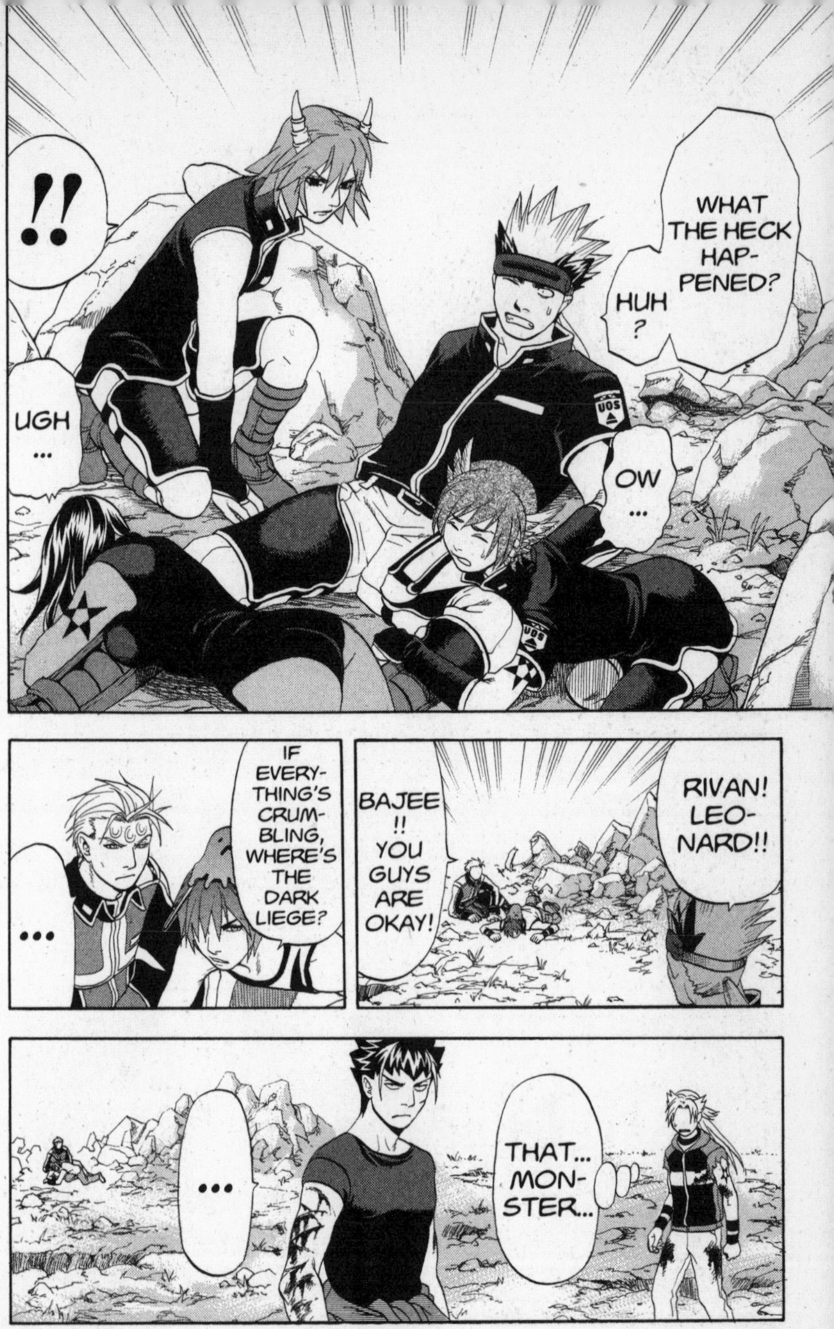
WHAT THE HECK HAP-PENED?
HUH?
!!
OW...
UGH...
RIVAN! LEO-NARD!!
BAJEE!! YOU GUYS ARE OKAY!
IF EVERY-THING'S CRUM-BLING, WHERE'S THE DARK LIEGE?
...
THAT... MON-STER...
...

READ THIS WAY

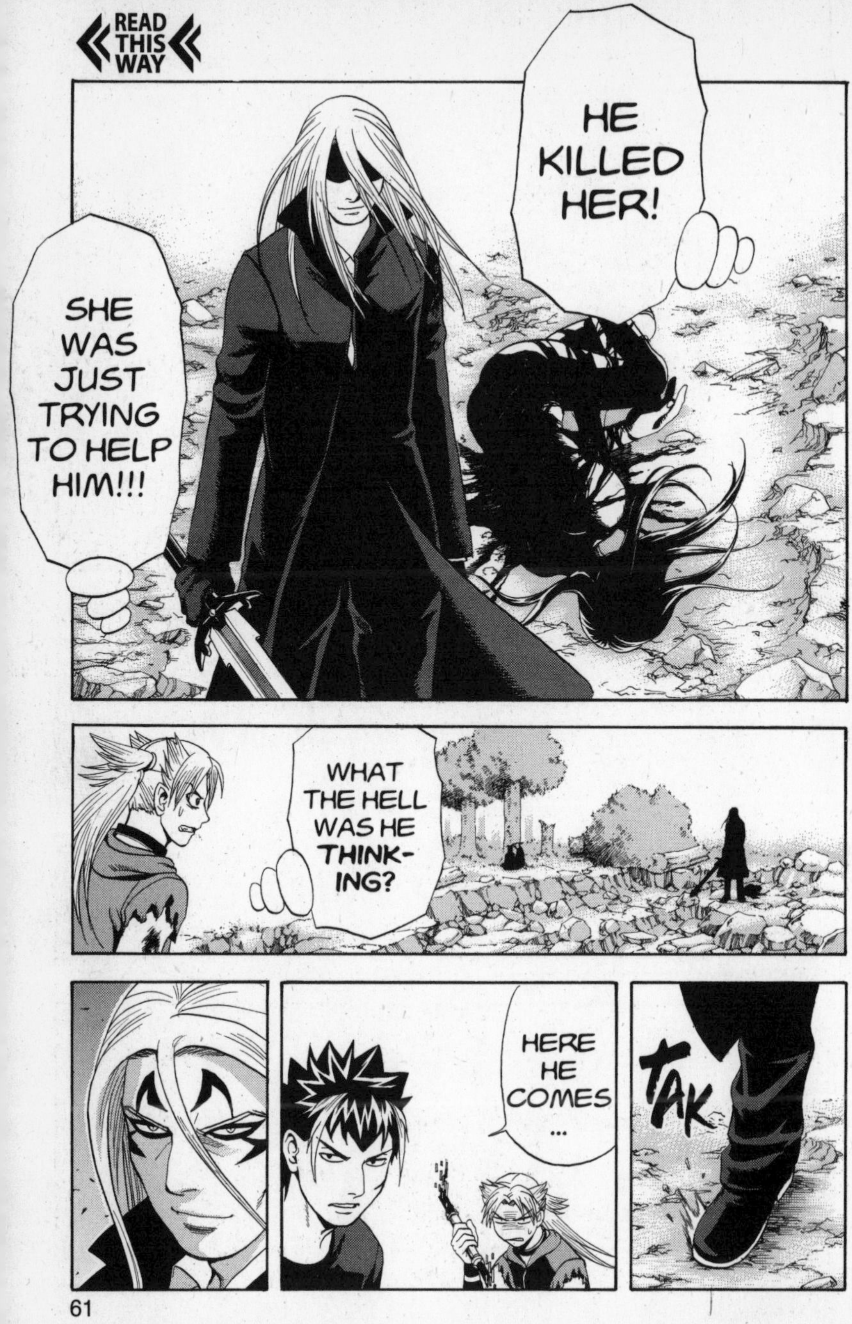
HE KILLED HER!
SHE WAS JUST TRYING TO HELP HIM!!!
WHAT THE HELL WAS HE THINK-ING?
TAK
HERE HE COMES ...

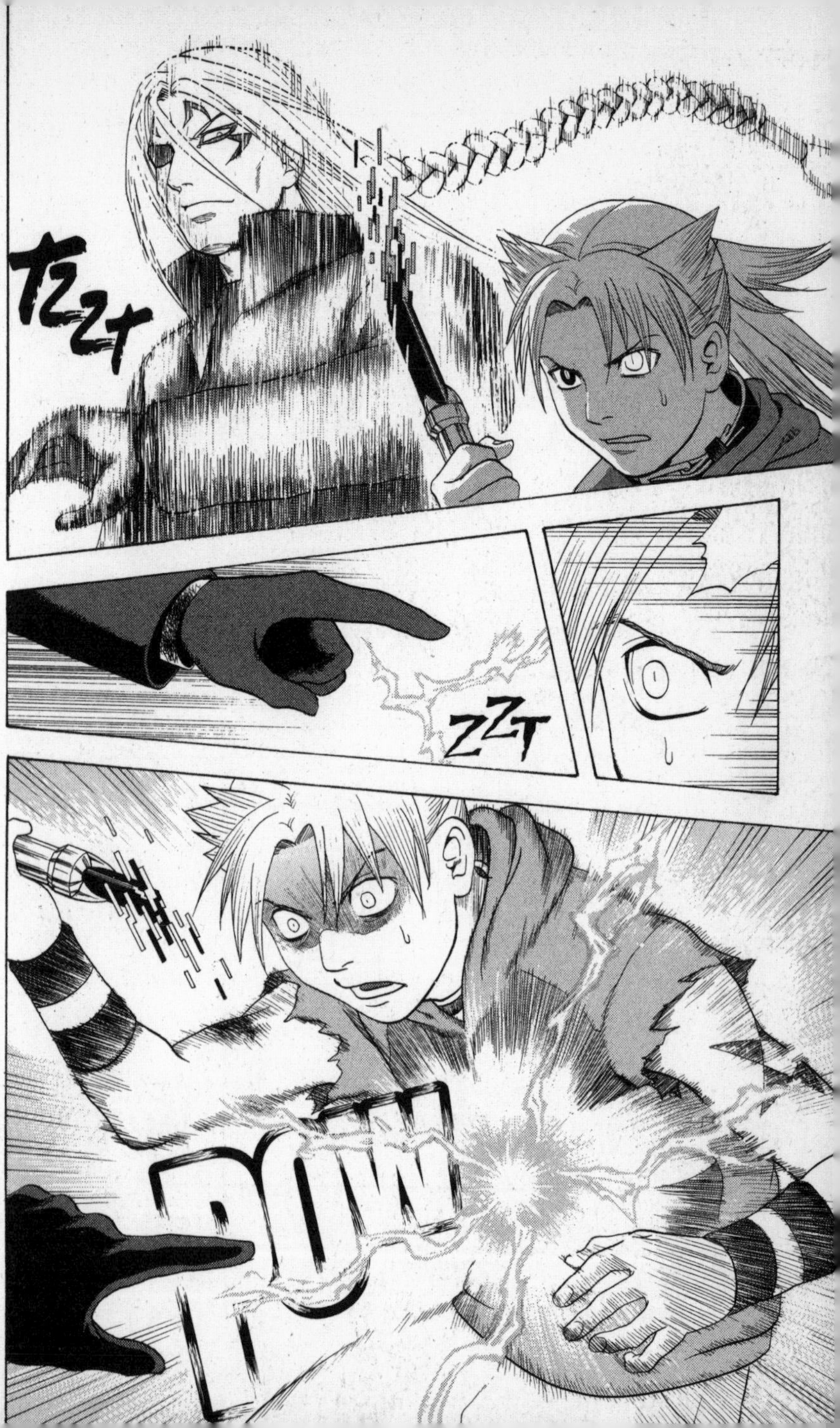
TZZT
ZZT
POW

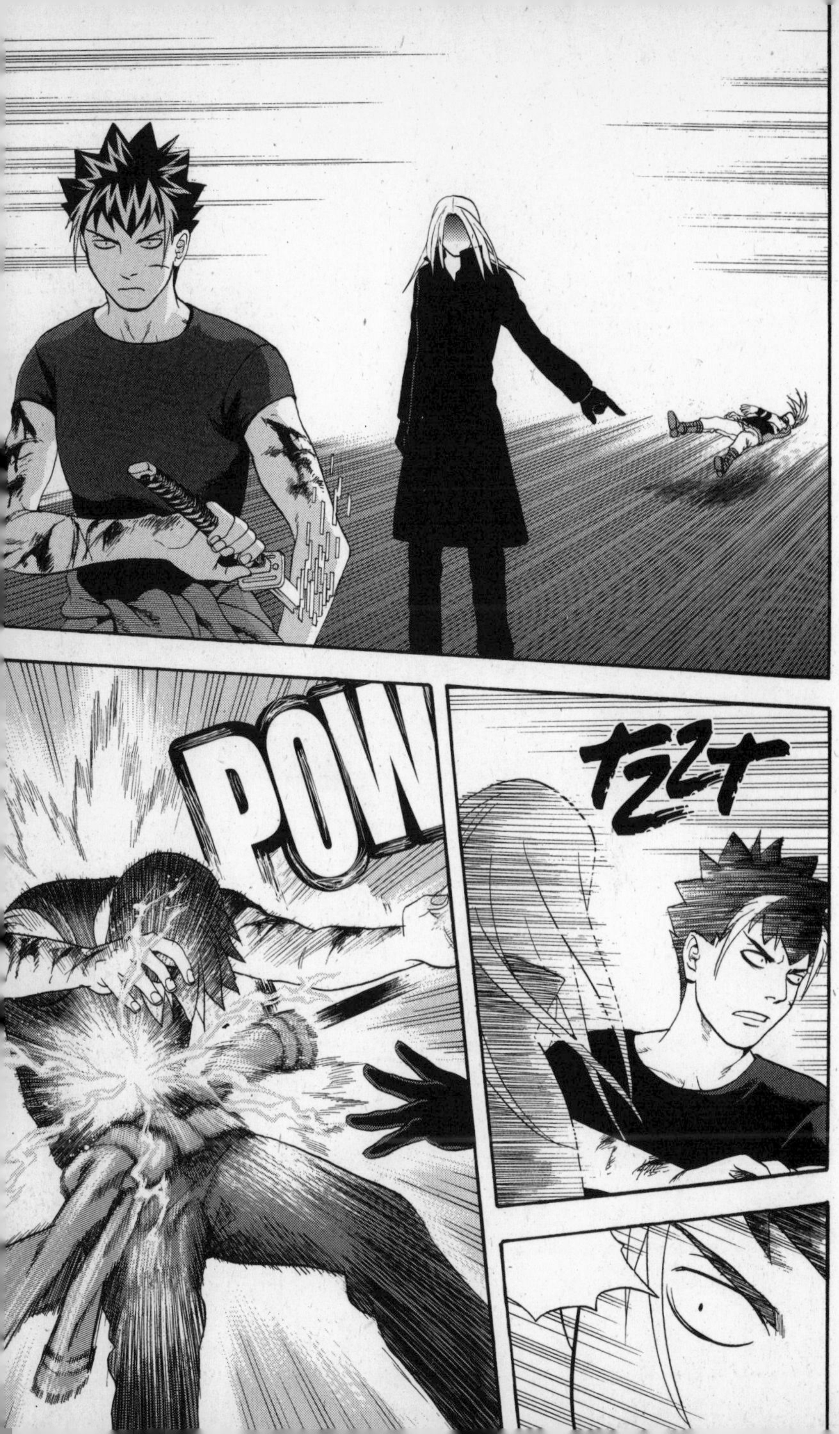
TZZT
POW

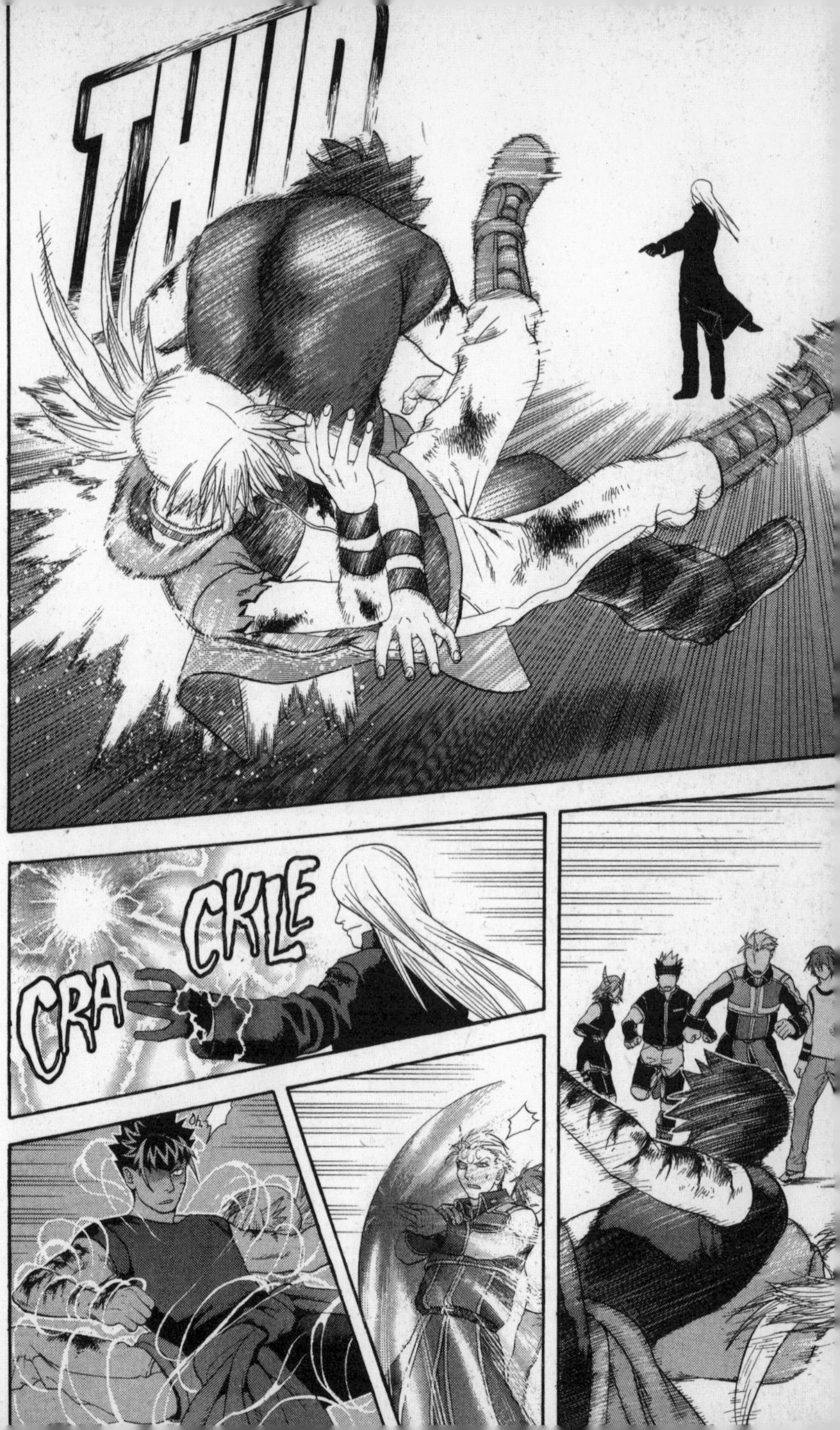
THUD
CRACKLE
Oh...

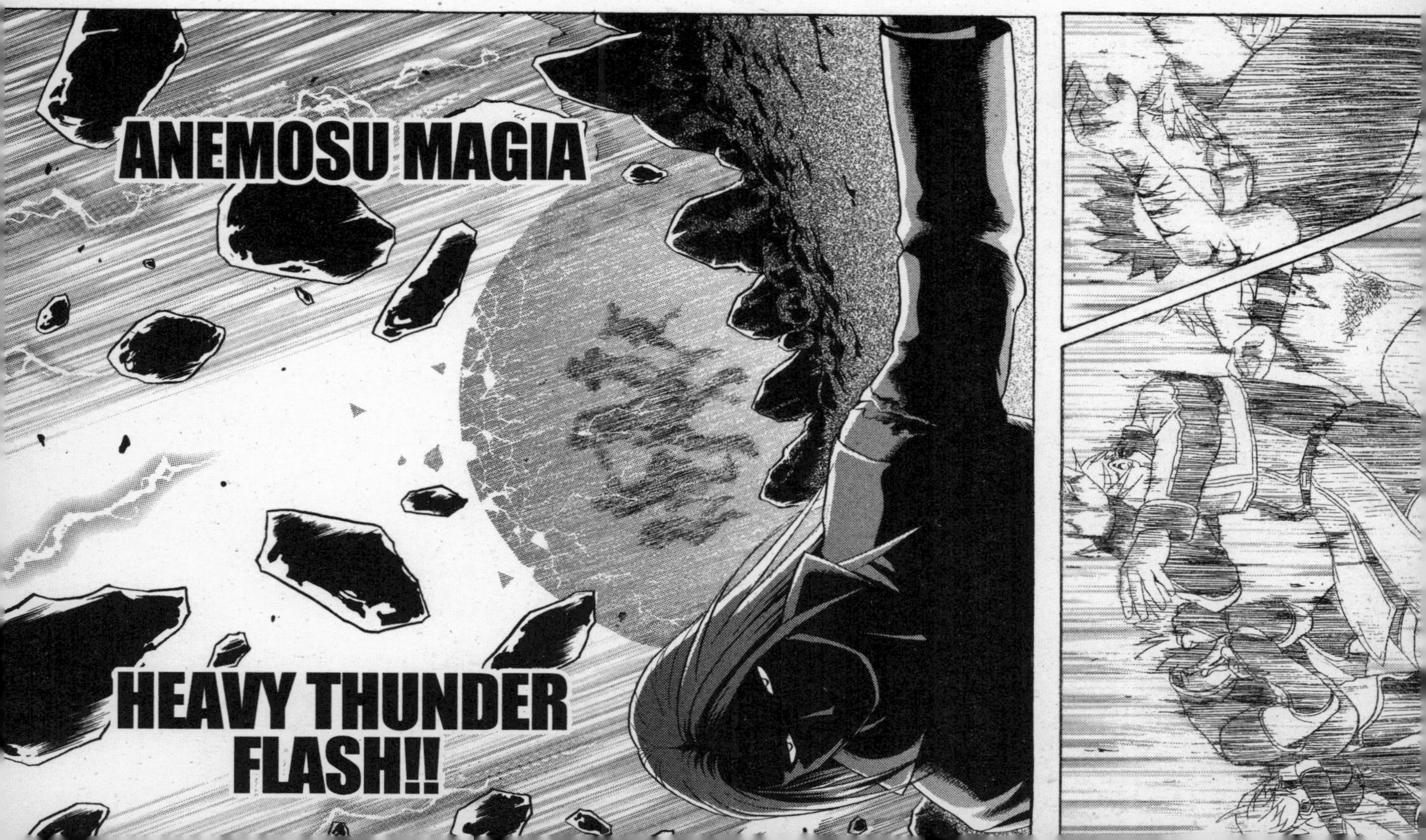
ANEMOSU MAGIA
HEAVY THUNDER FLASH!!

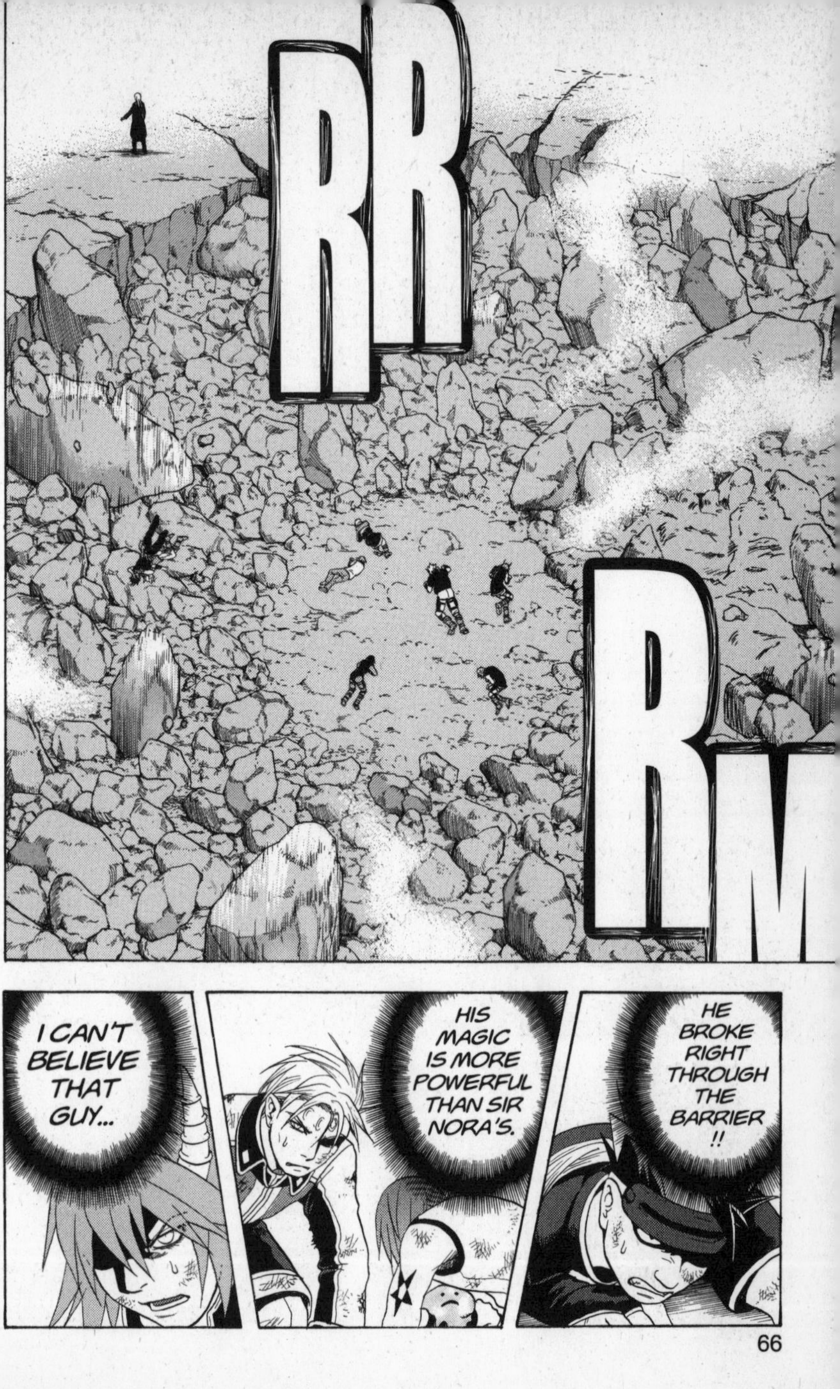
RR
RM
HE BROKE RIGHT THROUGH THE BARRIER!!
HIS MAGIC IS MORE POWERFUL THAN SIR NORA'S.
I CAN'T BELIEVE THAT GUY...

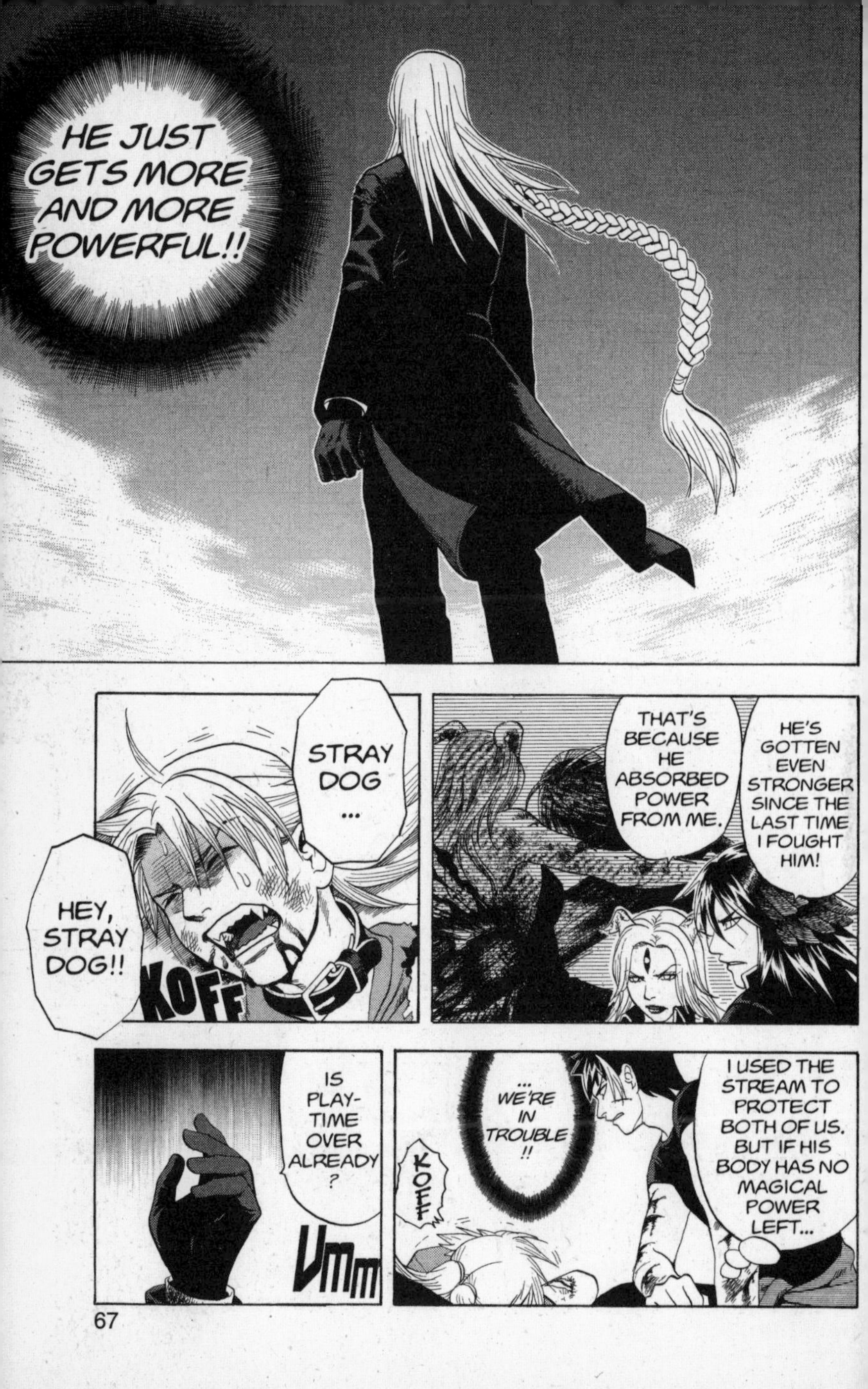
HE JUST GETS MORE AND MORE POWERFUL!!
HE'S GOTTEN EVEN STRONGER SINCE THE LAST TIME I FOUGHT HIM!
THAT'S BECAUSE HE ABSORBED POWER FROM ME.
STRAY DOG ...
HEY, STRAY DOG!!
KOFF
I USED THE STREAM TO PROTECT BOTH OF US. BUT IF HIS BODY HAS NO MAGICAL POWER LEFT...
... WE'RE IN TROUBLE !!
KOFF
IS PLAY-TIME OVER ALREADY?
VMM

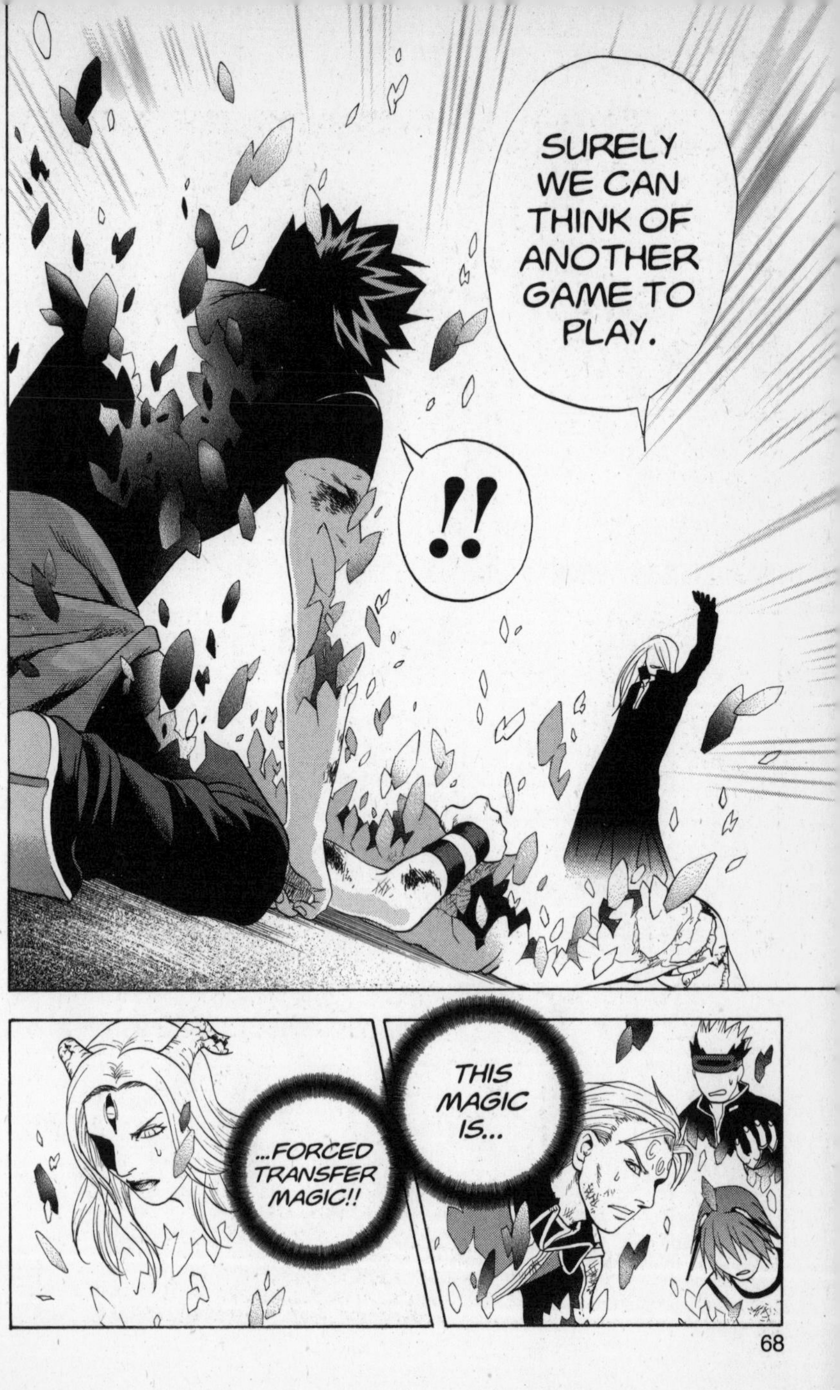
SURELY WE CAN THINK OF ANOTHER GAME TO PLAY.
!!
THIS MAGIC IS...
...FORCED TRANSFER MAGIC!!

READ THIS WAY

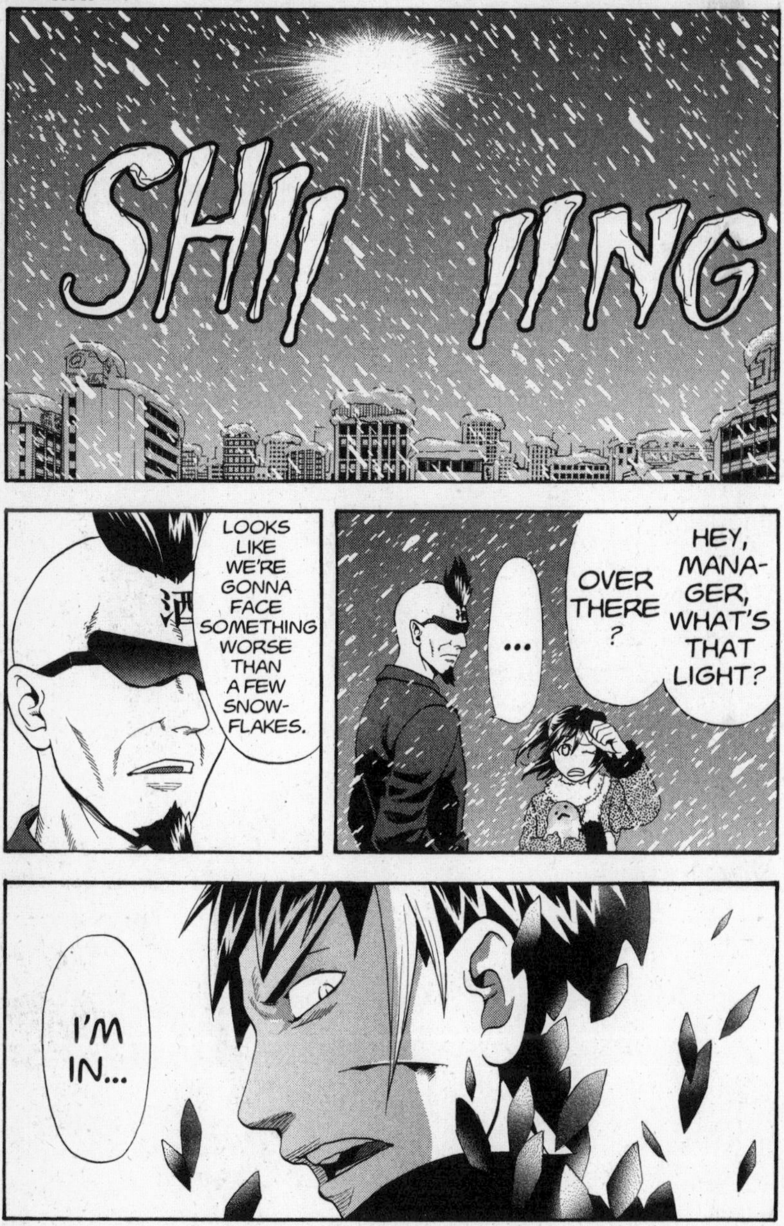
SHIIIING
HEY, MANAGER, WHAT'S THAT LIGHT?
OVER THERE?
...
LOOKS LIKE WE'RE GONNA FACE SOMETHING WORSE THAN A FEW SNOWFLAKES.
I'M IN...

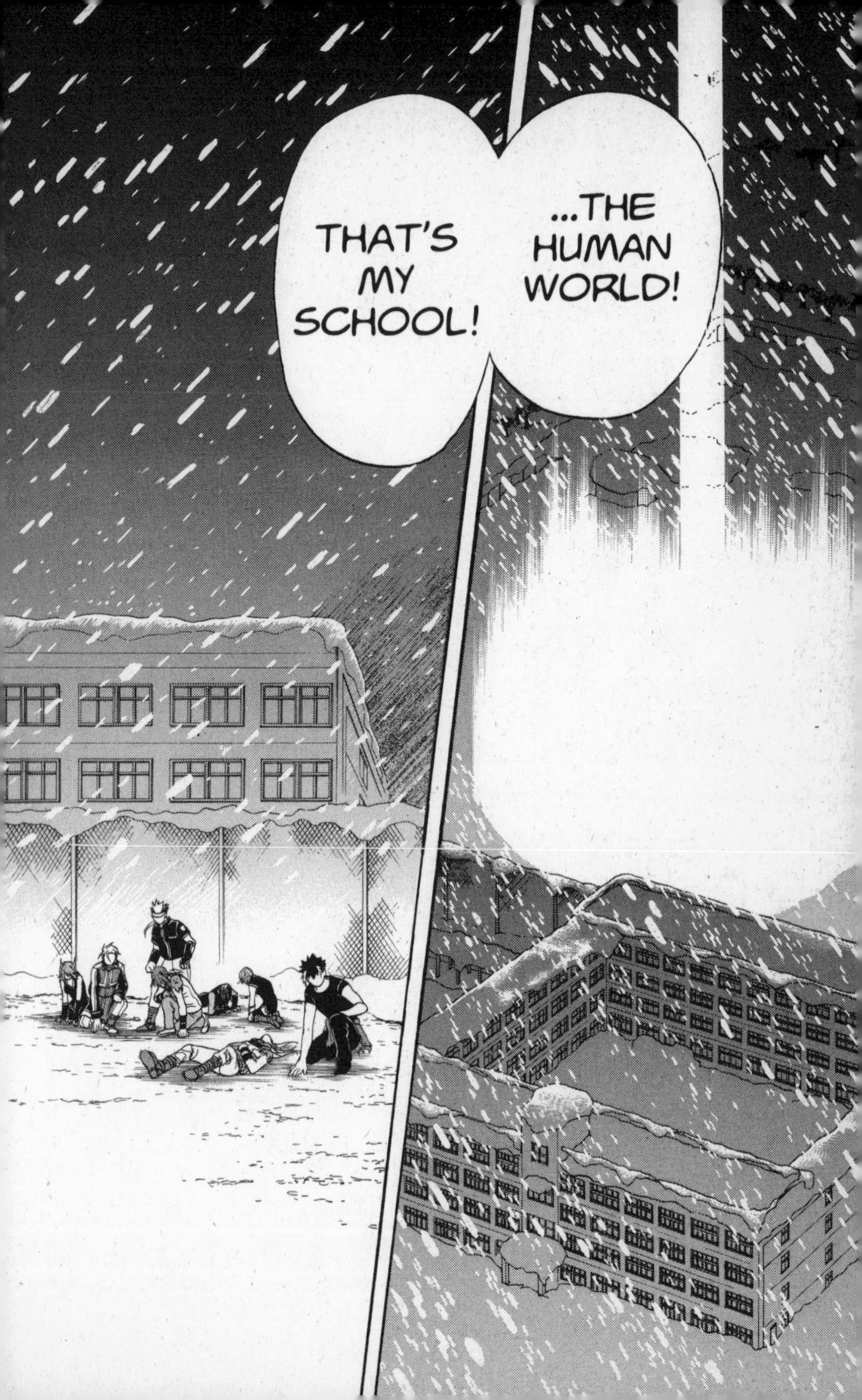
THAT'S MY SCHOOL!
...THE HUMAN WORLD!

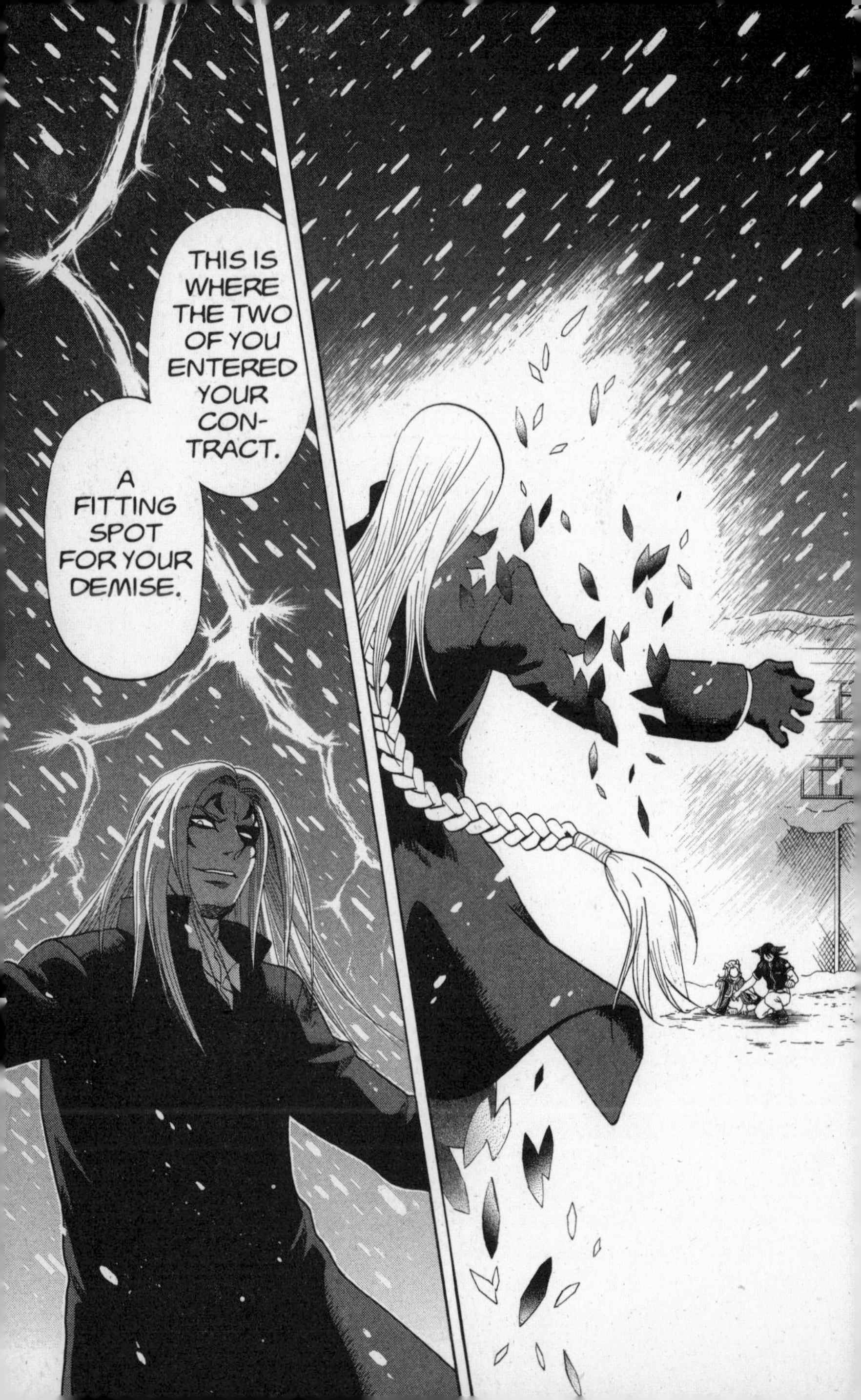
THIS IS WHERE THE TWO OF YOU ENTERED YOUR CON-TRACT.
A FITTING SPOT FOR YOUR DEMISE.

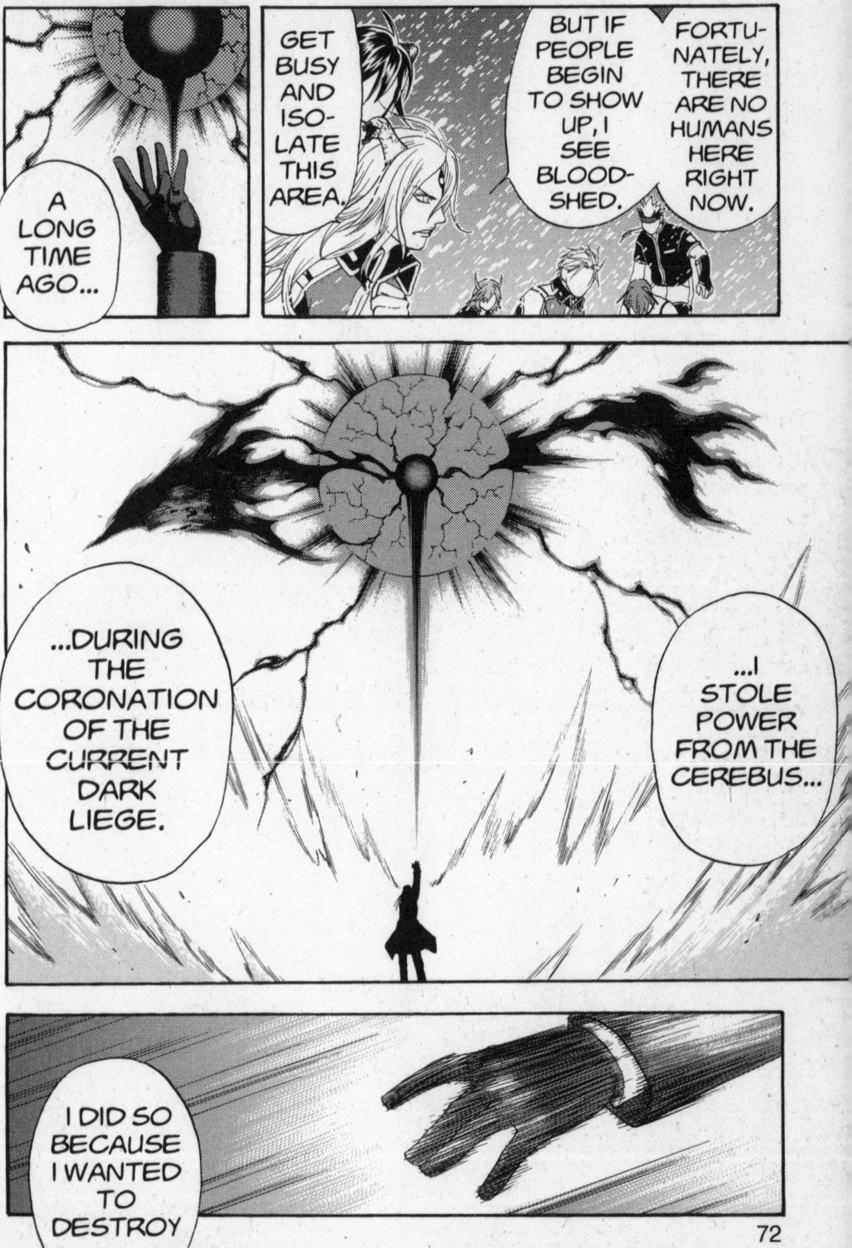
FORTUNATELY, THERE ARE NO HUMANS HERE RIGHT NOW.
BUT IF PEOPLE BEGIN TO SHOW UP, I SEE BLOODSHED.
GET BUSY AND ISOLATE THIS AREA.
A LONG TIME AGO...
...I STOLE POWER FROM THE CEREBUS...
...DURING THE CORONATION OF THE CURRENT DARK LIEGE.
I DID SO BECAUSE I WANTED TO DESTROY ...

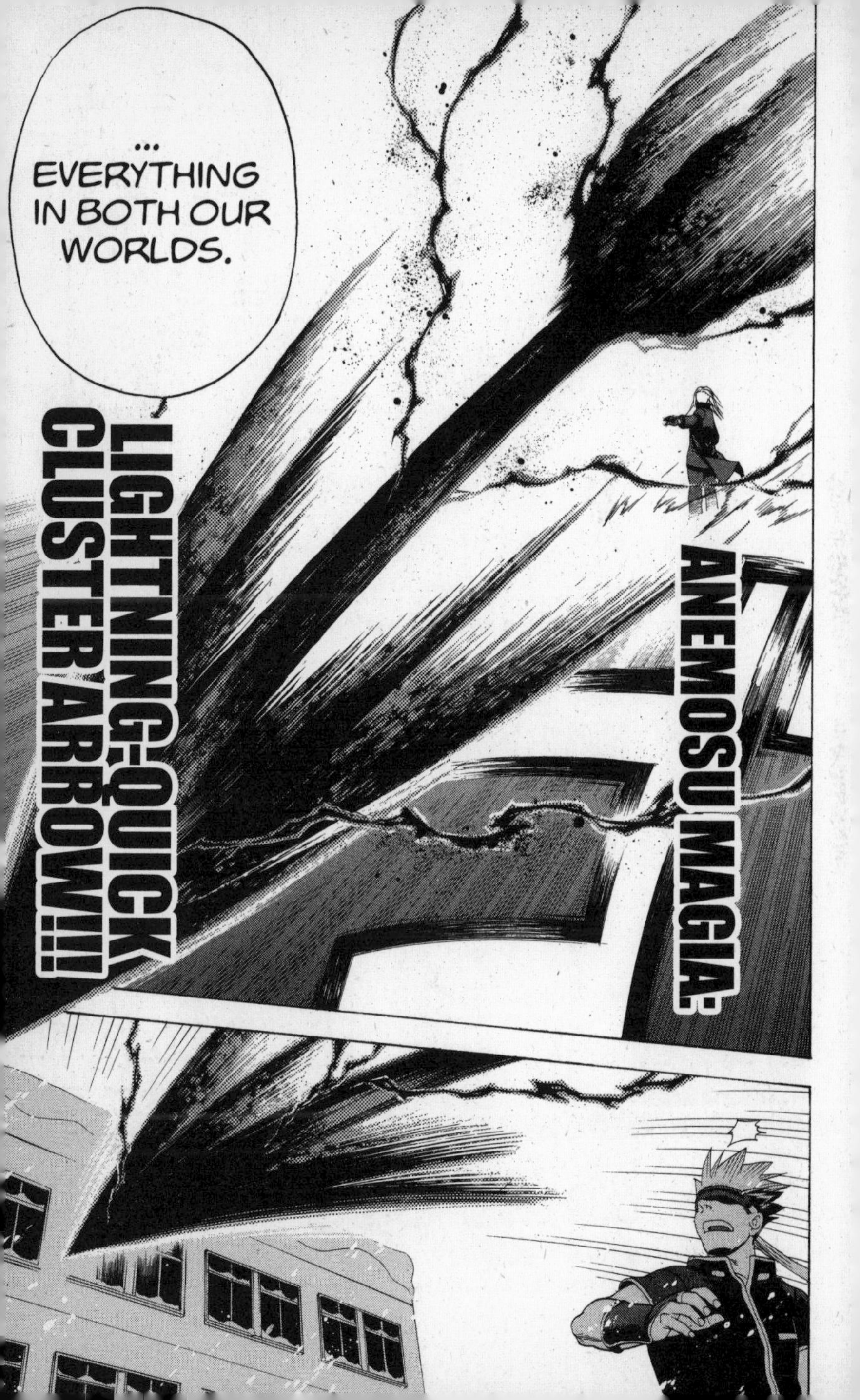
... EVERYTHING IN BOTH OUR WORLDS.
ANEMOSU MAGIA:
LIGHTNING-QUICK CLUSTER ARROW!!!

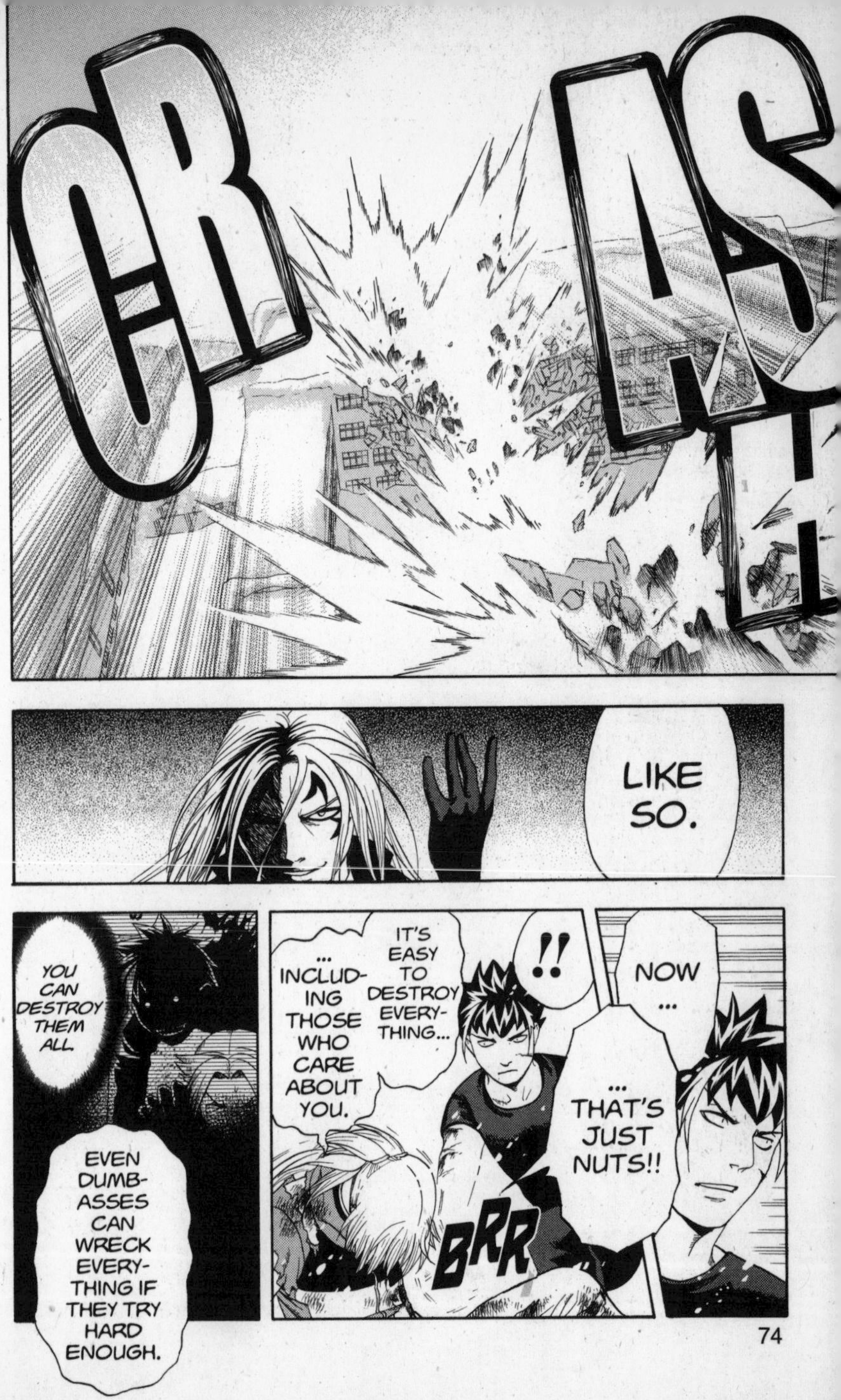
CRAS
LIKE SO.
NOW ...
... THAT'S JUST NUTS!!
!!
IT'S EASY TO DESTROY EVERYTHING...
... INCLUDING THOSE WHO CARE ABOUT YOU.
BRR
YOU CAN DESTROY THEM ALL.
EVEN DUMBASSES CAN WRECK EVERYTHING IF THEY TRY HARD ENOUGH.

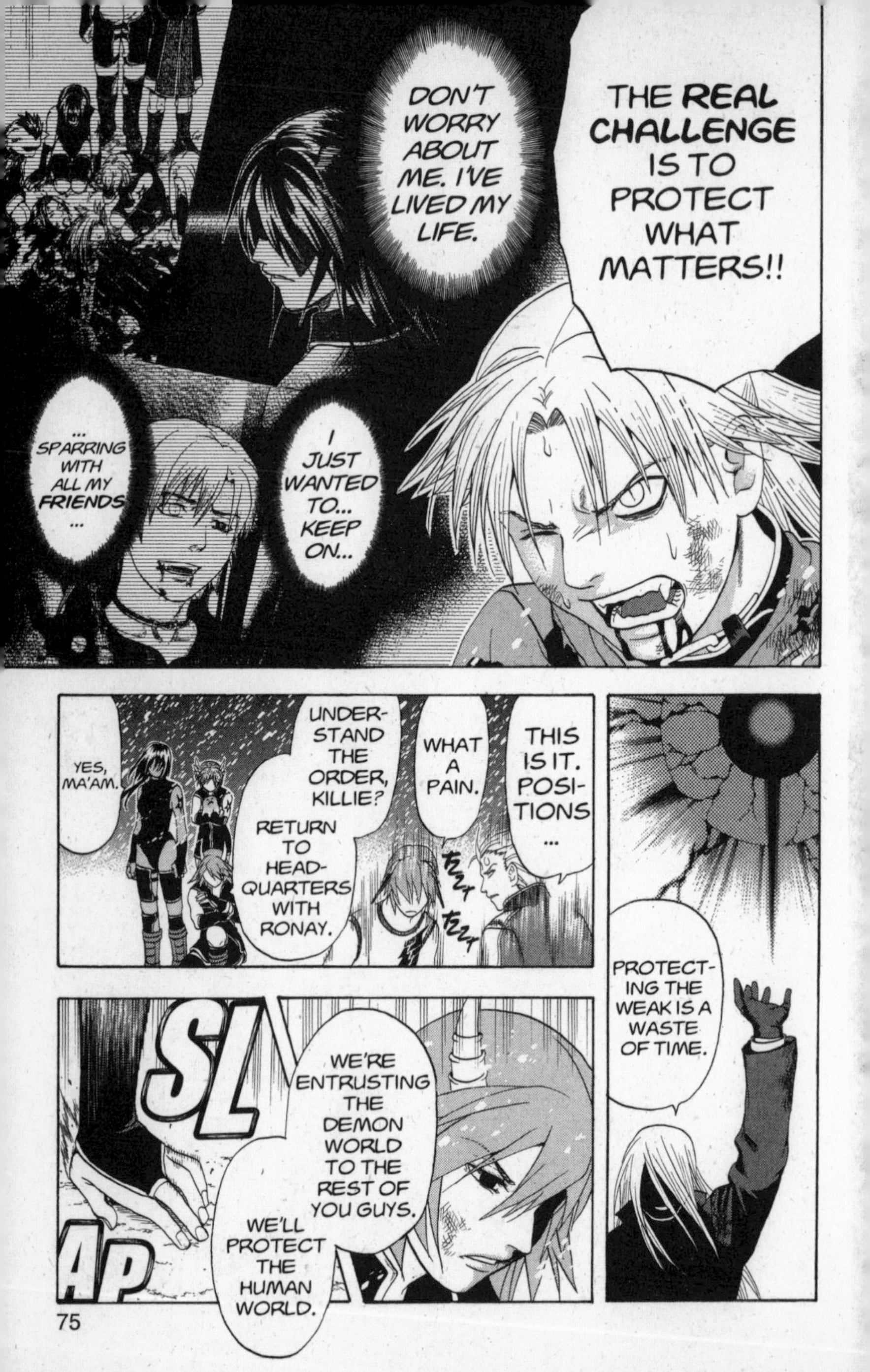
THE REAL CHALLENGE IS TO PROTECT WHAT MATTERS!!
DON'T WORRY ABOUT ME. I'VE LIVED MY LIFE.
I JUST WANTED TO... KEEP ON...
...SPARRING WITH ALL MY FRIENDS...
PROTECTING THE WEAK IS A WASTE OF TIME.
THIS IS IT. POSITIONS...
WHAT A PAIN.
UNDERSTAND THE ORDER, KILLIE?
RETURN TO HEADQUARTERS WITH RONAY.
YES, MA'AM.
SLAP
WE'RE ENTRUSTING THE DEMON WORLD TO THE REST OF YOU GUYS.
WE'LL PROTECT THE HUMAN WORLD.

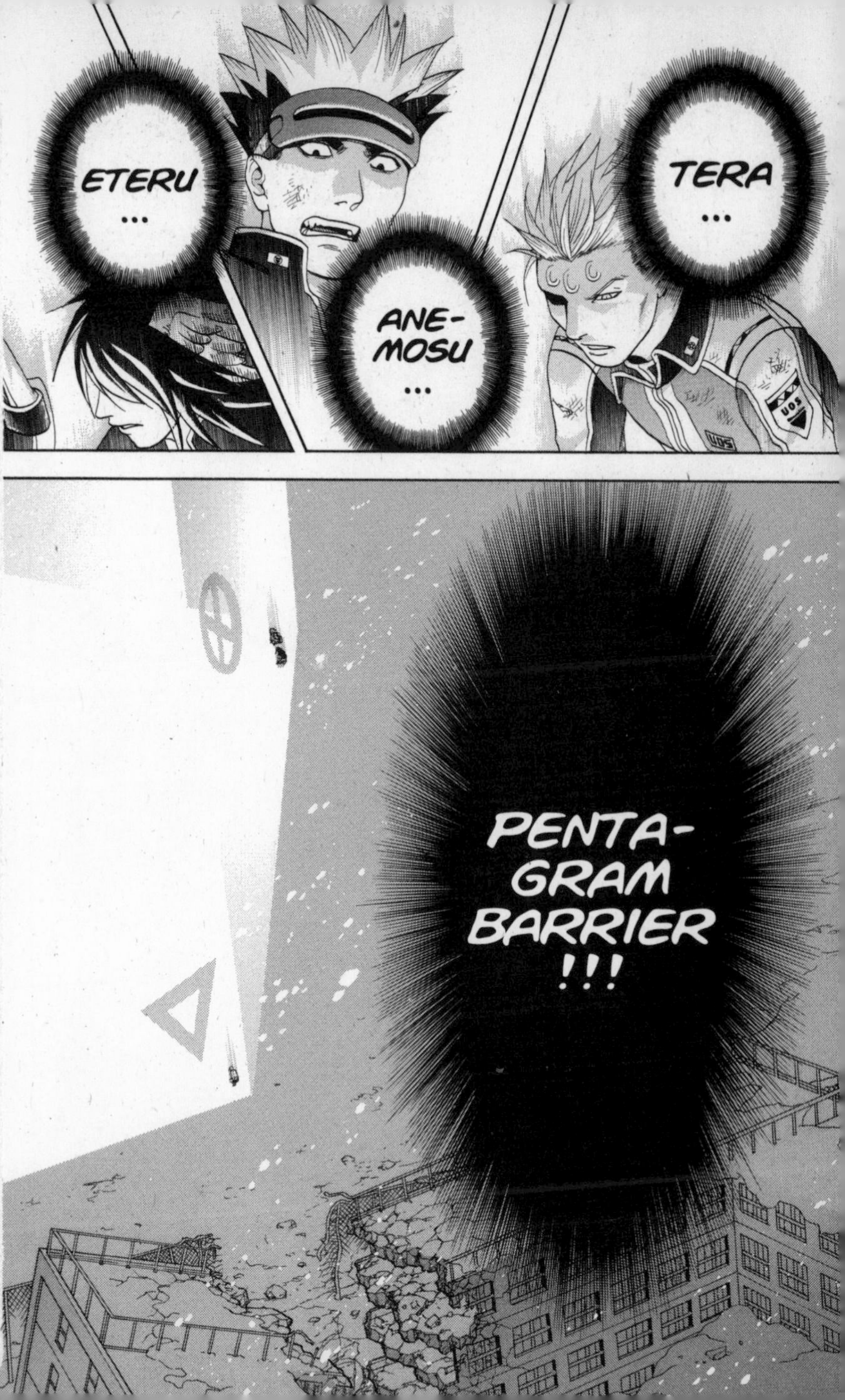
TERA ...
ANE-MOSU ...
ETERU ...
PENTA-GRAM BARRIER !!!

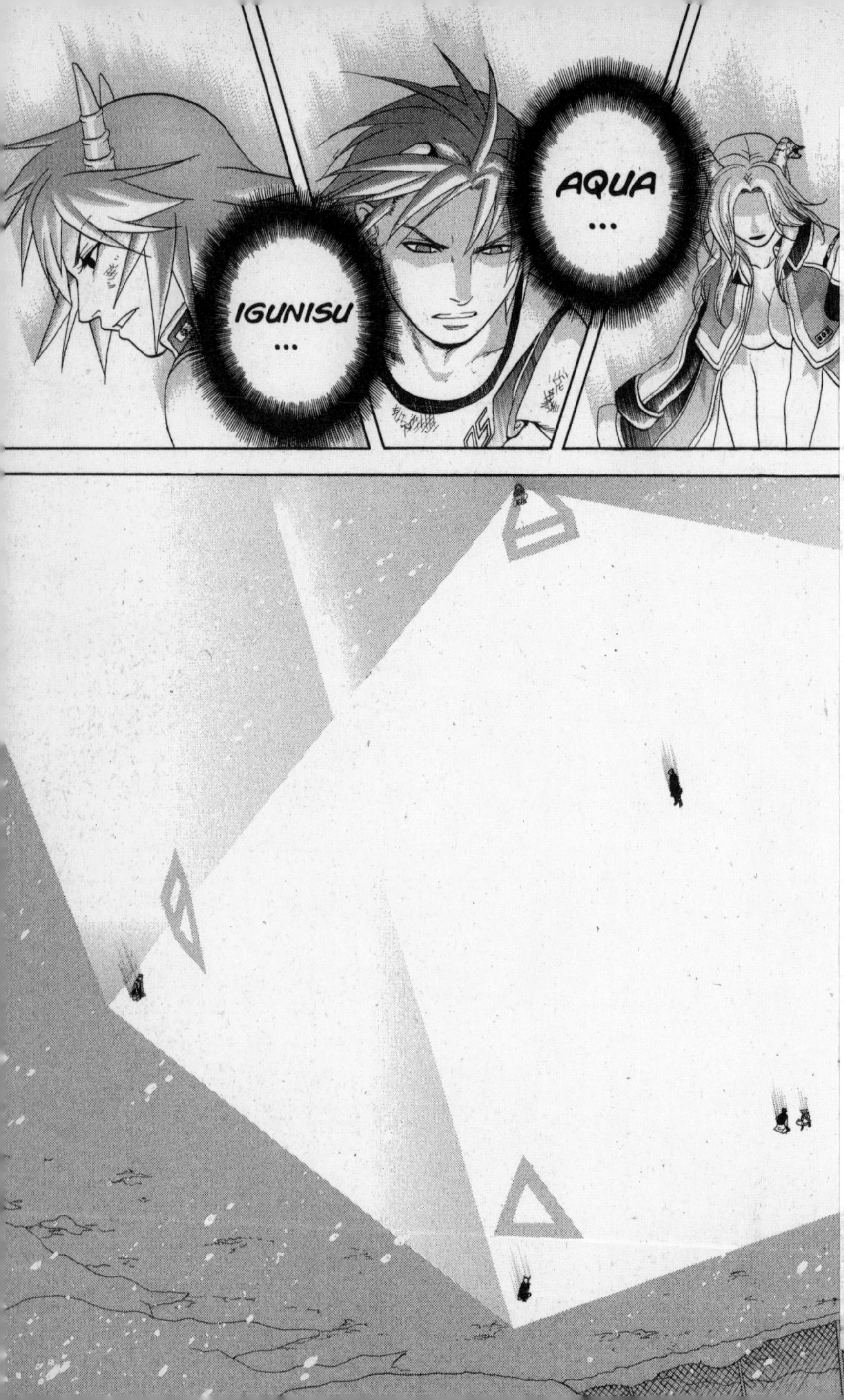
AQUA ...
IGUNISU ...

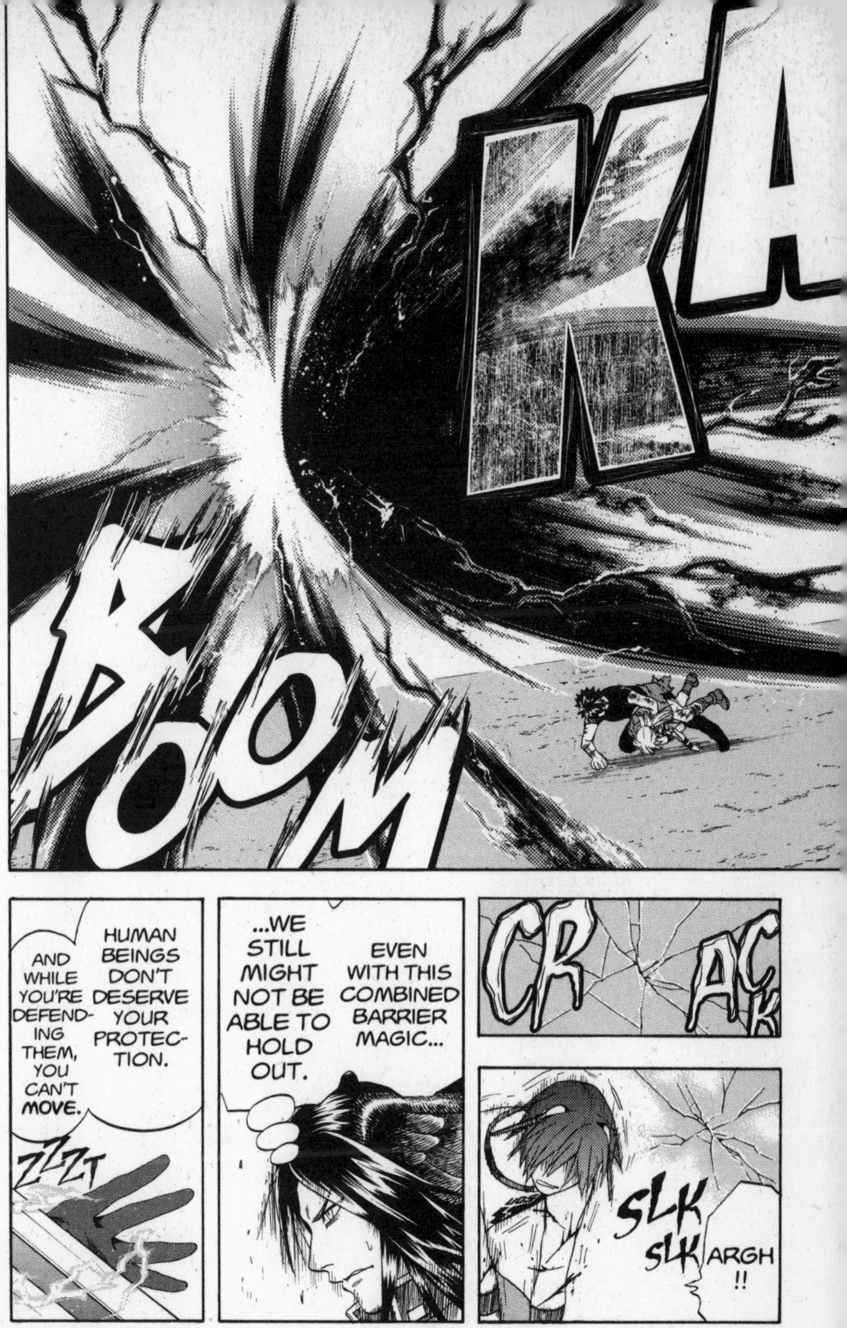
KA
BOOM
CRACK
SLK SLK
ARGH!!
EVEN WITH THIS COMBINED BARRIER MAGIC...
...WE STILL MIGHT NOT BE ABLE TO HOLD OUT.
HUMAN BEINGS DON'T DESERVE YOUR PROTECTION.
AND WHILE YOU'RE DEFENDING THEM, YOU CAN'T MOVE.
ZZZT

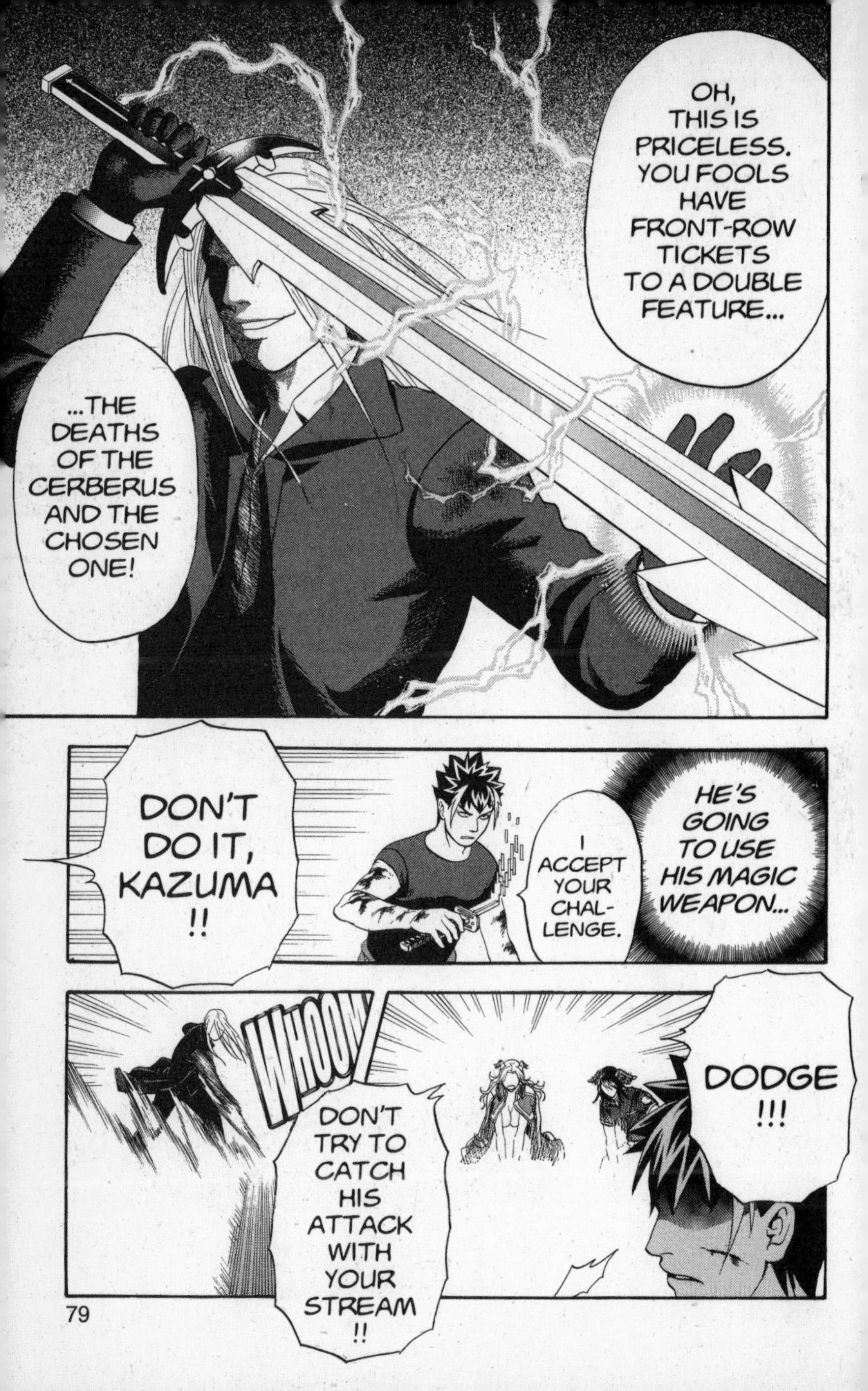
OH, THIS IS PRICELESS. YOU FOOLS HAVE FRONT-ROW TICKETS TO A DOUBLE FEATURE...
...THE DEATHS OF THE CERBERUS AND THE CHOSEN ONE!
HE'S GOING TO USE HIS MAGIC WEAPON...
I ACCEPT YOUR CHAL-LENGE.
DON'T DO IT, KAZUMA !!
DODGE !!!
DON'T TRY TO CATCH HIS ATTACK WITH YOUR STREAM !!
WHOOM

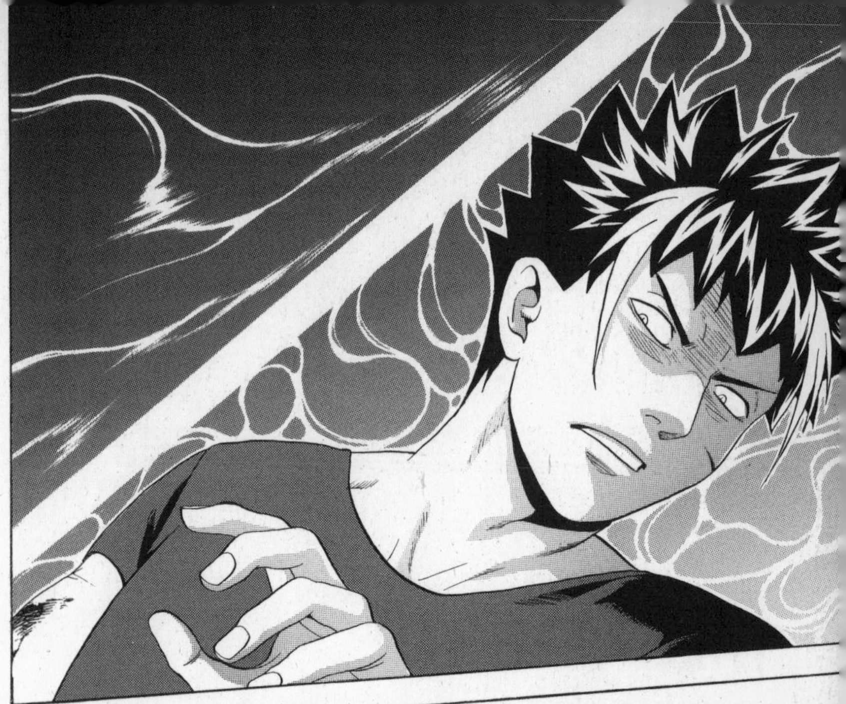

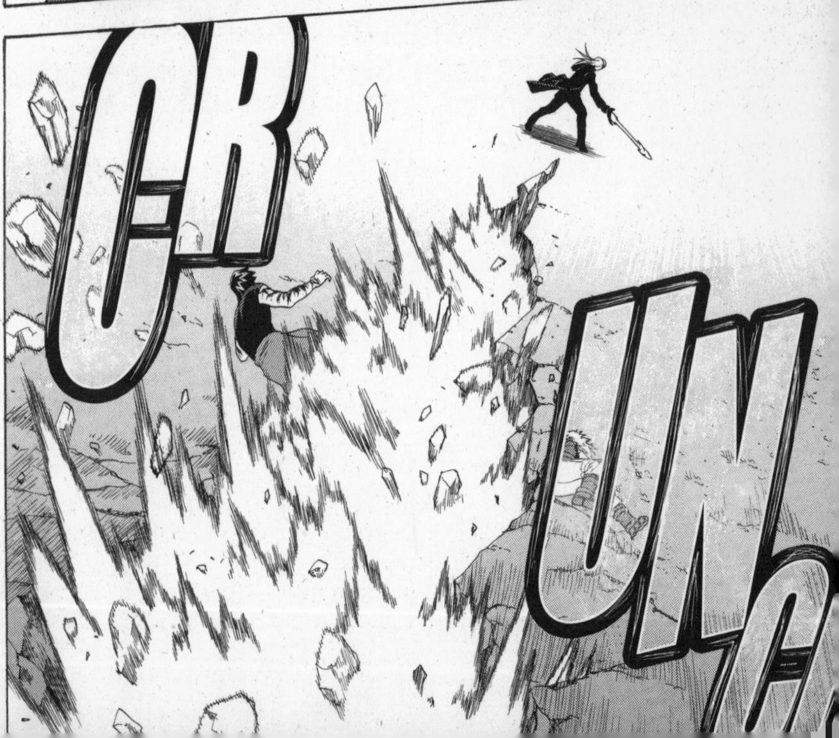
CR
UN

READ THIS WAY

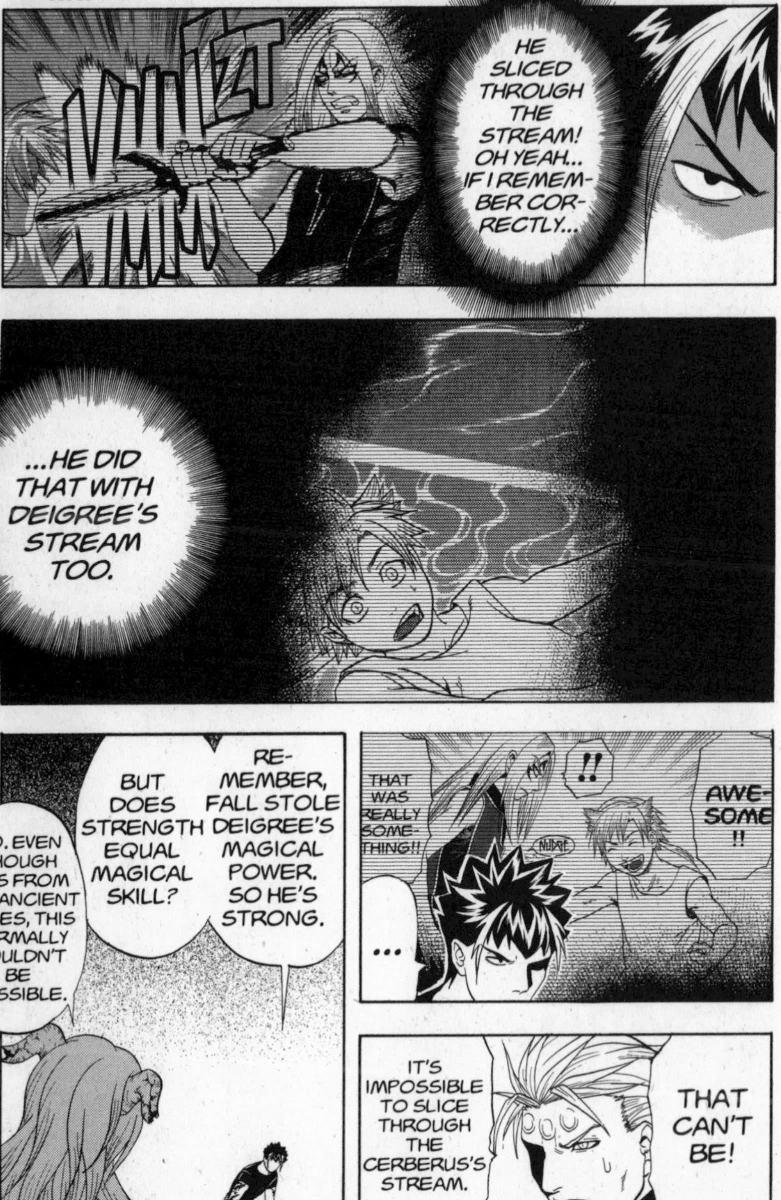
HE SLICED THROUGH THE STREAM! OH YEAH... IF I REMEMBER CORRECTLY...
...HE DID THAT WITH DEIGREE'S STREAM TOO.
AWESOME!!
!!
THAT WAS REALLY SOMETHING!!
...
THAT CAN'T BE!
IT'S IMPOSSIBLE TO SLICE THROUGH THE CERBERUS'S STREAM.
REMEMBER, FALL STOLE DEIGREE'S MAGICAL POWER. SO HE'S STRONG.
BUT DOES STRENGTH EQUAL MAGICAL SKILL?
NO. EVEN THOUGH HE'S FROM THE ANCIENT RACES, THIS NORMALLY WOULDN'T BE POSSIBLE.

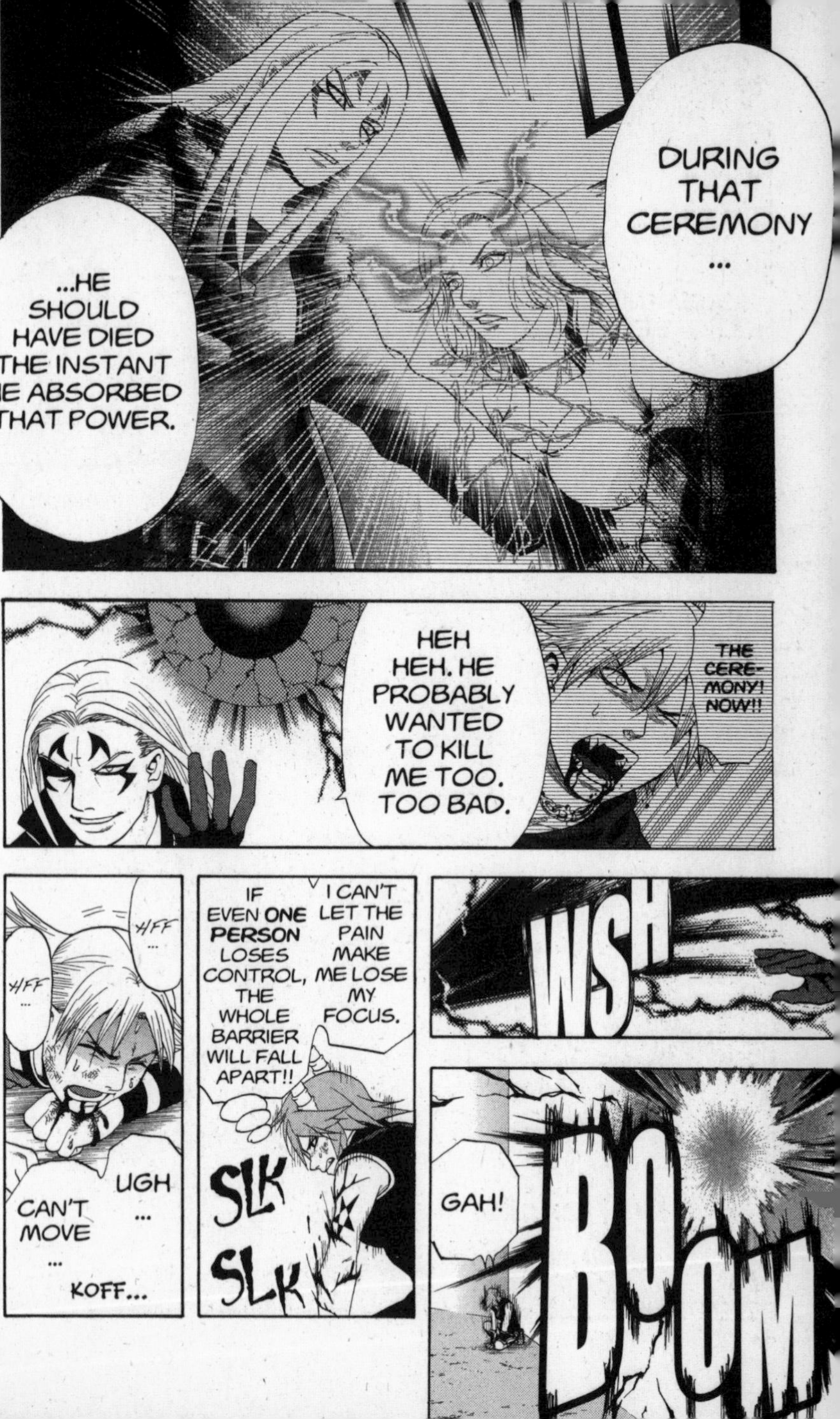
DURING THAT CEREMONY ...
...HE SHOULD HAVE DIED THE INSTANT HE ABSORBED THAT POWER.
THE CEREMONY! NOW!!
HEH HEH. HE PROBABLY WANTED TO KILL ME TOO. TOO BAD.
WSH
GAH!
BOOM
I CAN'T LET THE PAIN MAKE ME LOSE MY FOCUS.
IF EVEN ONE PERSON LOSES CONTROL, THE WHOLE BARRIER WILL FALL APART!!
SLK
SLK
HFF ...
HFF ...
UGH ...
CAN'T MOVE ...
KOFF...

READ THIS WAY

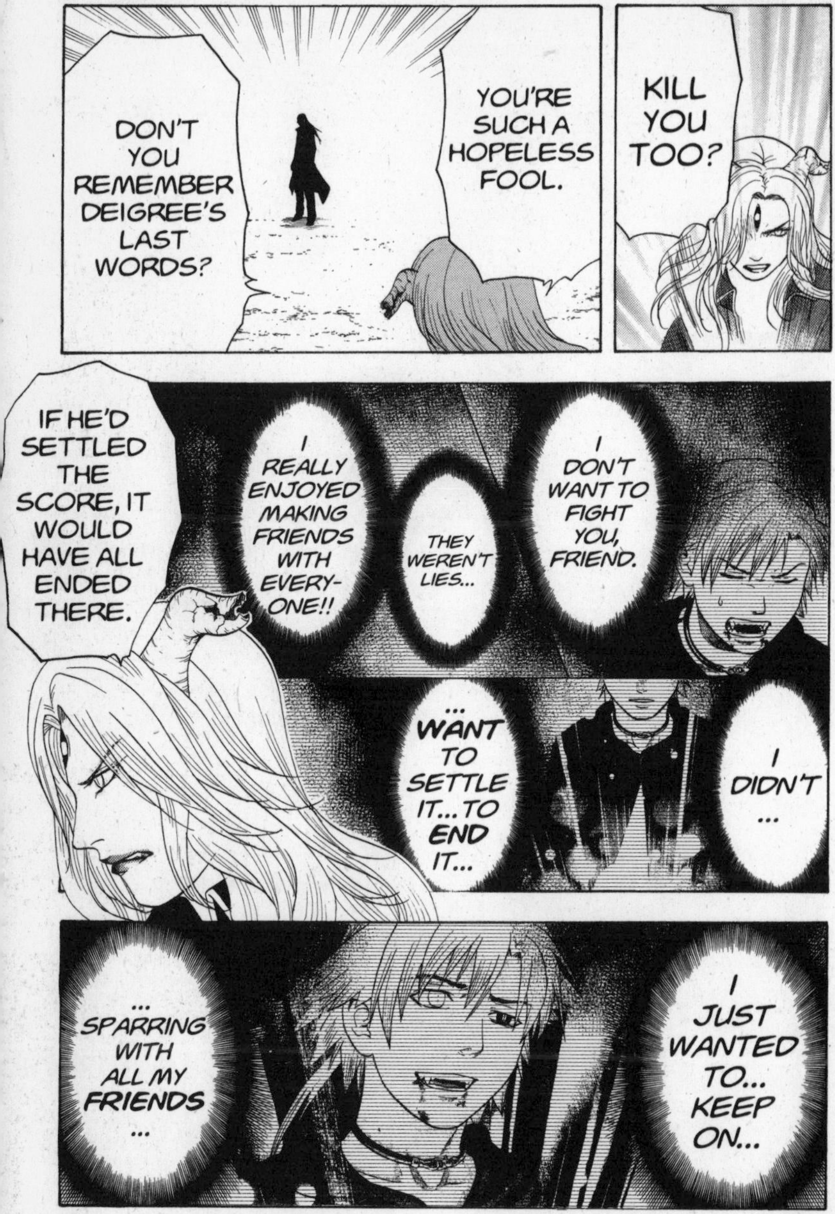
KILL YOU TOO?
YOU'RE SUCH A HOPELESS FOOL.
DON'T YOU REMEMBER DEIGREE'S LAST WORDS?
I DON'T WANT TO FIGHT YOU, FRIEND.
THEY WEREN'T LIES...
I REALLY ENJOYED MAKING FRIENDS WITH EVERY-ONE!!
IF HE'D SETTLED THE SCORE, IT WOULD HAVE ALL ENDED THERE.
I DIDN'T...
...WANT TO SETTLE IT...TO END IT...
I JUST WANTED TO... KEEP ON...
...SPARRING WITH ALL MY FRIENDS...

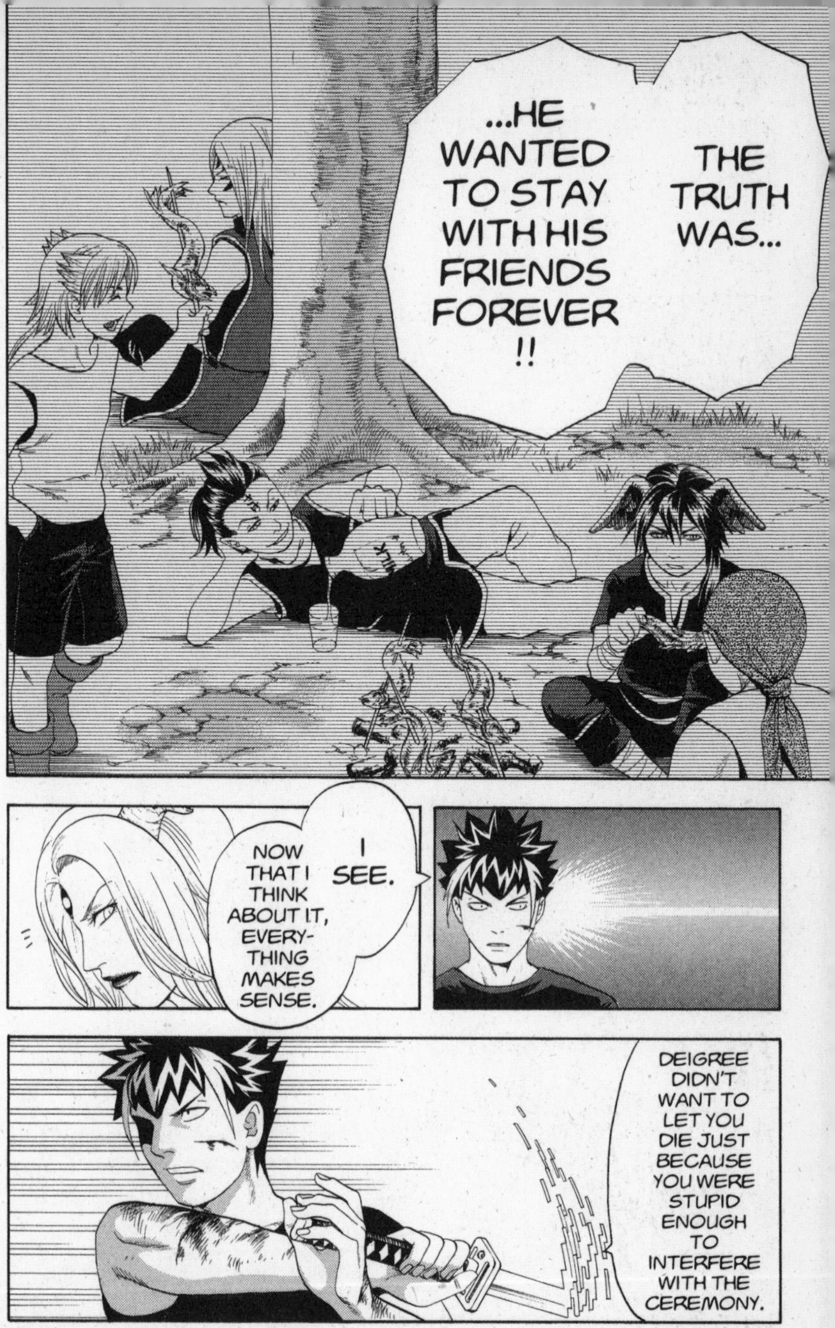
THE TRUTH WAS...
...HE WANTED TO STAY WITH HIS FRIENDS FOREVER!!
MILK
I SEE.
NOW THAT I THINK ABOUT IT, EVERYTHING MAKES SENSE.
DEIGREE DIDN'T WANT TO LET YOU DIE JUST BECAUSE YOU WERE STUPID ENOUGH TO INTERFERE WITH THE CEREMONY.

READ THIS WAY

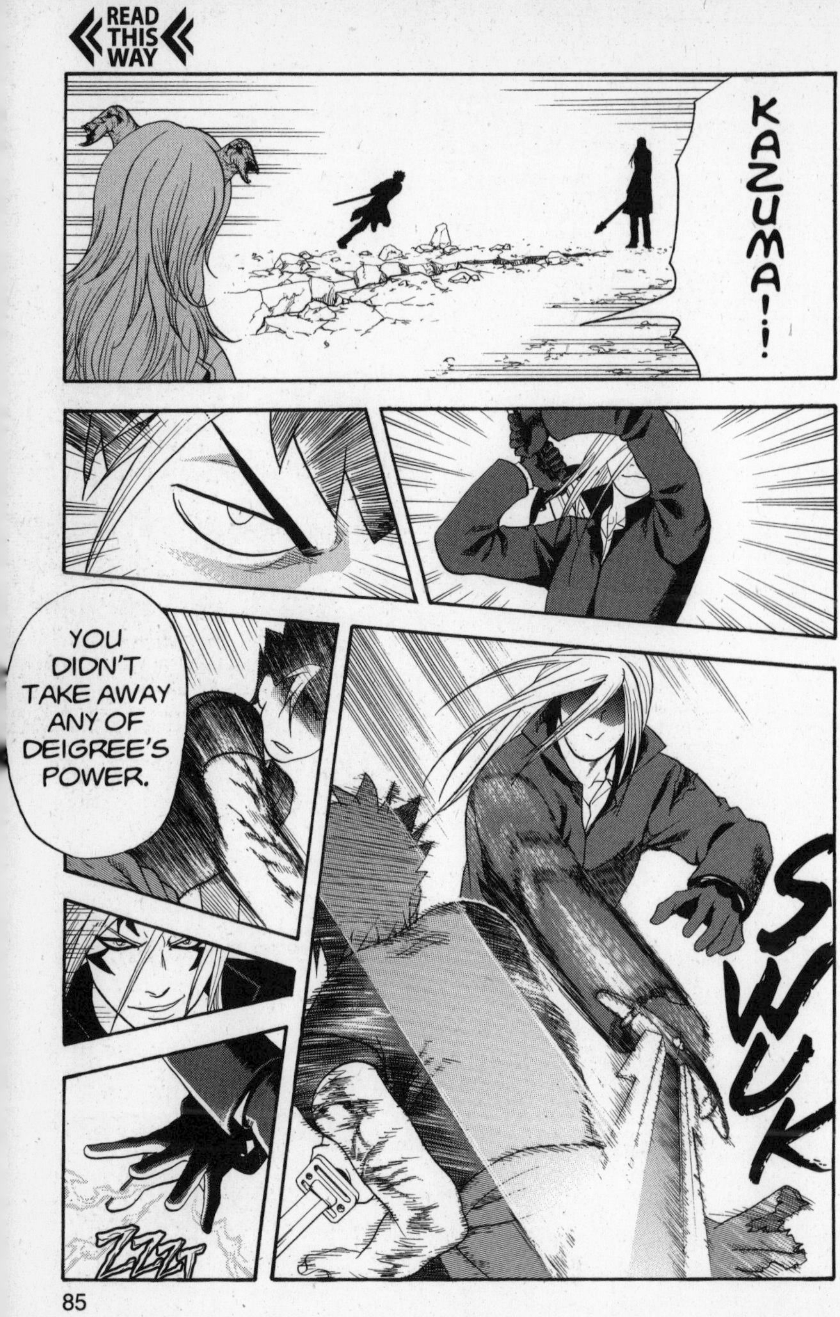
KAZUMA!!
SWUK
YOU DIDN'T TAKE AWAY ANY OF DEIGREE'S POWER.
ZZZT

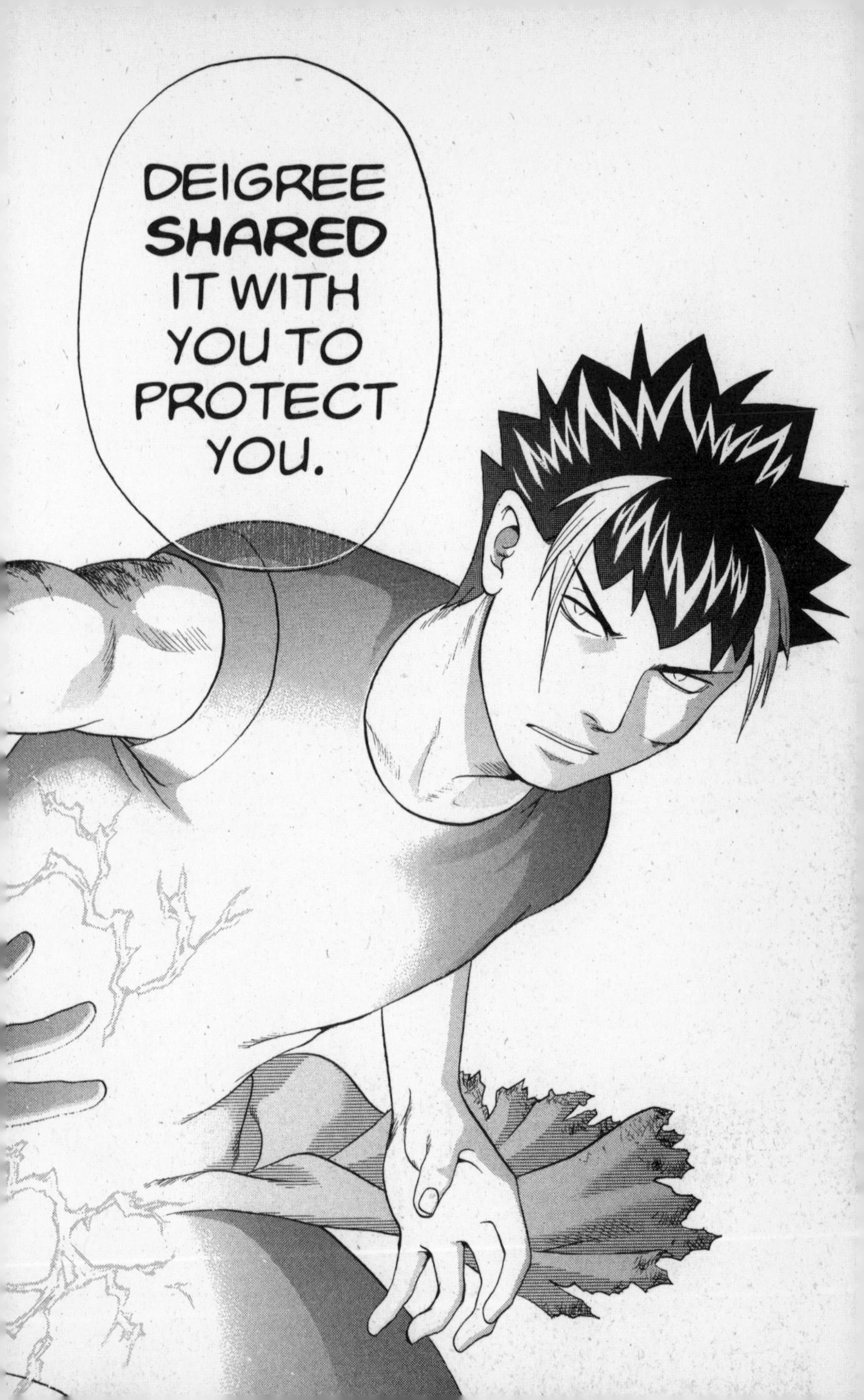
DEIGREE SHARED IT WITH YOU TO PROTECT YOU.

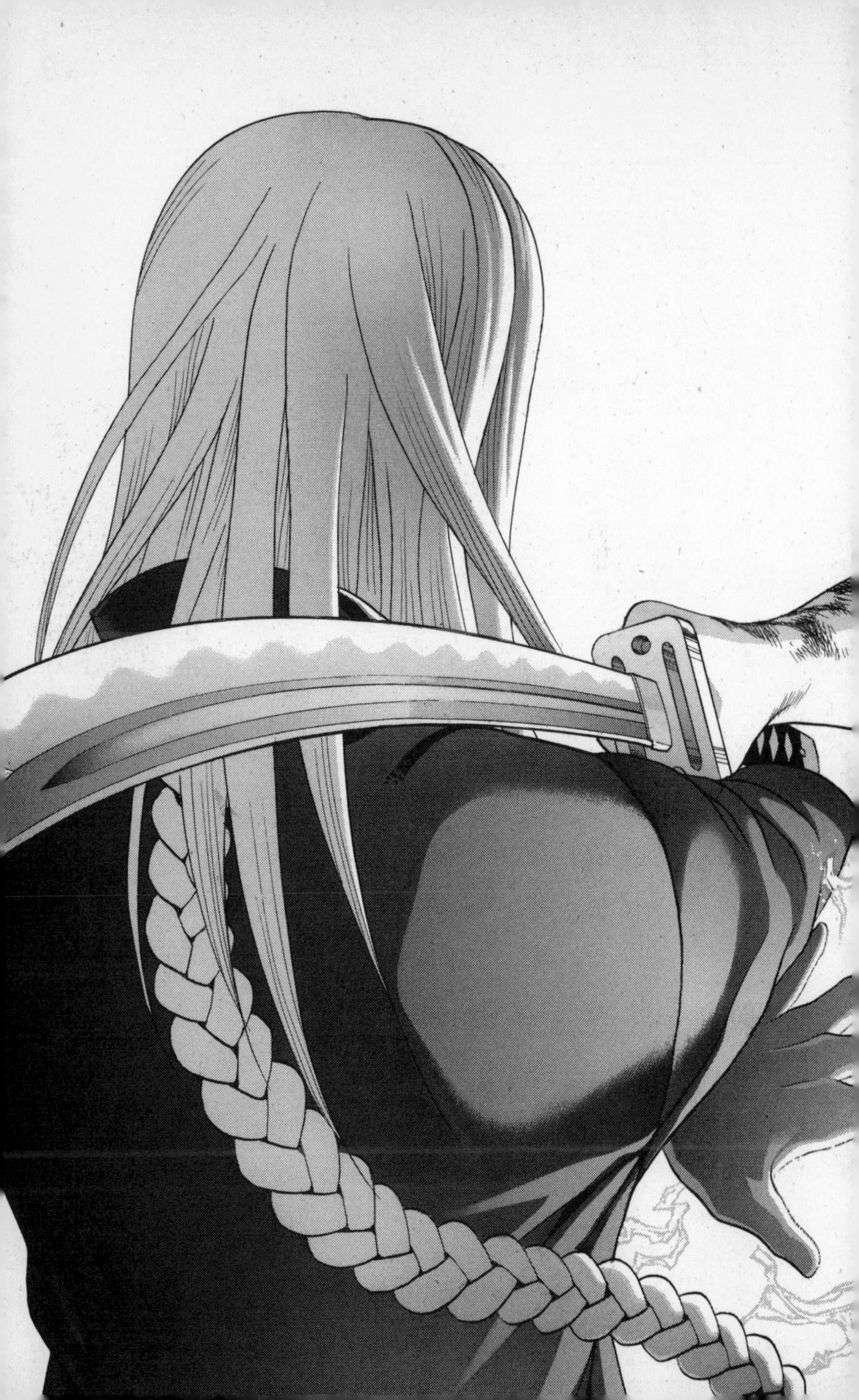

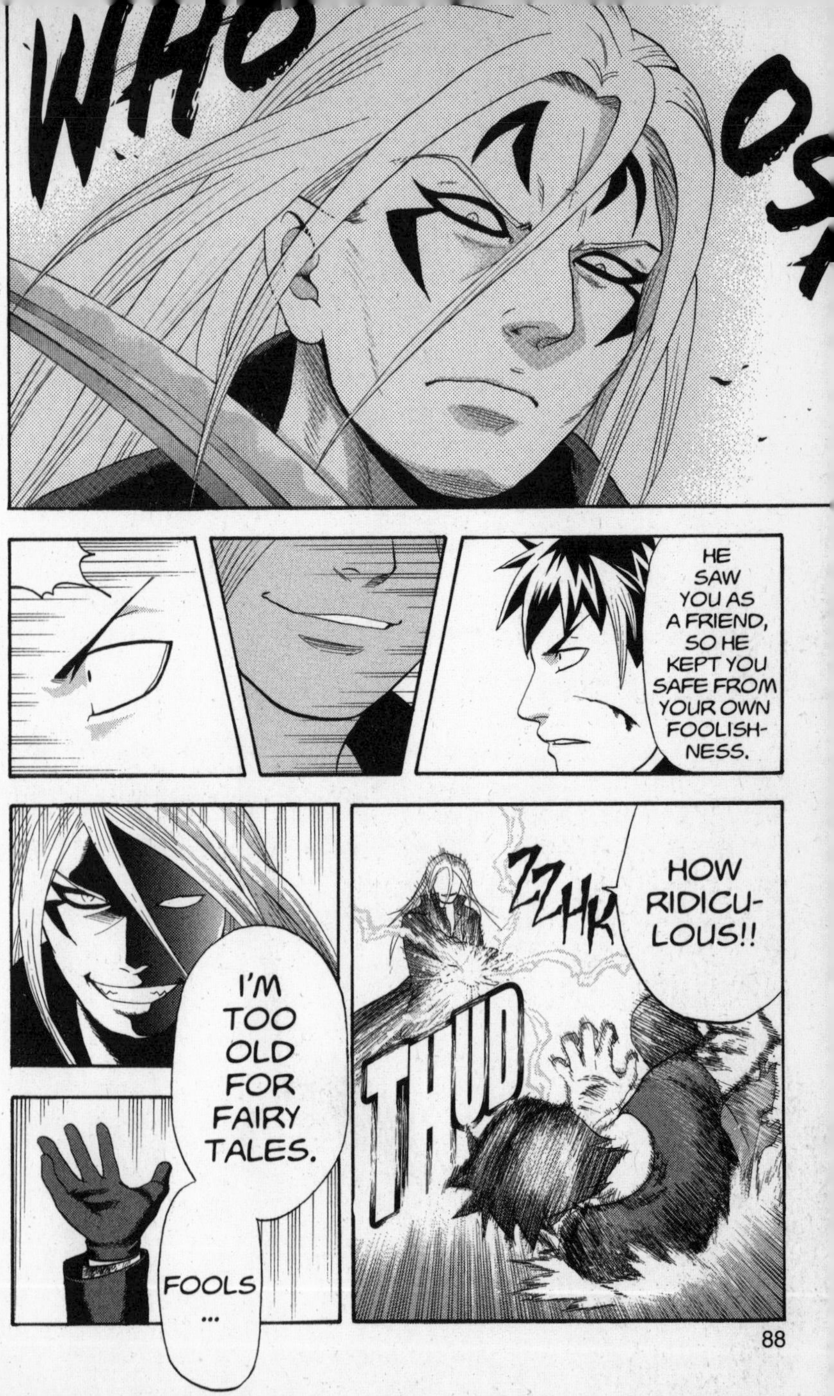
WHOOSH
HE SAW YOU AS A FRIEND, SO HE KEPT YOU SAFE FROM YOUR OWN FOOLISH-NESS.
HOW RIDICU-LOUS!!
ZZHK
THUD
I'M TOO OLD FOR FAIRY TALES.
FOOLS ...

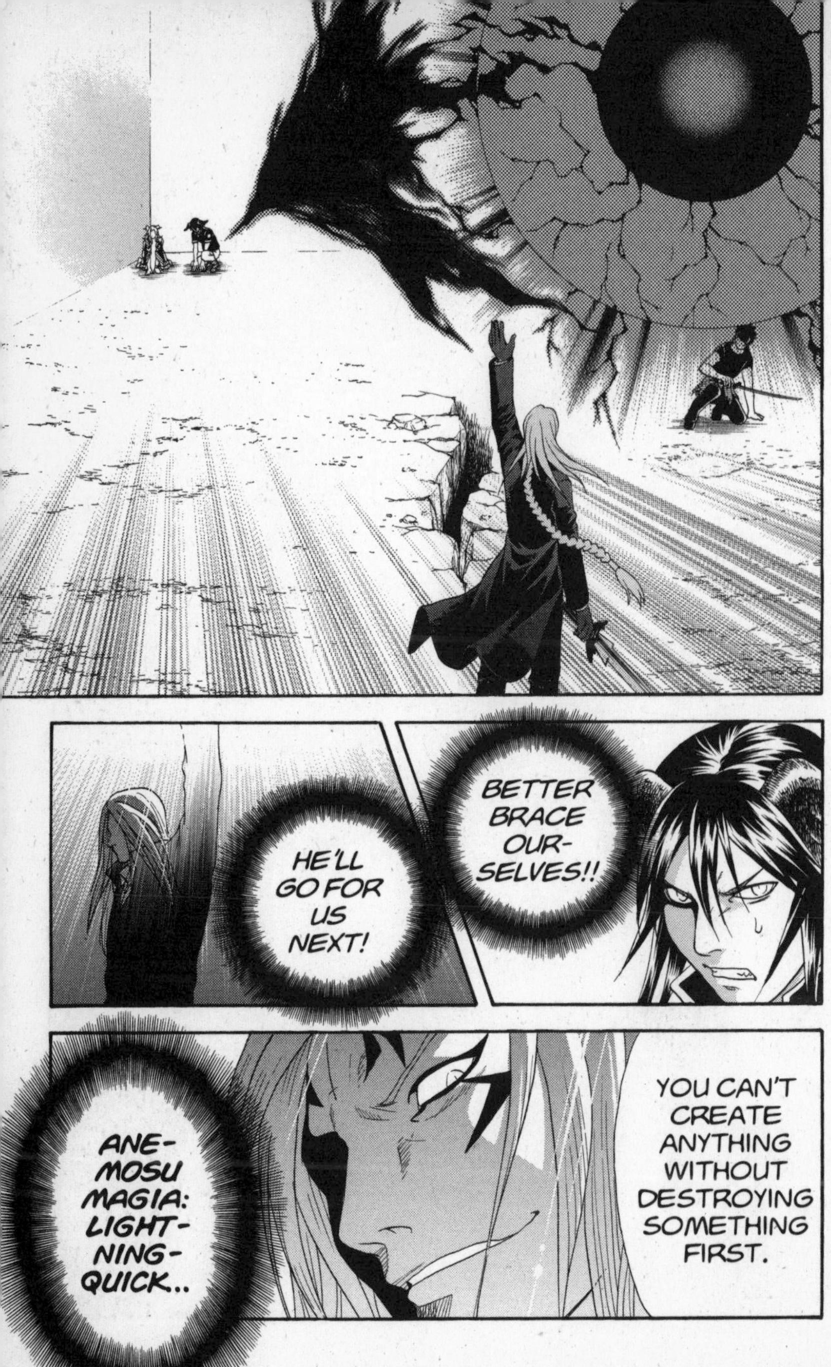
BETTER BRACE OUR-SELVES!!
HE'LL GO FOR US NEXT!
YOU CAN'T CREATE ANYTHING WITHOUT DESTROYING SOMETHING FIRST.
ANE-MOSU MAGIA: LIGHT-NING-QUICK...

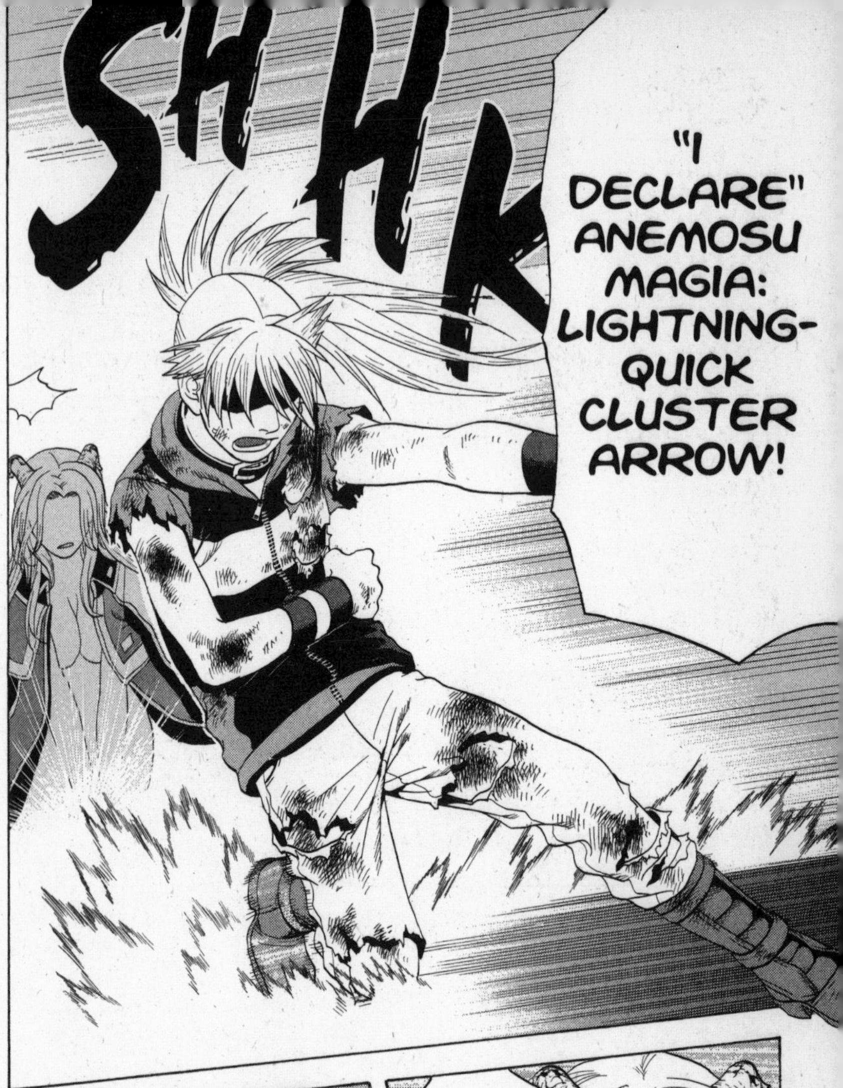
SHHK
"I DECLARE" ANEMOSU MAGIA: LIGHTNING-QUICK CLUSTER ARROW!

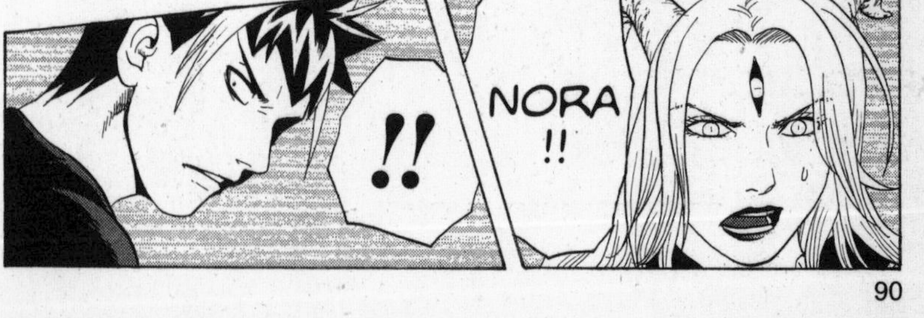
NORA !!
!!

READ THIS WAY

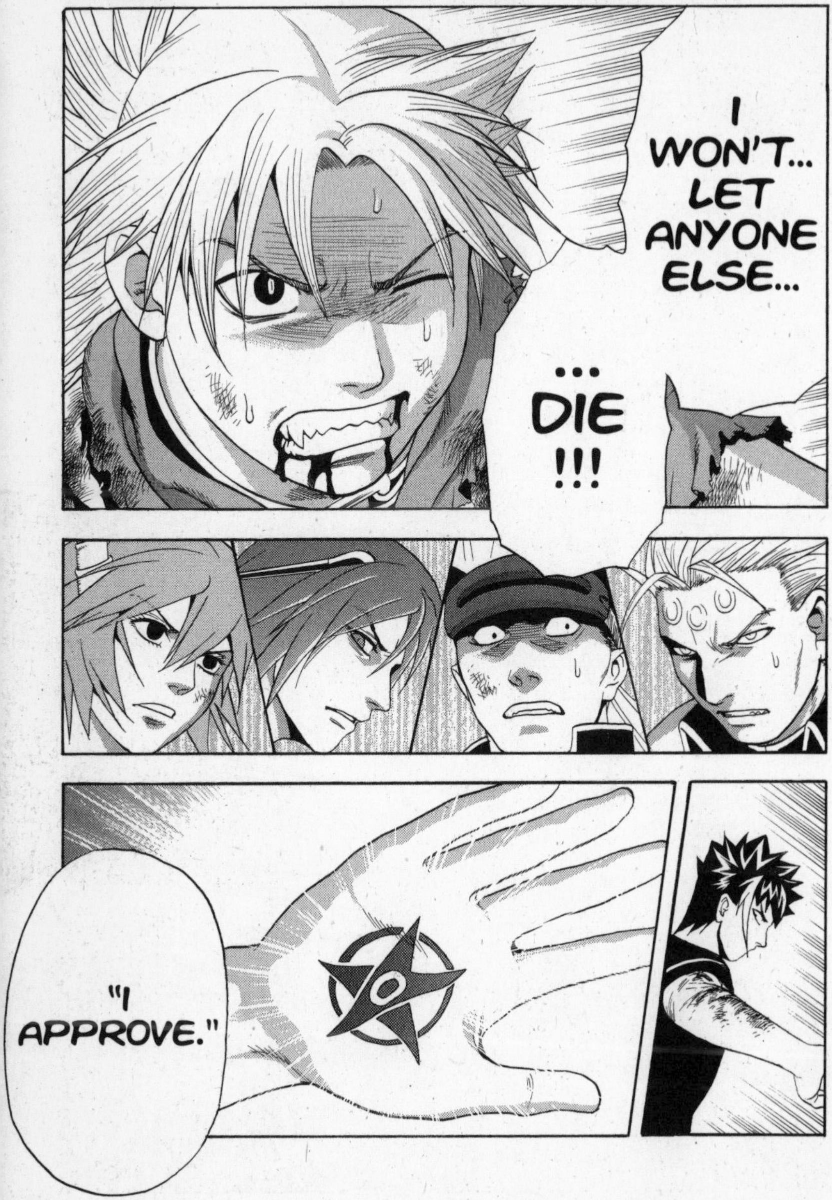
I WON'T... LET ANYONE ELSE...
...DIE!!!
"I APPROVE."

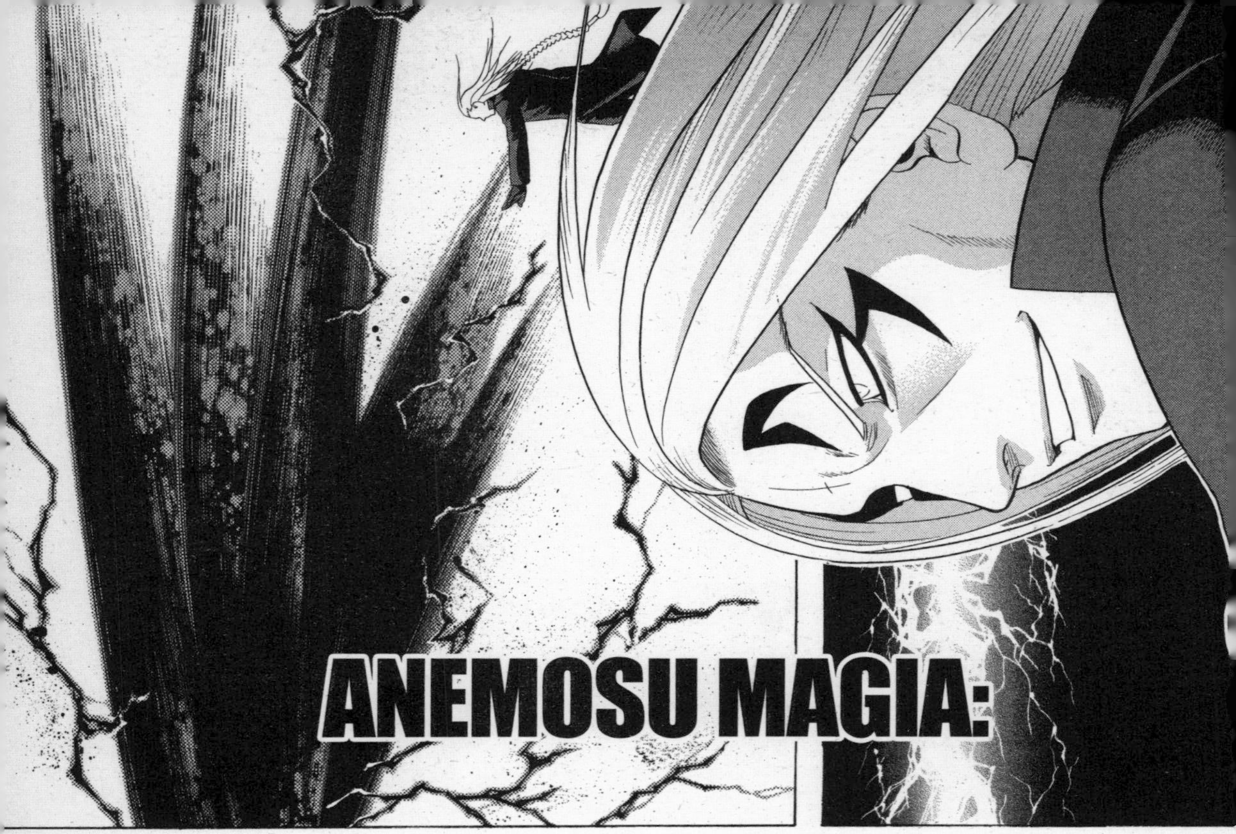
ANEMOSU MAGIA:

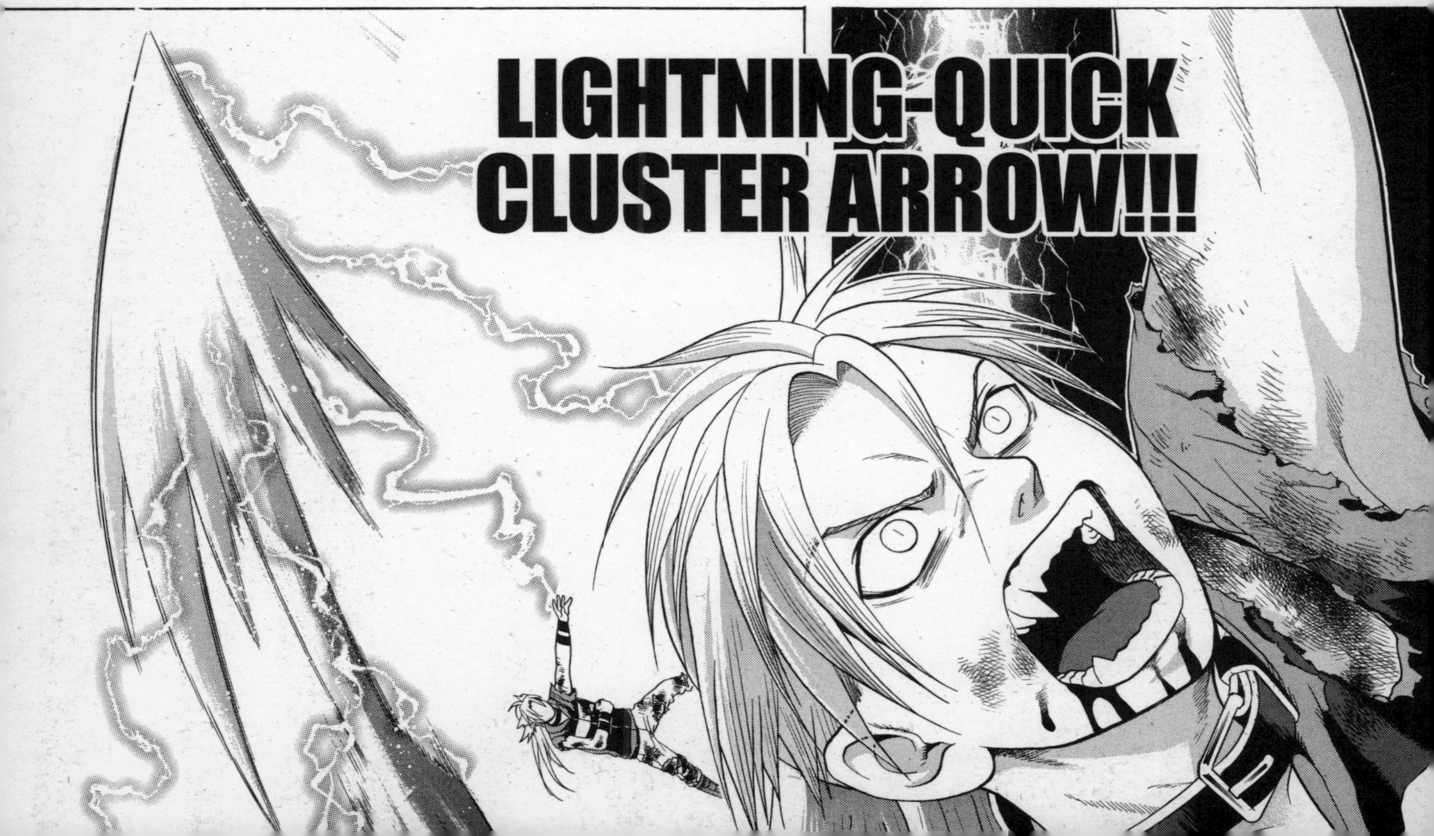
LIGHTNING-QUICK CLUSTER ARROW!!!

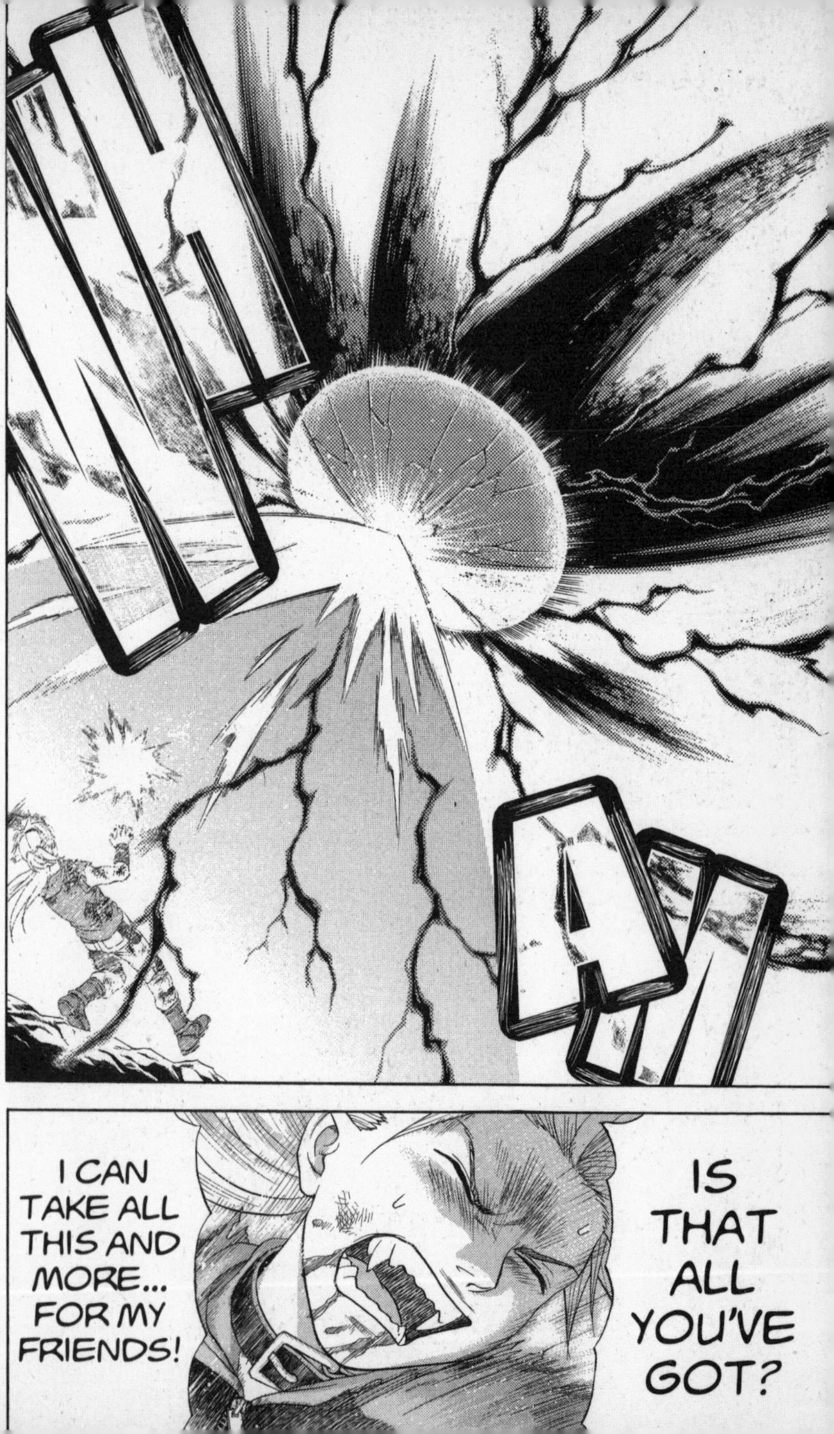
IS THAT ALL YOU'VE GOT?
I CAN TAKE ALL THIS AND MORE... FOR MY FRIENDS!

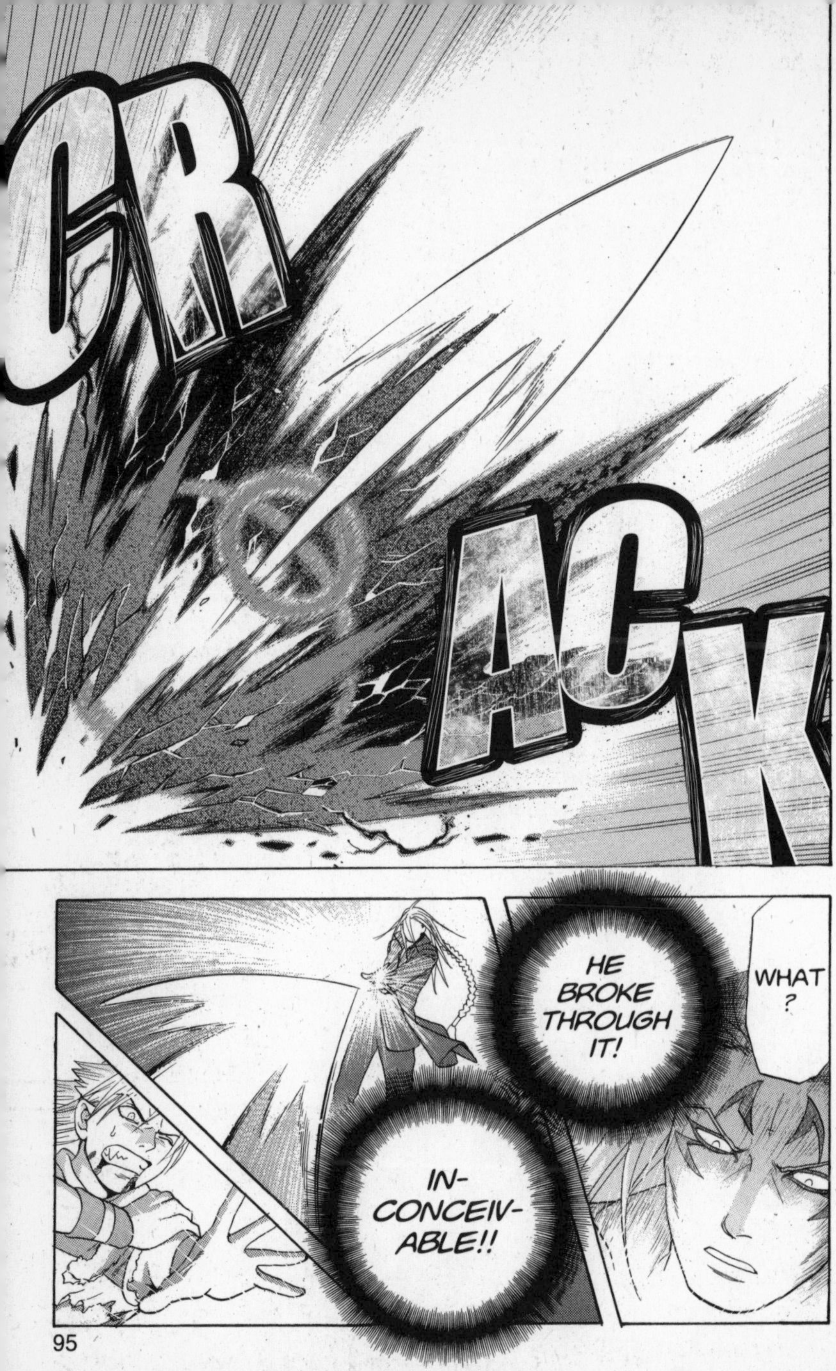
CRACK
WHAT?
HE BROKE THROUGH IT!
IN-CONCEIV-ABLE!!

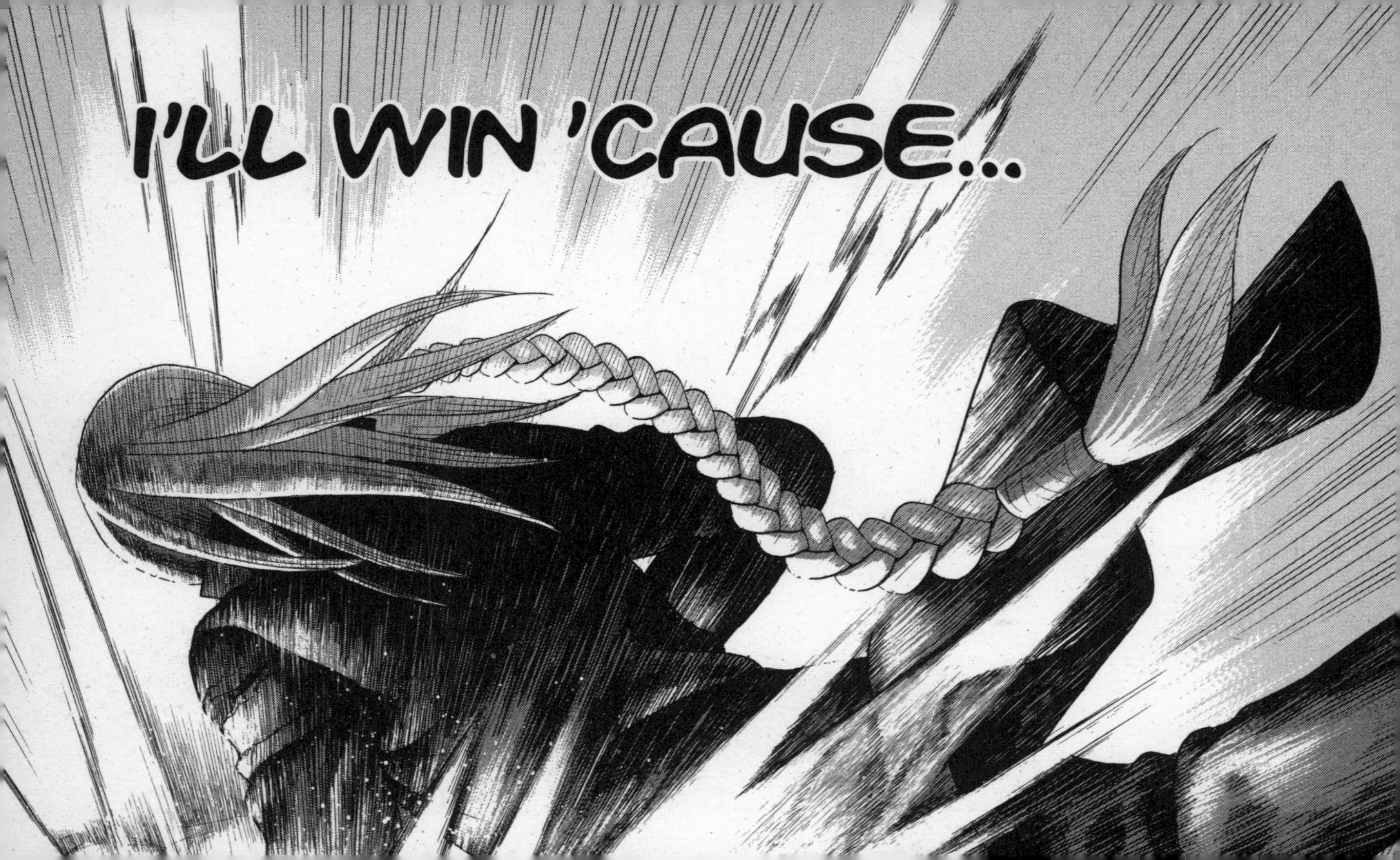
I'LL WIN 'CAUSE...

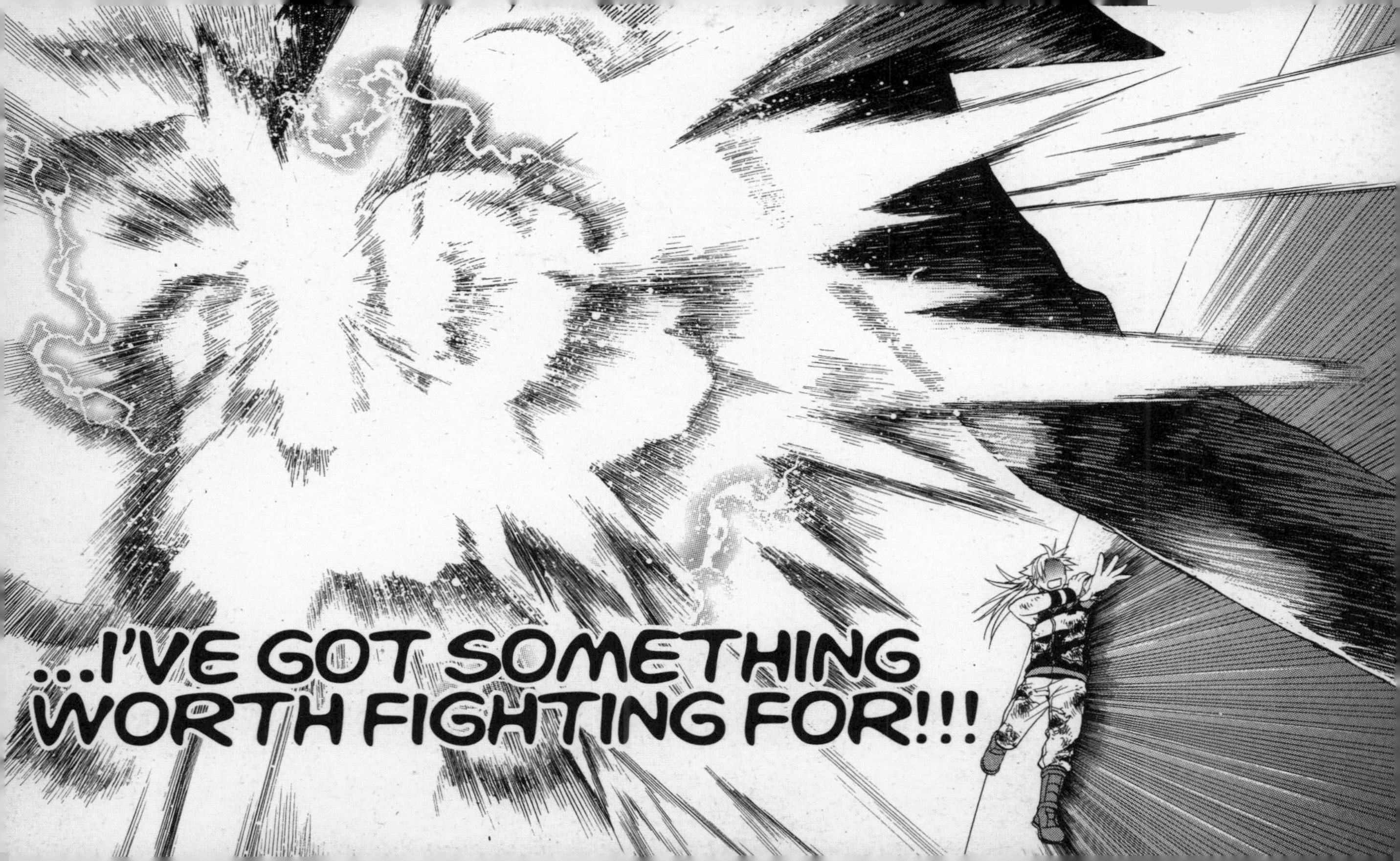
...I'VE GOT SOMETHING WORTH FIGHTING FOR!!!

Story 31: The Shout of the Soul

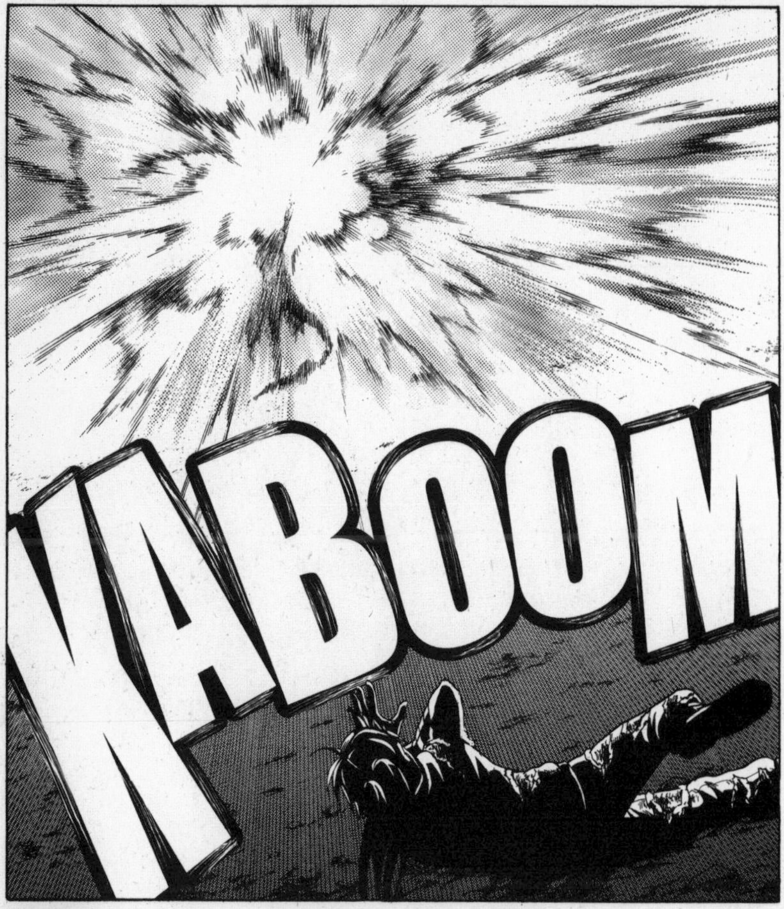
KABOOM

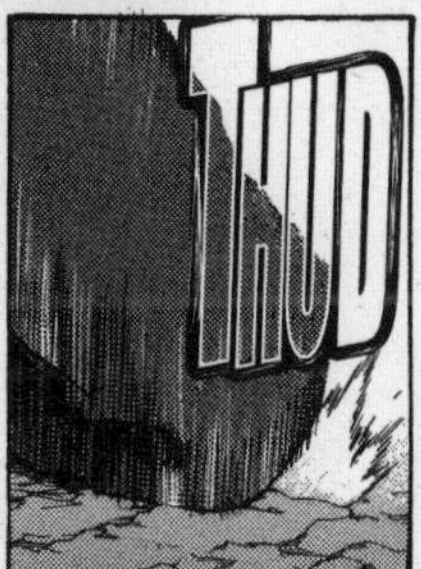
THUD

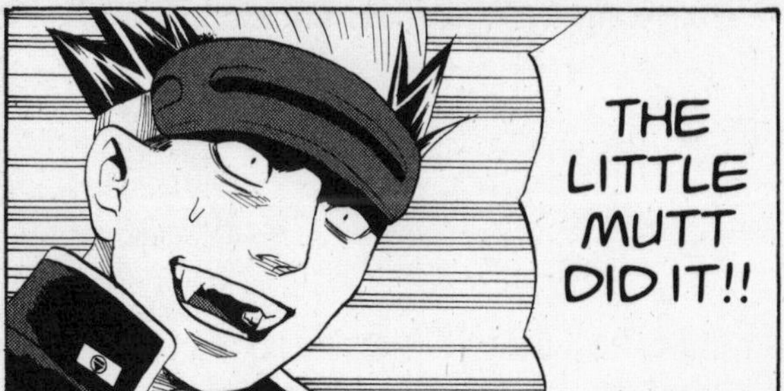
THE LITTLE MUTT DID IT!!

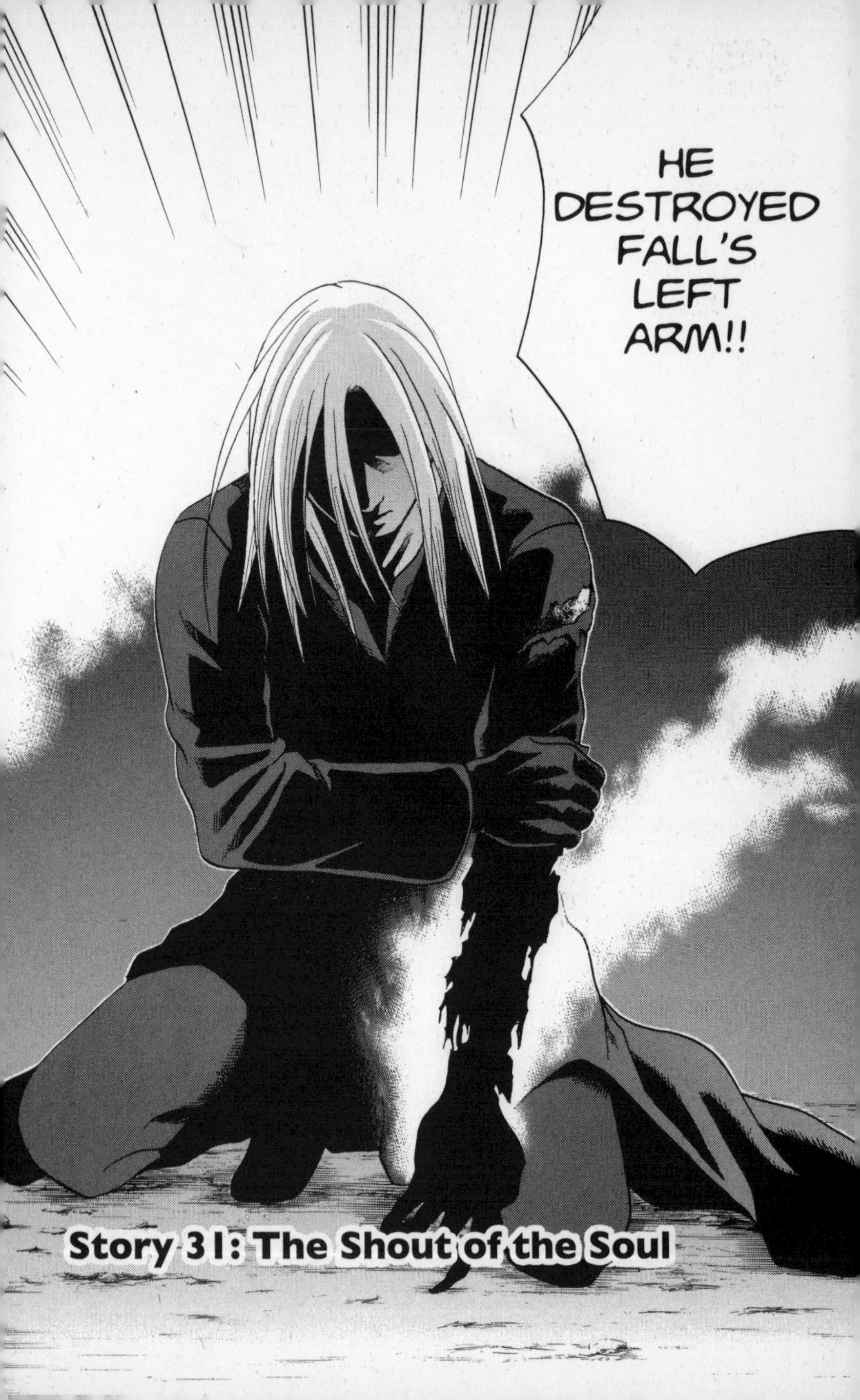
HE DESTROYED FALL'S LEFT ARM!!
Story 31: The Shout of the Soul

READ THIS WAY

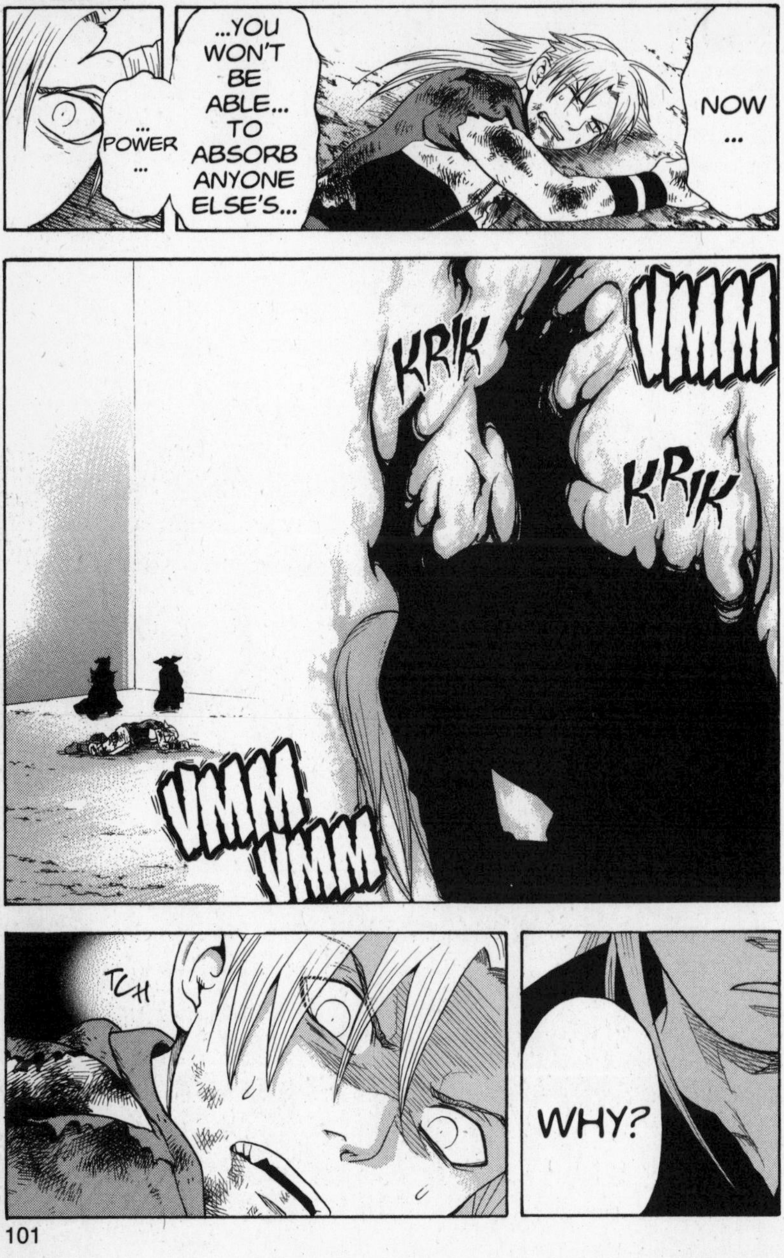
NOW ...
...YOU WON'T BE ABLE... TO ABSORB ANYONE ELSE'S...
... POWER ...
VMM
KRIK
KRIK
VMM VMM
WHY?
TCH

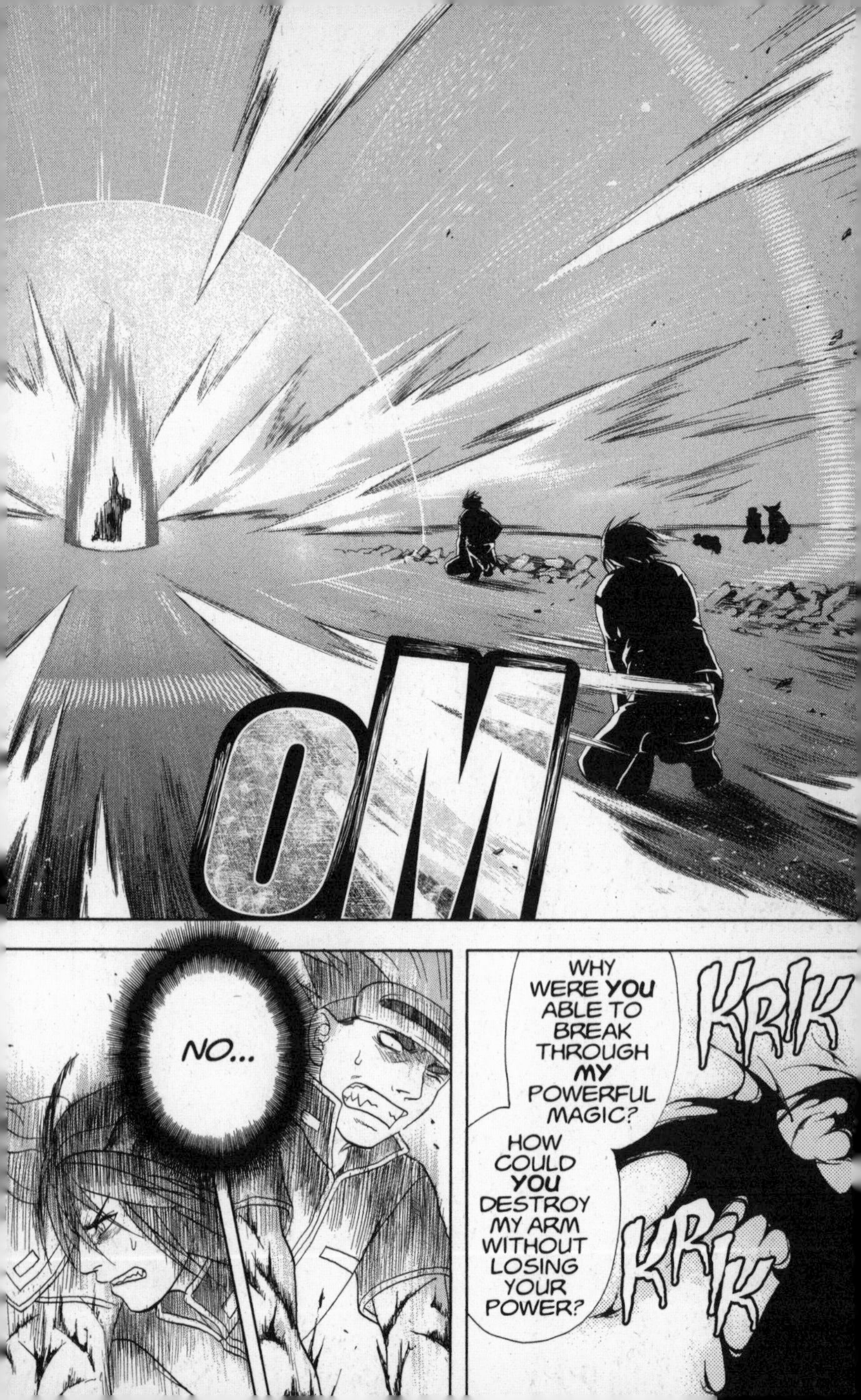
OM
WHY WERE YOU ABLE TO BREAK THROUGH MY POWERFUL MAGIC?
HOW COULD YOU DESTROY MY ARM WITHOUT LOSING YOUR POWER?
KRIK
KRIK
NO...

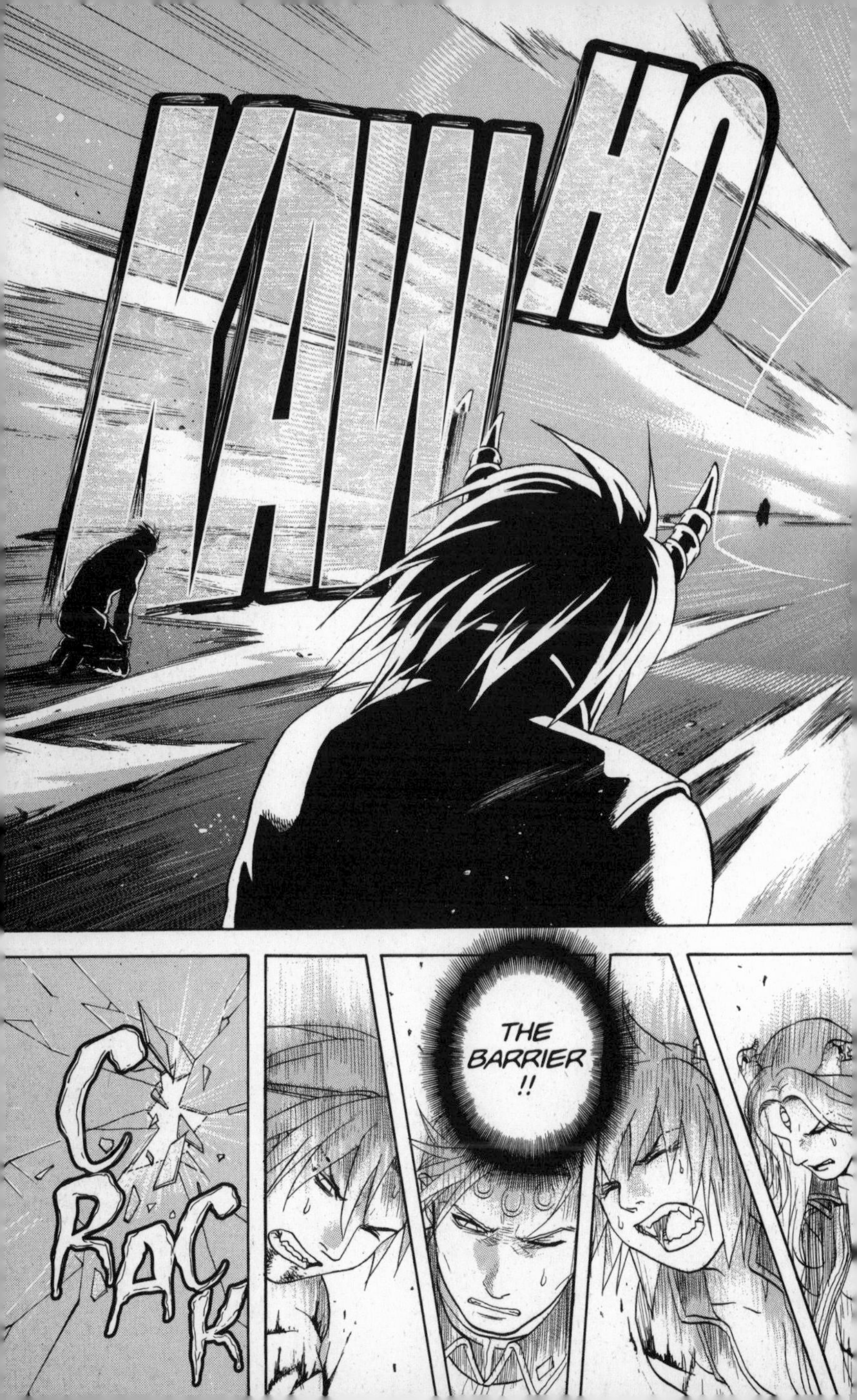
KAWHO
THE BARRIER !!
CRACK

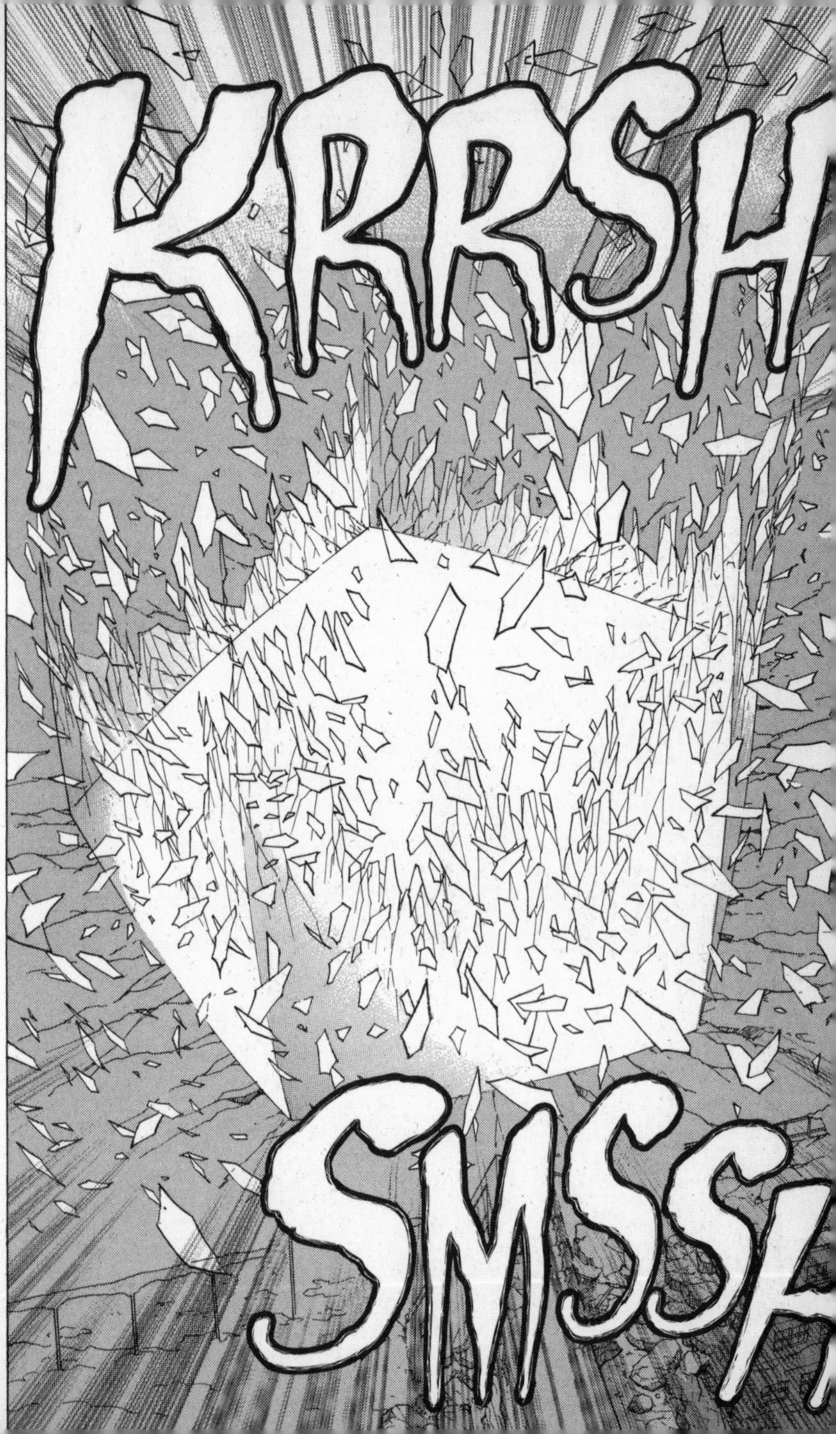
KRRSH
SMSSH

READ THIS WAY

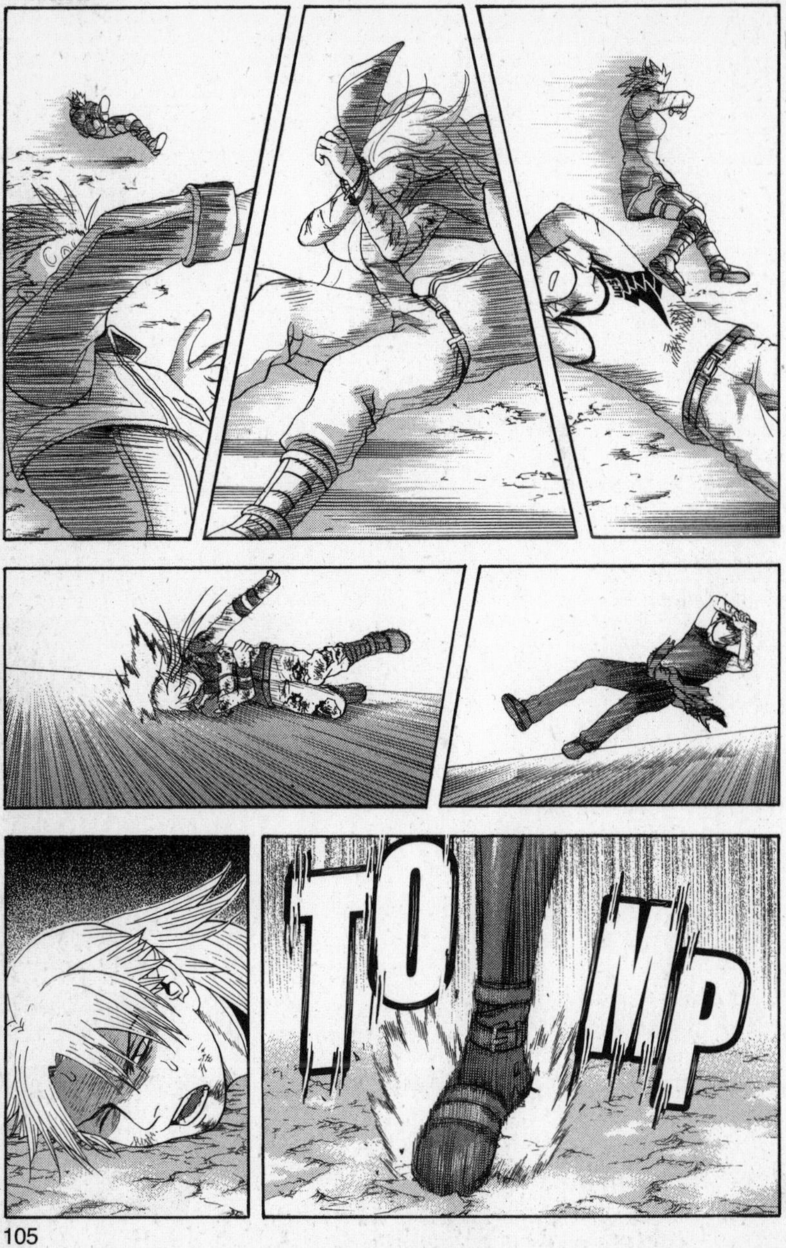
TO MP

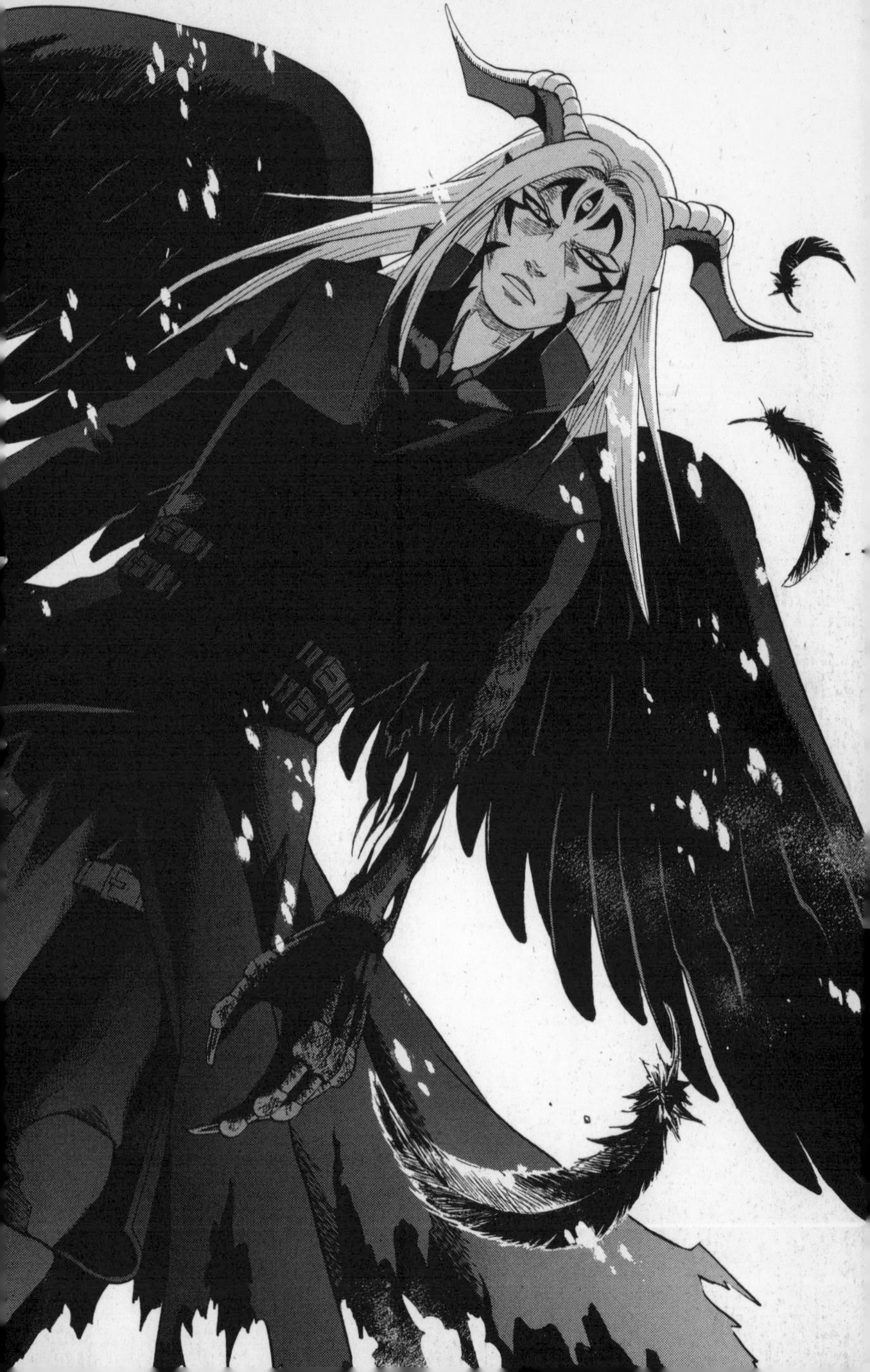

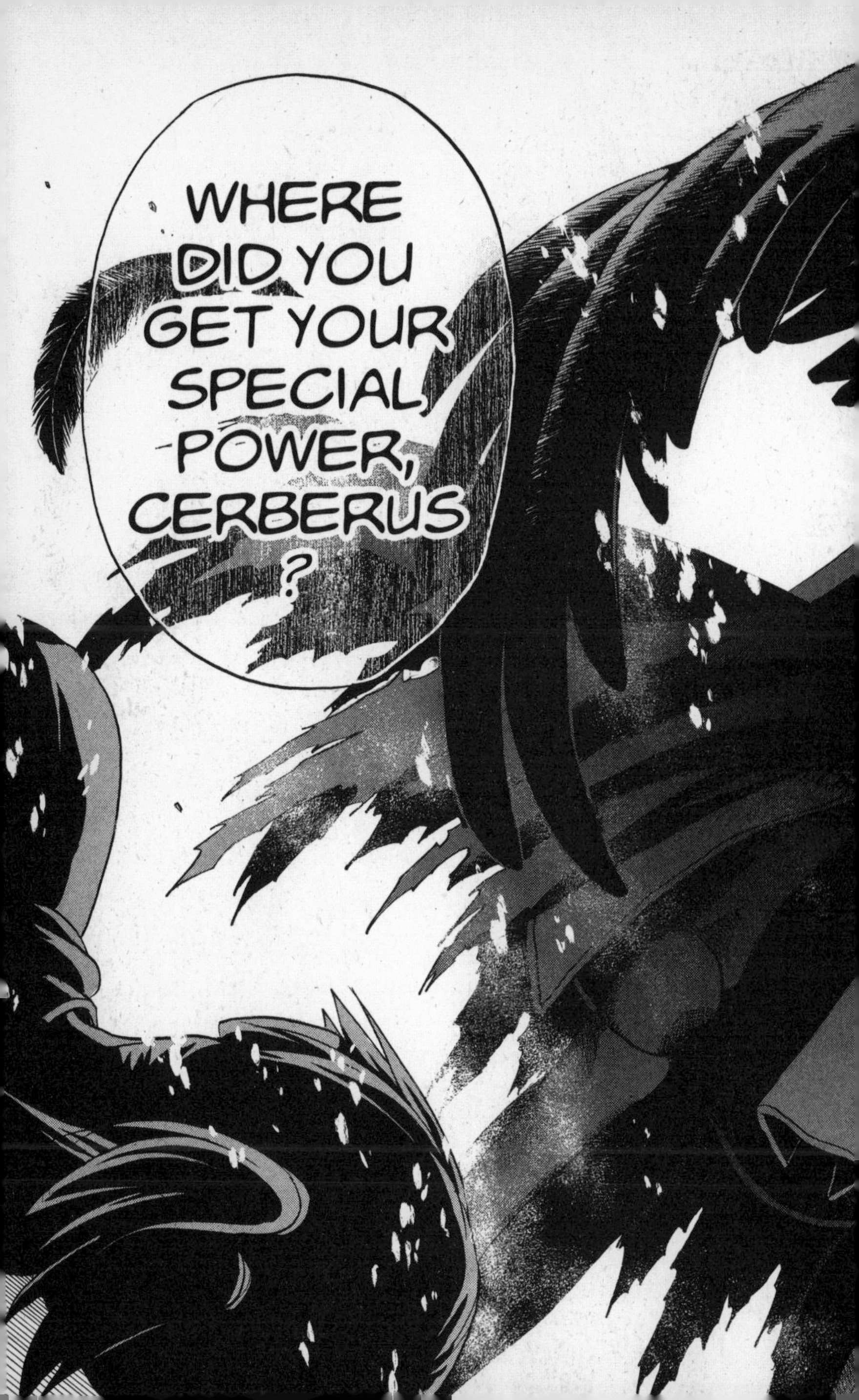
WHERE DID YOU GET YOUR SPECIAL POWER, CERBERUS ?

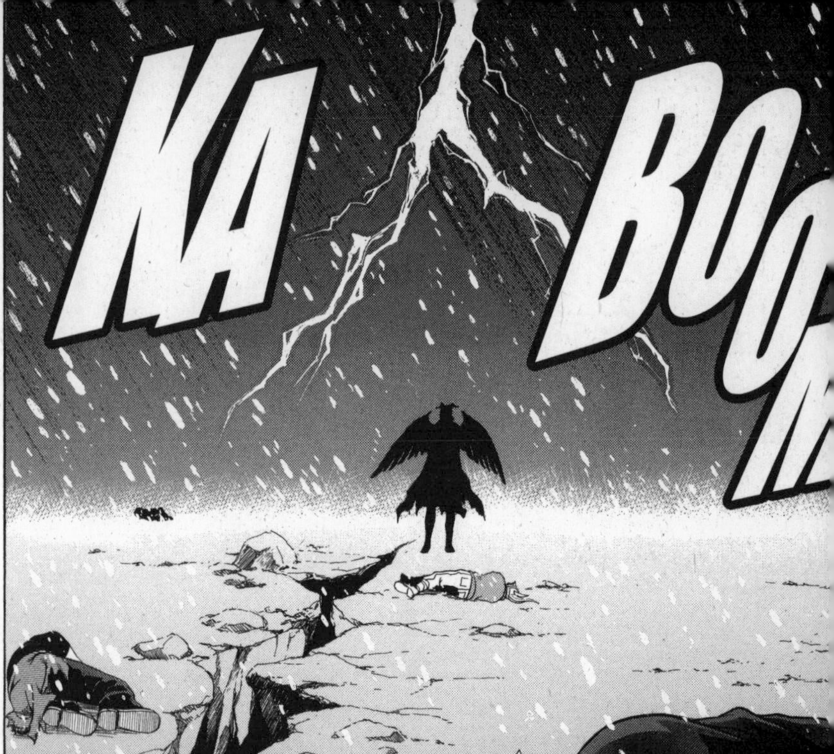
KA
BO

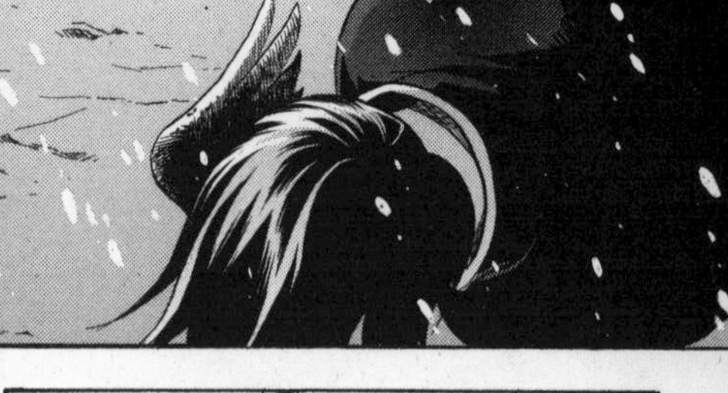
THAT'S HIS...
... TRUE FORM.

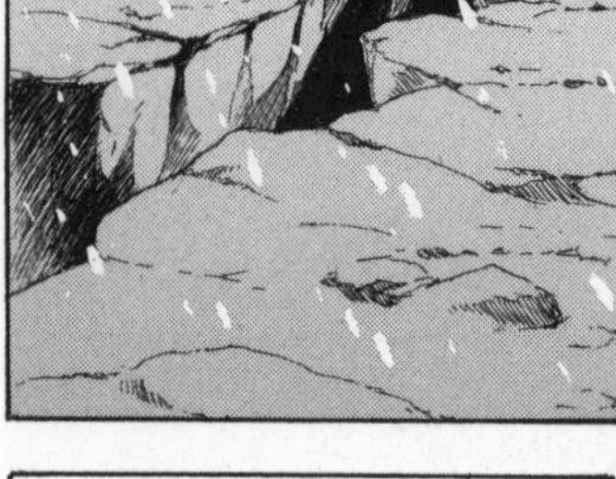
DAMN ...

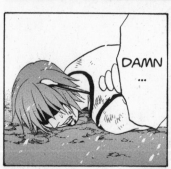

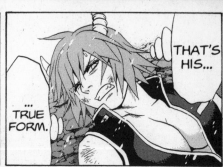

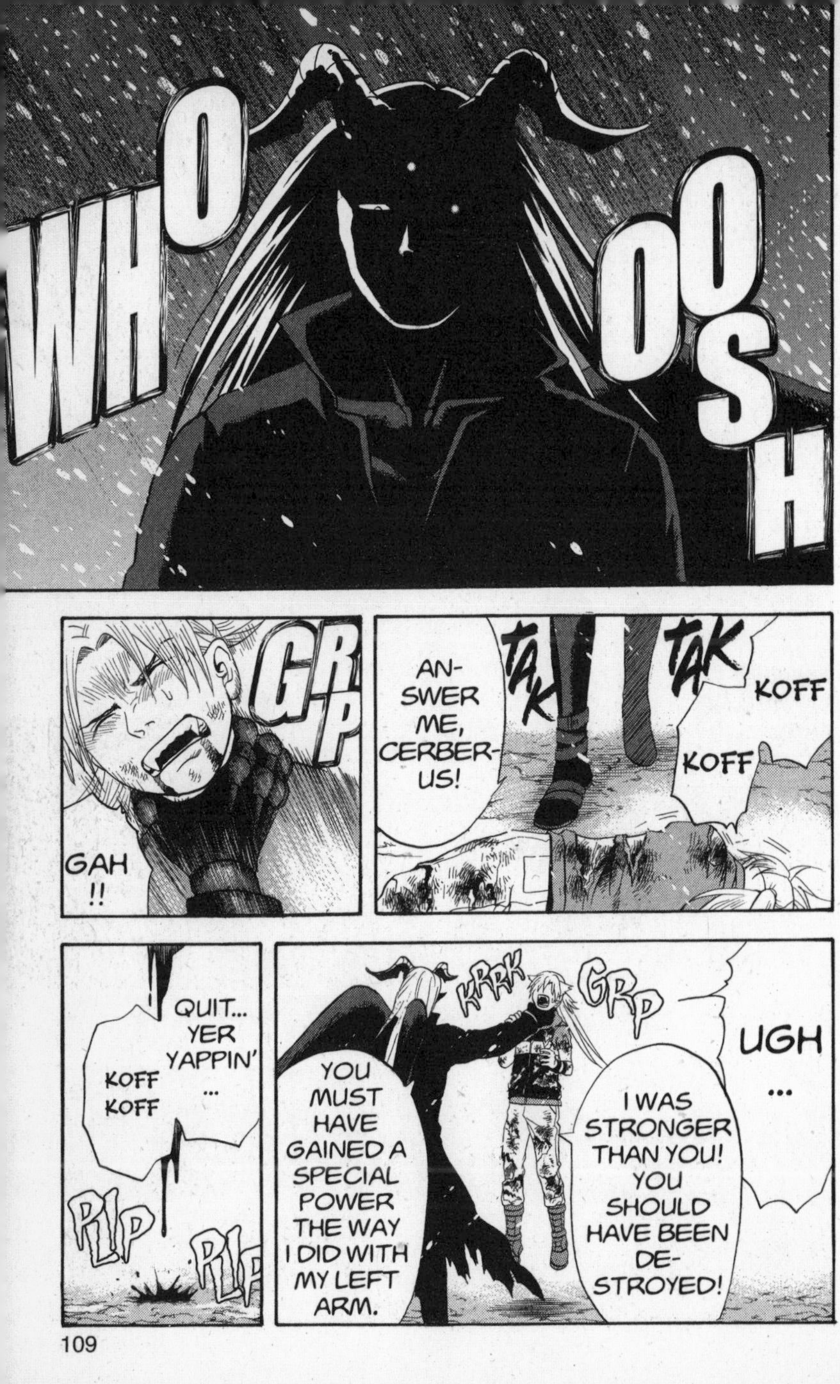
WHOOOOSH
TAK
TAK
AN-SWER ME, CERBER-US!
KOFF
KOFF
GRP
GAH !!
UGH ...
GRP
KRRK
I WAS STRONGER THAN YOU! YOU SHOULD HAVE BEEN DE-STROYED!
YOU MUST HAVE GAINED A SPECIAL POWER THE WAY I DID WITH MY LEFT ARM.
QUIT... YER YAPPIN' ...
KOFF KOFF
PLIP
PLIP

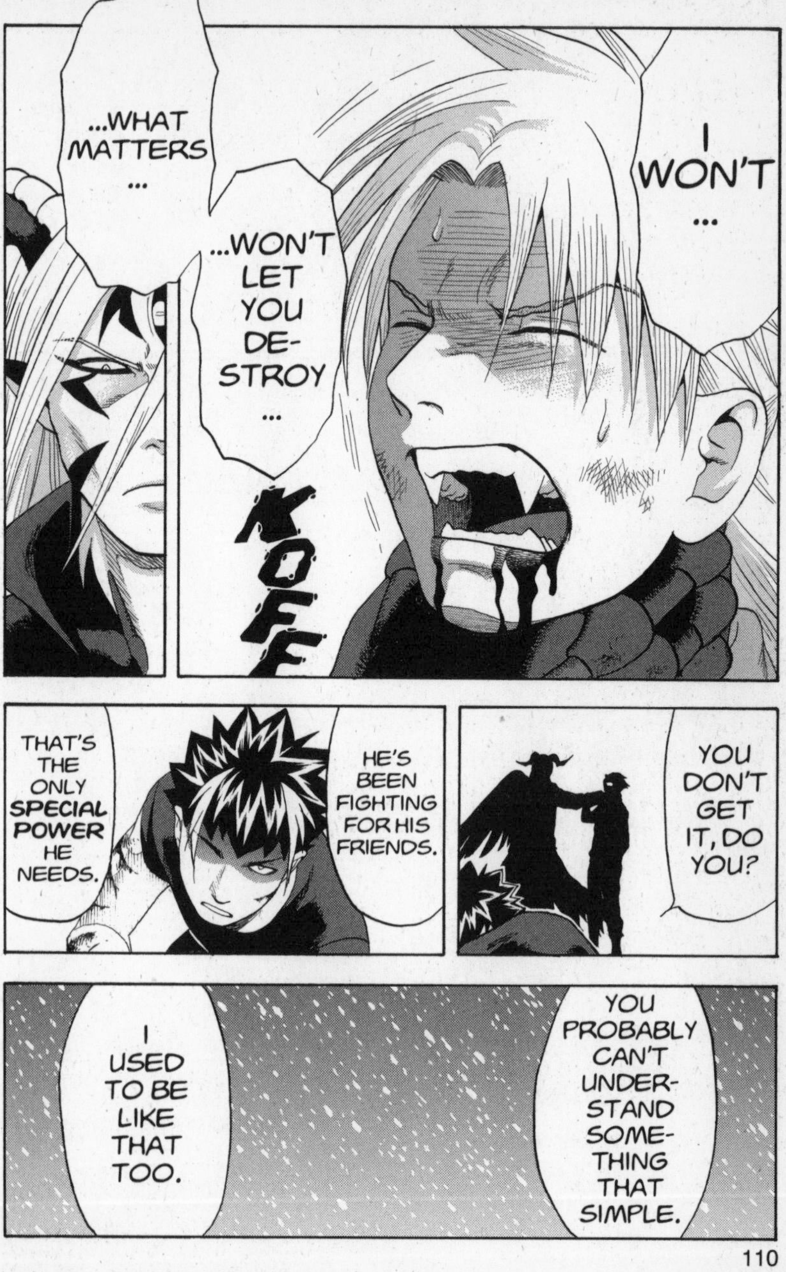
I WON'T ...
...WON'T LET YOU DE-STROY ...
KOFF
...WHAT MATTERS ...
YOU DON'T GET IT, DO YOU?
HE'S BEEN FIGHTING FOR HIS FRIENDS.
THAT'S THE ONLY **SPECIAL POWER** HE NEEDS.
YOU PROBABLY CAN'T UNDER-STAND SOME-THING THAT SIMPLE.
I USED TO BE LIKE THAT TOO.

READ THIS WAY

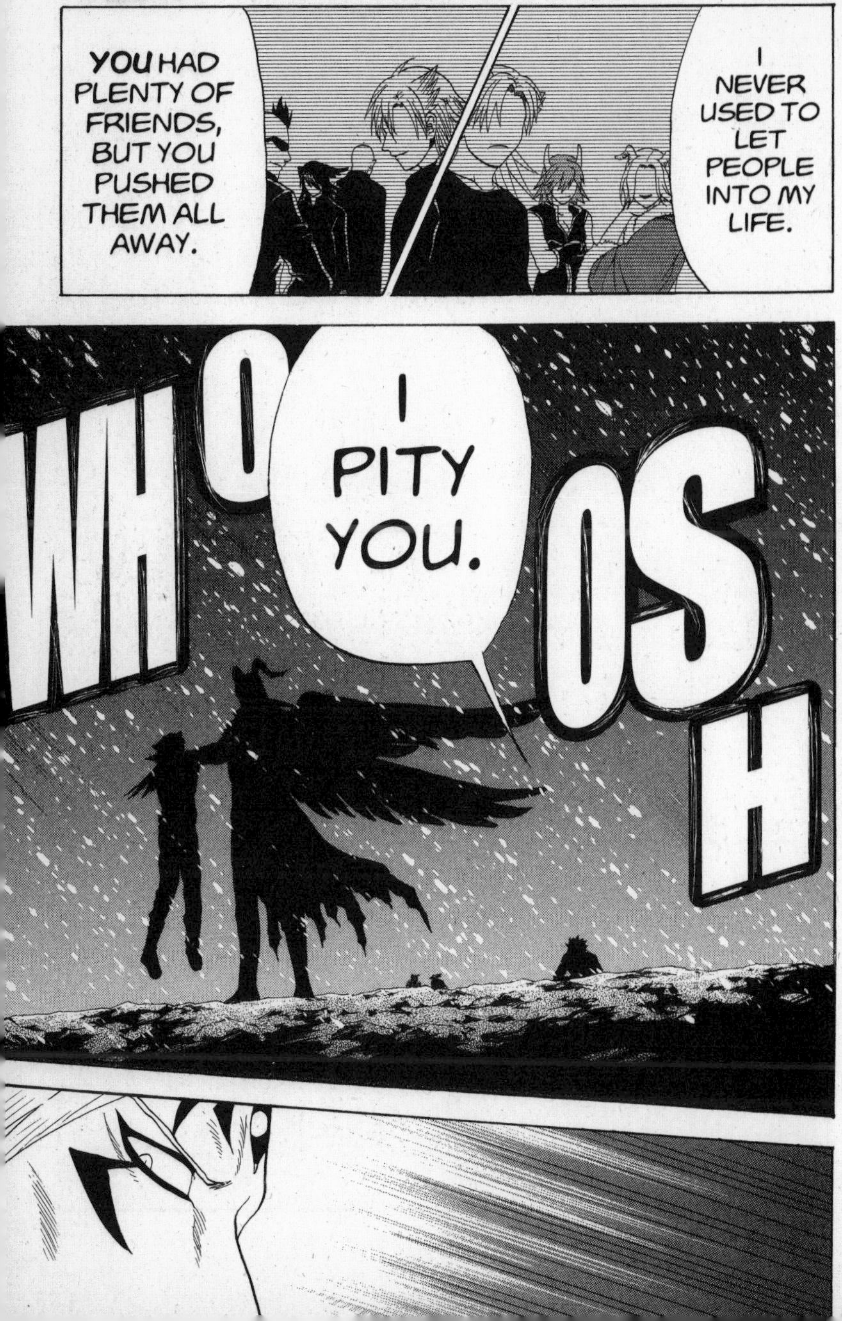
I NEVER USED TO LET PEOPLE INTO MY LIFE.
YOU HAD PLENTY OF FRIENDS, BUT YOU PUSHED THEM ALL AWAY.
WHOOSH
I PITY YOU.

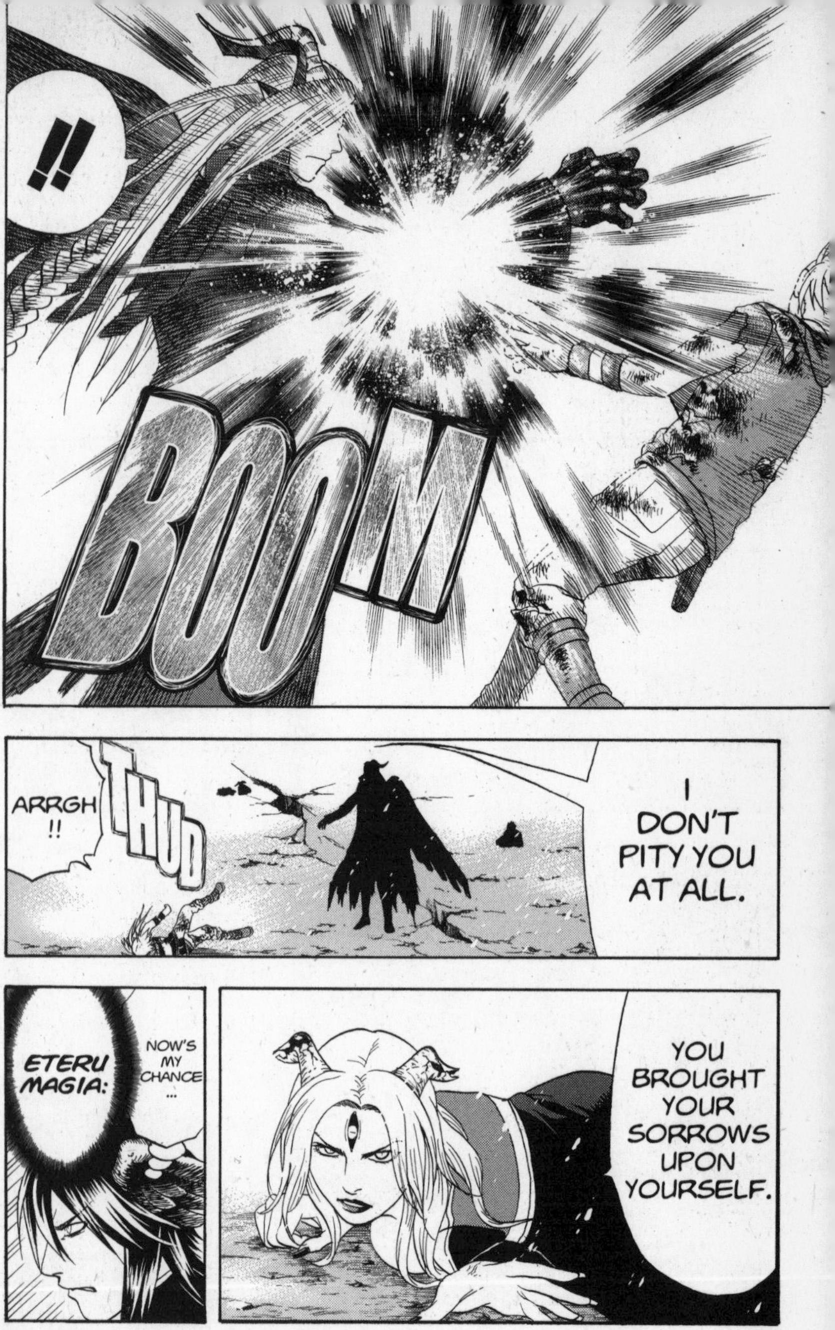
!!
BOOM
I DON'T PITY YOU AT ALL.
THUD
ARRGH !!
YOU BROUGHT YOUR SORROWS UPON YOURSELF.
NOW'S MY CHANCE ...
ETERU MAGIA:

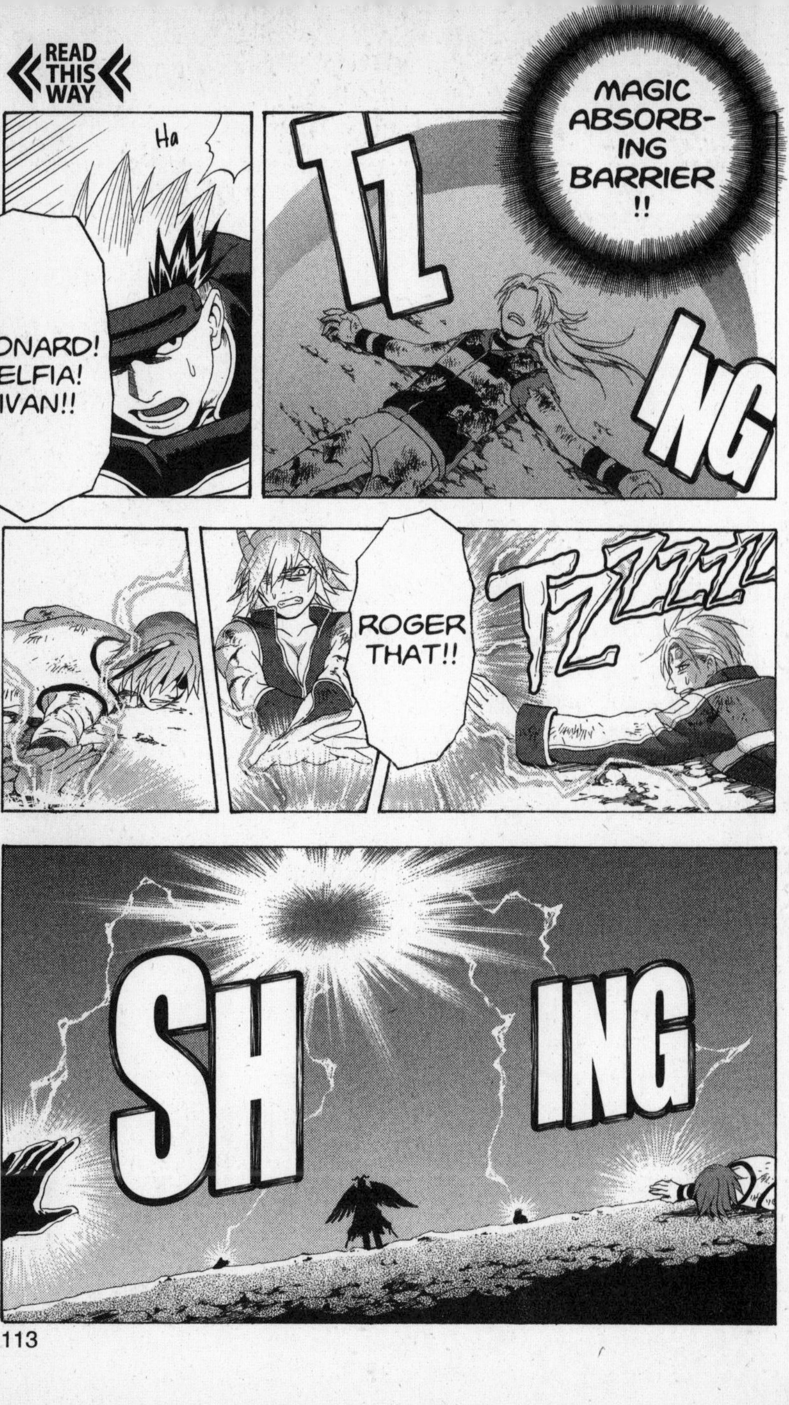
READ THIS WAY
MAGIC ABSORB-ING BARRIER!!
TZ
ING
Ha
LEONARD! MELFIA! RIVAN!!
TZZZZ
ROGER THAT!!
SH
ING

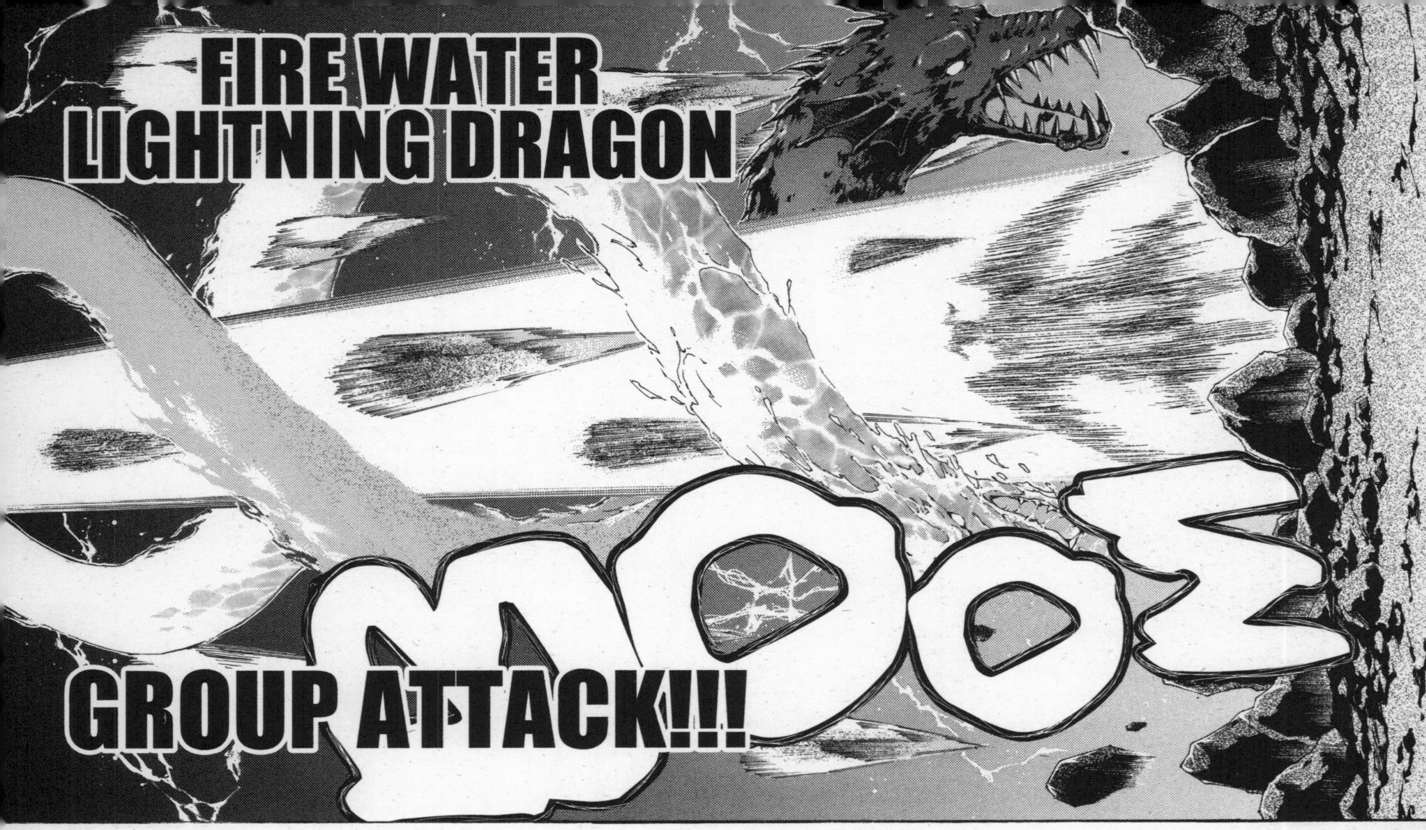
FIRE WATER
LIGHTNING DRAGON
GROUP ATTACK!!!

READ THIS WAY

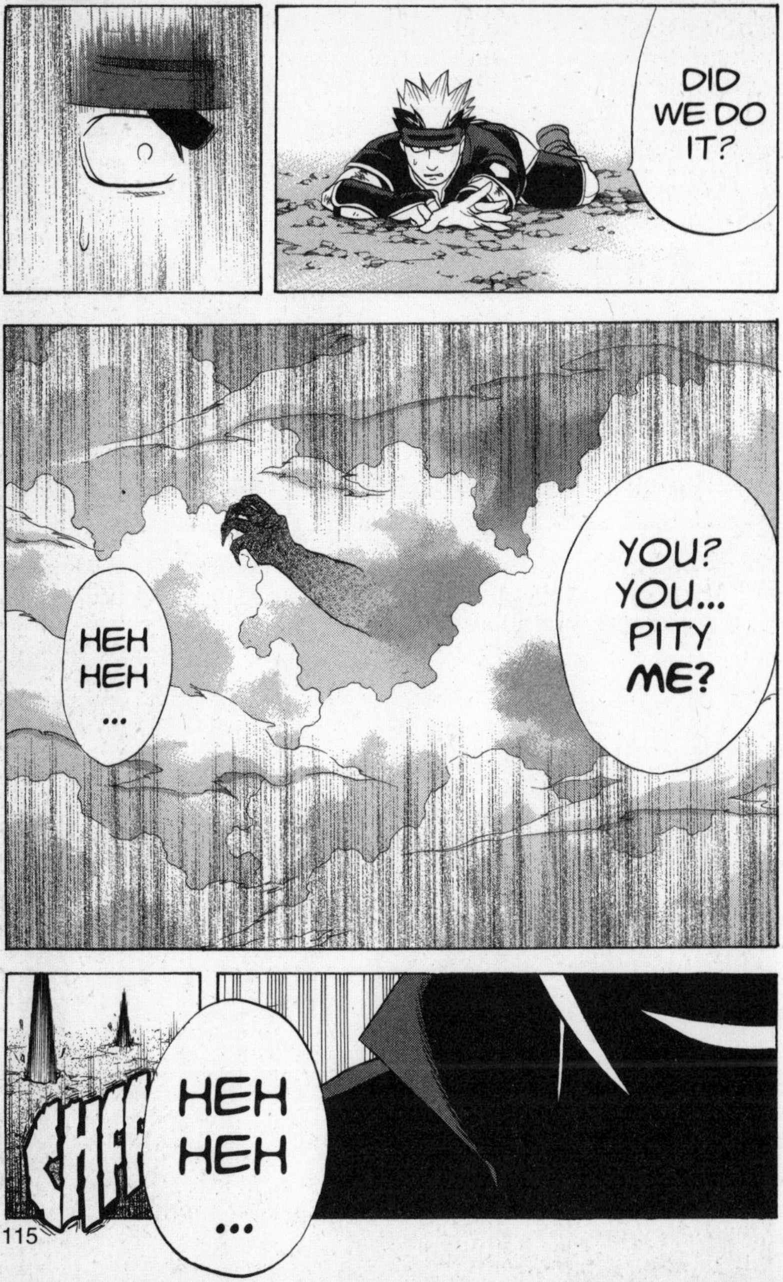
DID WE DO IT?
YOU? YOU... PITY ME?
HEH HEH ...
HEH HEH ...
CHFF

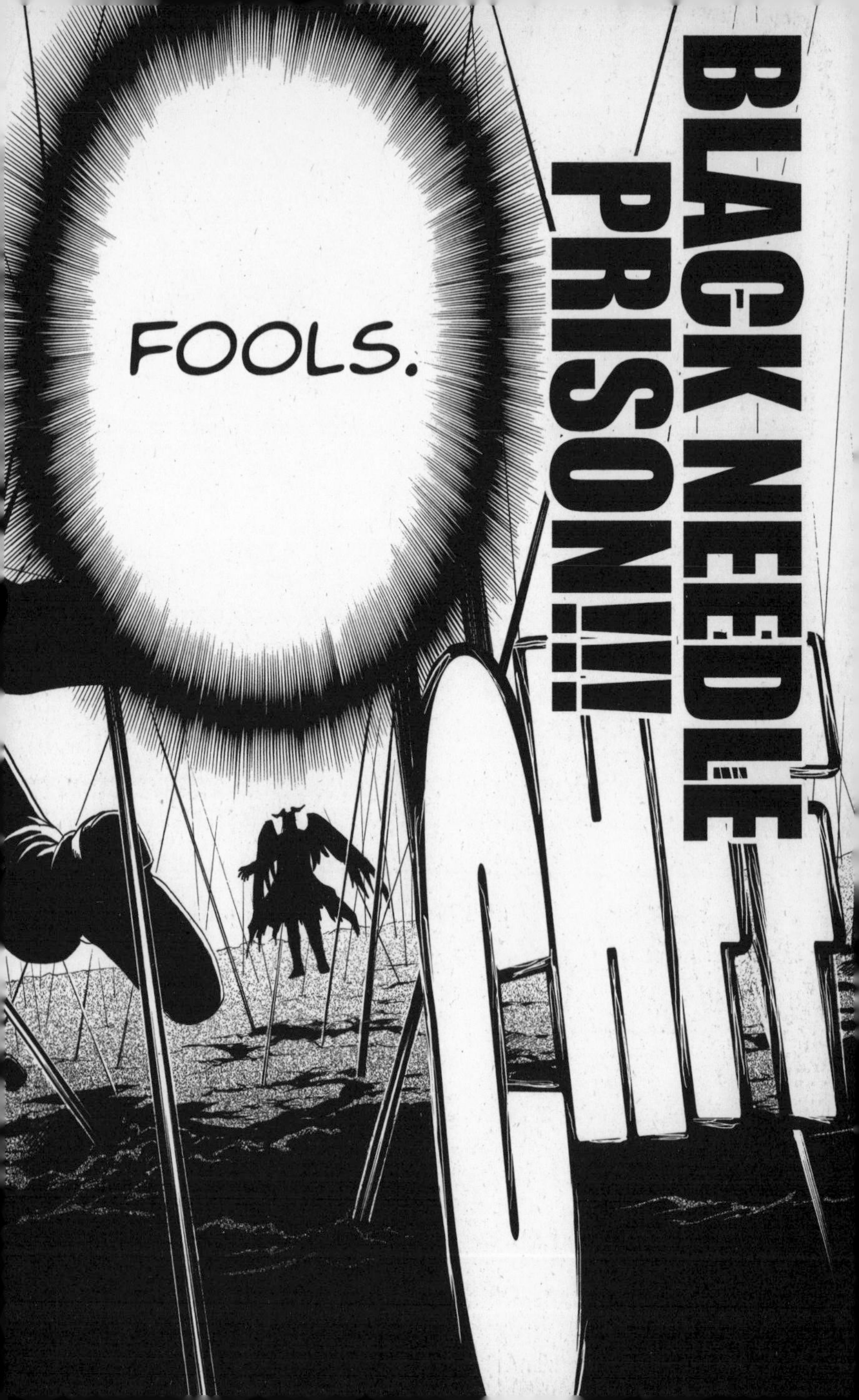
BLACK NEEDLE PRISON!!!
FOOLS.

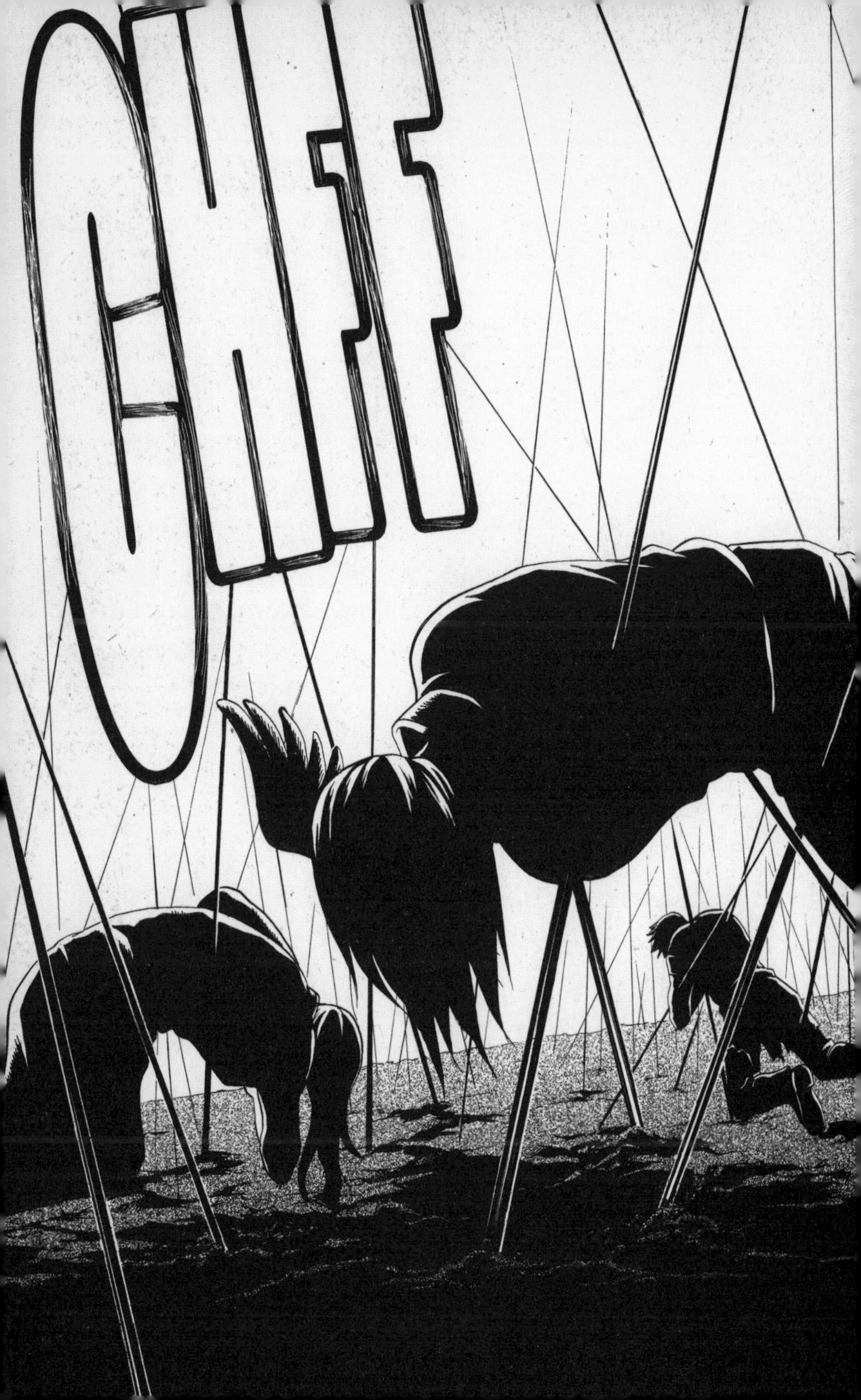

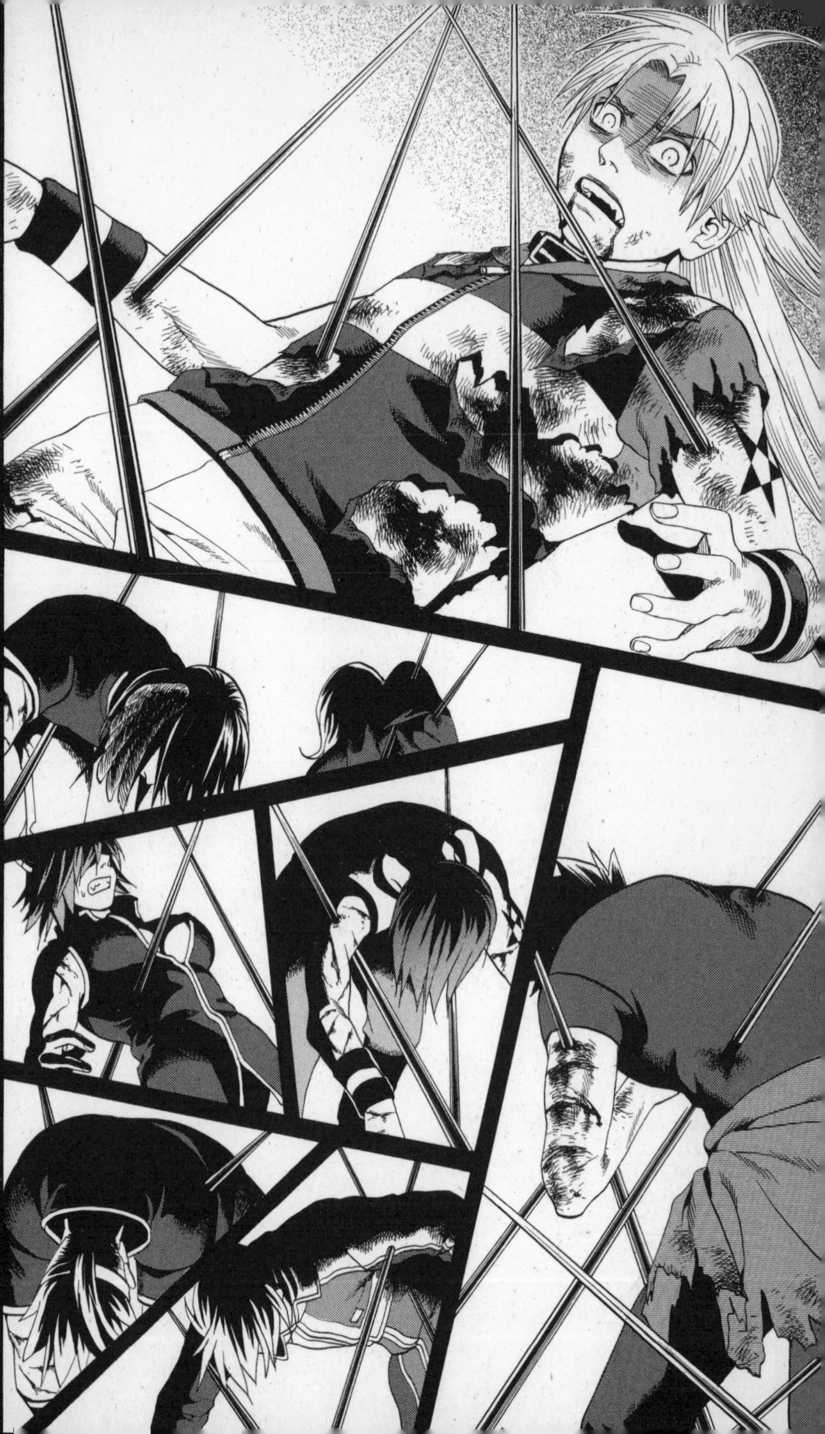

READ THIS WAY

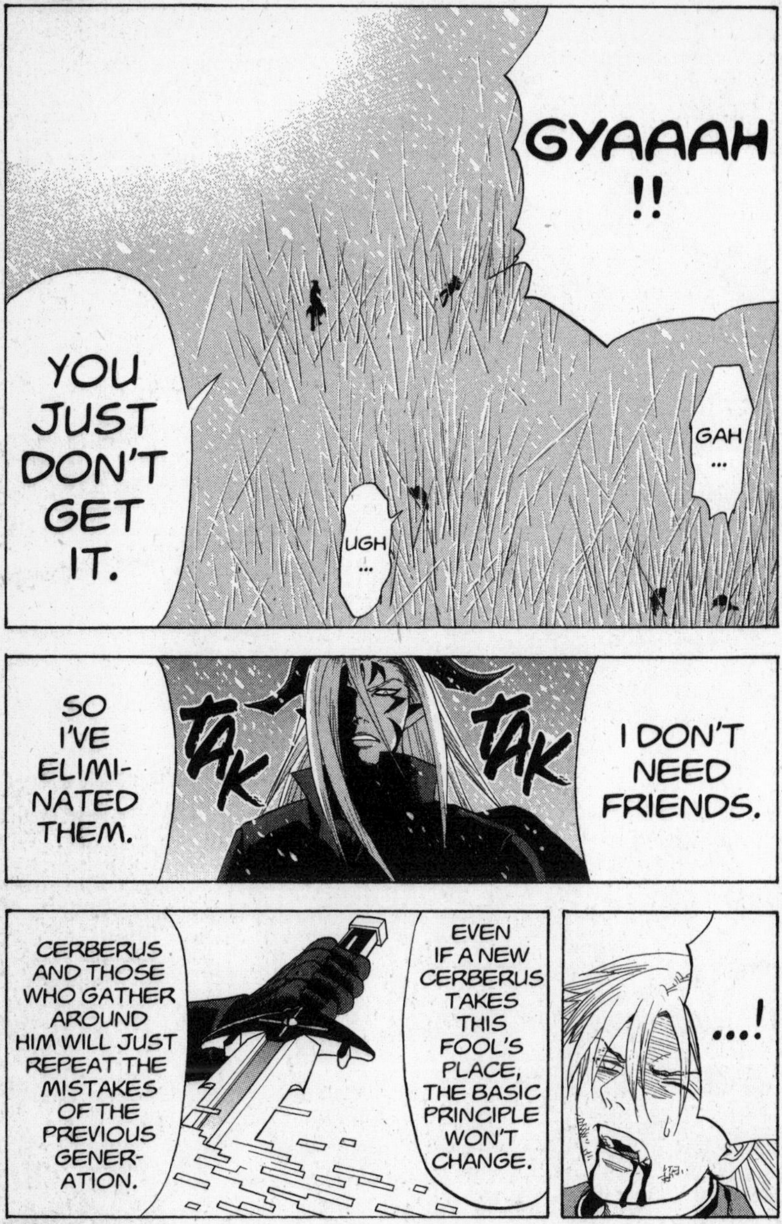
GYAAAH!!
GAH...
UGH...
YOU JUST DON'T GET IT.
I DON'T NEED FRIENDS.
TAK
TAK
SO I'VE ELIMINATED THEM.
...!
EVEN IF A NEW CERBERUS TAKES THIS FOOL'S PLACE, THE BASIC PRINCIPLE WON'T CHANGE.
CERBERUS AND THOSE WHO GATHER AROUND HIM WILL JUST REPEAT THE MISTAKES OF THE PREVIOUS GENERATION.

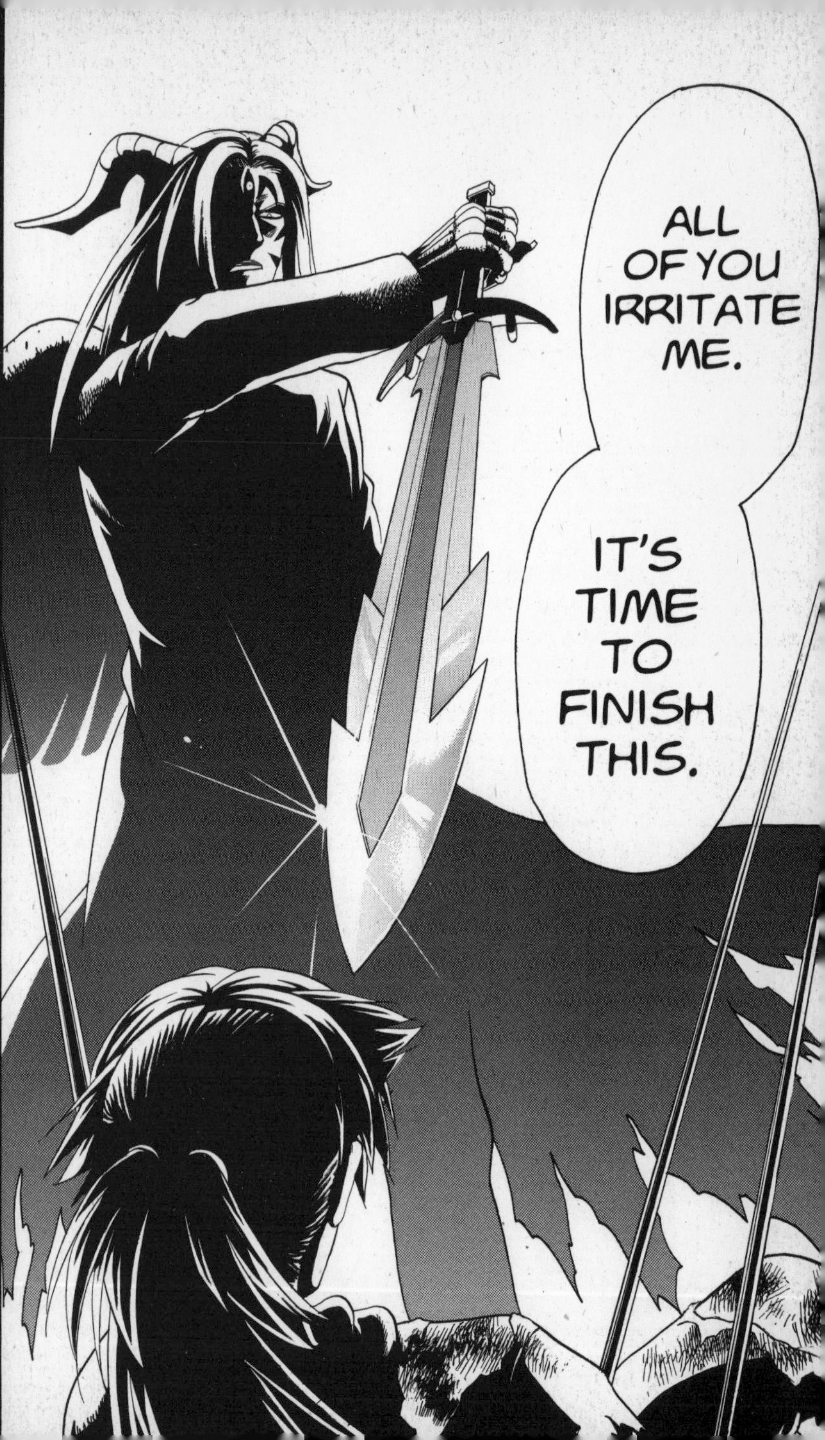
ALL OF YOU IRRITATE ME.
IT'S TIME TO FINISH THIS.

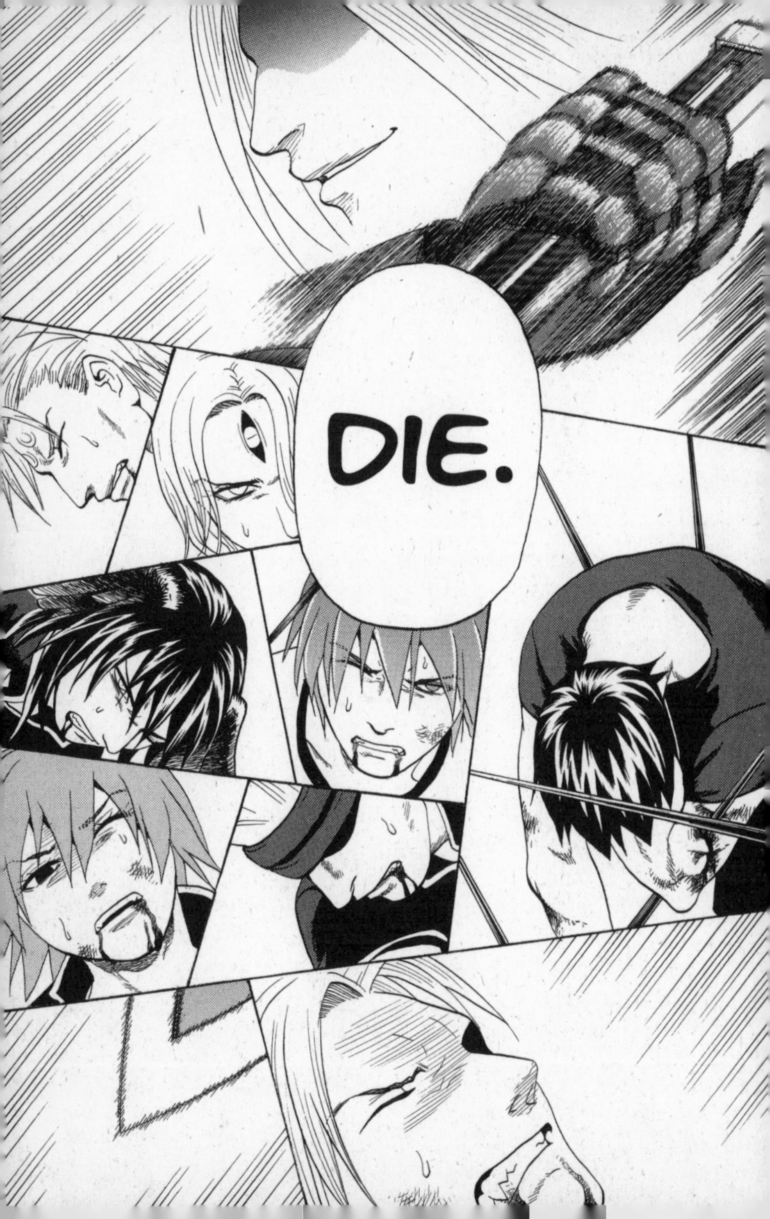
DIE.

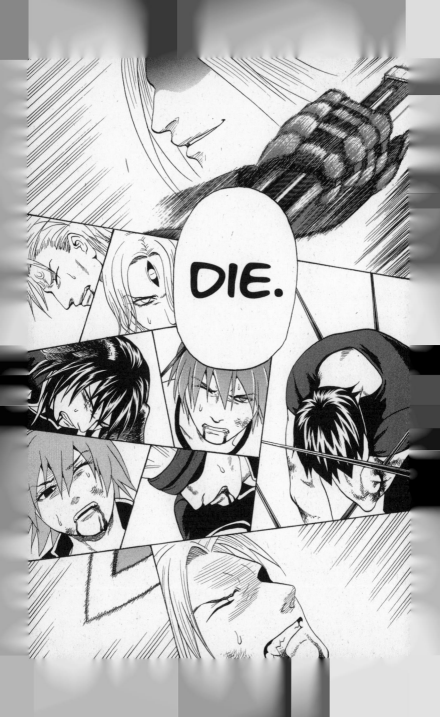

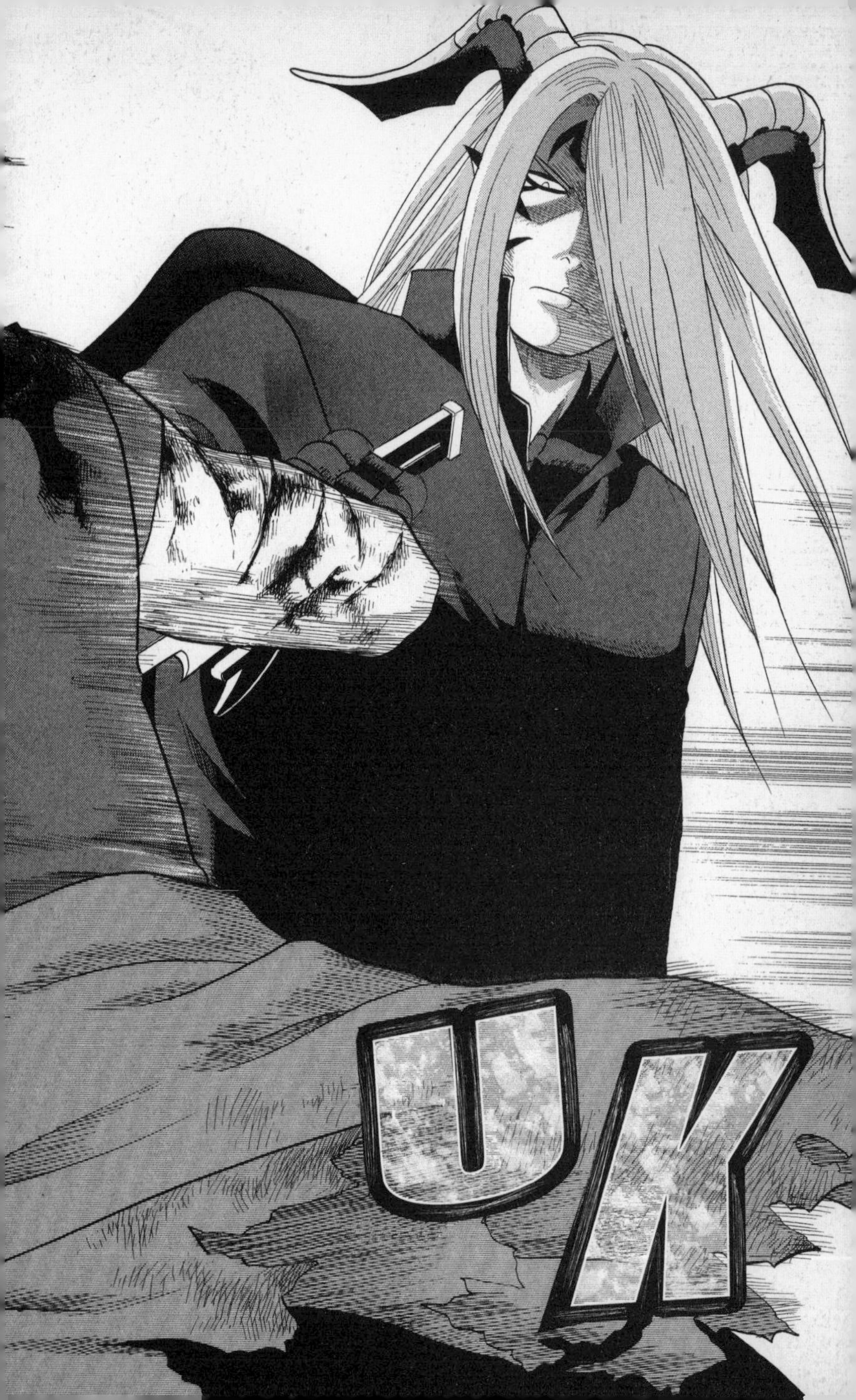
UK

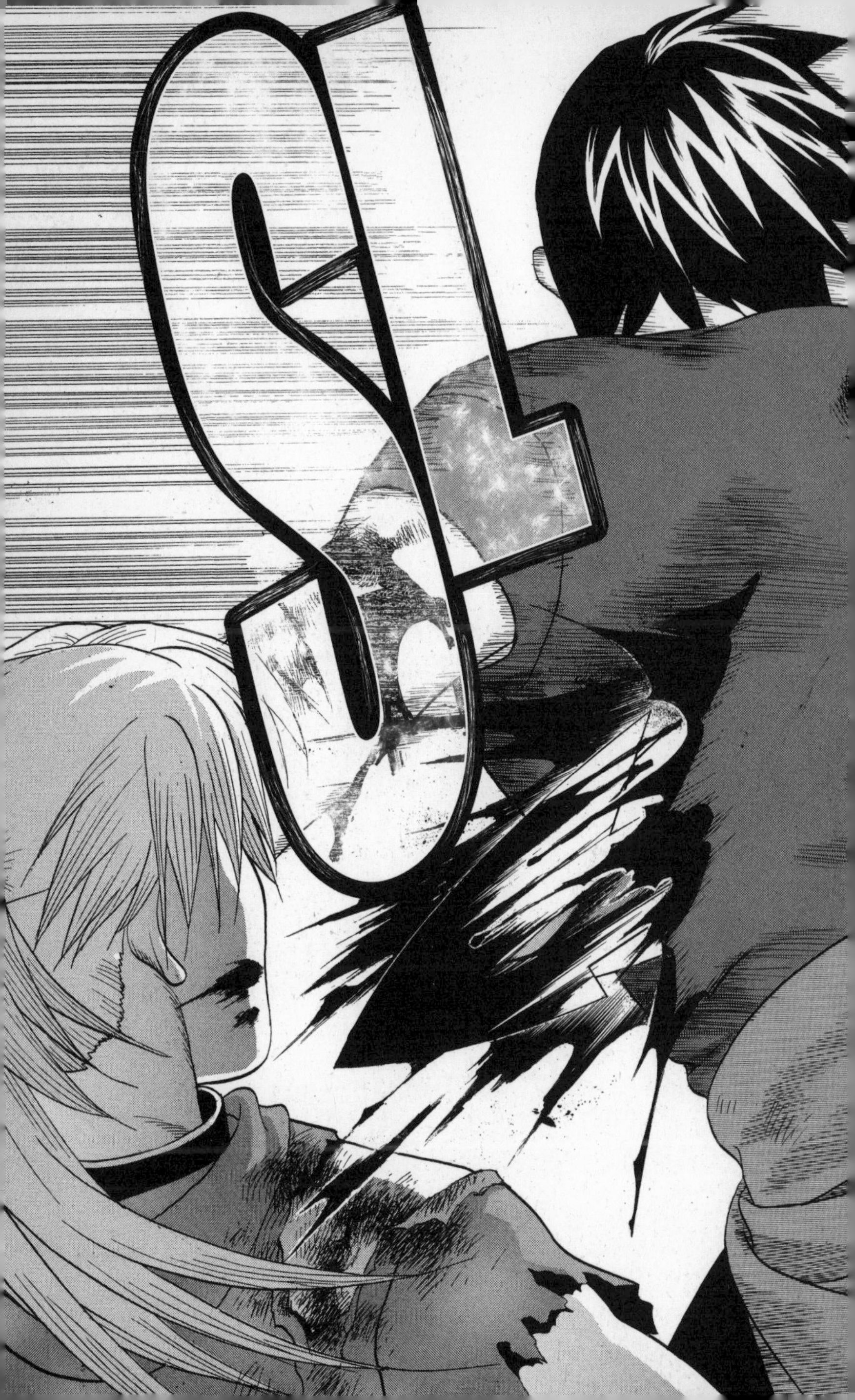

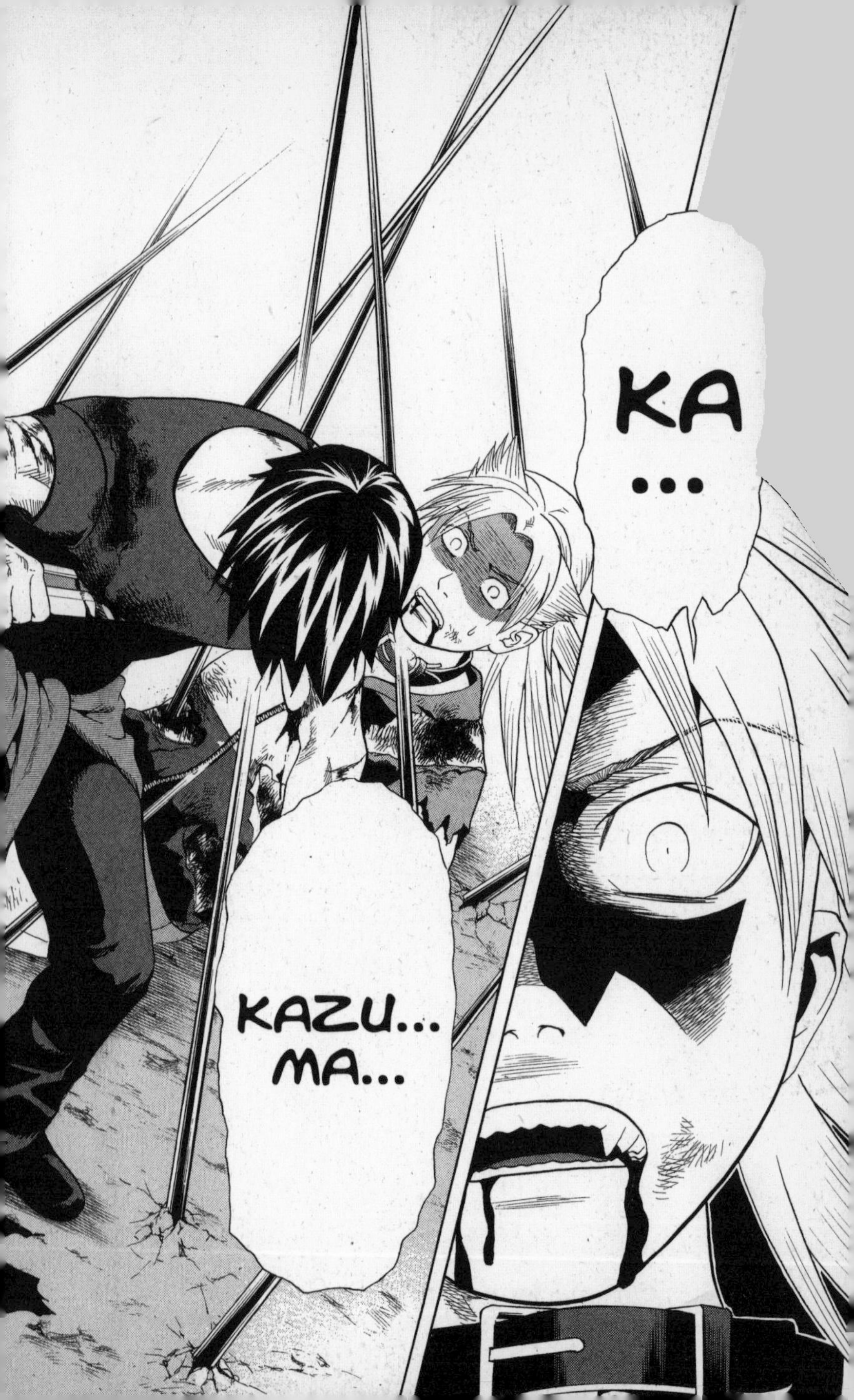
KA...
KAZU... MA...

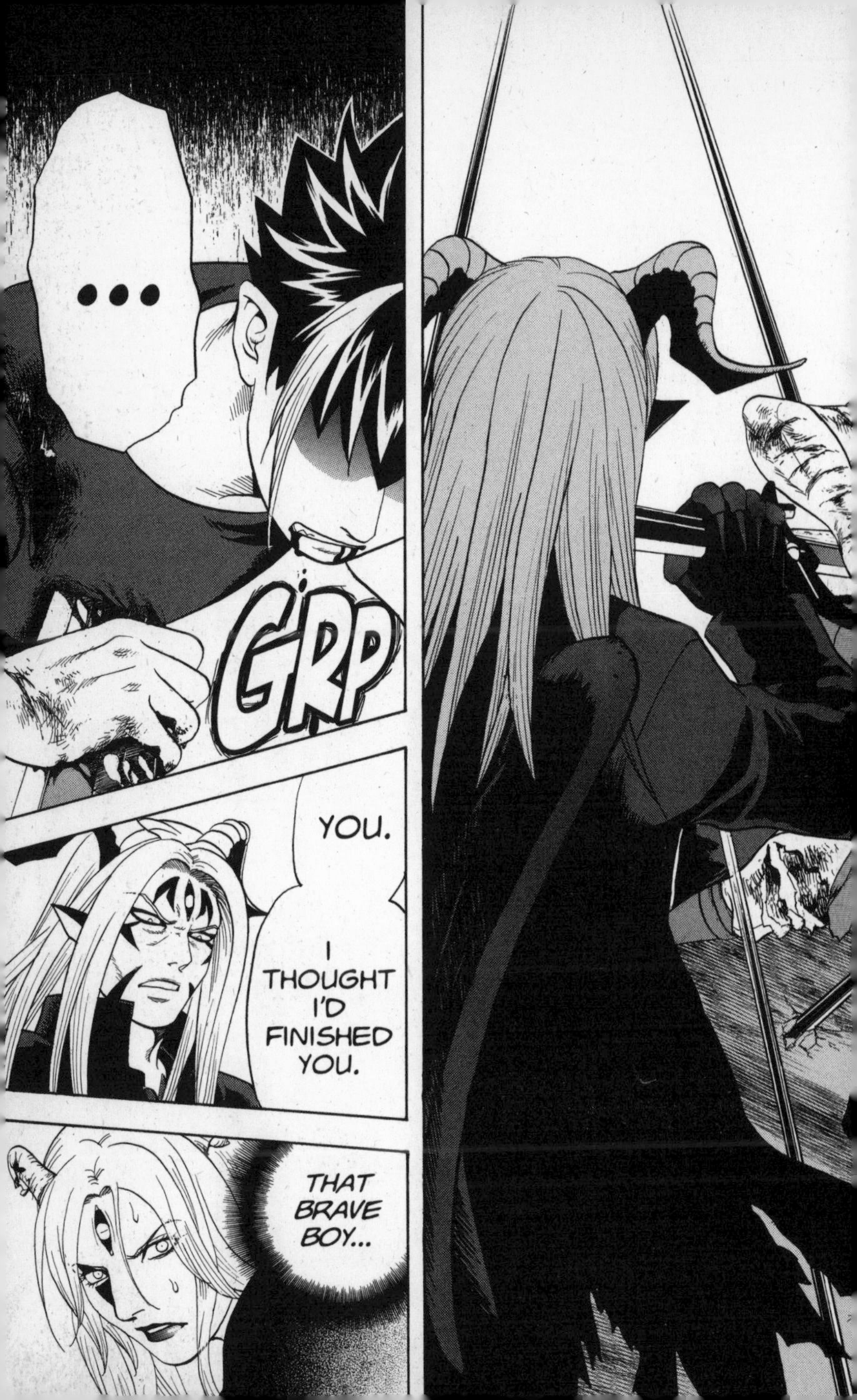
...
GRP
YOU.
I THOUGHT I'D FINISHED YOU.
THAT BRAVE BOY...

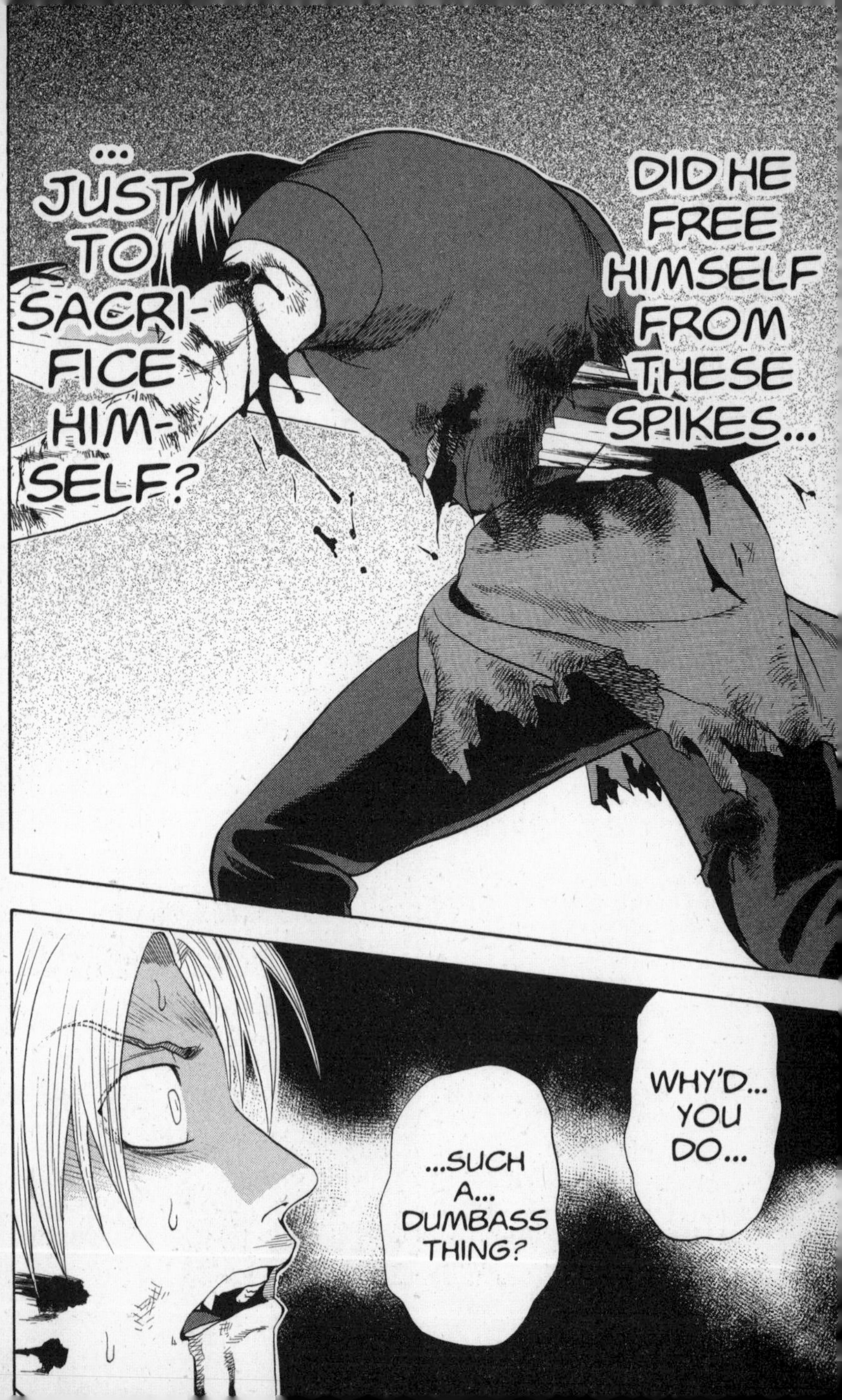
DID HE FREE HIMSELF FROM THESE SPIKES...
...JUST TO SACRIFICE HIMSELF?
WHY'D... YOU DO...
...SUCH A... DUMBASS THING?

READ THIS WAY

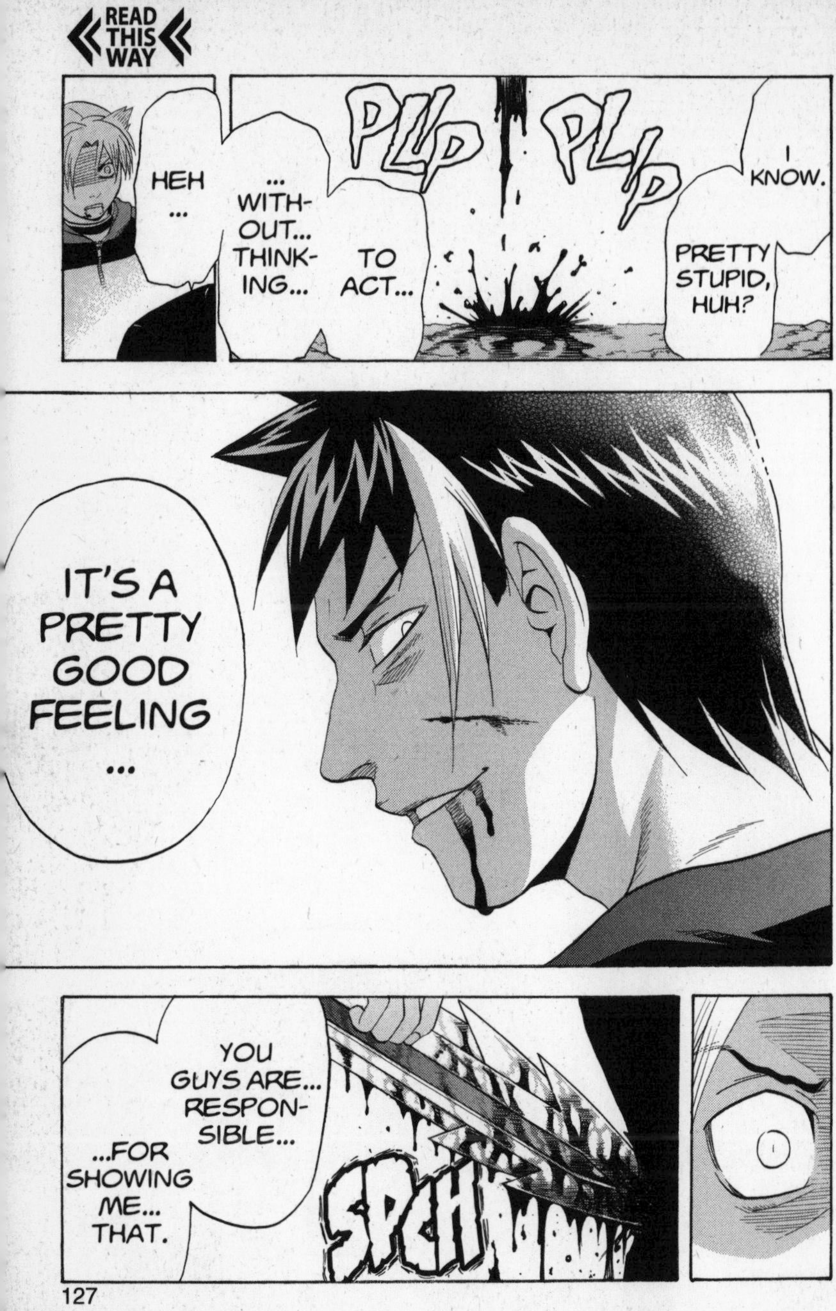
I KNOW.
PRETTY STUPID, HUH?
PLIP PLIP
TO ACT...
... WITHOUT... THINKING...
HEH ...
IT'S A PRETTY GOOD FEELING ...
YOU GUYS ARE... RESPONSIBLE...
...FOR SHOWING ME... THAT.
SPCH

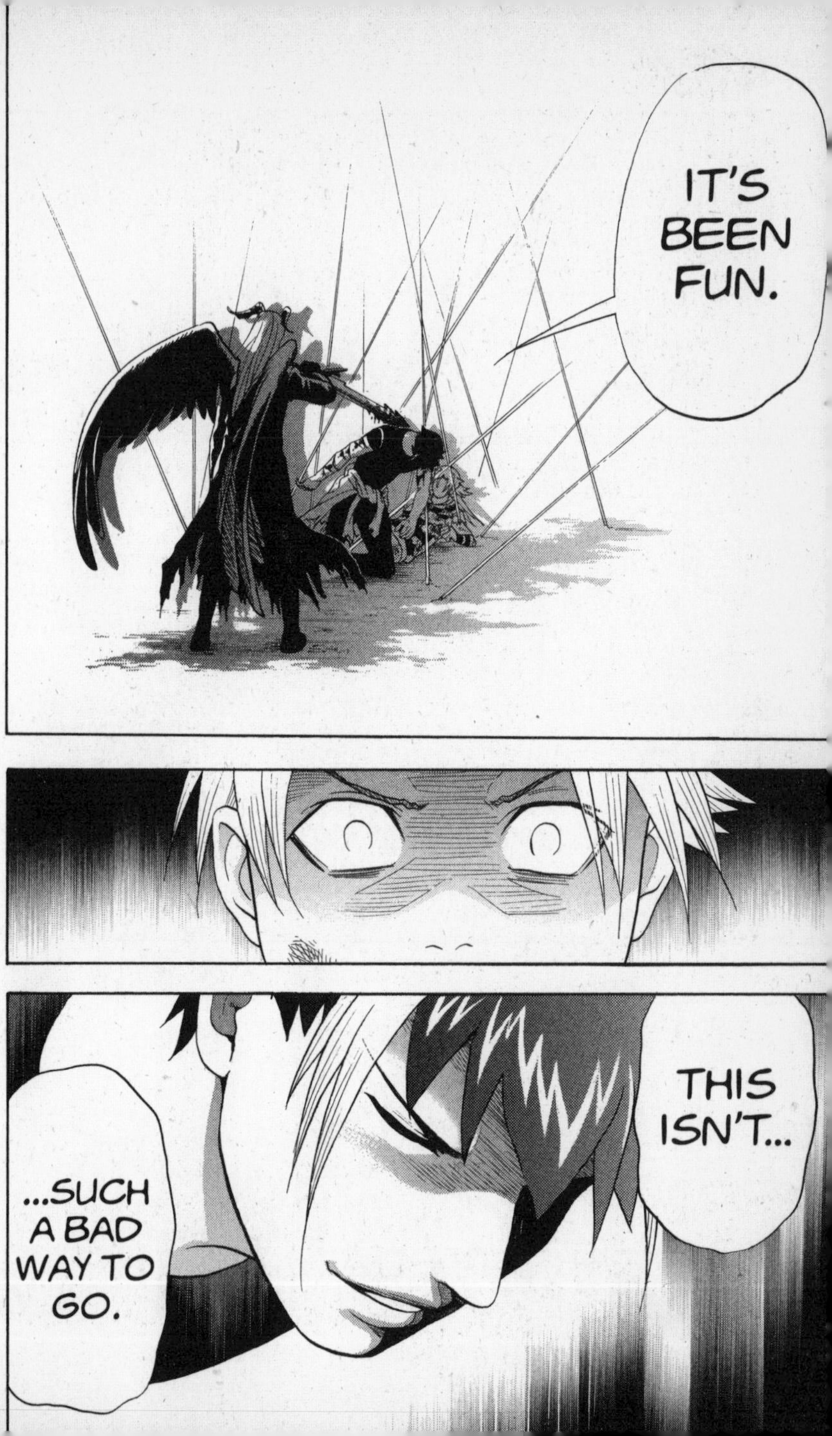
IT'S BEEN FUN.
THIS ISN'T...
...SUCH A BAD WAY TO GO.

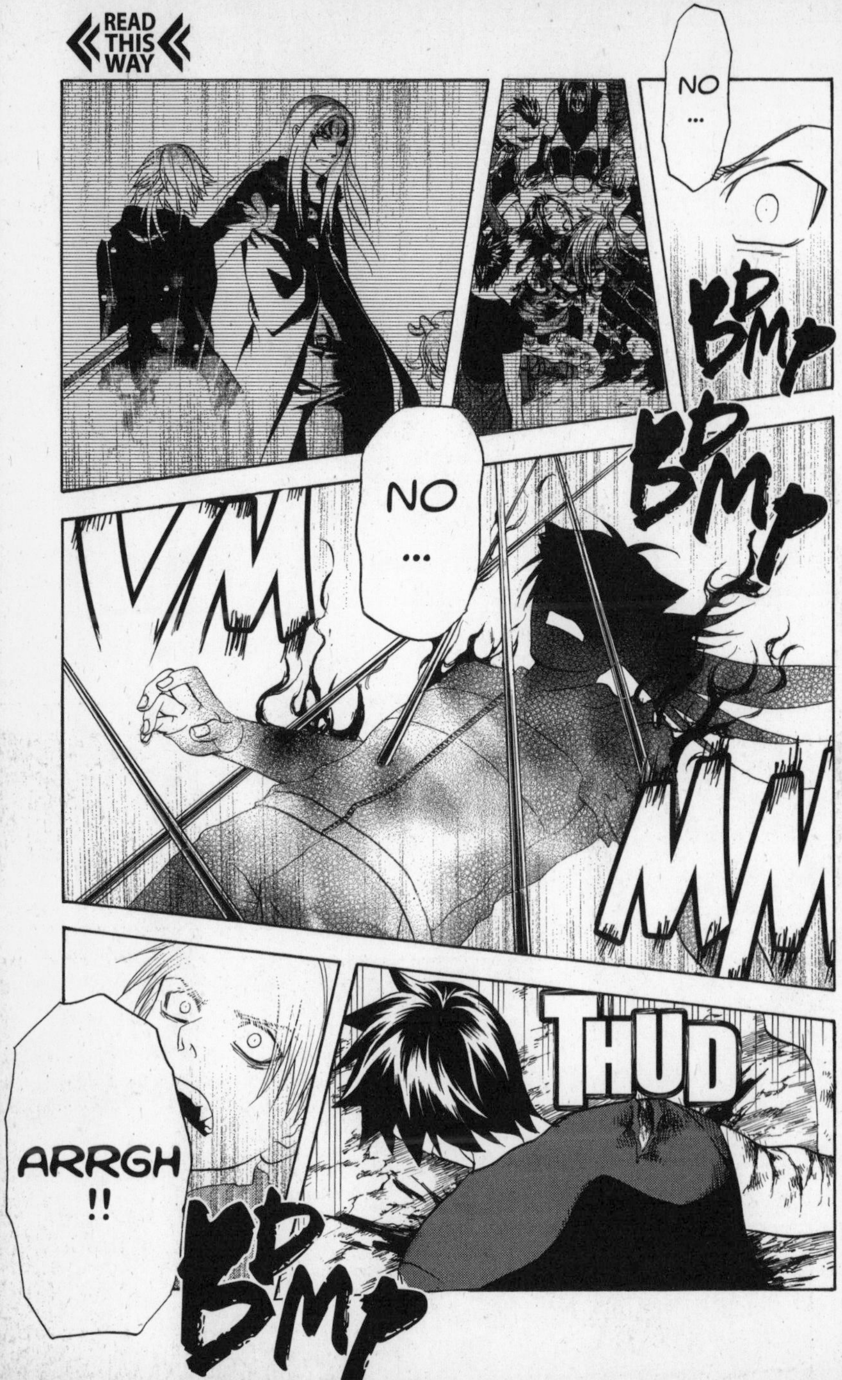
READ THIS WAY
NO ...
BDMP BDMP
NO ...
VMMM
THUD
ARRGH !!
BDMP

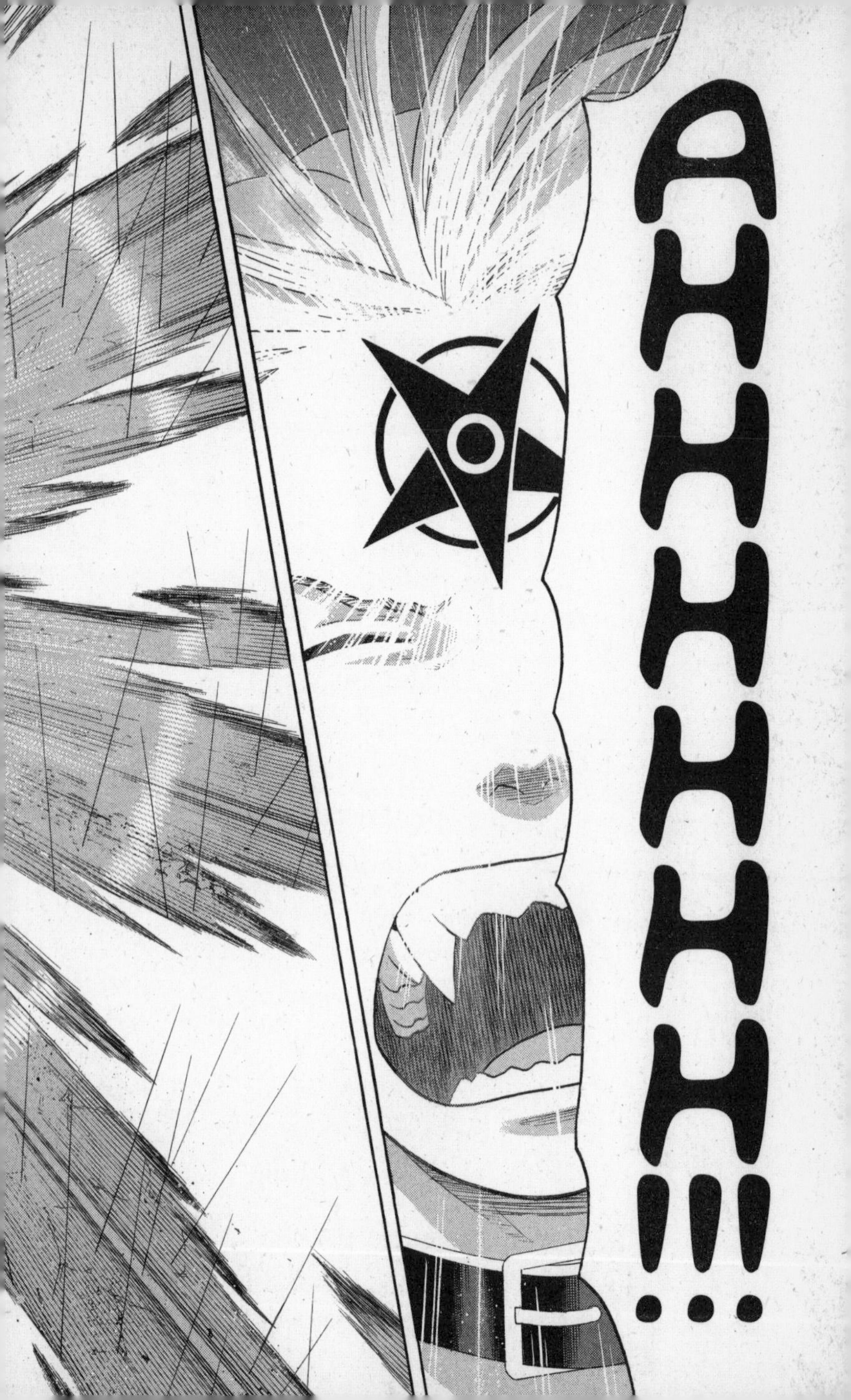
AHHHHHHH!!!

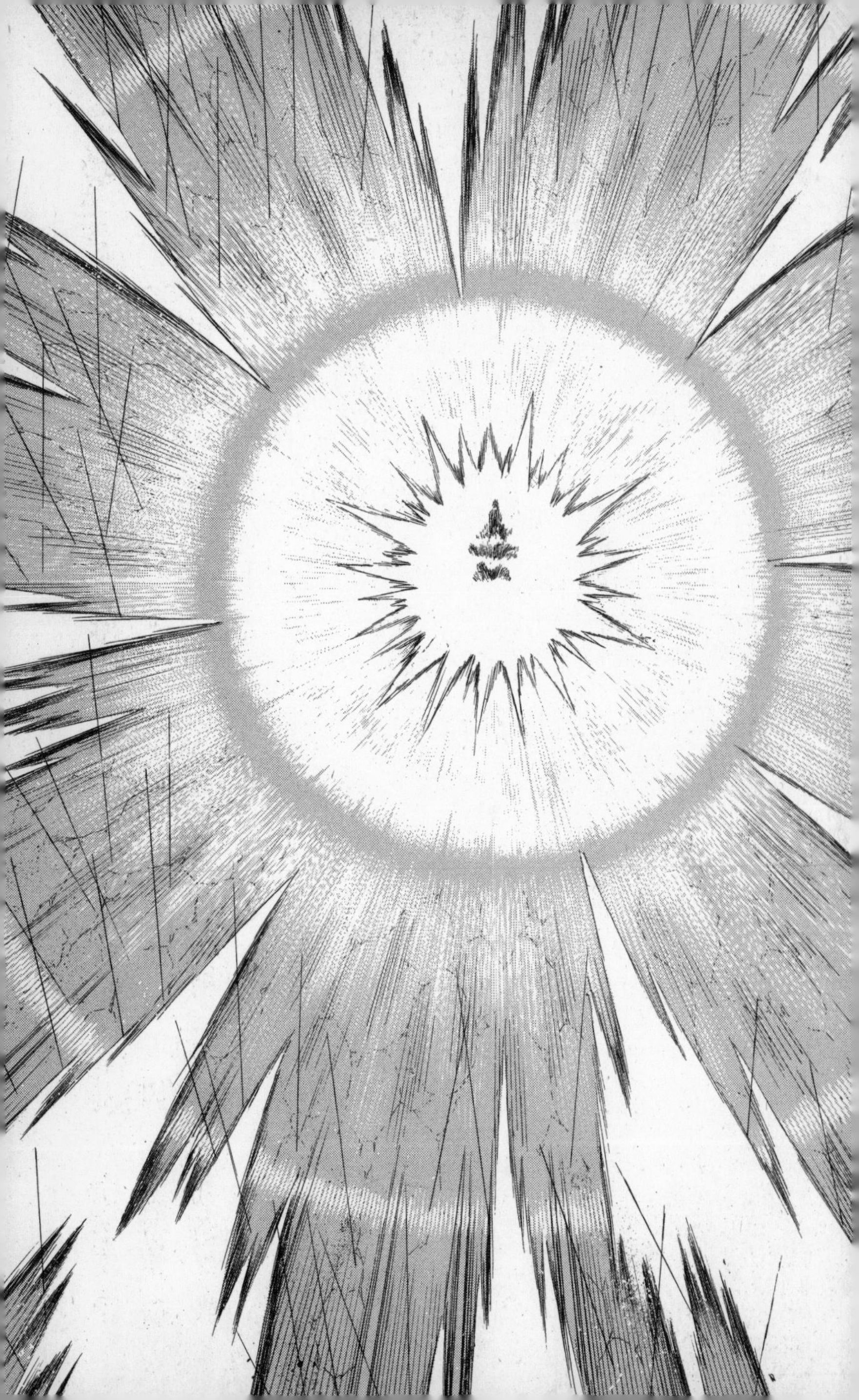

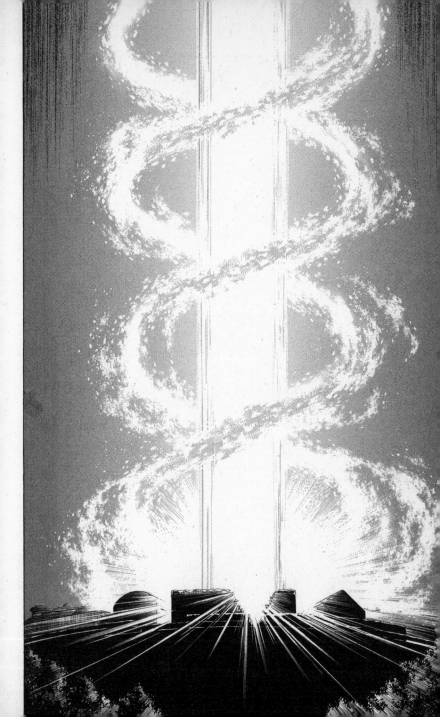

READ THIS WAY

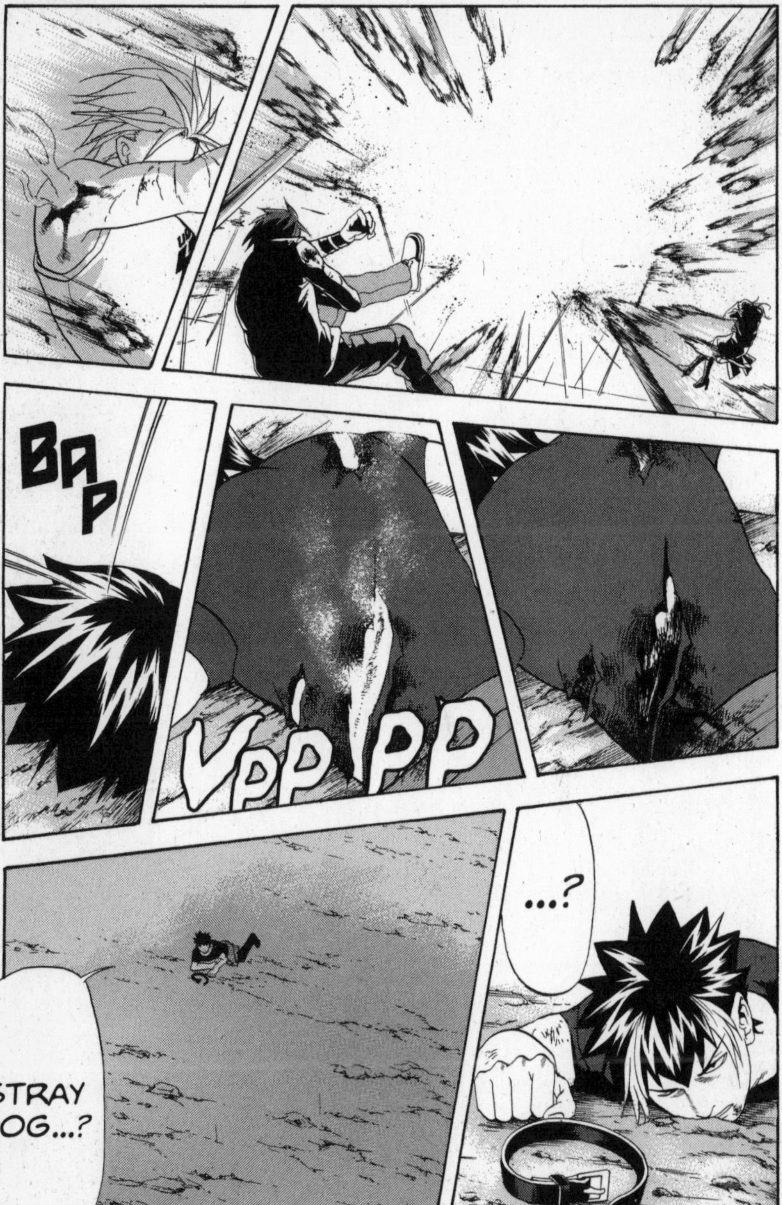
VPP PP
BAP
...?
STRAY DOG...?

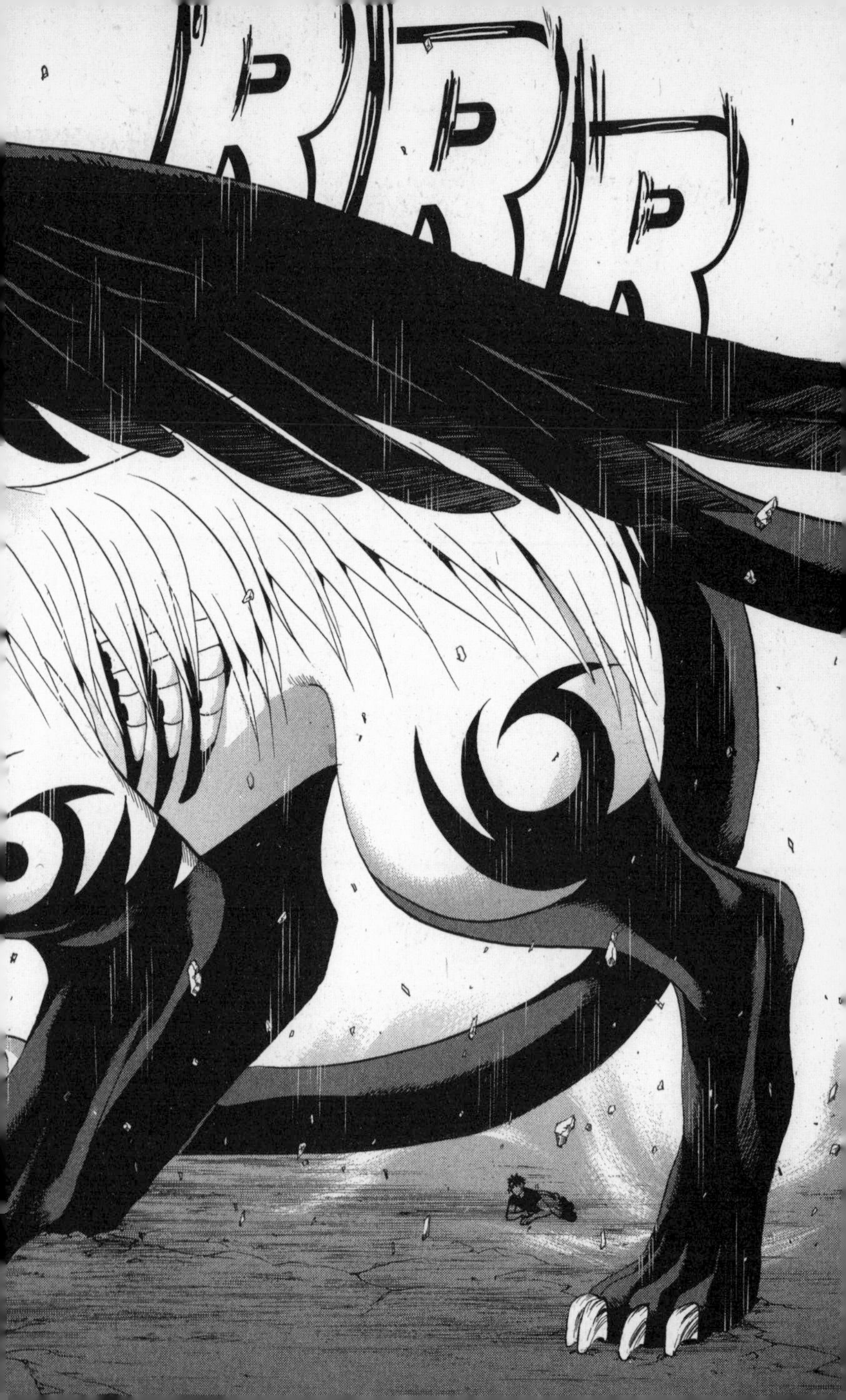
RRRR

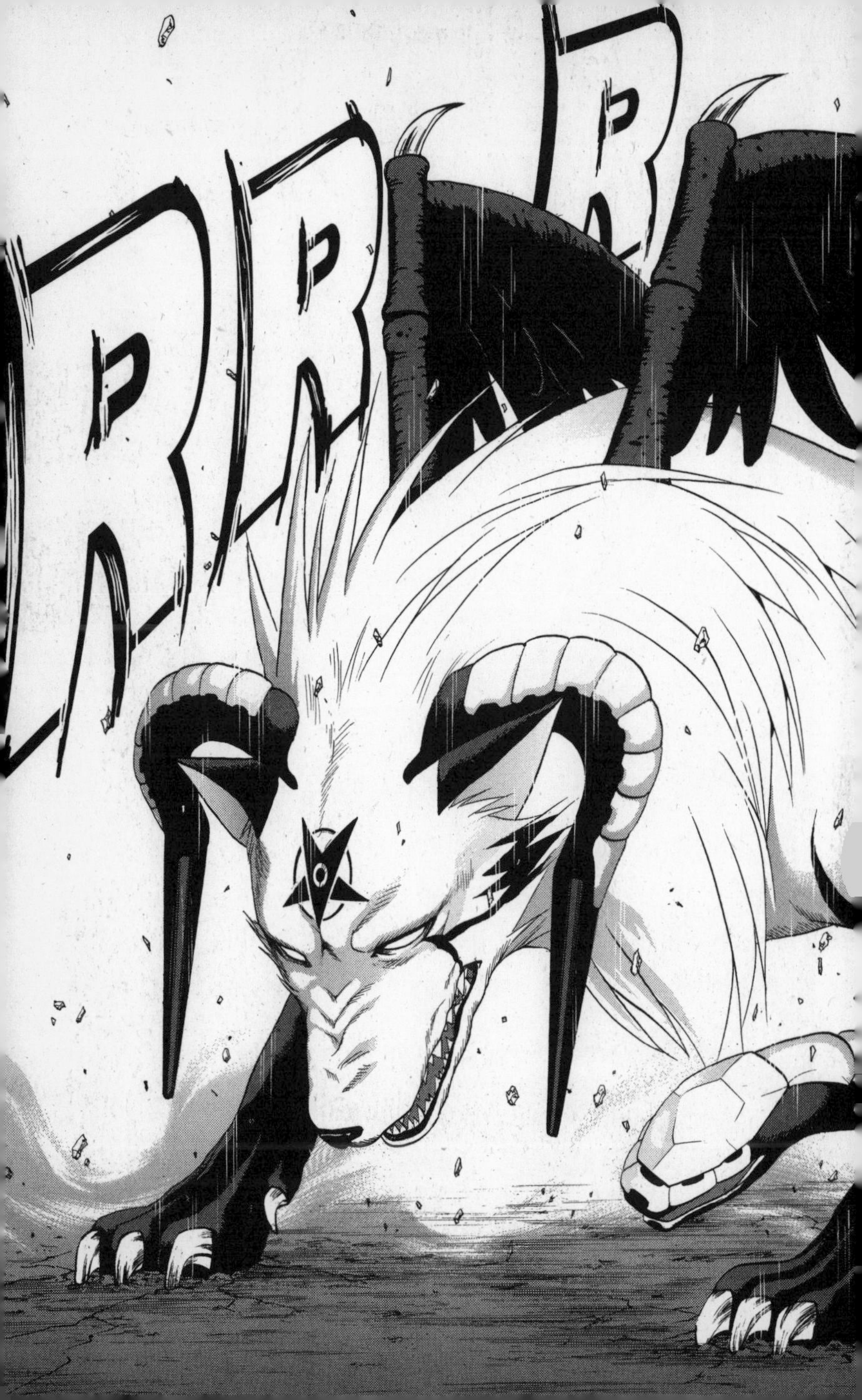
RRRR

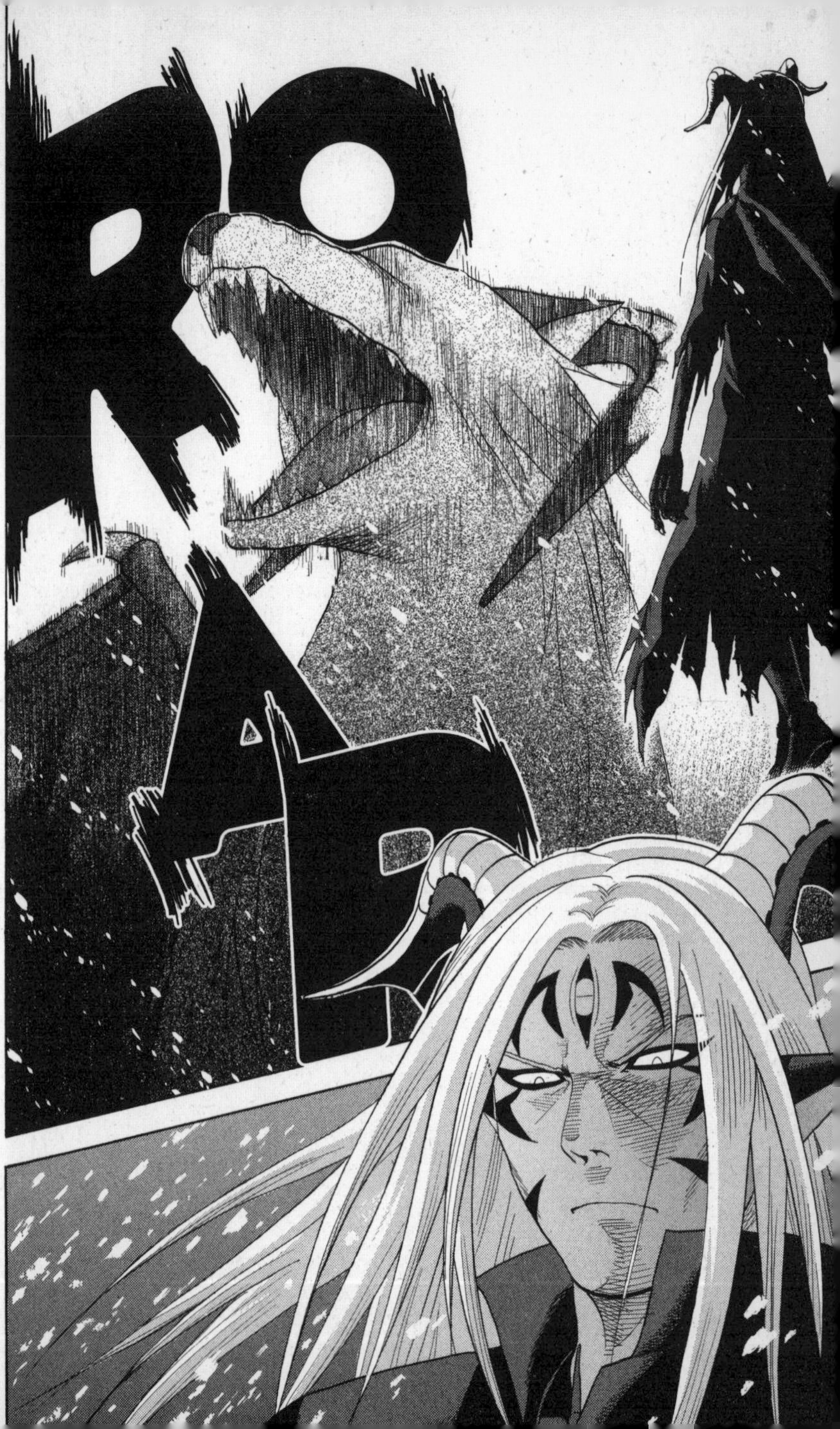
ROAR

READ THIS WAY

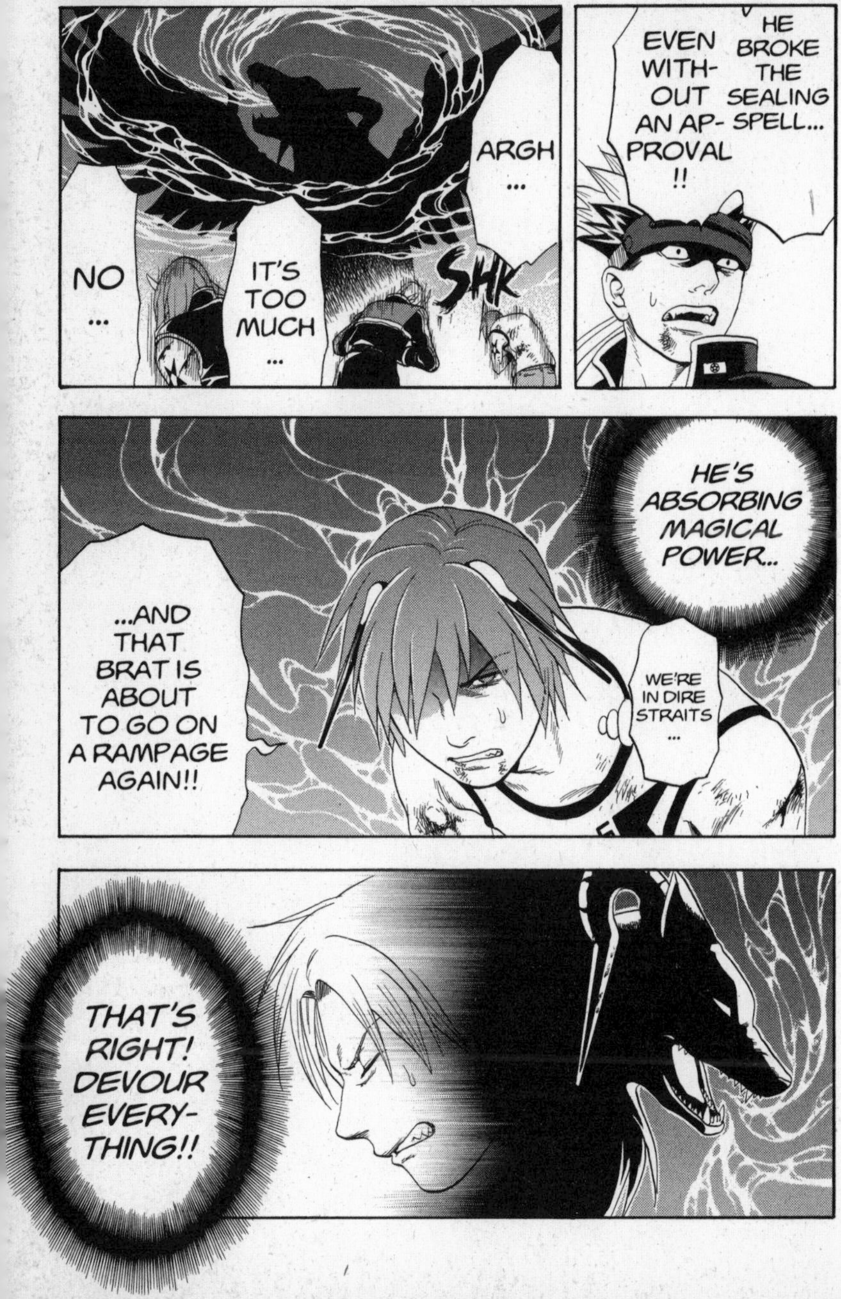
HE BROKE THE SEALING SPELL...
EVEN WITHOUT AN APPROVAL !!
ARGH ...
SHK
IT'S TOO MUCH ...
NO ...
HE'S ABSORBING MAGICAL POWER...
WE'RE IN DIRE STRAITS ...
...AND THAT BRAT IS ABOUT TO GO ON A RAMPAGE AGAIN!!
THAT'S RIGHT! DEVOUR EVERYTHING!!

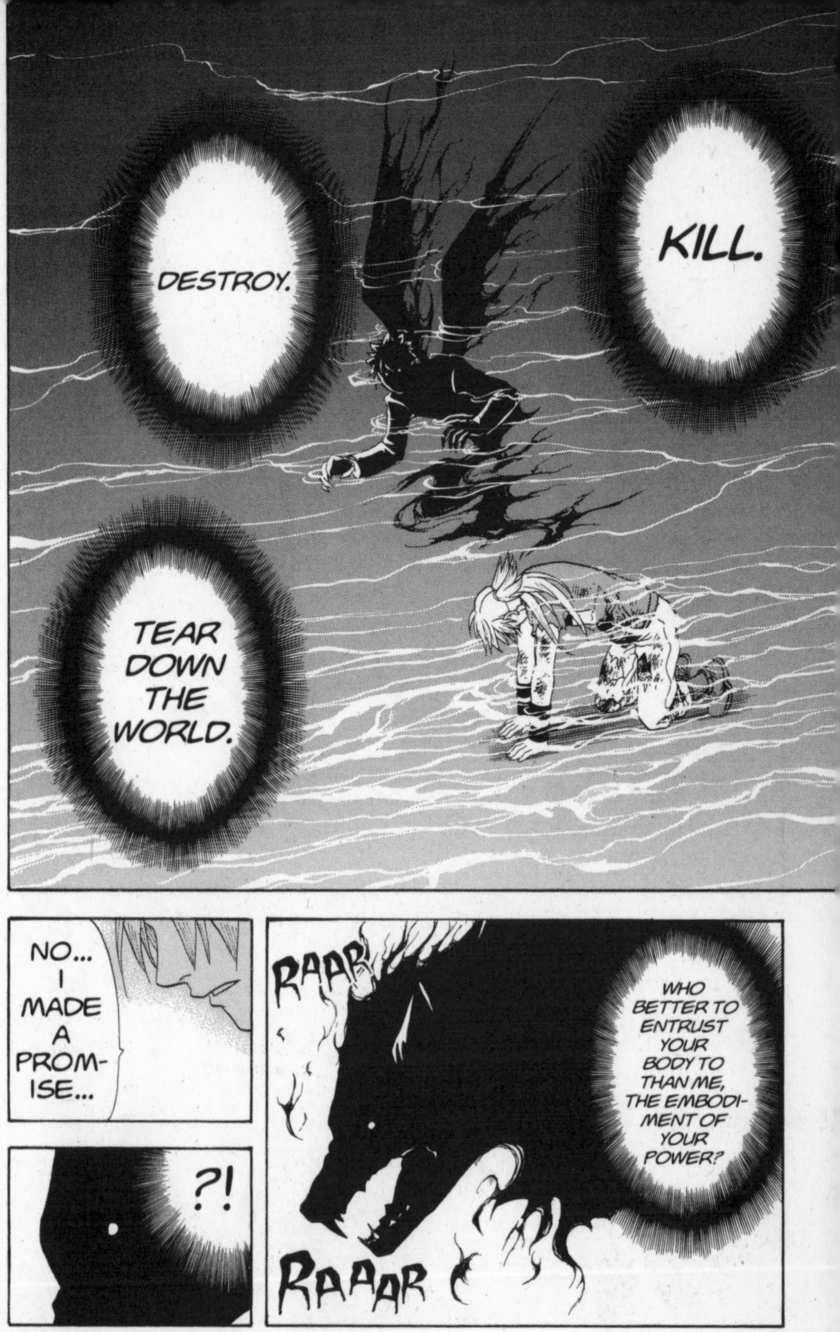
KILL.
DESTROY.
TEAR DOWN THE WORLD.
RAAR
WHO BETTER TO ENTRUST YOUR BODY TO THAN ME, THE EMBODIMENT OF YOUR POWER?
RAAAR
NO... I MADE A PROMISE...
?!

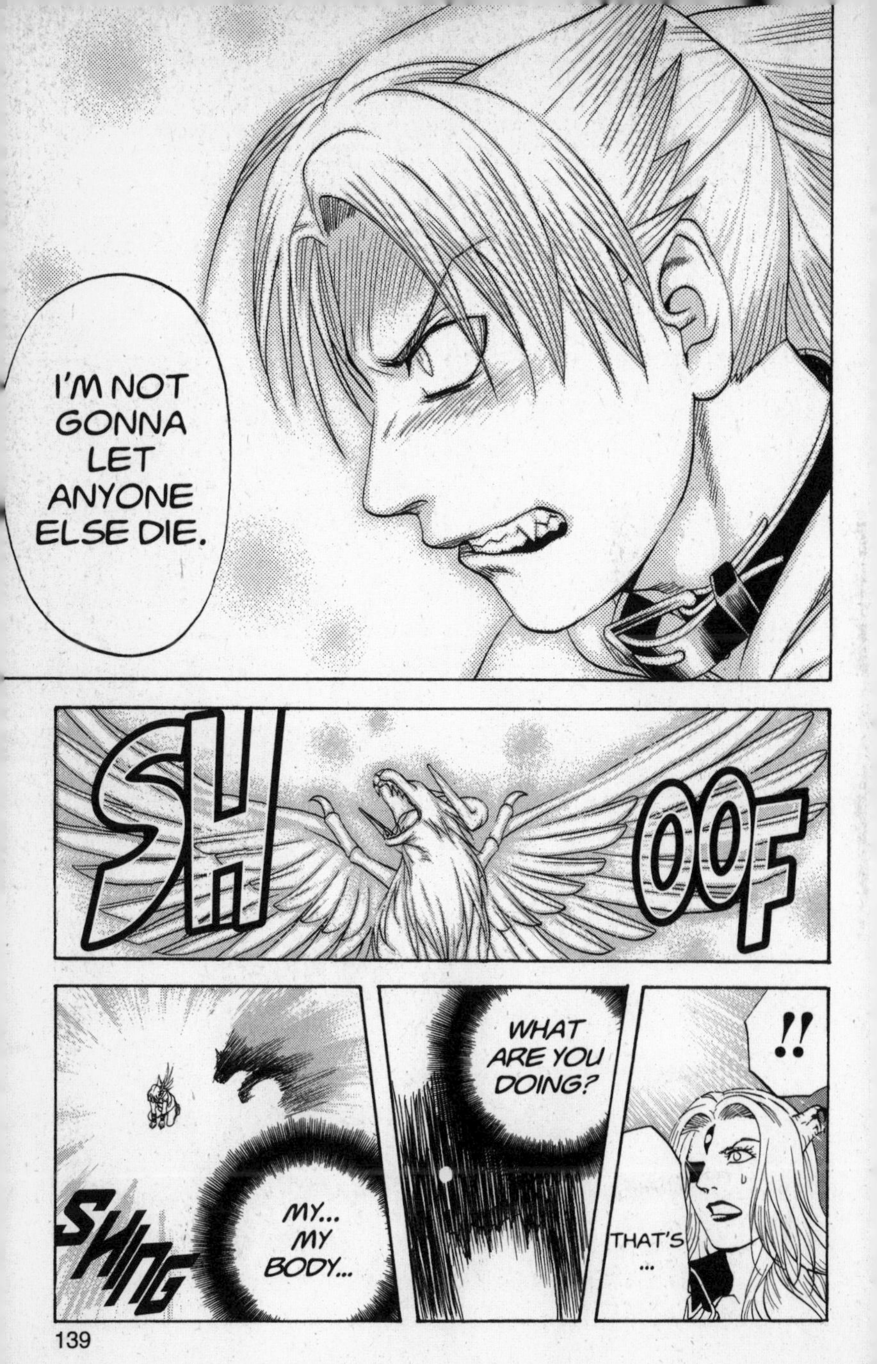
I'M NOT GONNA LET ANYONE ELSE DIE.
SHOOF
!!
THAT'S ...
WHAT ARE YOU DOING?
MY... MY BODY...
SHING

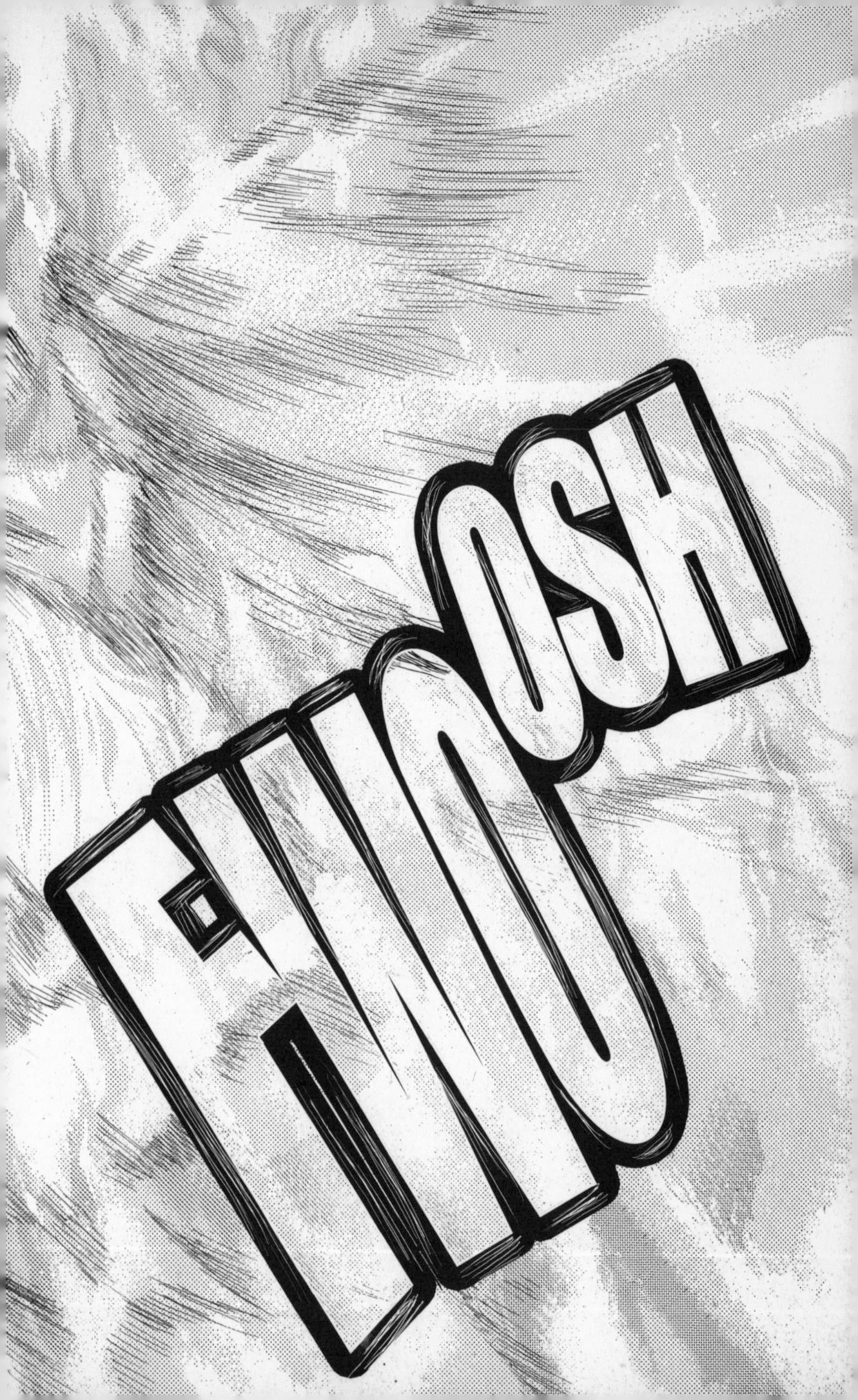
FWOOSH

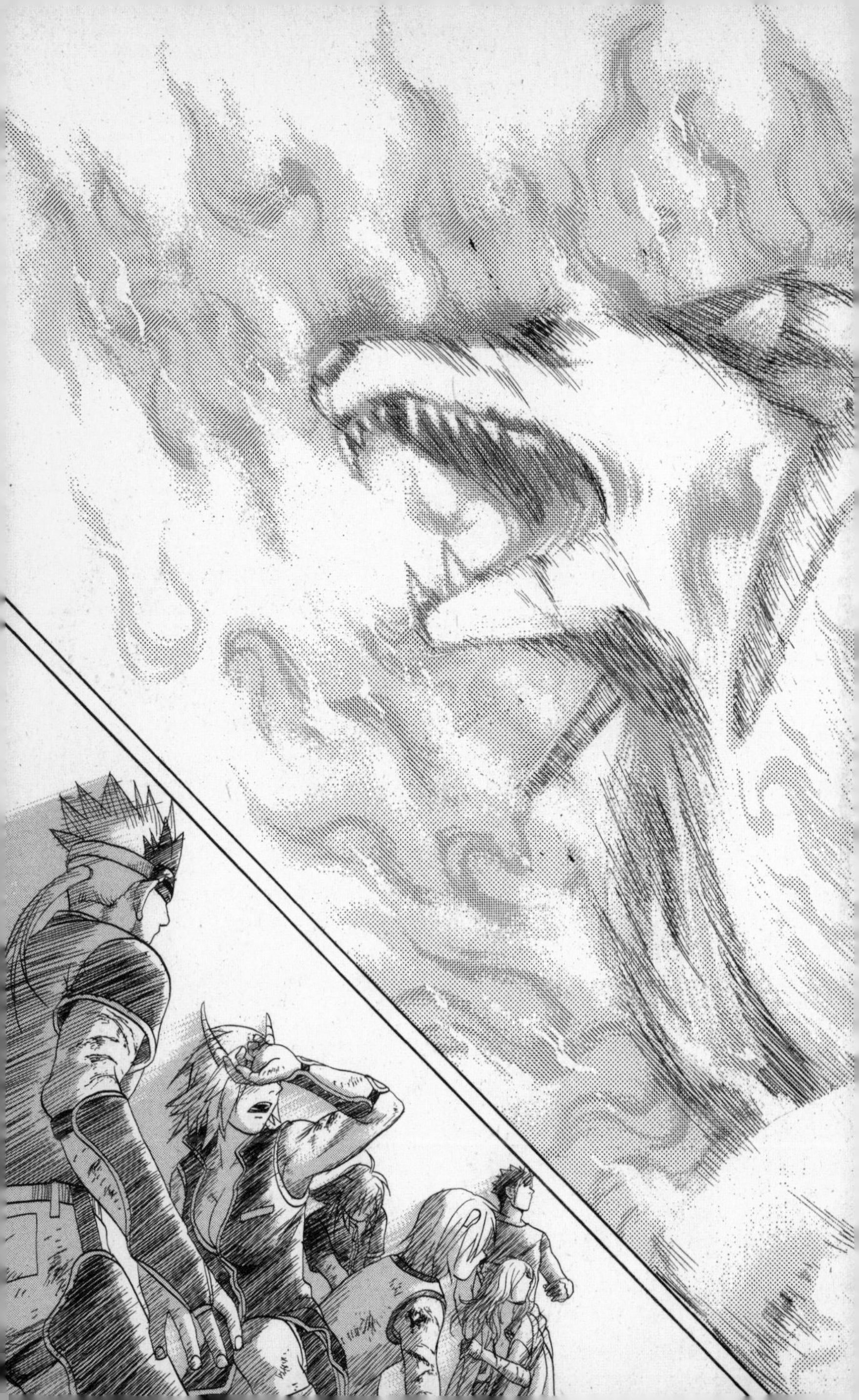

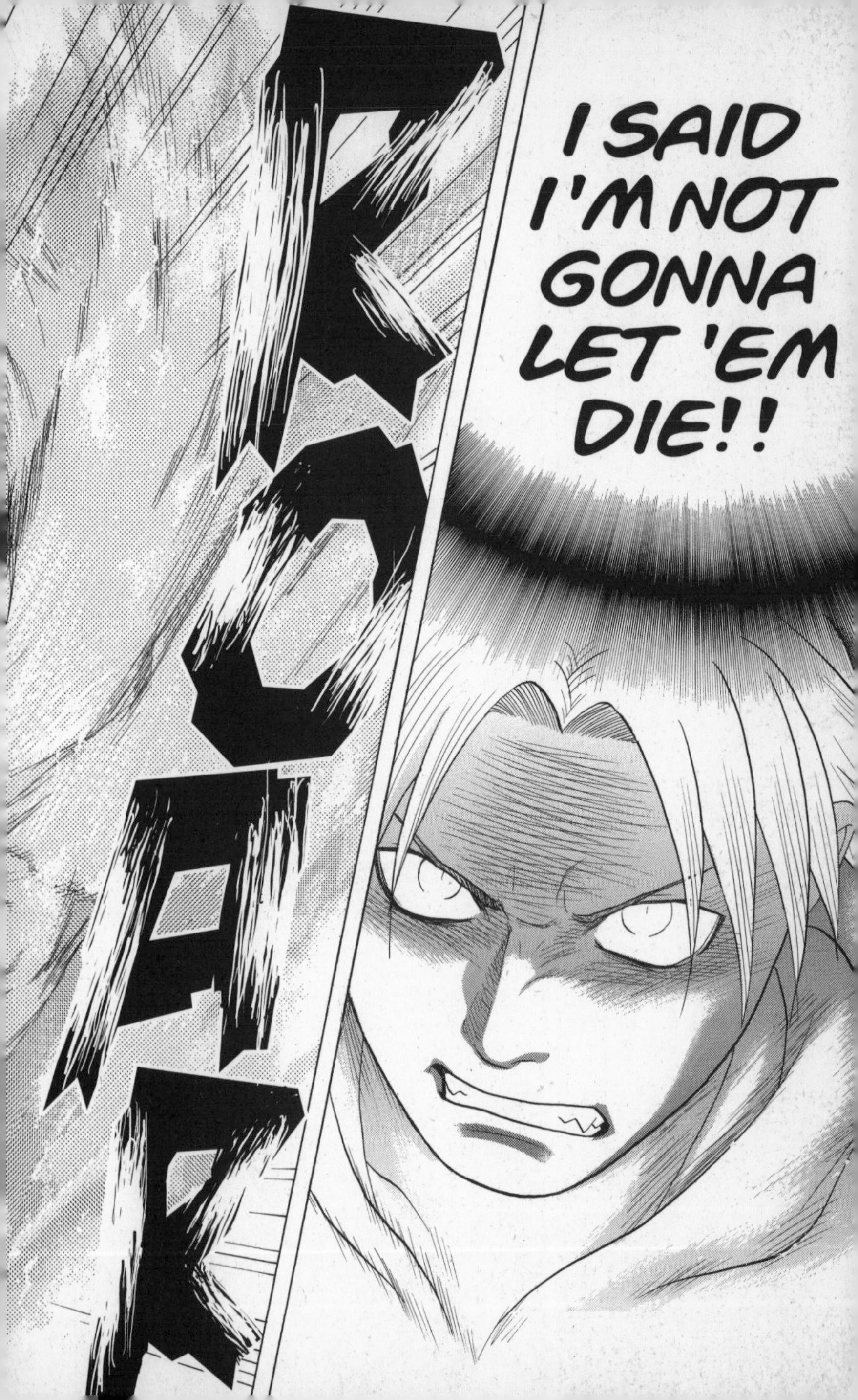
I SAID I'M NOT GONNA LET 'EM DIE!!

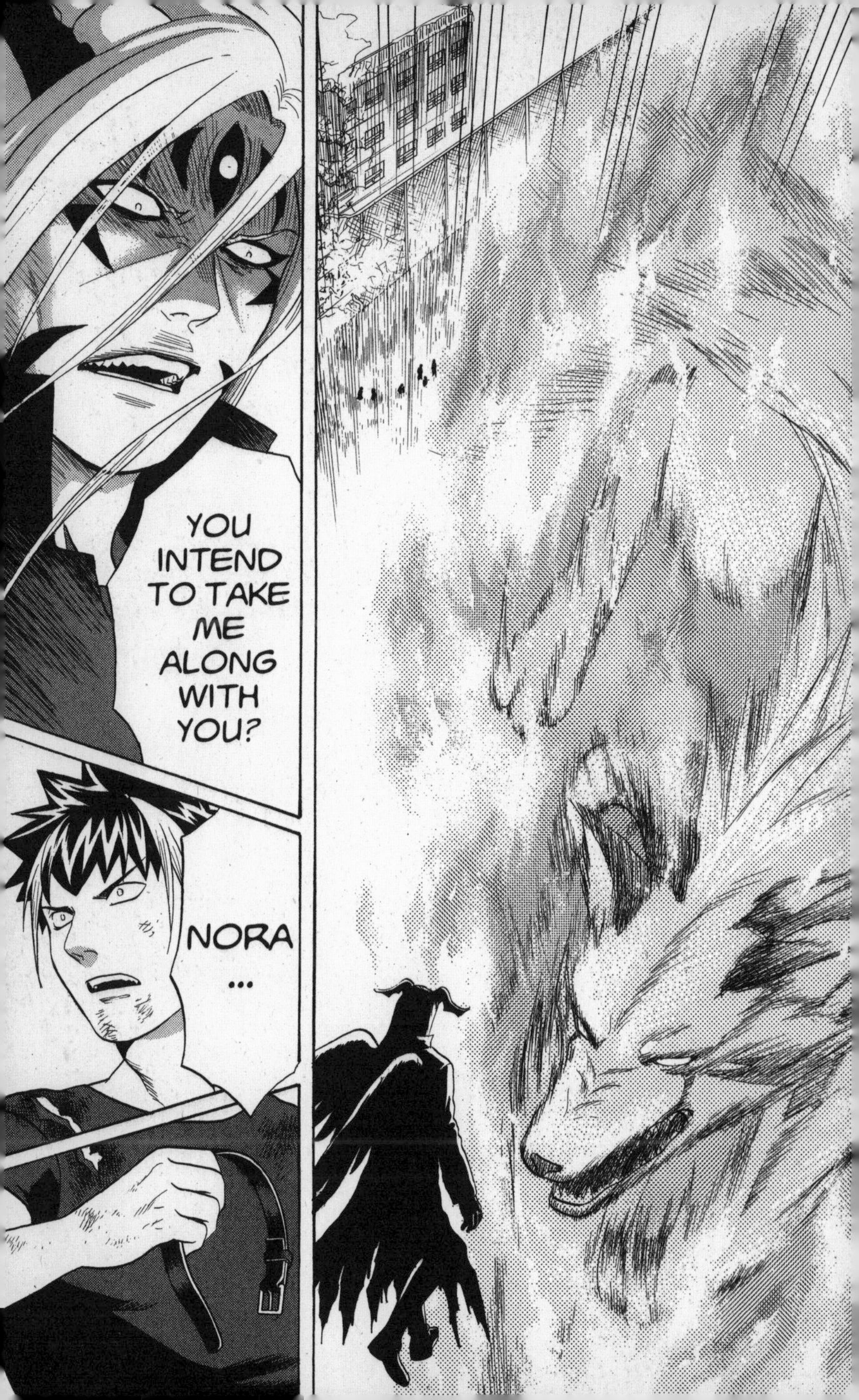
YOU INTEND TO TAKE ME ALONG WITH YOU?
NORA ...

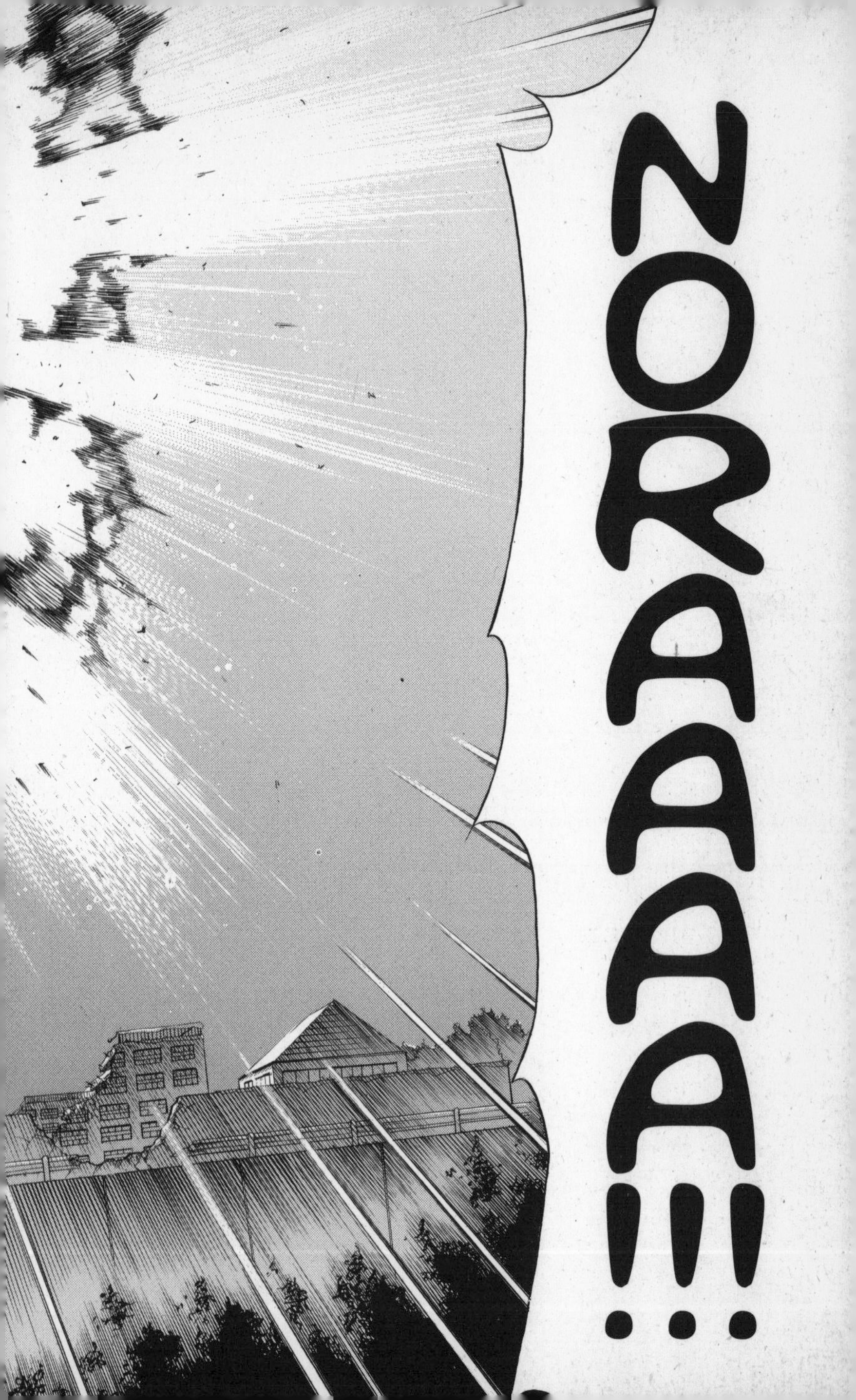
NORAAAA!!!

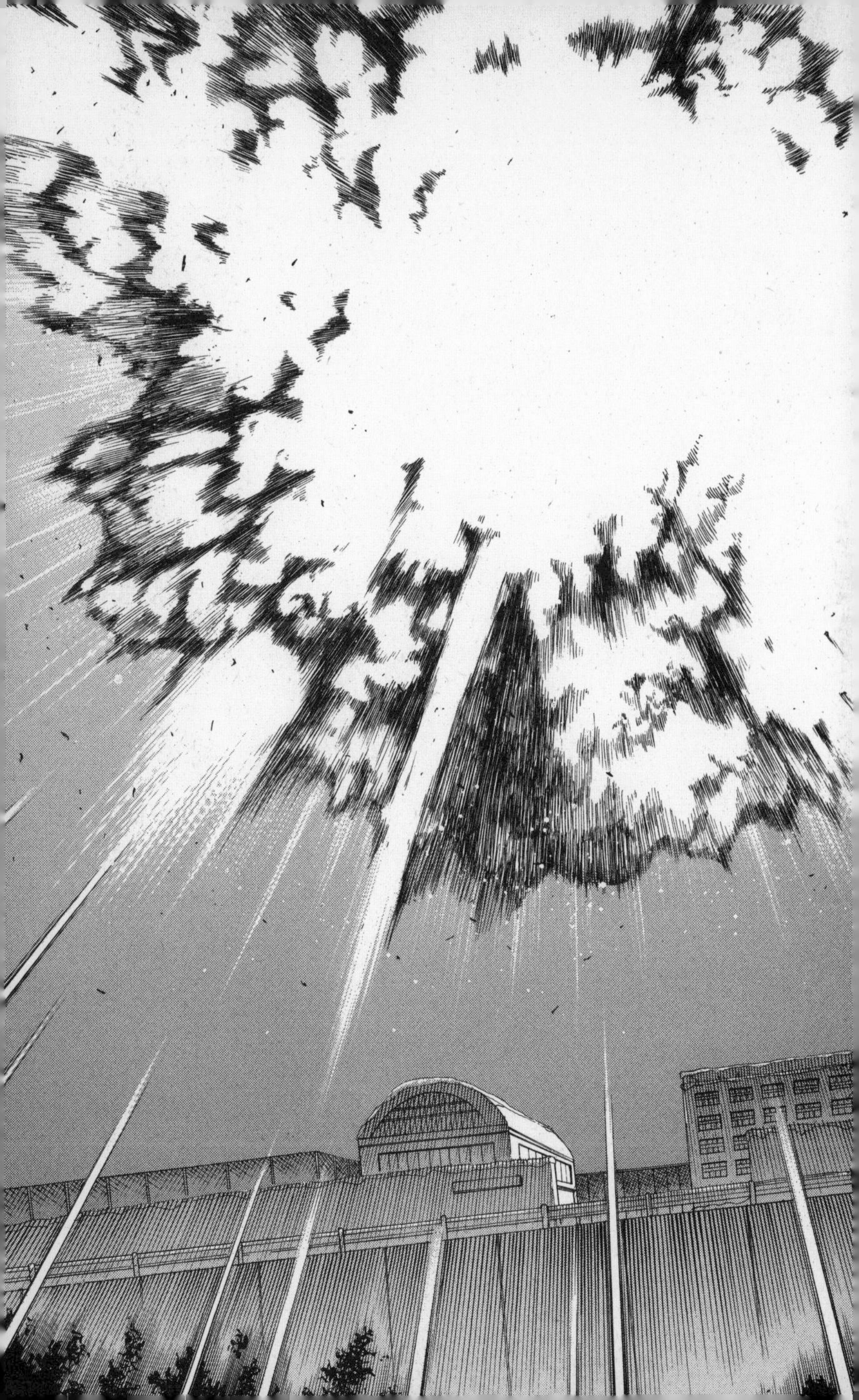

IN CASE YOU WERE WONDERING, KAKEI IS STANDING IN THE AUTHOR PAGE PHOTO IN VOLUME 7.

Story 32: True Intention

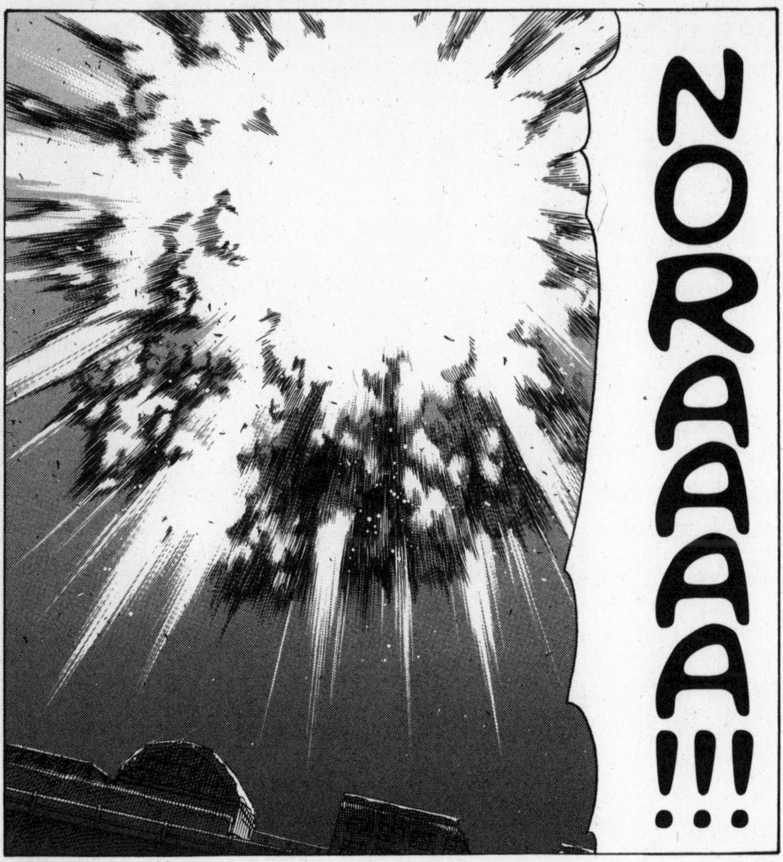
NORAAAA!!!

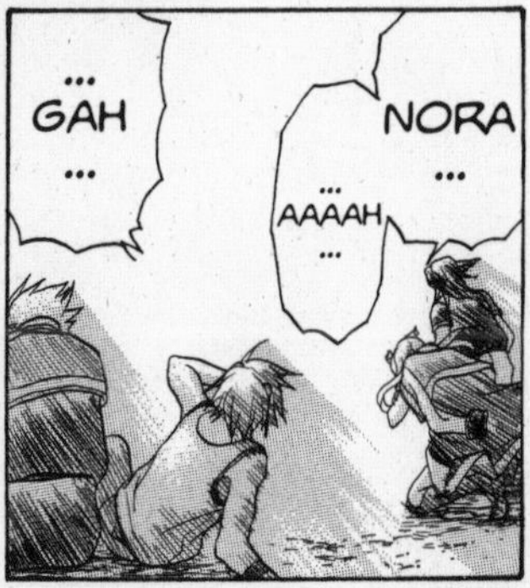
NORA ...
... AAAAH ...
... GAH ...

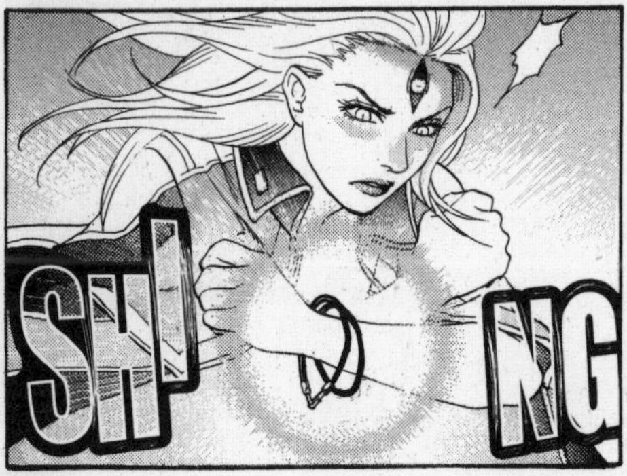
SHING

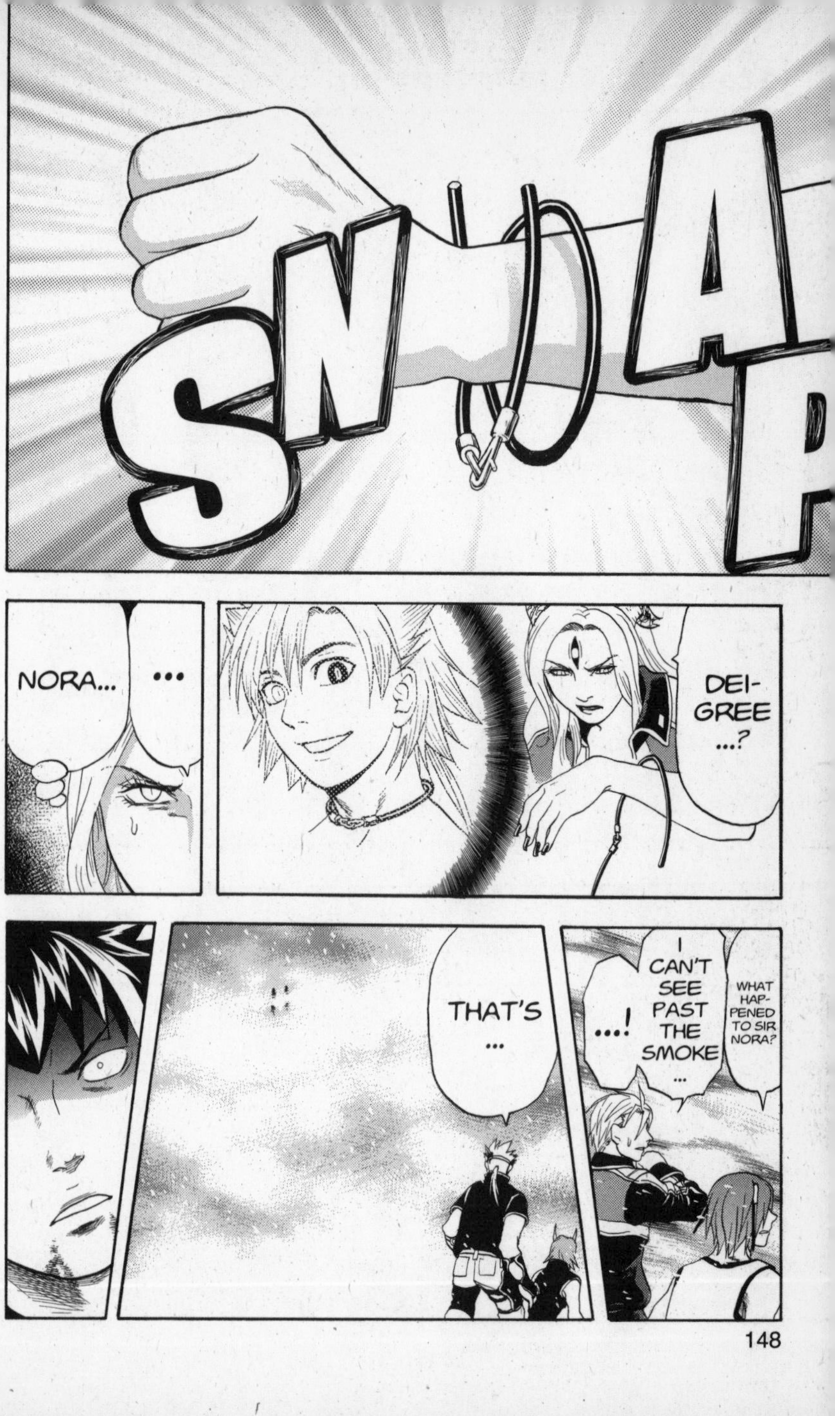
SNAP
DEI-GREE ...?
...
NORA...
WHAT HAP-PENED TO SIR NORA?
I CAN'T SEE PAST THE SMOKE ...
...!
THAT'S ...

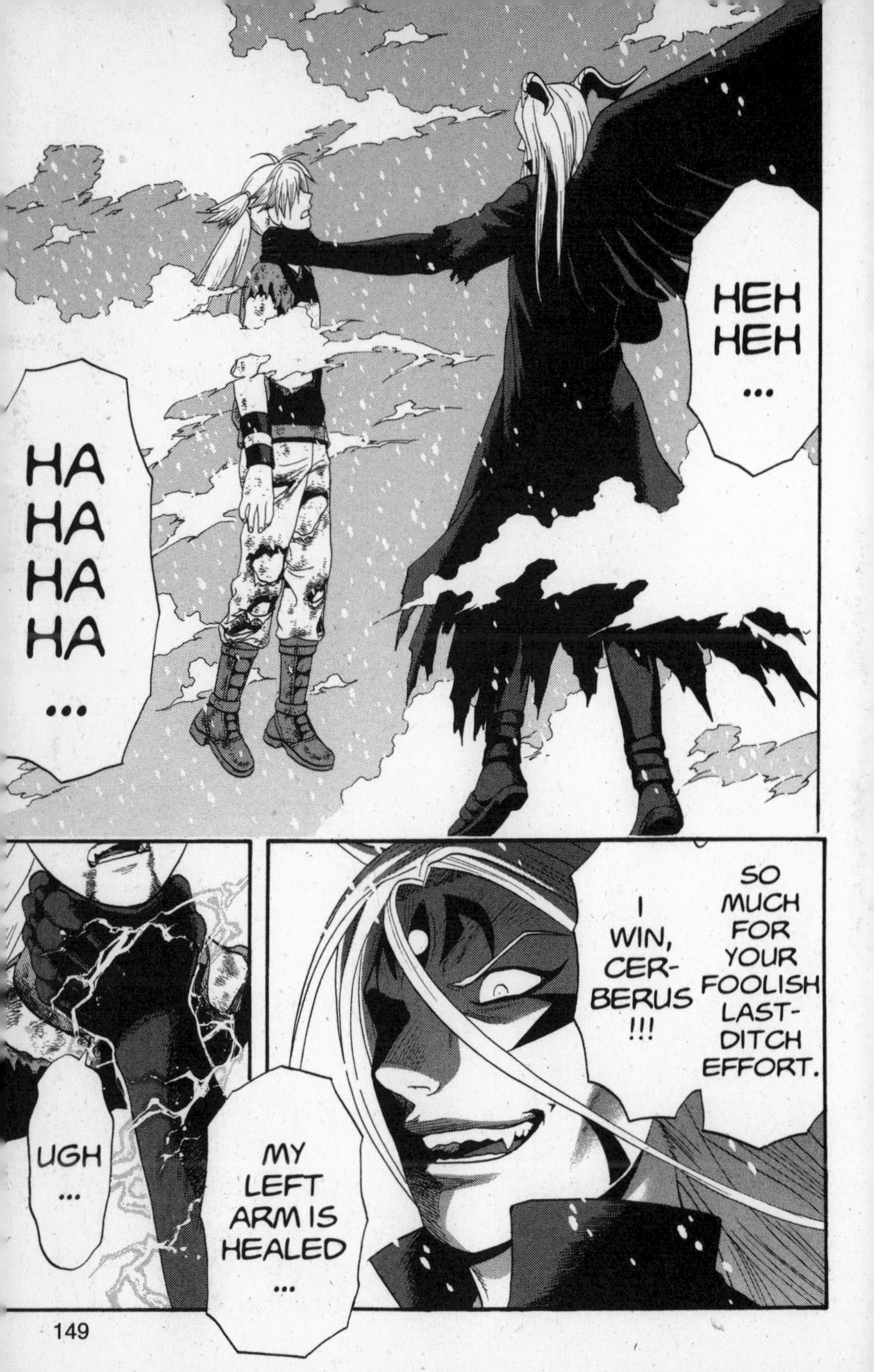
HEH HEH ...
HA HA HA HA ...
SO MUCH FOR YOUR FOOLISH LAST-DITCH EFFORT.
I WIN, CERBERUS!!!
MY LEFT ARM IS HEALED ...
UGH ...

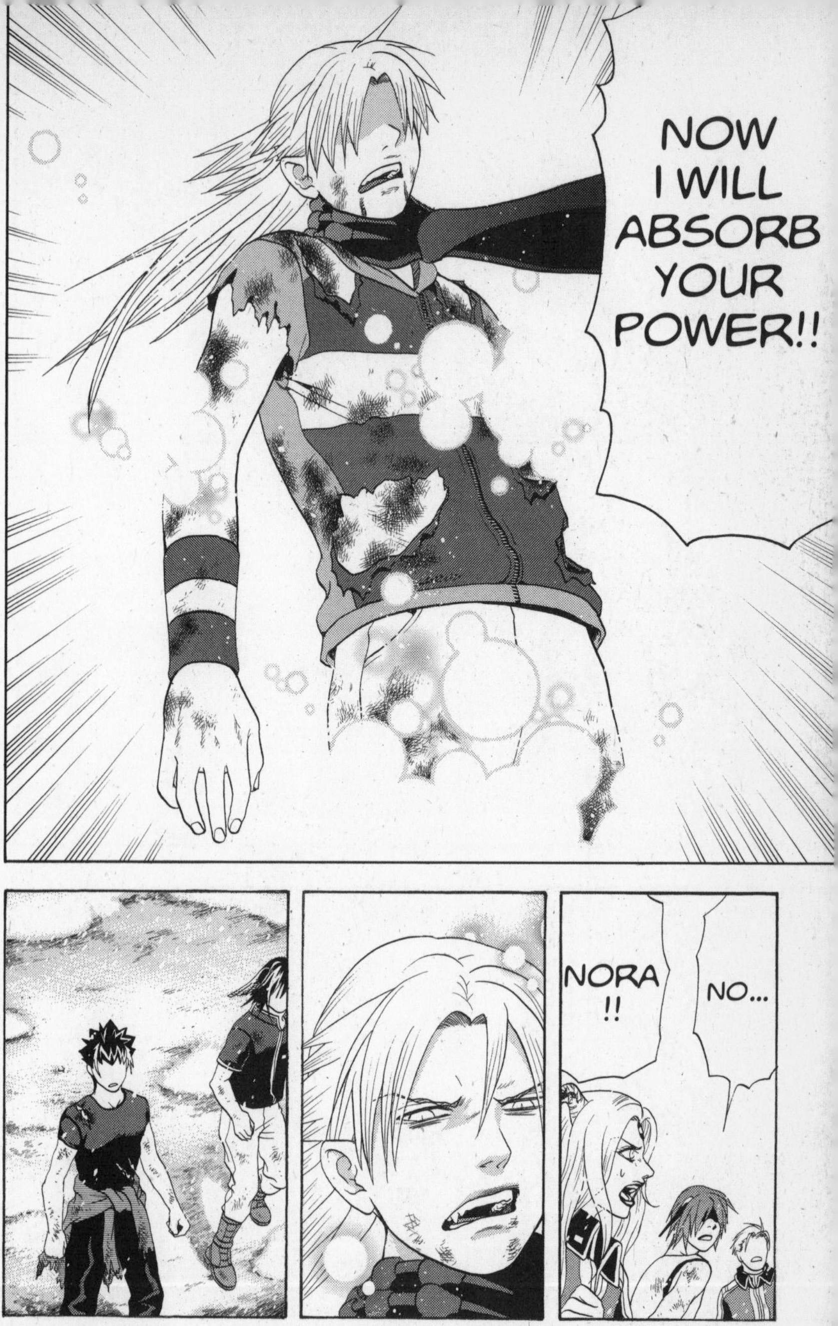
NOW I WILL ABSORB YOUR POWER!!
NO...
NORA !!

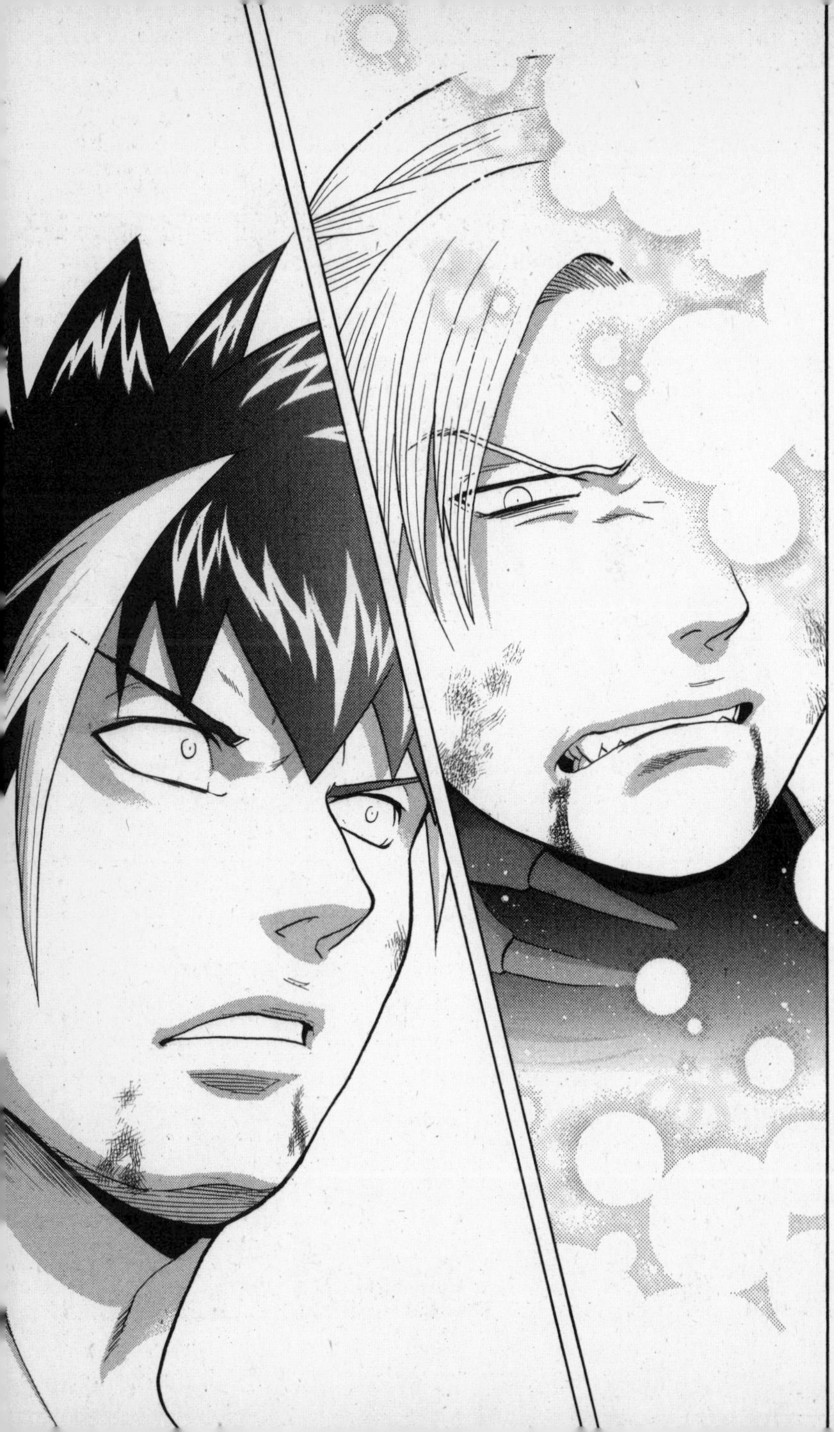

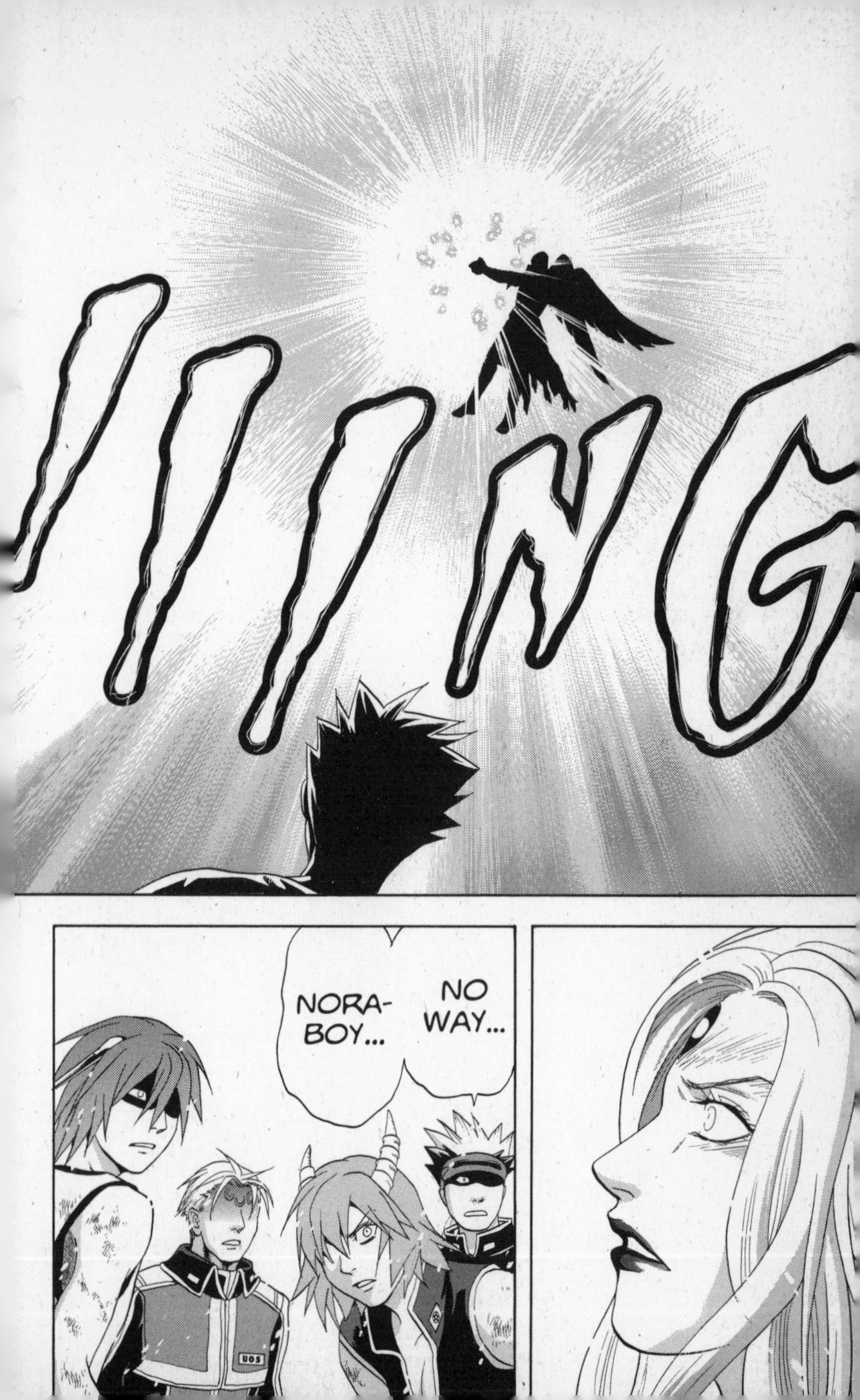
NO WAY...
NORA-BOY...

SH

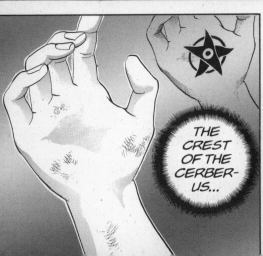

THE
CREST
OF THE
CERBER-
US...

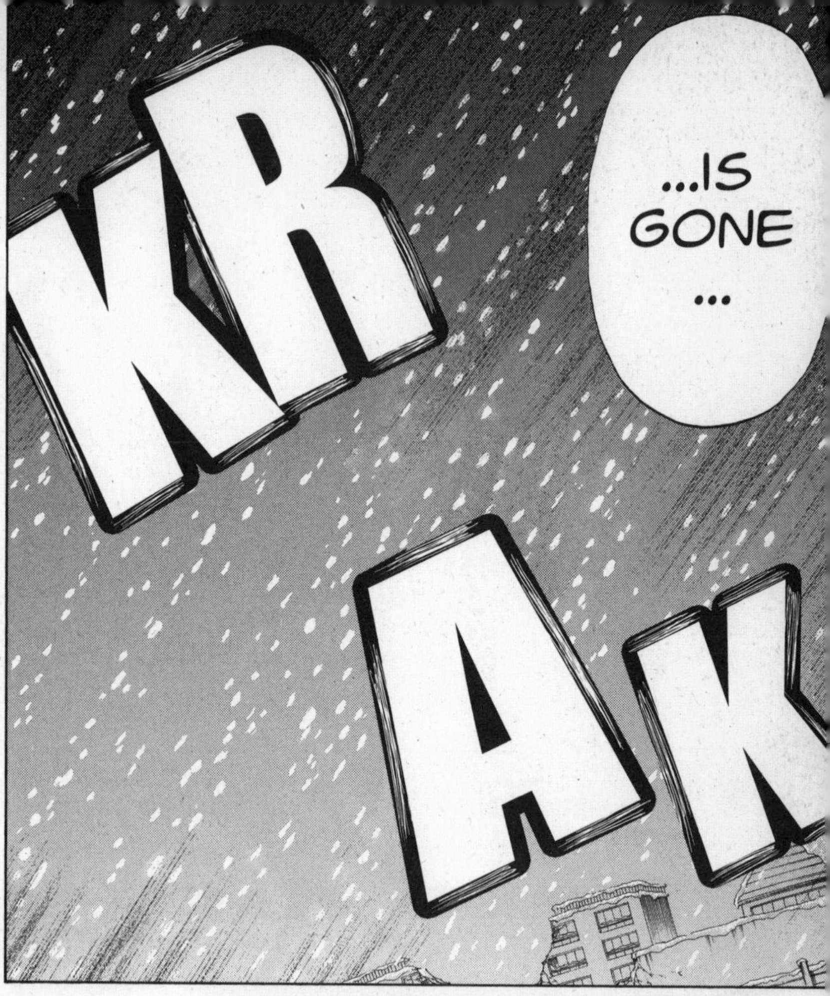
...IS GONE ...
KRAK
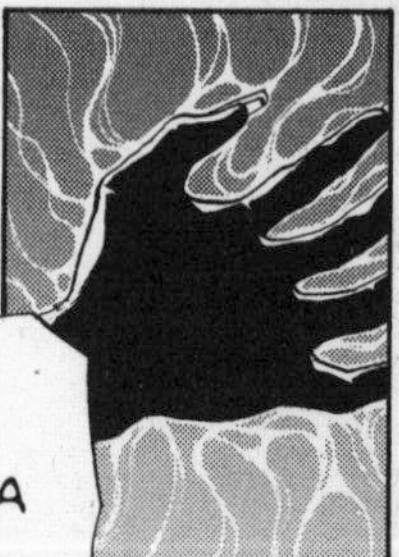
HA HA...
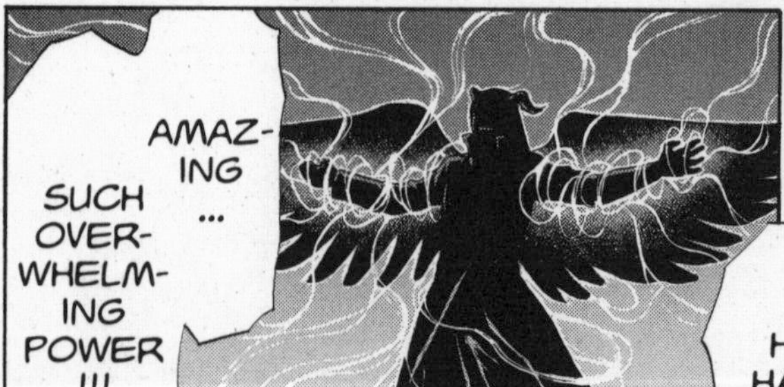
AMAZING ...
SUCH OVERWHELMING POWER !!!

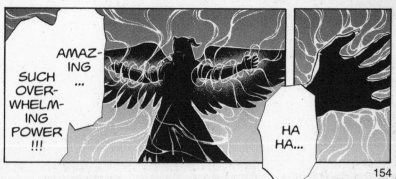

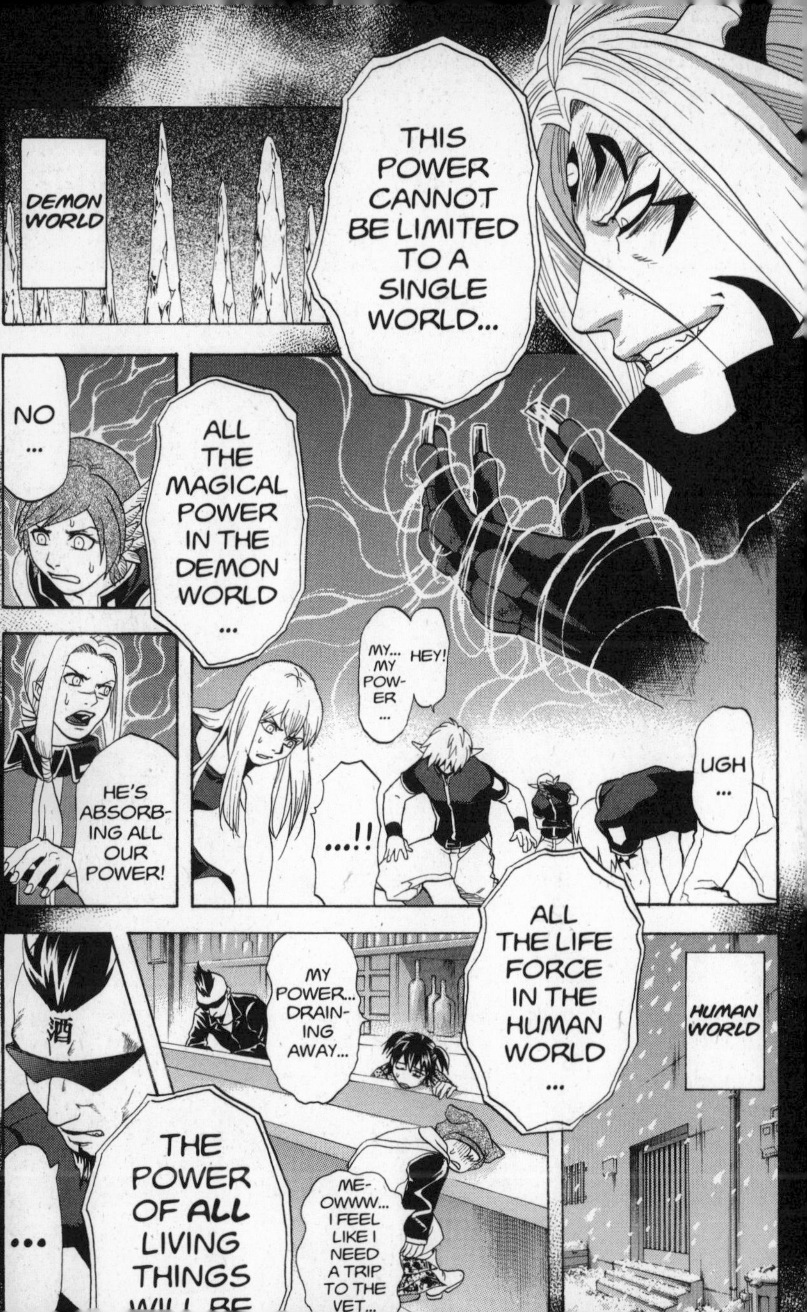
THIS POWER CANNOT BE LIMITED TO A SINGLE WORLD...
DEMON WORLD
ALL THE MAGICAL POWER IN THE DEMON WORLD...
NO...
HEY!
MY... MY POWER...
UGH...
...!!
HE'S ABSORBING ALL OUR POWER!
HUMAN WORLD
ALL THE LIFE FORCE IN THE HUMAN WORLD...
MY POWER... DRAINING AWAY...
MEOWWW... I FEEL LIKE I NEED A TRIP TO THE VET...
THE POWER OF **ALL** LIVING THINGS
...

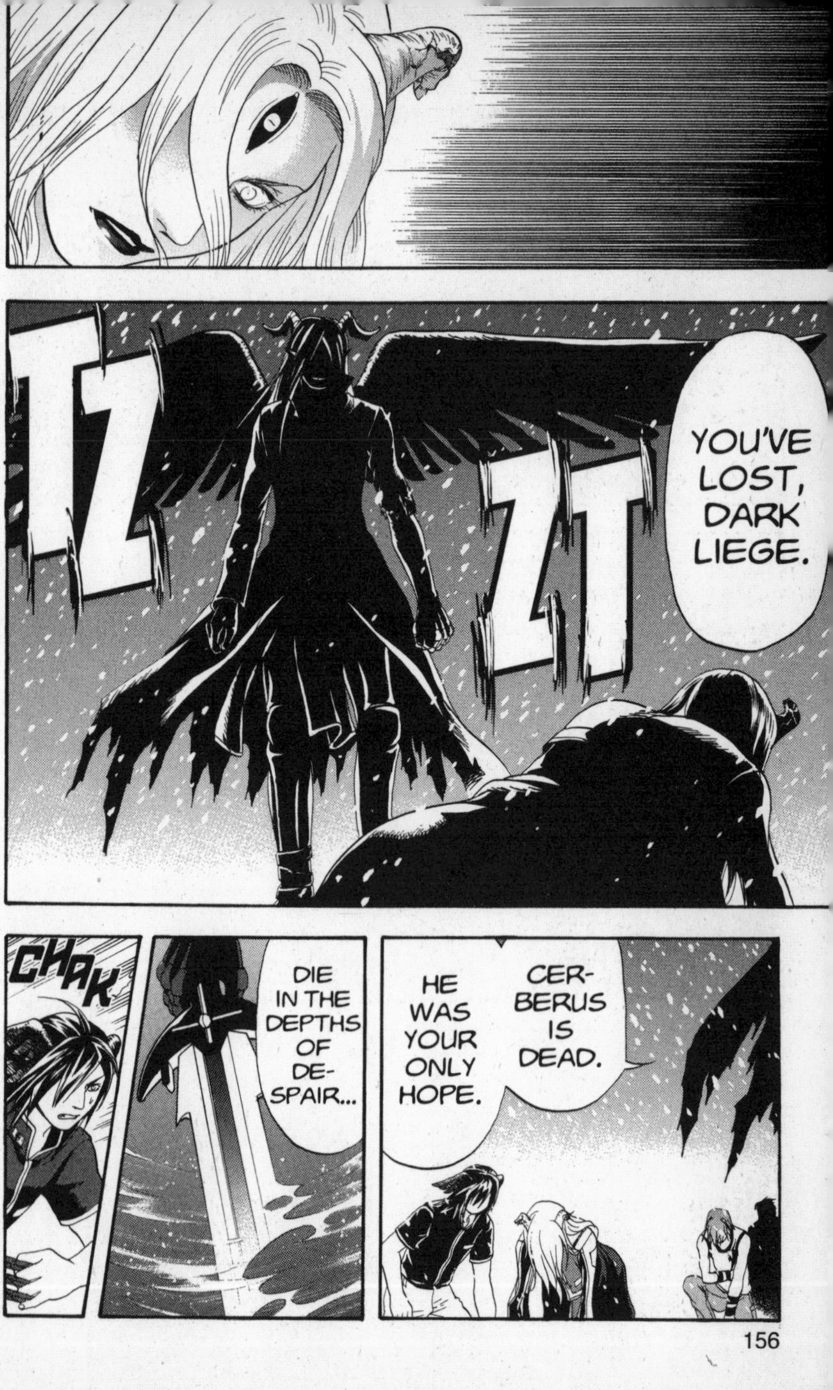
YOU'VE LOST, DARK LIEGE.
CERBERUS IS DEAD.
HE WAS YOUR ONLY HOPE.
DIE IN THE DEPTHS OF DESPAIR...
CHAK

READ THIS WAY

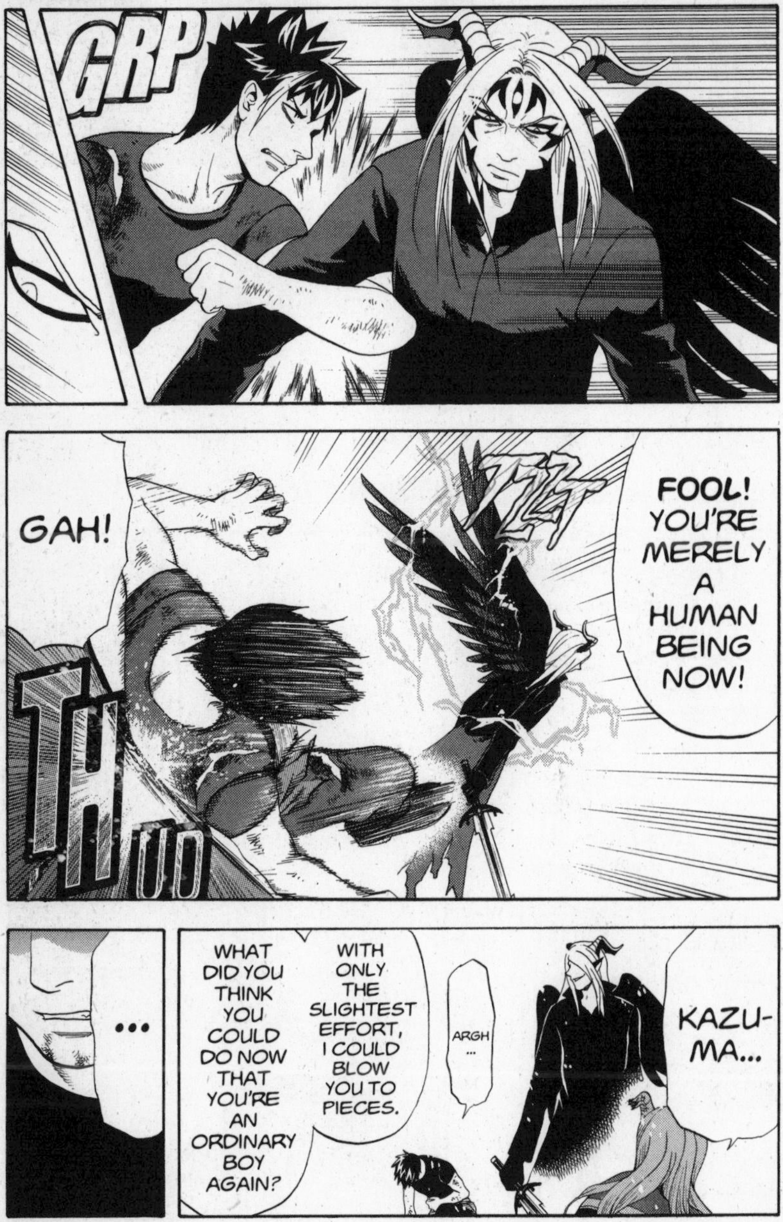
GRP
FOOL! YOU'RE MERELY A HUMAN BEING NOW!
TZZT
GAH!
THUD
KAZUMA...
ARGH...
WITH ONLY THE SLIGHTEST EFFORT, I COULD BLOW YOU TO PIECES.
WHAT DID YOU THINK YOU COULD DO NOW THAT YOU'RE AN ORDINARY BOY AGAIN?
...

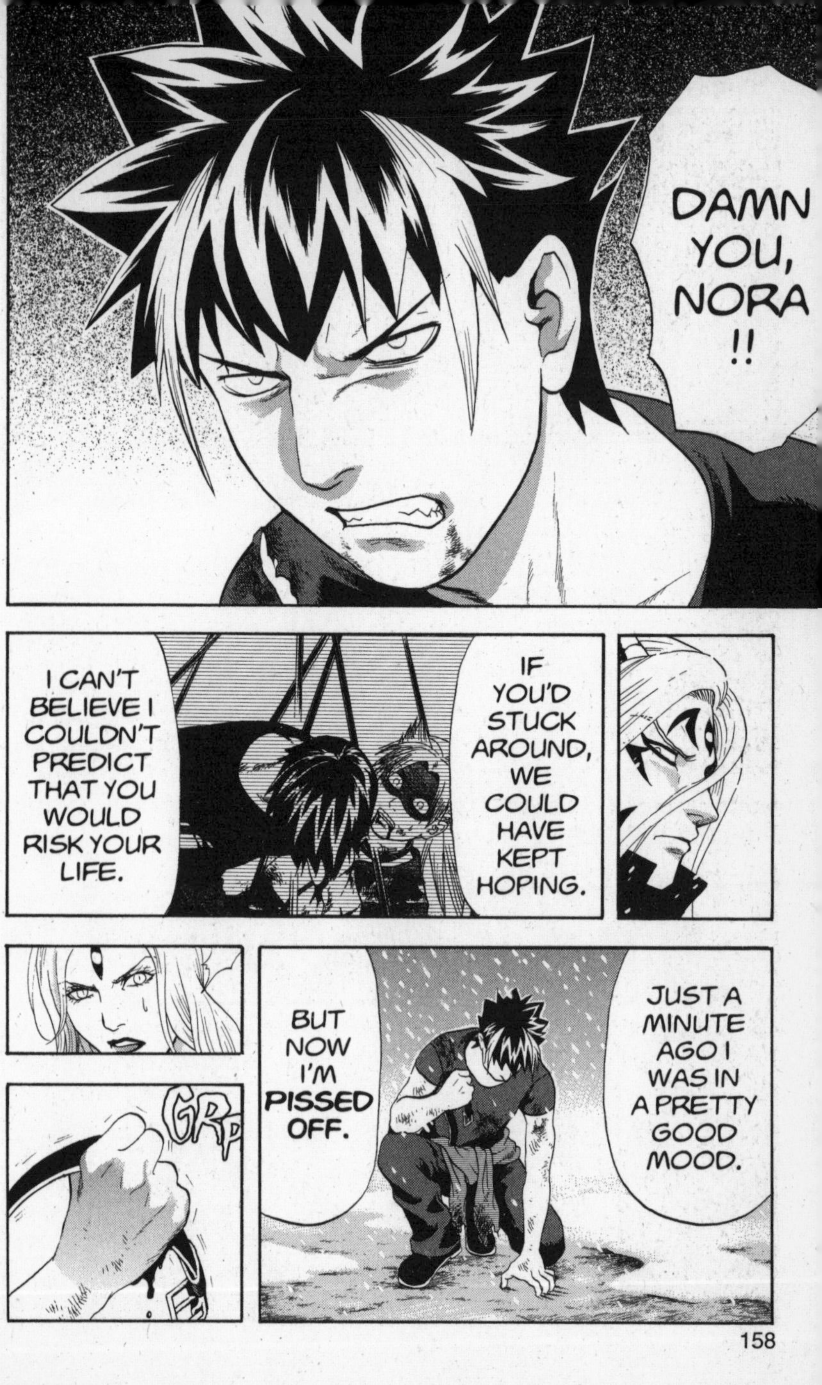
DAMN YOU, NORA!!
IF YOU'D STUCK AROUND, WE COULD HAVE KEPT HOPING.
I CAN'T BELIEVE I COULDN'T PREDICT THAT YOU WOULD RISK YOUR LIFE.
JUST A MINUTE AGO I WAS IN A PRETTY GOOD MOOD.
BUT NOW I'M PISSED OFF.
GRP

READ THIS WAY

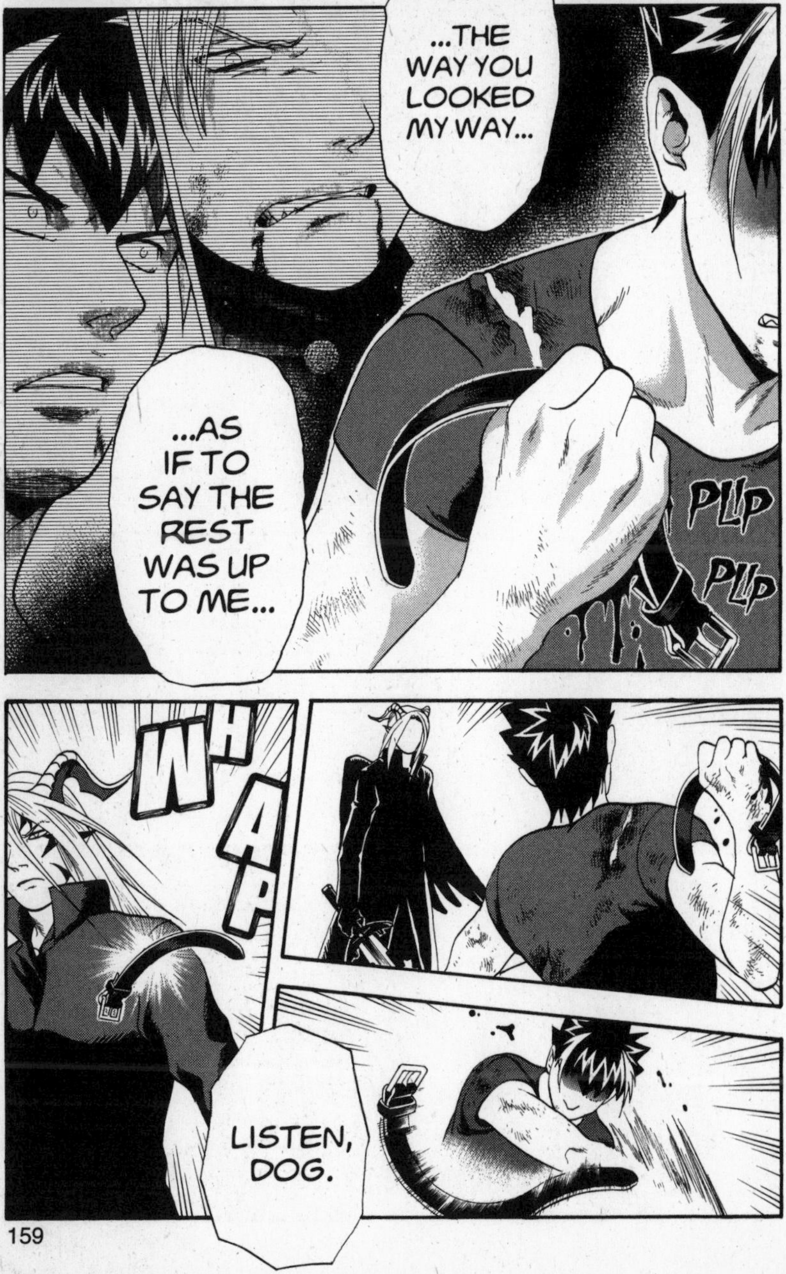
...THE WAY YOU LOOKED MY WAY...
...AS IF TO SAY THE REST WAS UP TO ME...
PLIP
PLIP
LISTEN, DOG.
WHAP

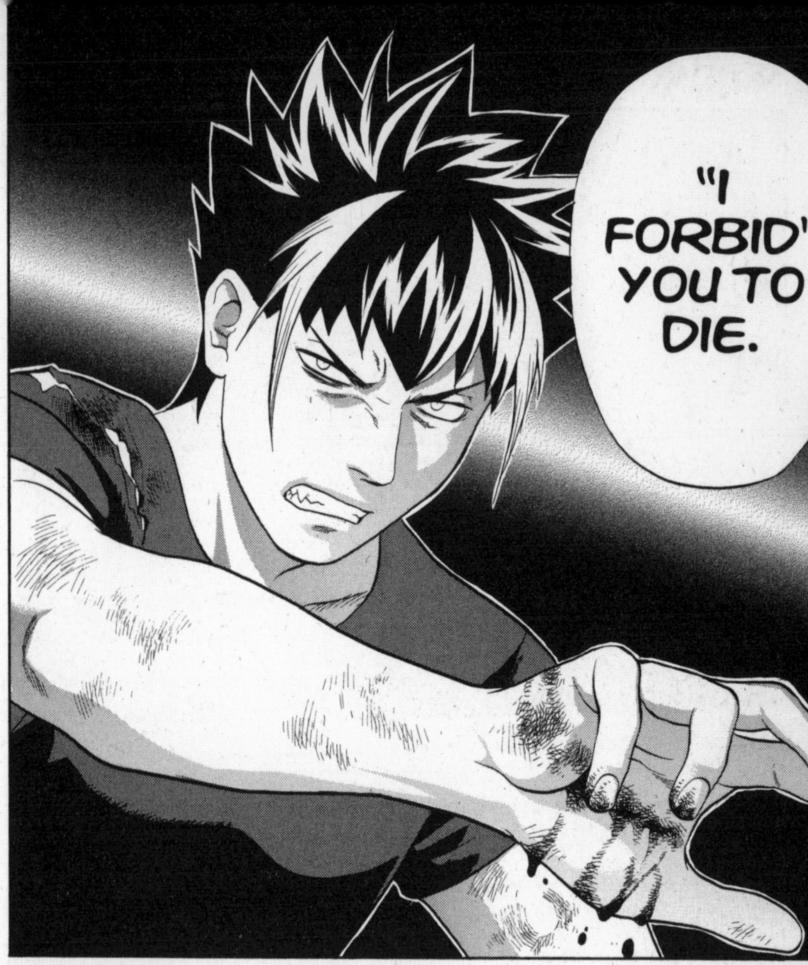
"I FORBID" YOU TO DIE.

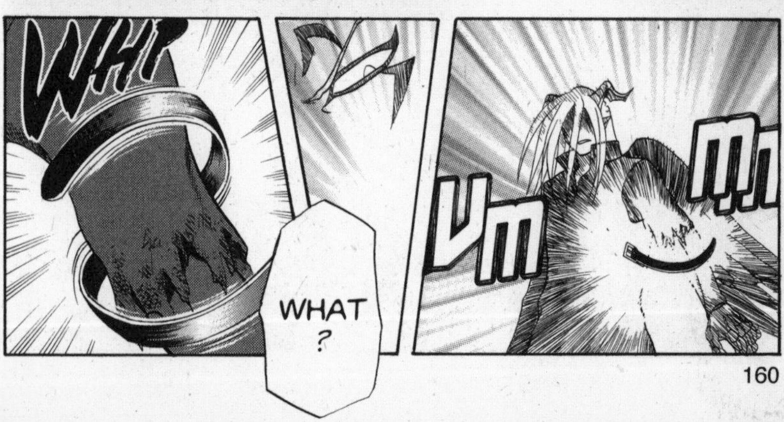
WHAT ?

READ THIS WAY

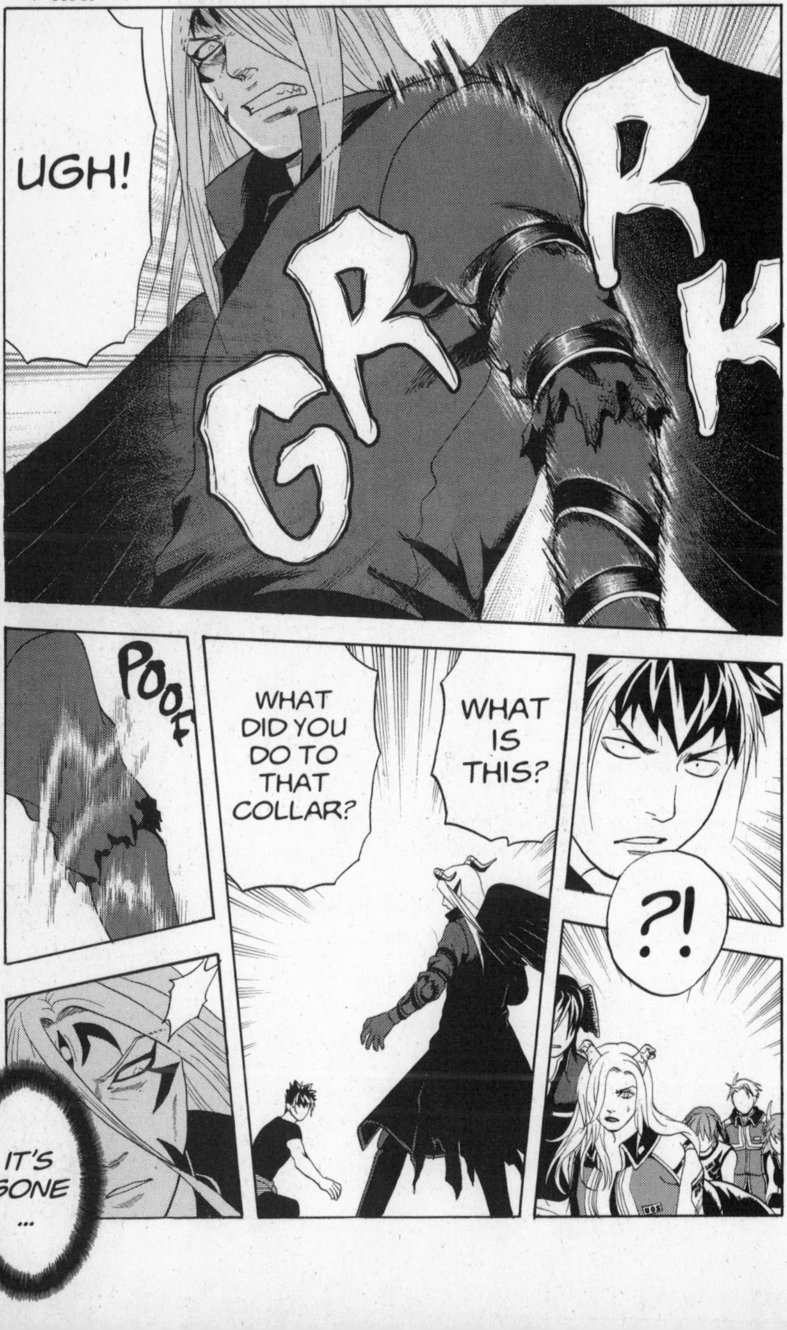
GRRK
UGH!
?!
WHAT IS THIS?
WHAT DID YOU DO TO THAT COLLAR?
POOF
IT'S GONE ...

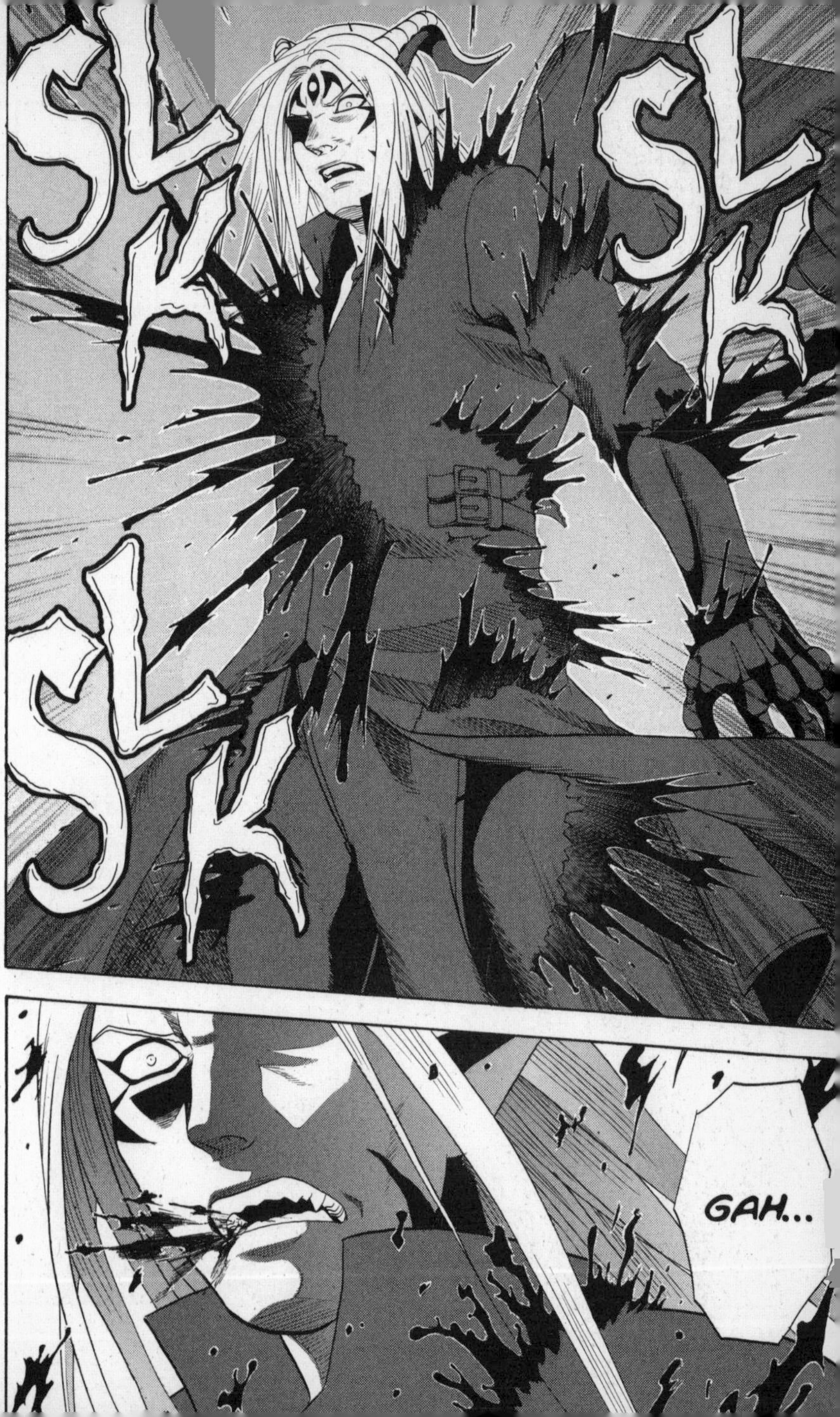
SLK
SLK
SLK
GAH...

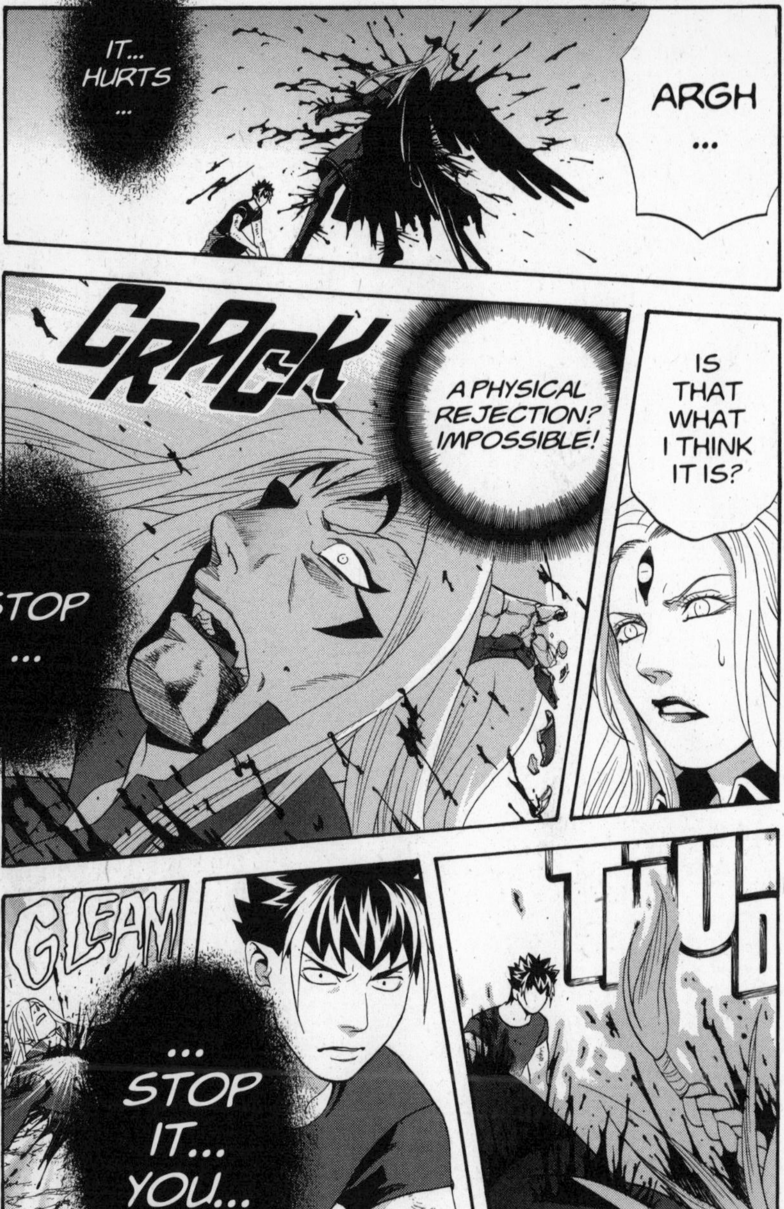
ARGH ...
IT... HURTS ...
IS THAT WHAT I THINK IT IS?
CRACK
A PHYSICAL REJECTION? IMPOSSIBLE!
STOP ...
THUD
GLEAM
... STOP IT... YOU...

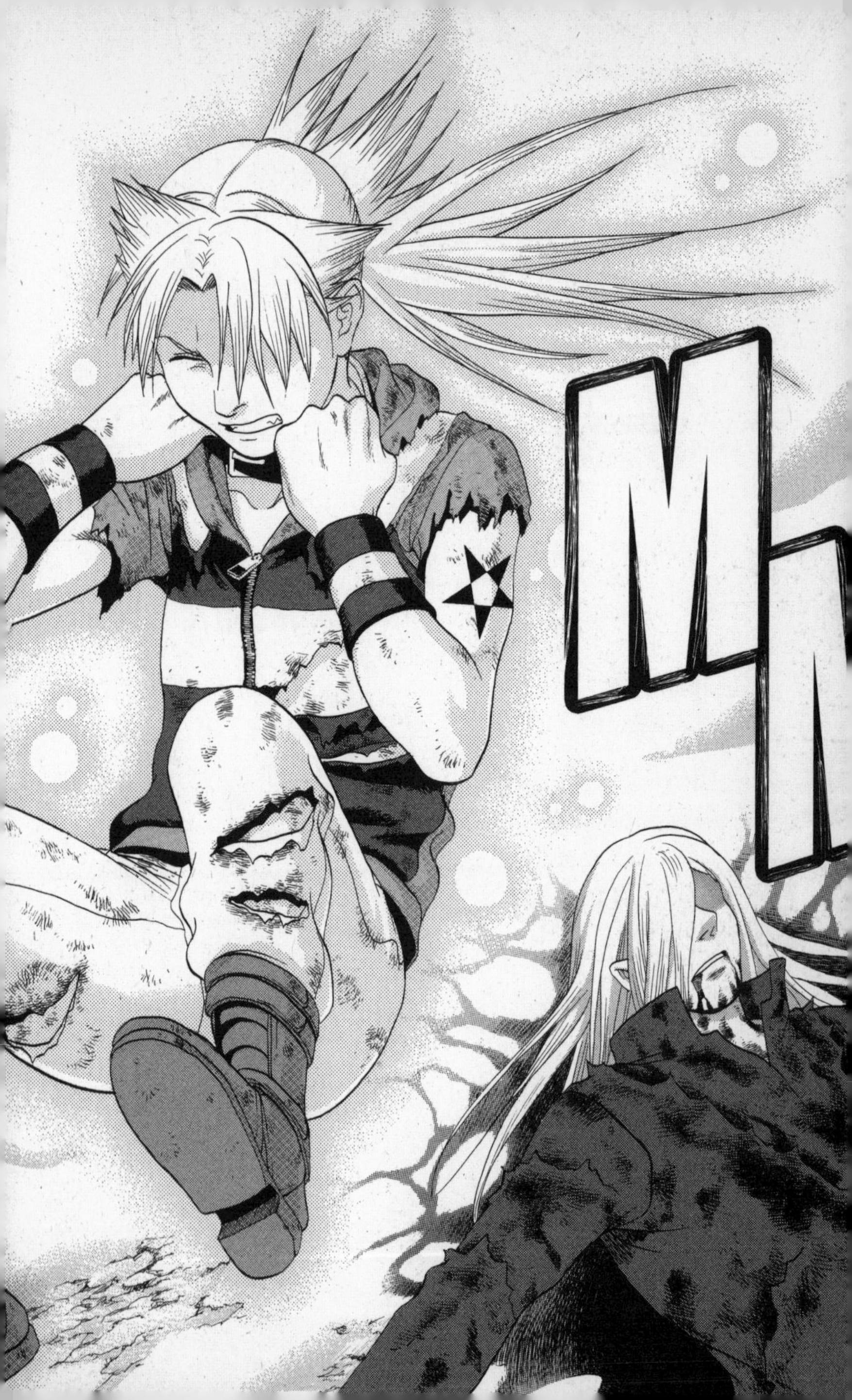
M

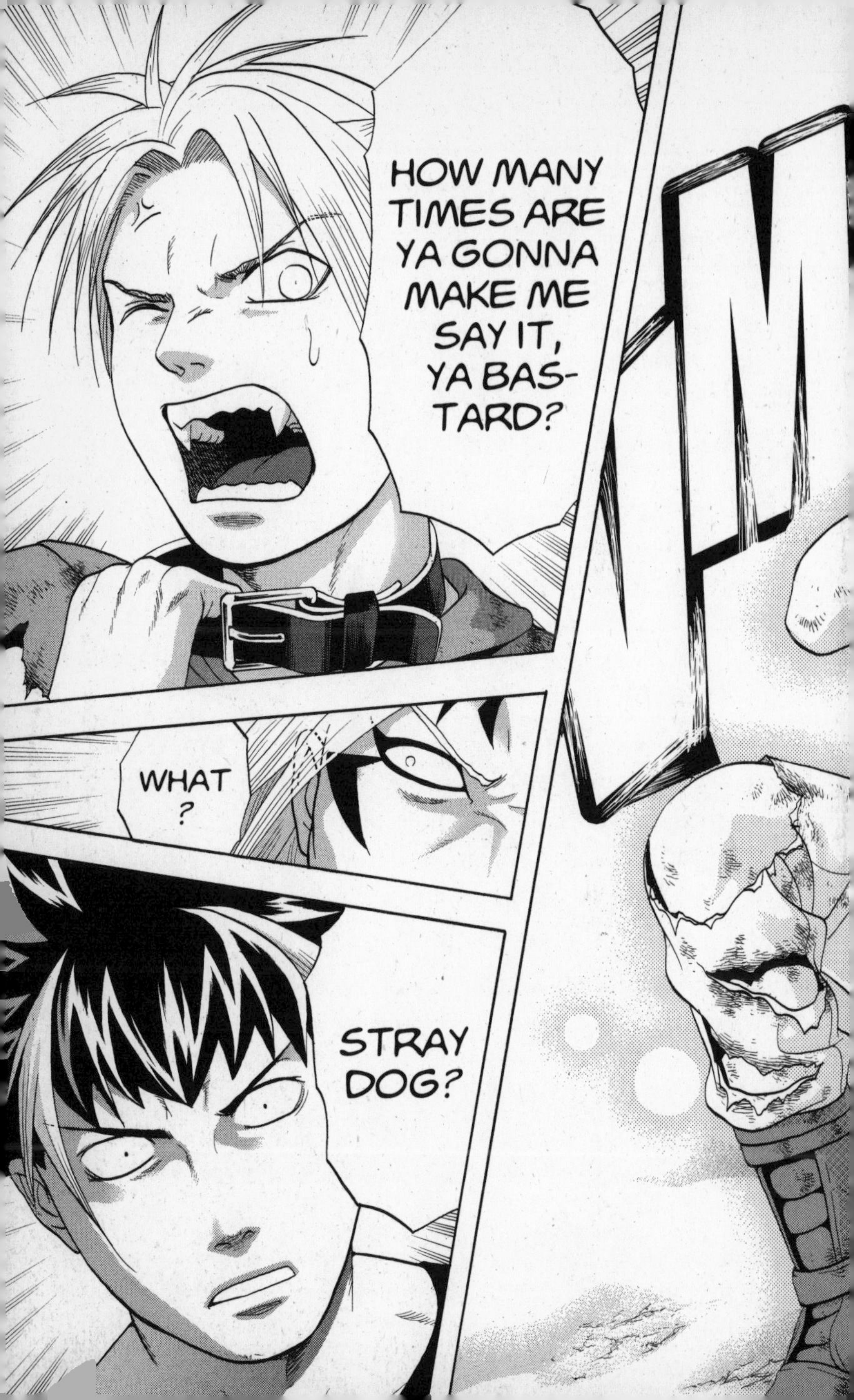
HOW MANY TIMES ARE YA GONNA MAKE ME SAY IT, YA BAS-TARD?
WHAT ?
STRAY DOG?

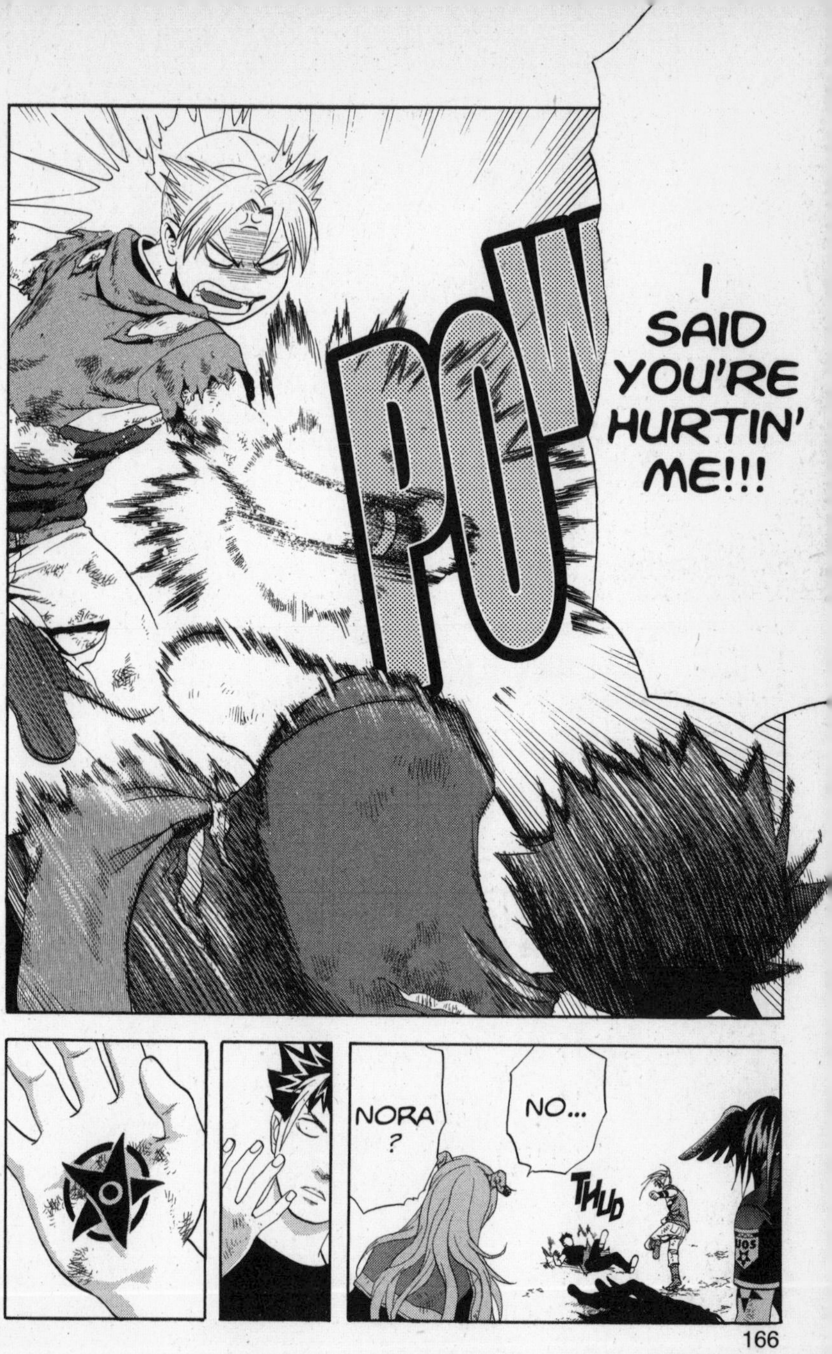
POW
I SAID YOU'RE HURTIN' ME!!!
NO...
NORA?
THUD

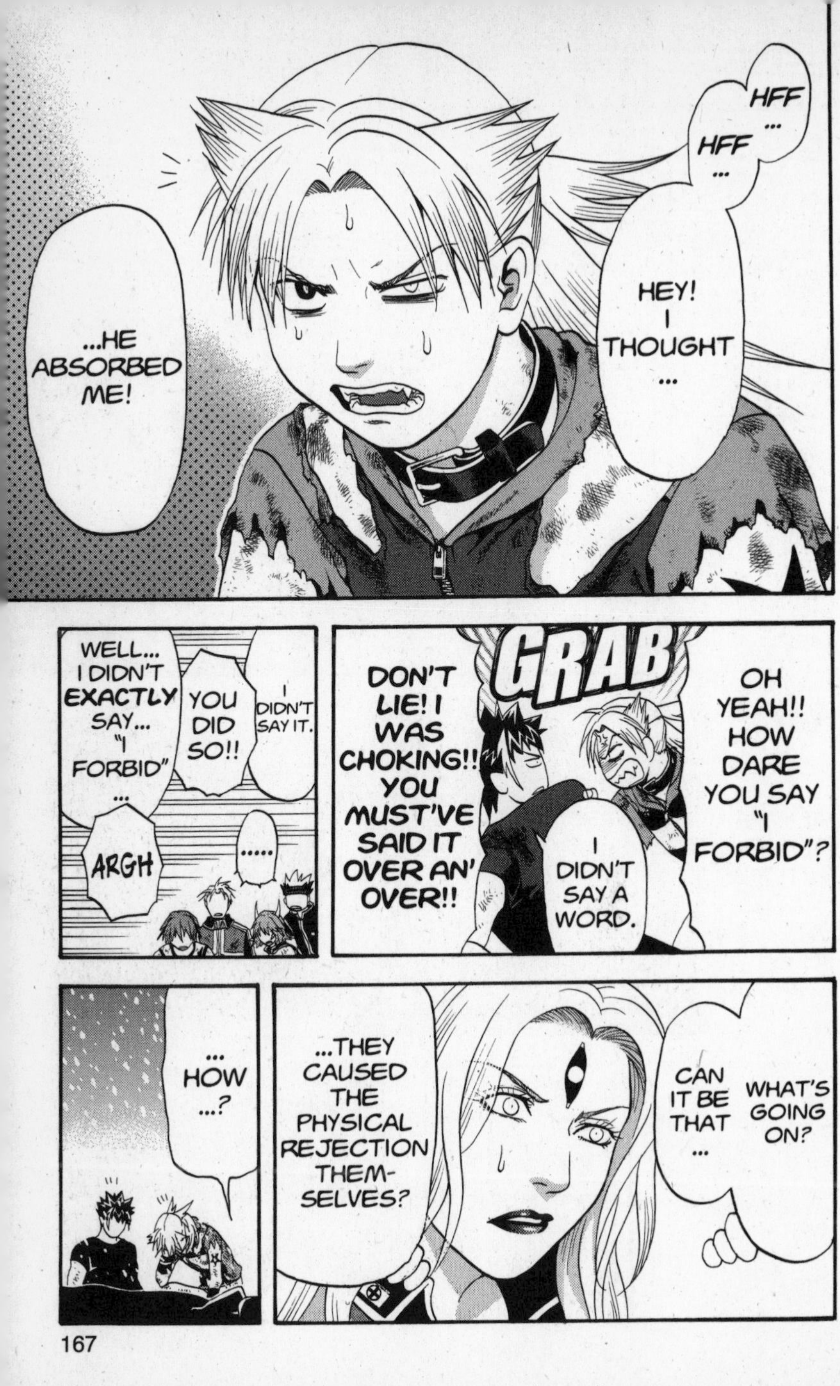
HFF... HFF...
HEY! I THOUGHT...
...HE ABSORBED ME!
GRAB
OH YEAH!! HOW DARE YOU SAY "I FORBID"?
I DIDN'T SAY A WORD.
DON'T LIE! I WAS CHOKING!! YOU MUST'VE SAID IT OVER AN' OVER!!
I DIDN'T SAY IT.
YOU DID SO!!
WELL... I DIDN'T EXACTLY SAY... "I FORBID"...
......
ARGH
WHAT'S GOING ON?
CAN IT BE THAT...
...THEY CAUSED THE PHYSICAL REJECTION THEM-SELVES?
... HOW ...?

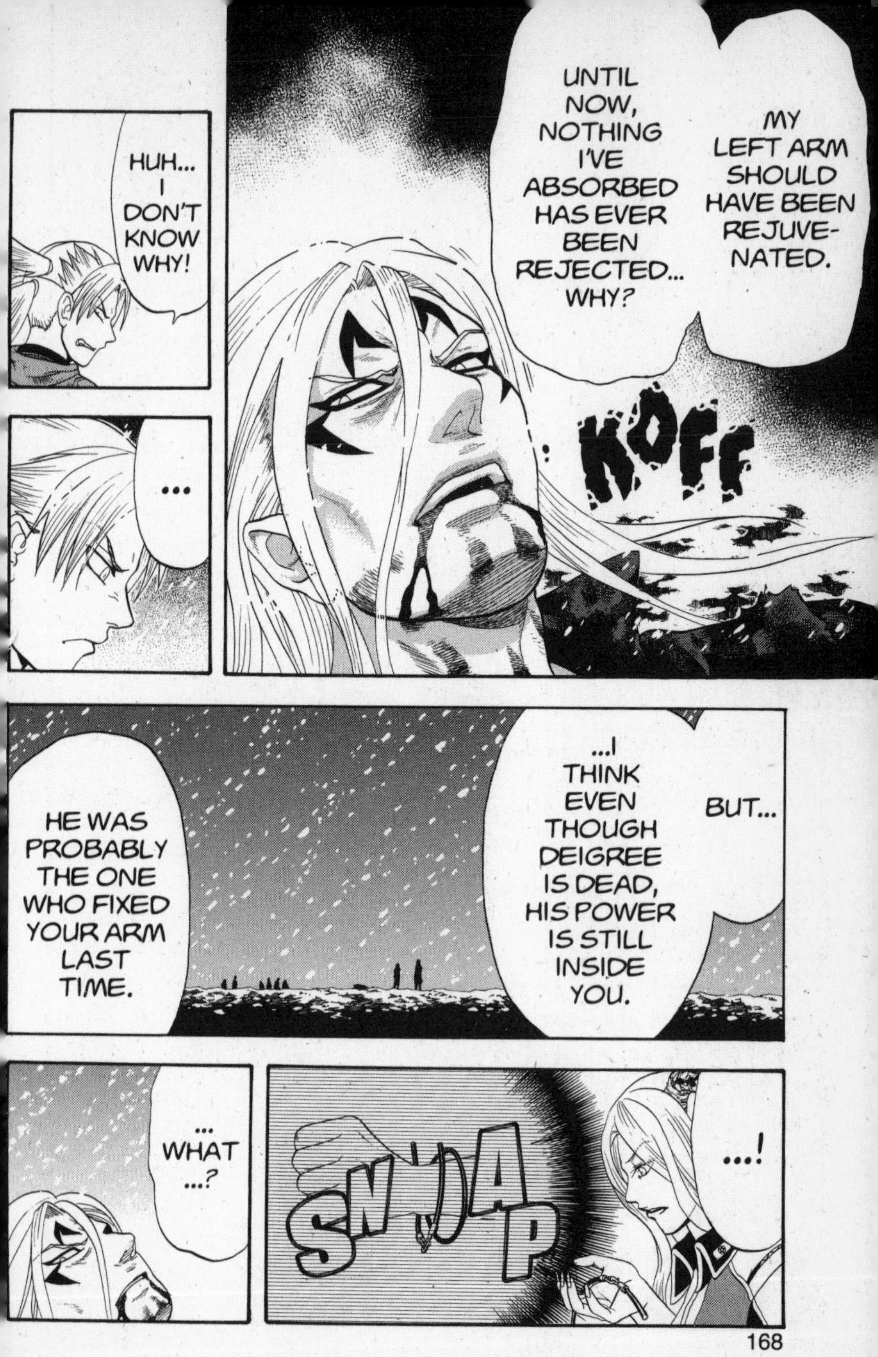
MY LEFT ARM SHOULD HAVE BEEN REJUVE- NATED.
UNTIL NOW, NOTHING I'VE ABSORBED HAS EVER BEEN REJECTED... WHY?
KOFF
HUH... I DON'T KNOW WHY!
...
BUT...
...I THINK EVEN THOUGH DEIGREE IS DEAD, HIS POWER IS STILL INSIDE YOU.
HE WAS PROBABLY THE ONE WHO FIXED YOUR ARM LAST TIME.
...!
SNAP
... WHAT ...?

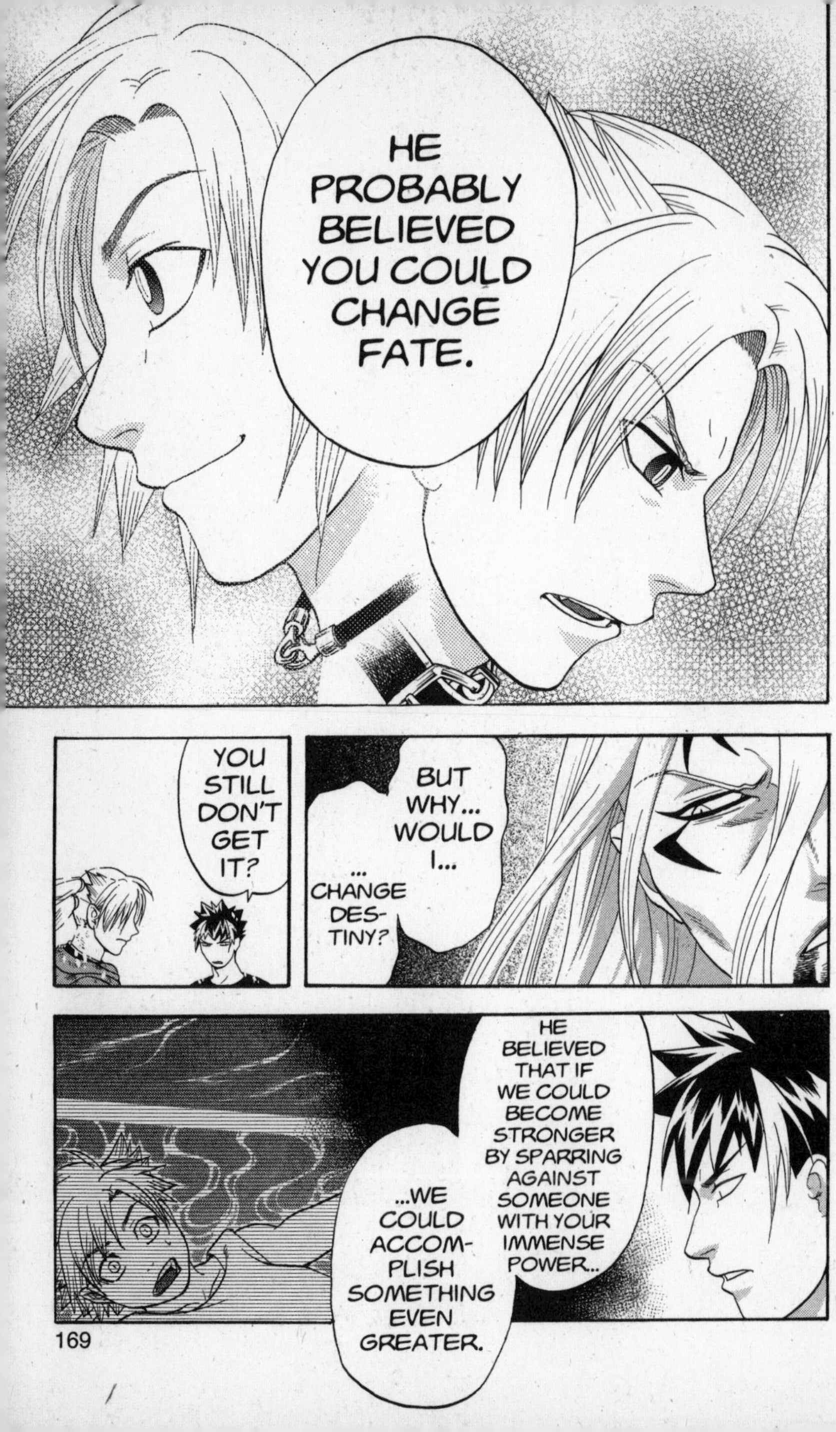
HE PROBABLY BELIEVED YOU COULD CHANGE FATE.
BUT WHY... WOULD I...
...CHANGE DES-TINY?
YOU STILL DON'T GET IT?
HE BELIEVED THAT IF WE COULD BECOME STRONGER BY SPARRING AGAINST SOMEONE WITH YOUR IMMENSE POWER...
...WE COULD ACCOM-PLISH SOMETHING EVEN GREATER.

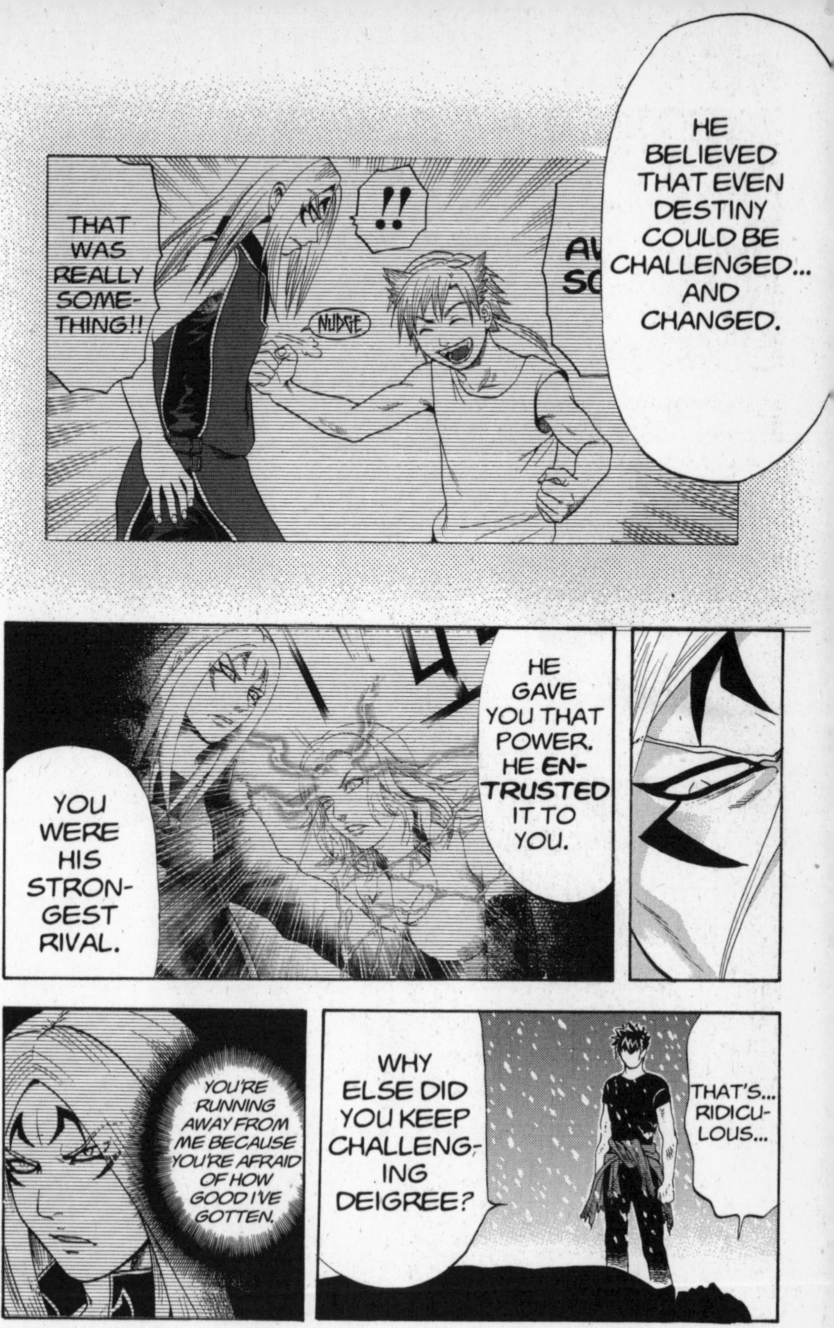
HE BELIEVED THAT EVEN DESTINY COULD BE CHALLENGED... AND CHANGED.
!!
THAT WAS REALLY SOME-THING!!
NUDGE
HE GAVE YOU THAT POWER. HE EN-TRUSTED IT TO YOU.
YOU WERE HIS STRON-GEST RIVAL.
THAT'S... RIDICU-LOUS...
WHY ELSE DID YOU KEEP CHALLENG-ING DEIGREE?
YOU'RE RUNNING AWAY FROM ME BECAUSE YOU'RE AFRAID OF HOW GOOD I'VE GOTTEN.

READ THIS WAY

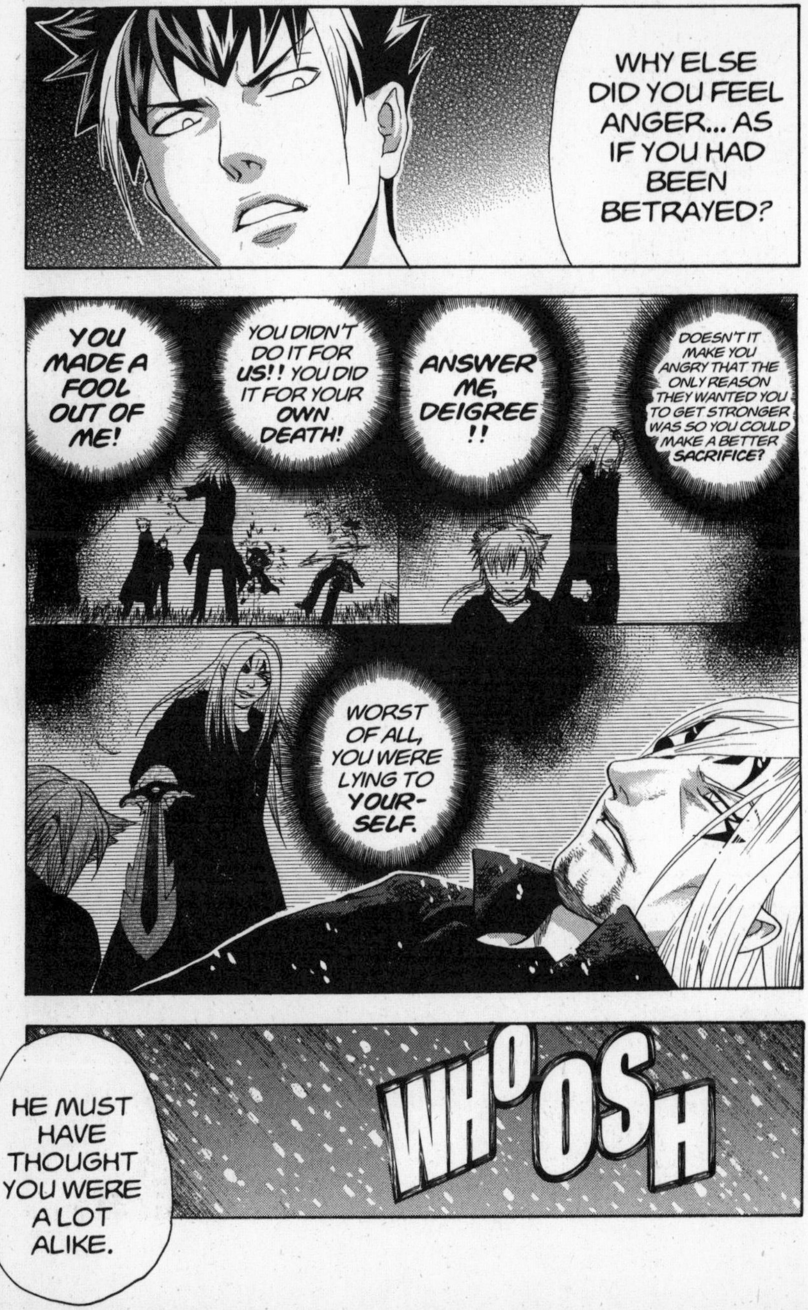
WHY ELSE DID YOU FEEL ANGER... AS IF YOU HAD BEEN BETRAYED?
DOESN'T IT MAKE YOU ANGRY THAT THE ONLY REASON THEY WANTED YOU TO GET STRONGER WAS SO YOU COULD MAKE A BETTER SACRIFICE?
ANSWER ME, DEIGREE!!
YOU DIDN'T DO IT FOR US!! YOU DID IT FOR YOUR OWN DEATH!
YOU MADE A FOOL OUT OF ME!
WORST OF ALL, YOU WERE LYING TO YOURSELF.
WHOOSH
HE MUST HAVE THOUGHT YOU WERE A LOT ALIKE.

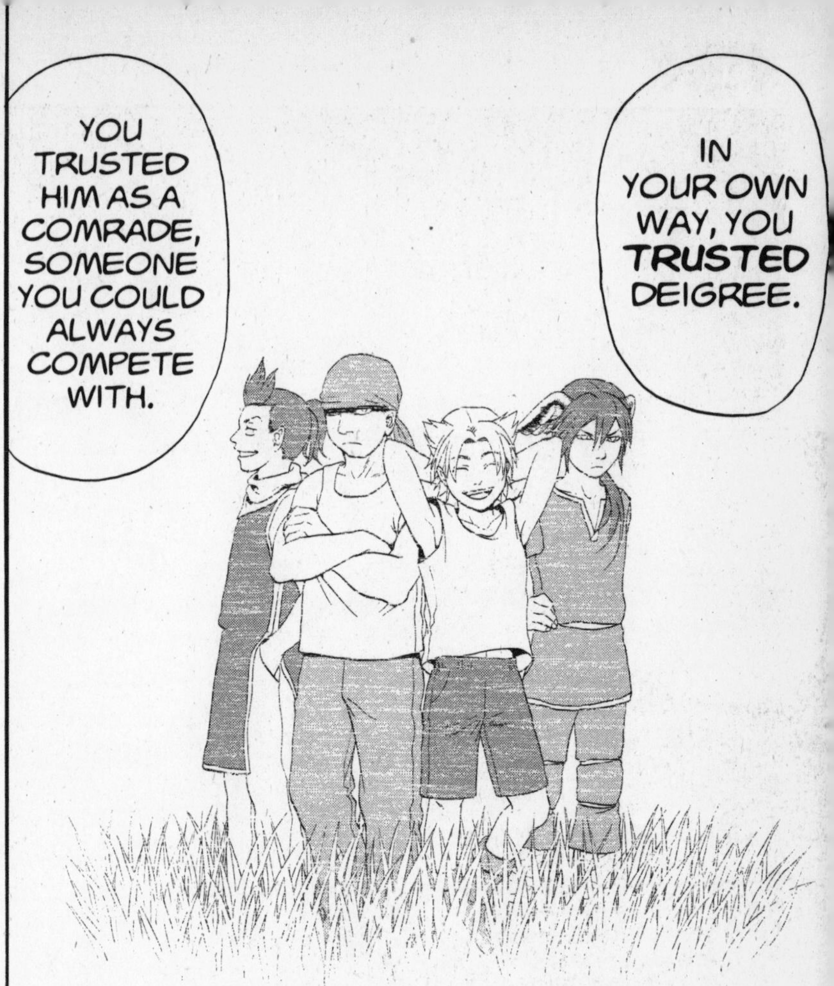
IN YOUR OWN WAY, YOU TRUSTED DEIGREE.
YOU TRUSTED HIM AS A COMRADE, SOMEONE YOU COULD ALWAYS COMPETE WITH.
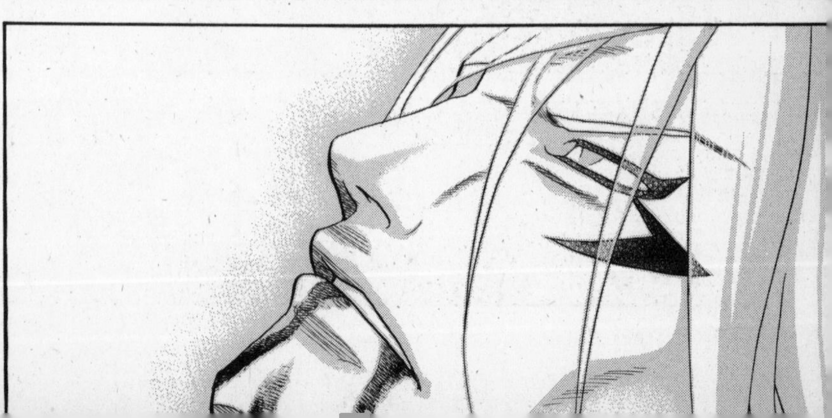

READ THIS WAY

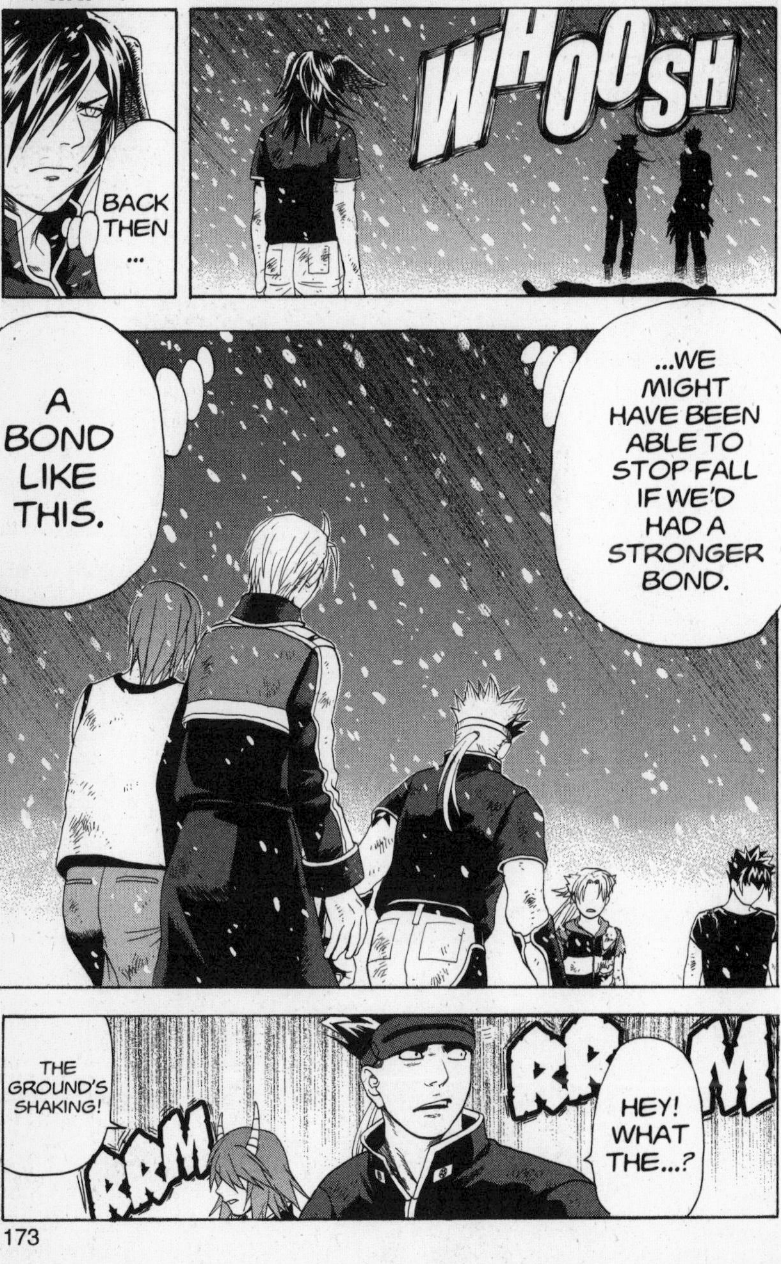
WHOOSH
BACK THEN ...
...WE MIGHT HAVE BEEN ABLE TO STOP FALL IF WE'D HAD A STRONGER BOND.
A BOND LIKE THIS.
HEY! WHAT THE...?
THE GROUND'S SHAKING!
RRM

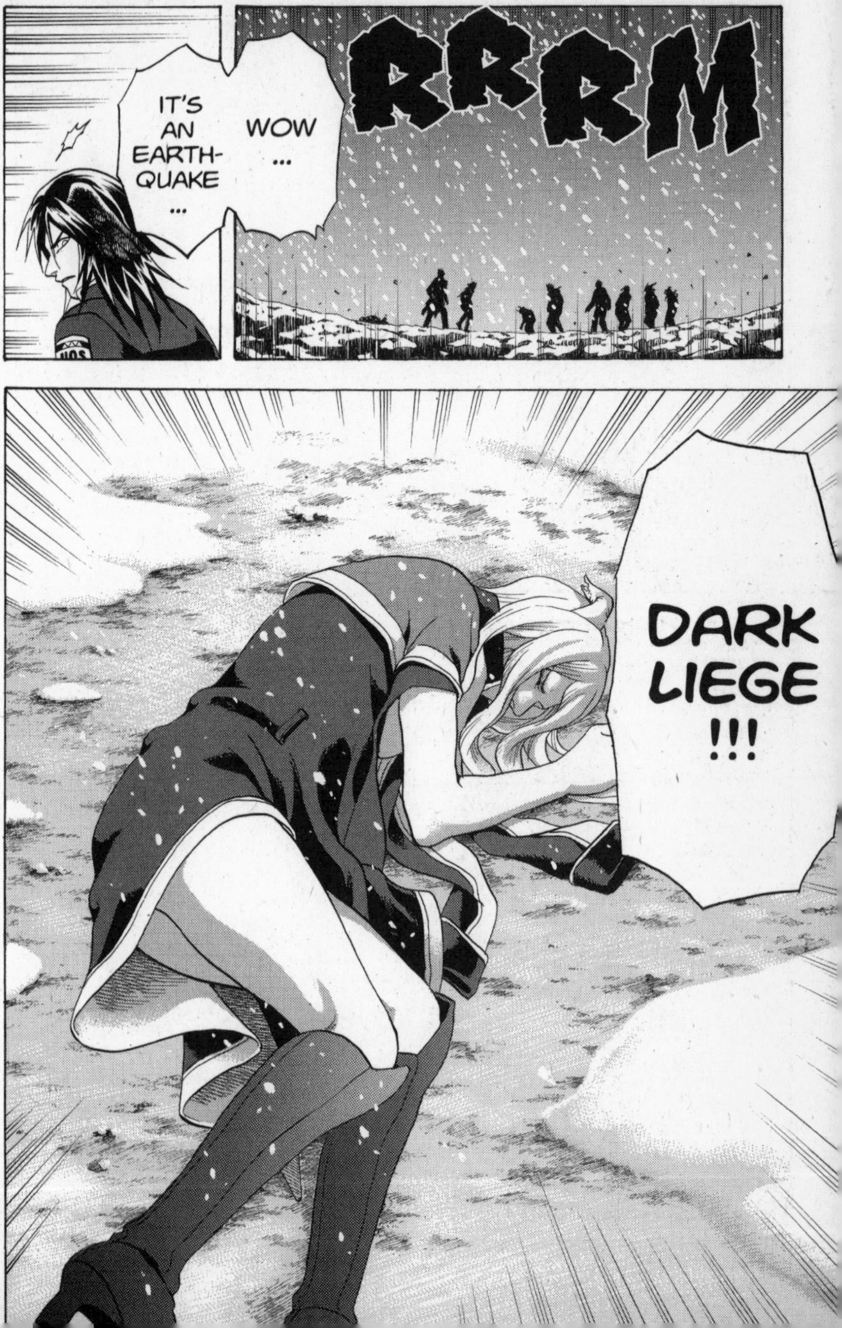
RRRM
WOW ...
IT'S AN EARTH-QUAKE ...
DARK LIEGE !!!

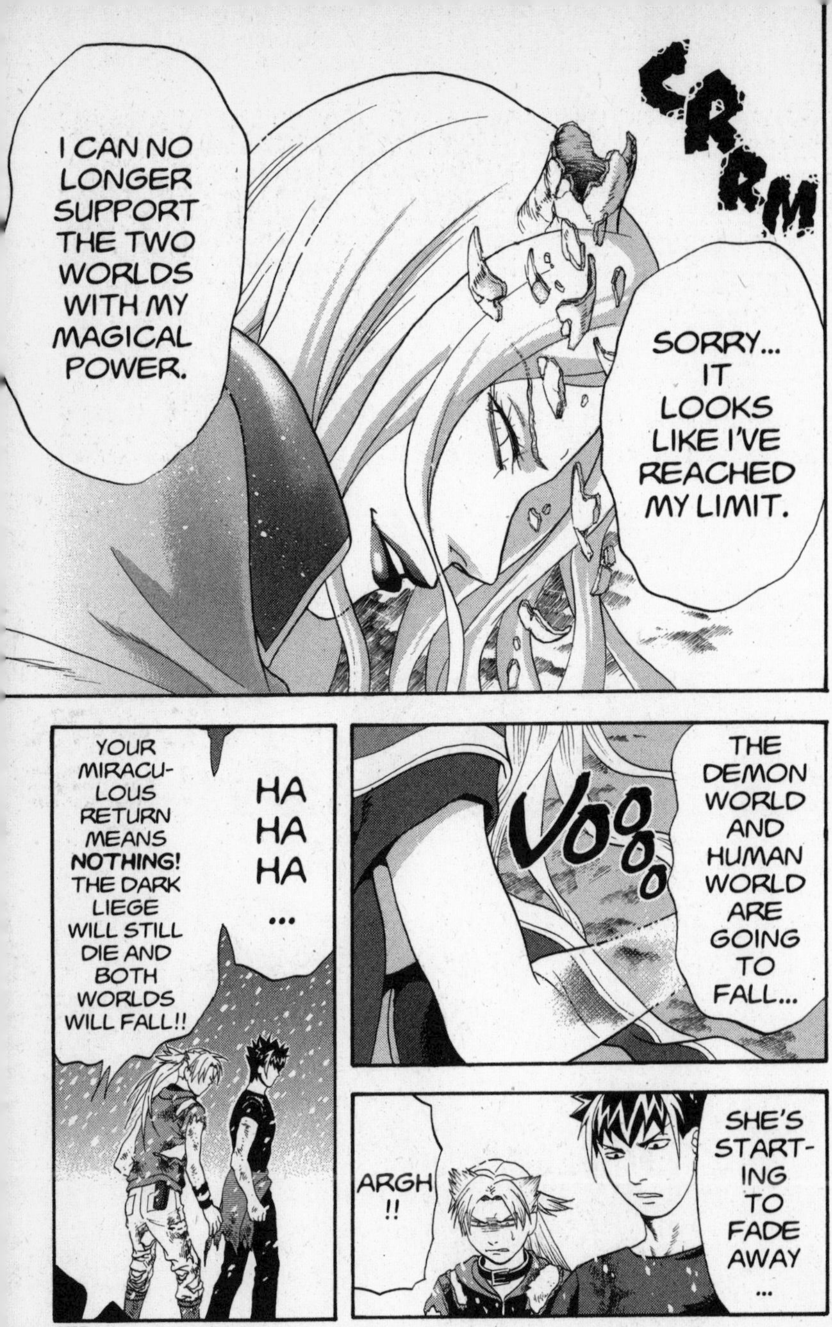
CRRM
SORRY... IT LOOKS LIKE I'VE REACHED MY LIMIT.
I CAN NO LONGER SUPPORT THE TWO WORLDS WITH MY MAGICAL POWER.
THE DEMON WORLD AND HUMAN WORLD ARE GOING TO FALL...
VOOOO
SHE'S STARTING TO FADE AWAY...
ARGH!!
HA HA HA...
YOUR MIRACULOUS RETURN MEANS NOTHING! THE DARK LIEGE WILL STILL DIE AND BOTH WORLDS WILL FALL!!

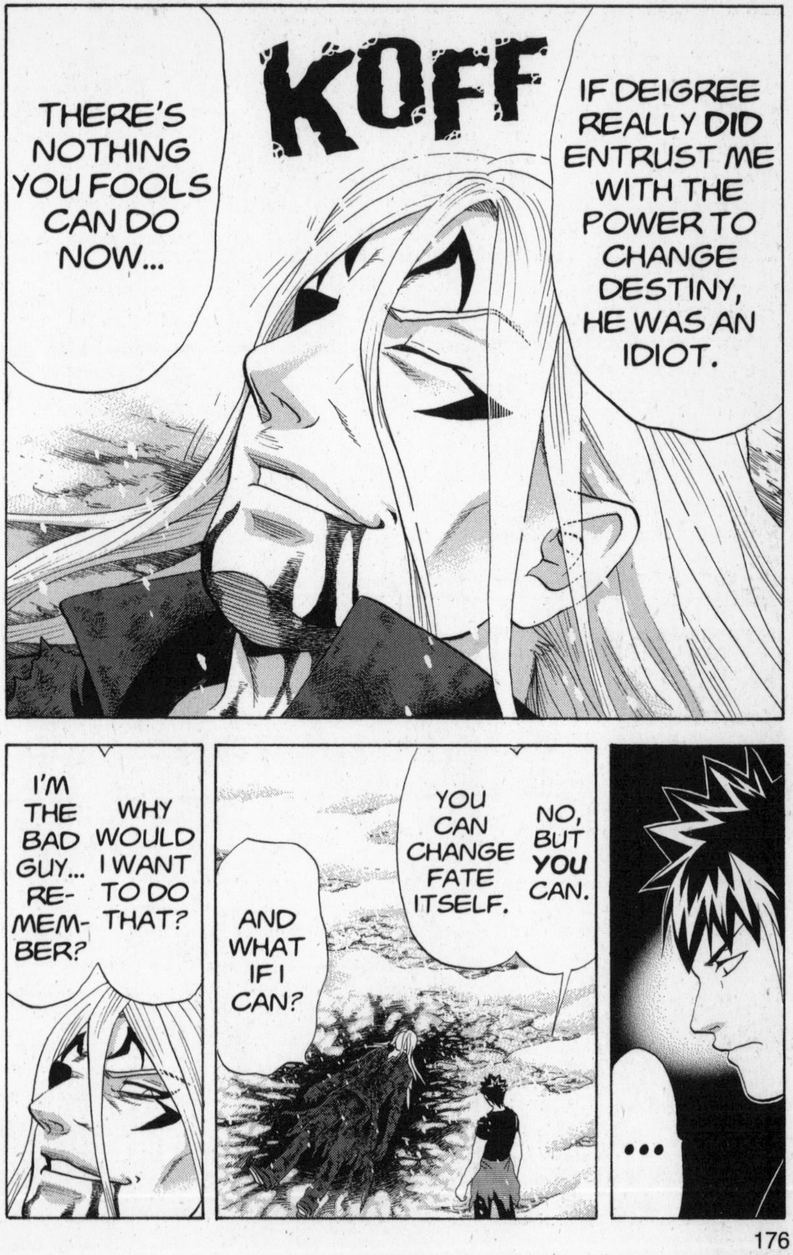
IF DEIGREE REALLY DID ENTRUST ME WITH THE POWER TO CHANGE DESTINY, HE WAS AN IDIOT.
KOFF
THERE'S NOTHING YOU FOOLS CAN DO NOW...
...
NO, BUT YOU CAN.
YOU CAN CHANGE FATE ITSELF.
AND WHAT IF I CAN?
WHY WOULD I WANT TO DO THAT?
I'M THE BAD GUY... RE-MEM-BER?

READ THIS WAY

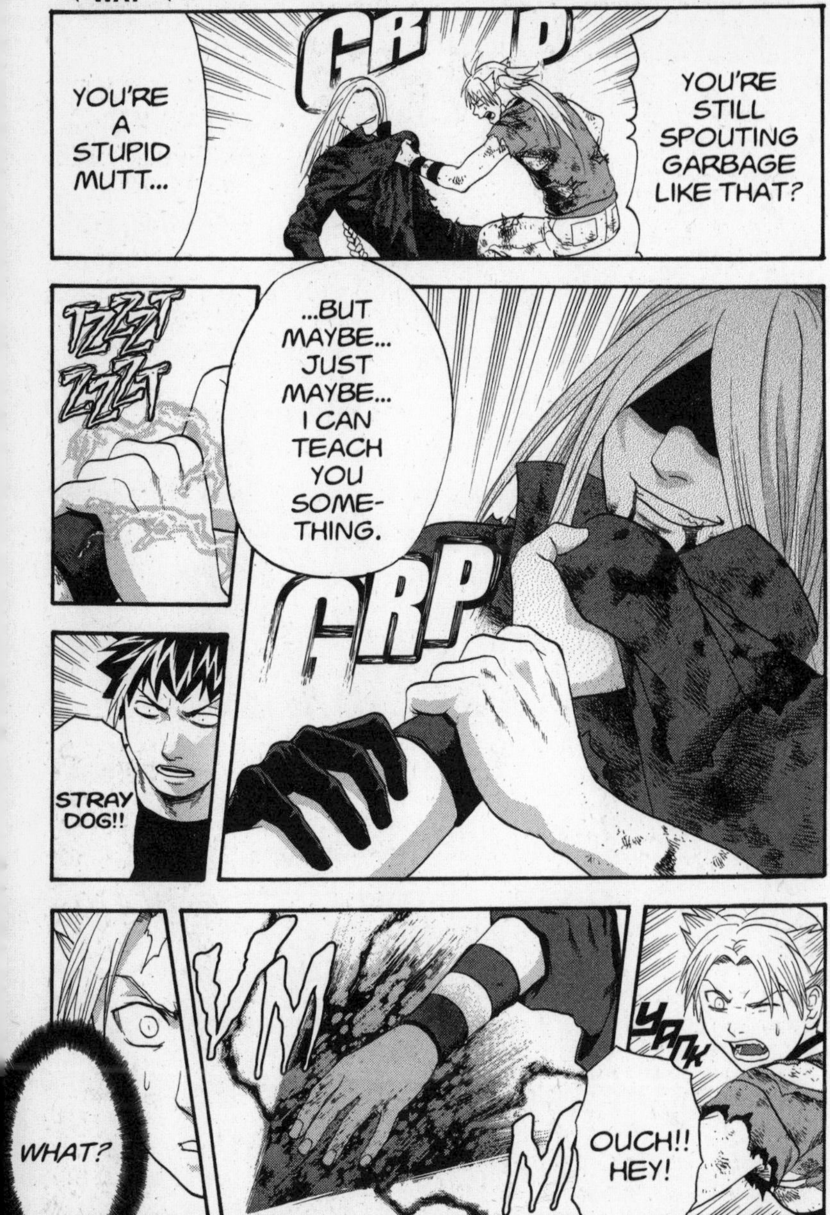
YOU'RE STILL SPOUTING GARBAGE LIKE THAT?
YOU'RE A STUPID MUTT...
...BUT MAYBE... JUST MAYBE... I CAN TEACH YOU SOME-THING.
CRP
TZZZT
ZZZT
STRAY DOG!!
YANK
OUCH!! HEY!
VMM
WHAT?

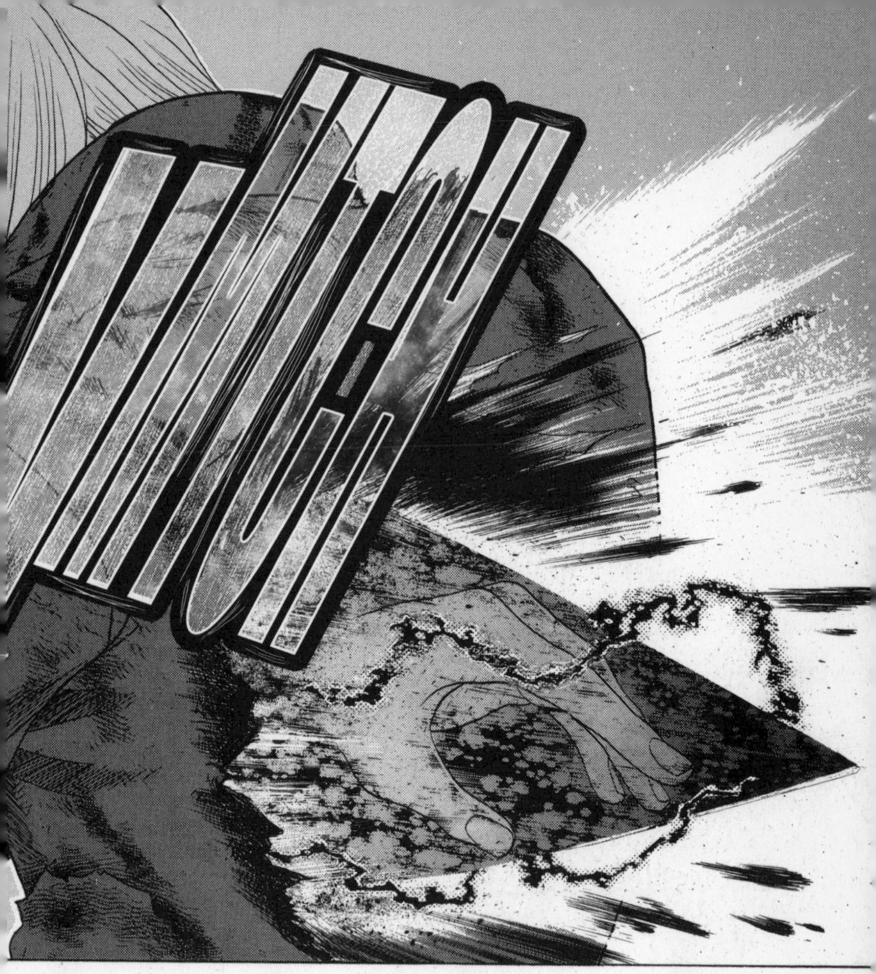
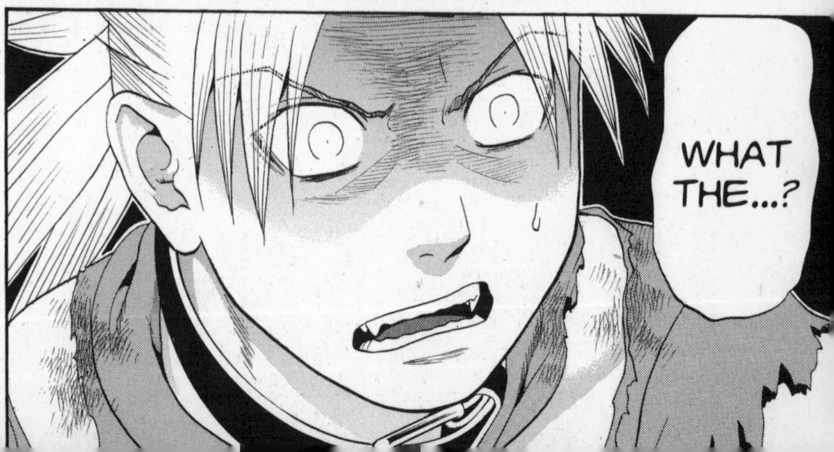
WHAT THE...?

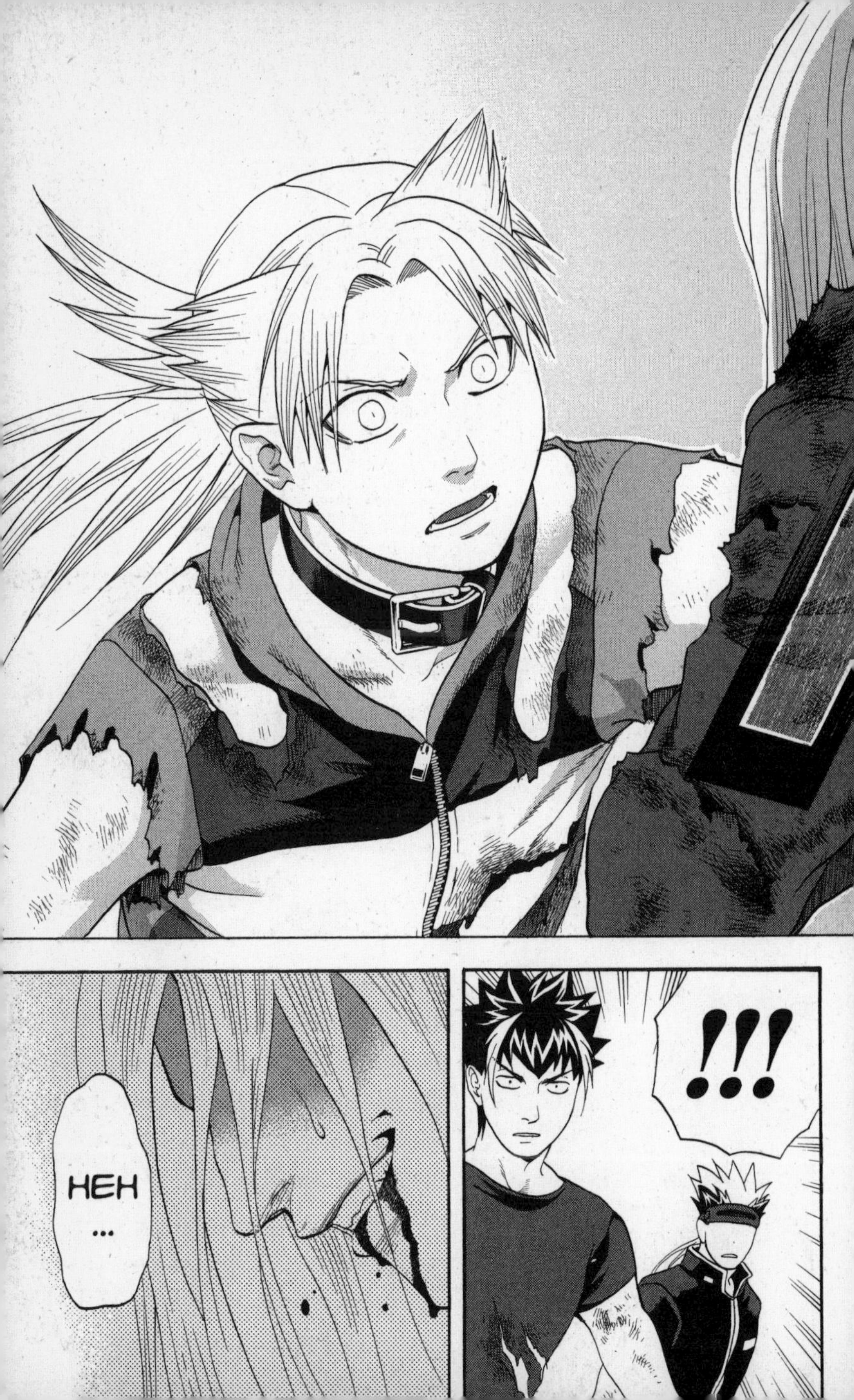
!!!
HEH ...

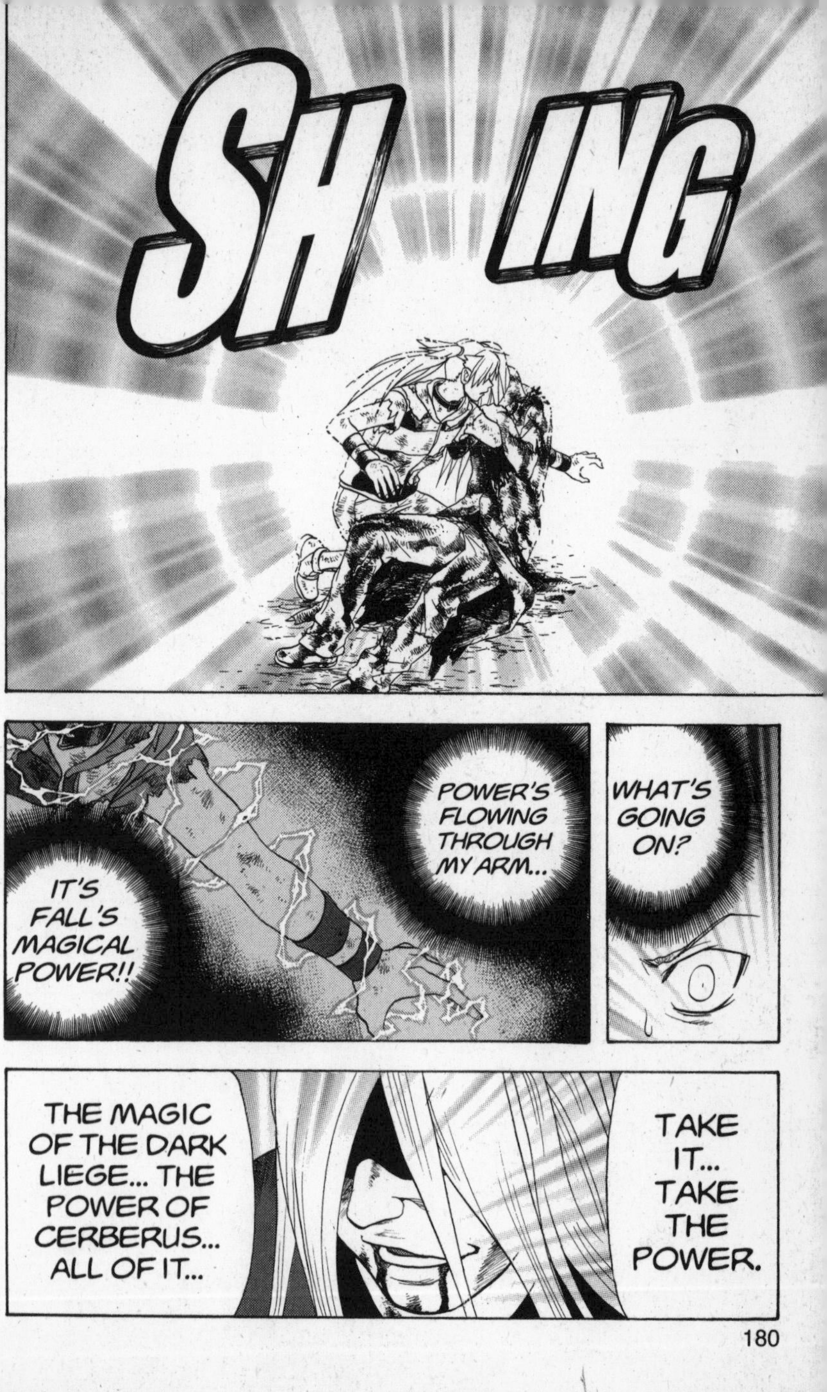
SH ING
WHAT'S GOING ON?
POWER'S FLOWING THROUGH MY ARM...
IT'S FALL'S MAGICAL POWER!!
TAKE IT... TAKE THE POWER.
THE MAGIC OF THE DARK LIEGE... THE POWER OF CERBERUS... ALL OF IT...

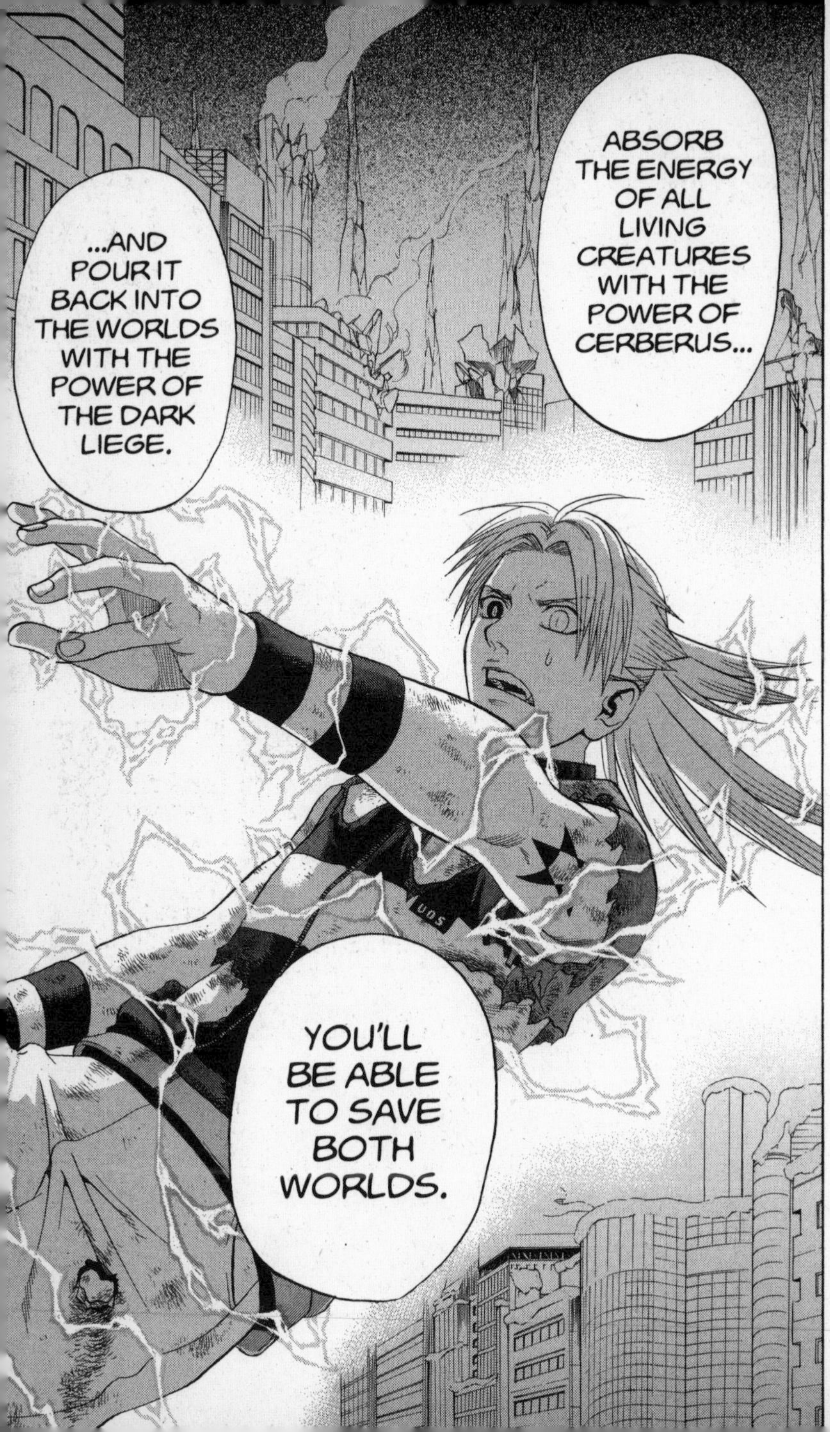
ABSORB THE ENERGY OF ALL LIVING CREATURES WITH THE POWER OF CERBERUS...
...AND POUR IT BACK INTO THE WORLDS WITH THE POWER OF THE DARK LIEGE.
YOU'LL BE ABLE TO SAVE BOTH WORLDS.

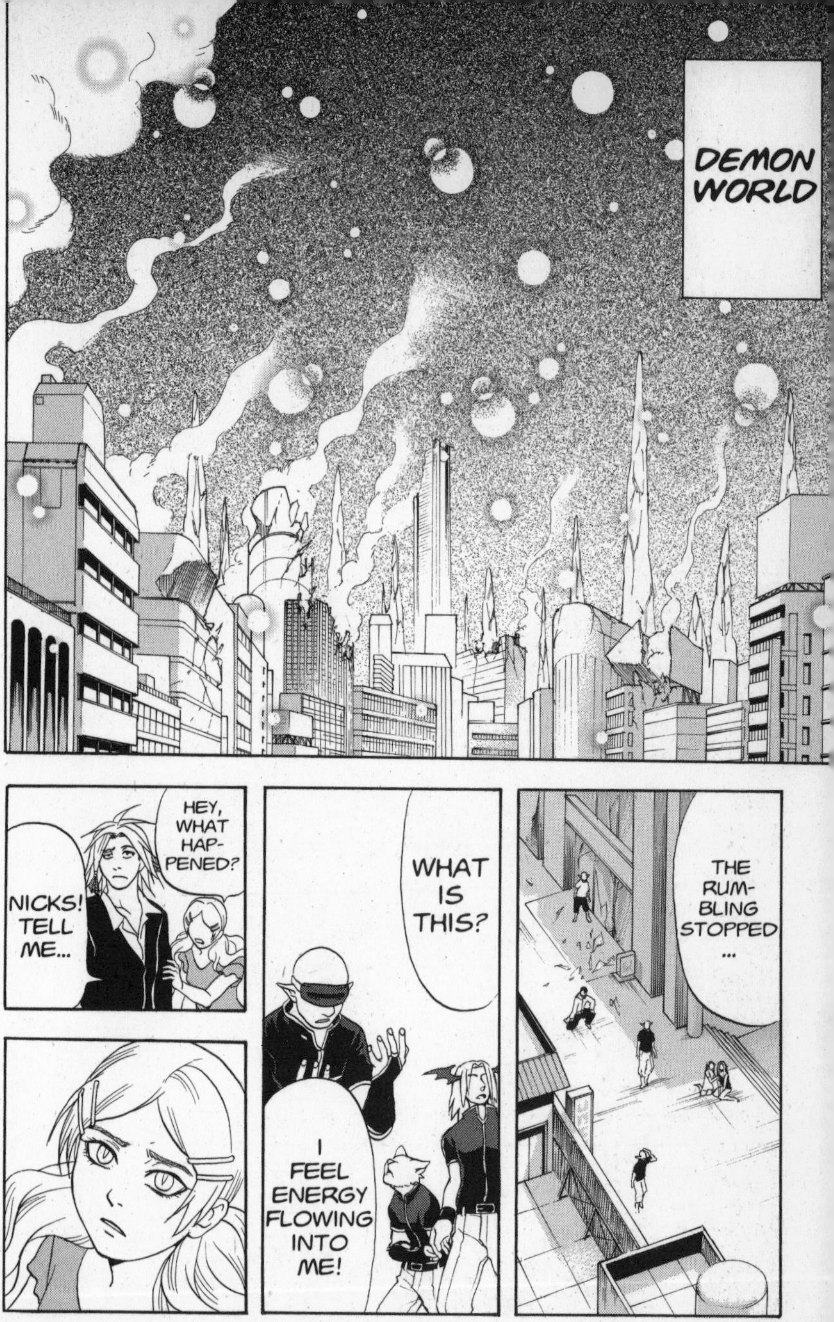
DEMON WORLD
THE RUMBLING STOPPED...
WHAT IS THIS?
I FEEL ENERGY FLOWING INTO ME!
HEY, WHAT HAPPENED?
NICKS! TELL ME...

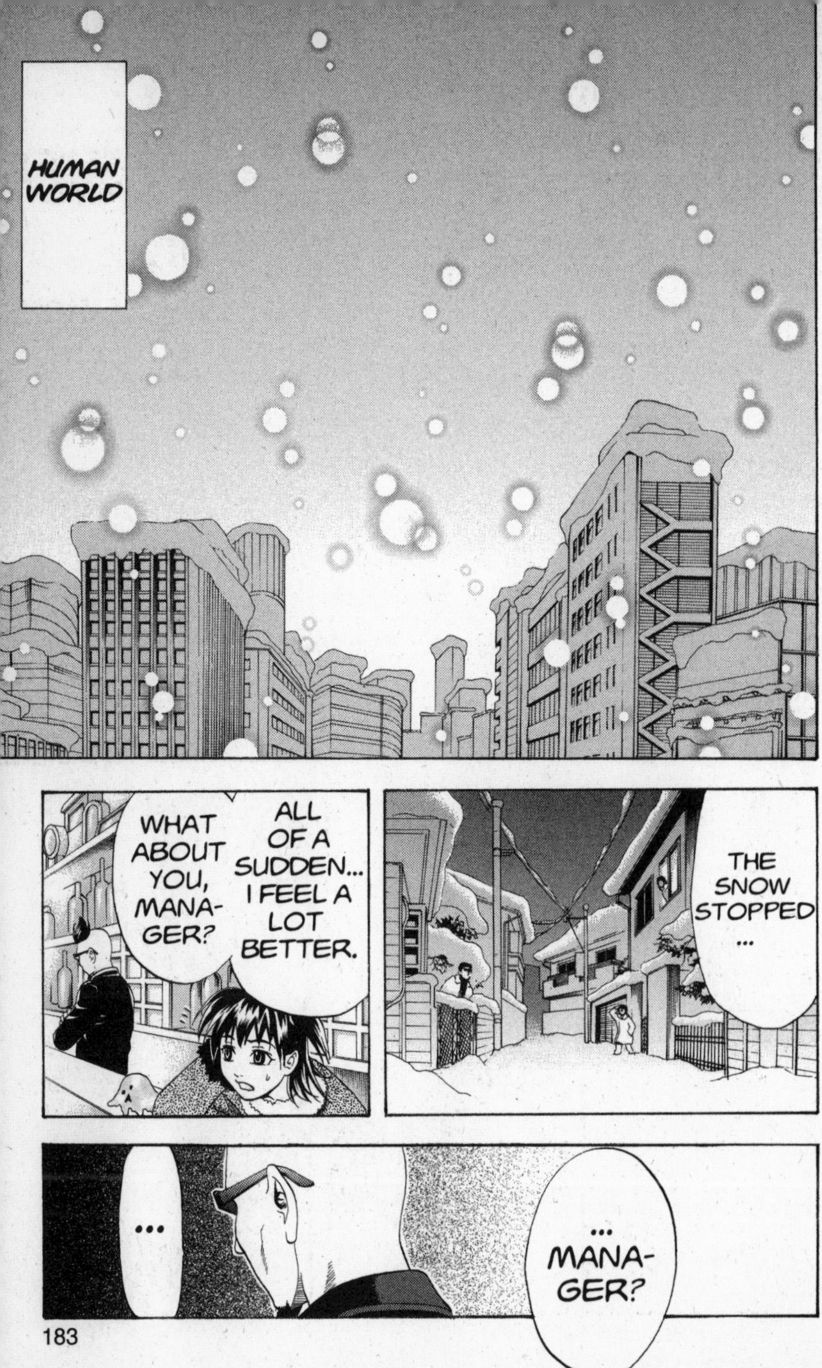
HUMAN WORLD
THE SNOW STOPPED ...
ALL OF A SUDDEN... I FEEL A LOT BETTER.
WHAT ABOUT YOU, MANAGER?
... MANAGER?
...

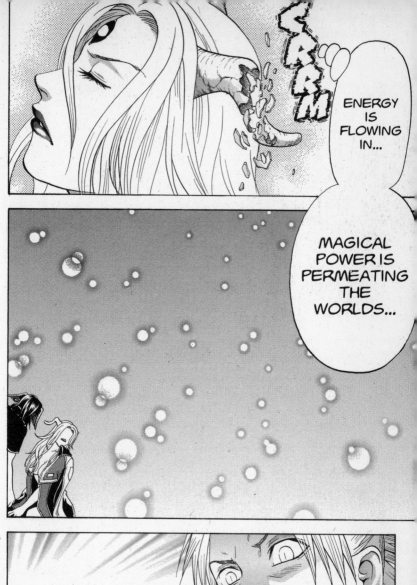

ENERGY IS FLOWING IN...

MAGICAL POWER IS PERMEATING THE WORLDS...

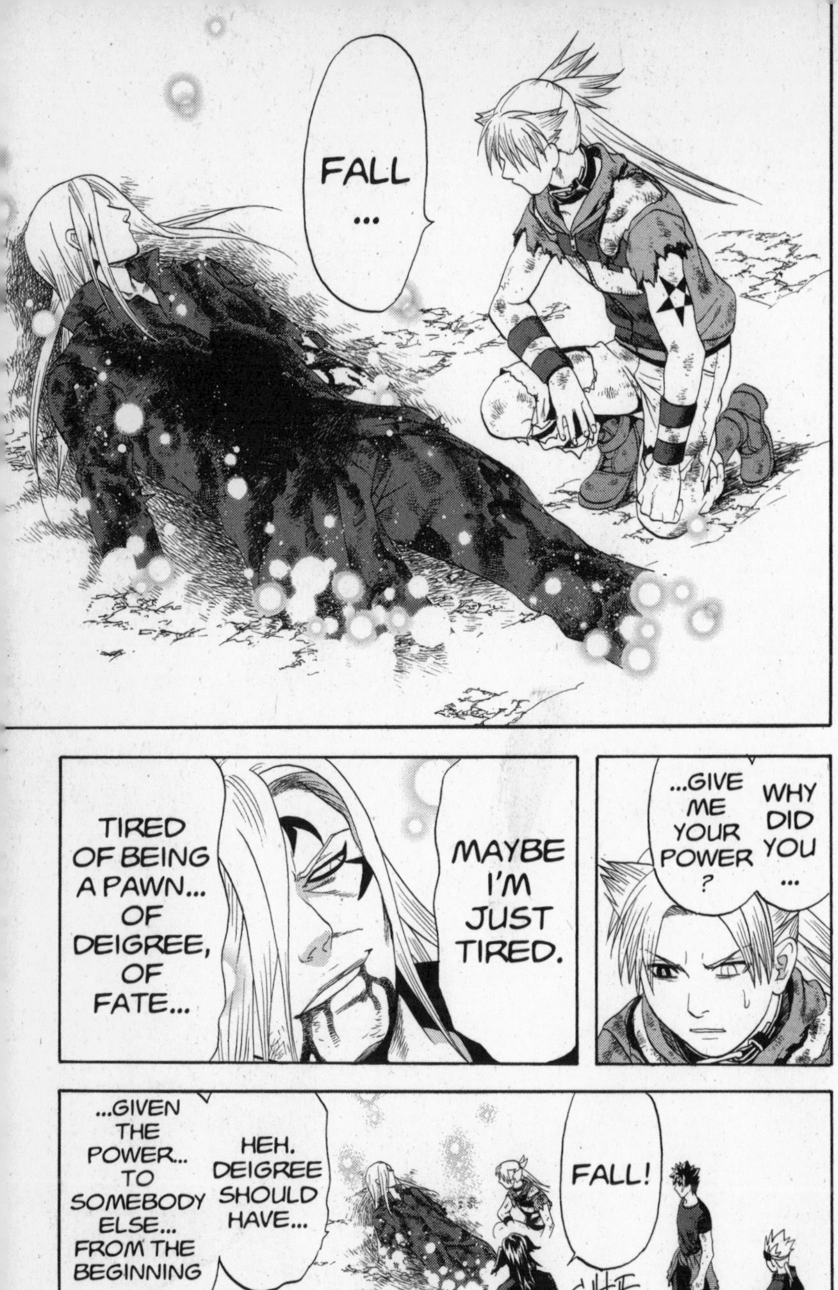
FALL ...
WHY DID YOU ...
...GIVE ME YOUR POWER ?
MAYBE I'M JUST TIRED.
TIRED OF BEING A PAWN... OF DEIGREE, OF FATE...
FALL!
CHF
HEH. DEIGREE SHOULD HAVE...
...GIVEN THE POWER... TO SOMEBODY ELSE... FROM THE BEGINNING ...

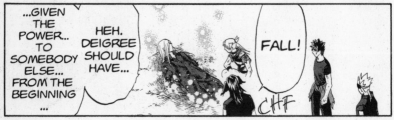

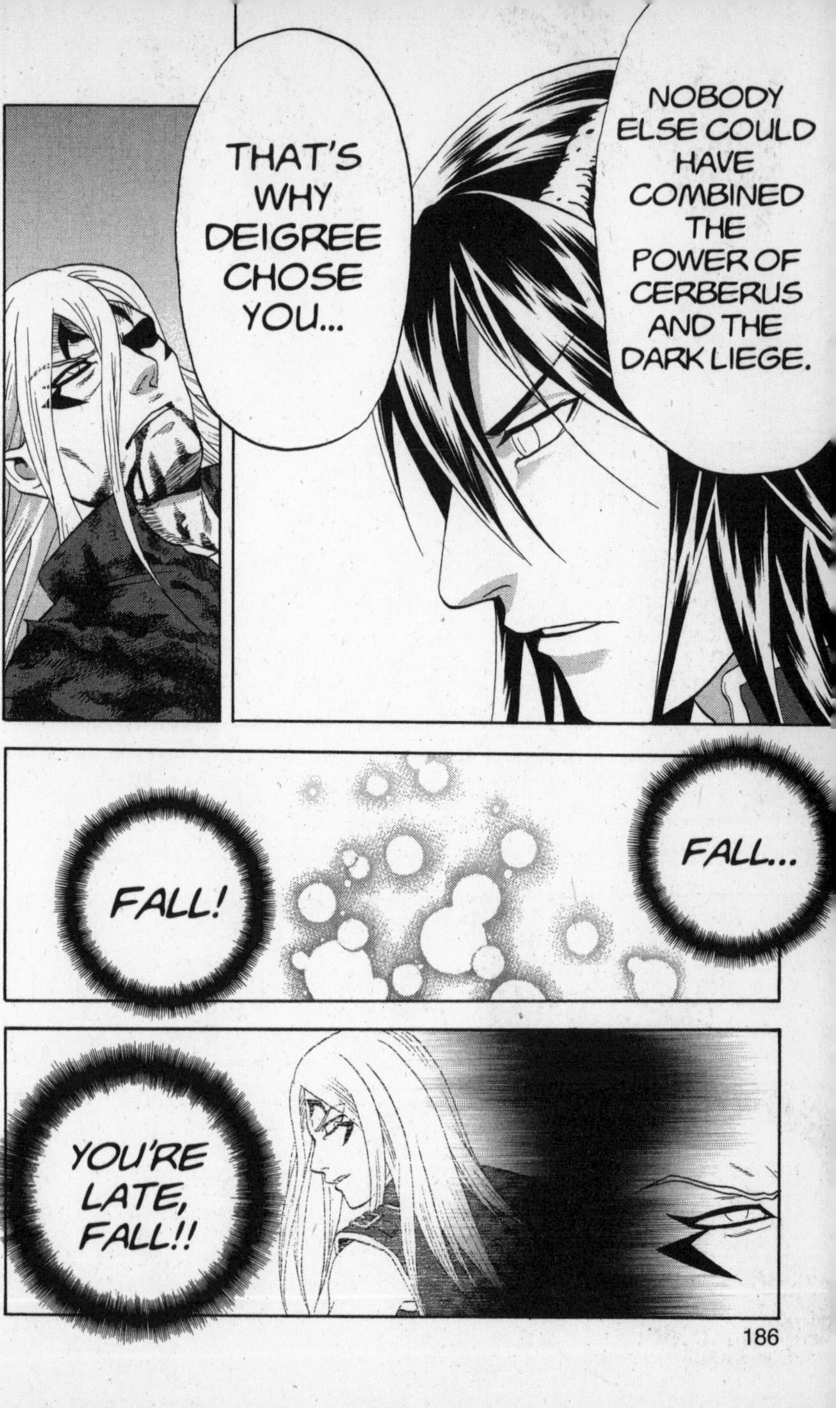
NOBODY ELSE COULD HAVE COMBINED THE POWER OF CERBERUS AND THE DARK LIEGE.
THAT'S WHY DEIGREE CHOSE YOU...
FALL...
FALL!
YOU'RE LATE, FALL!!

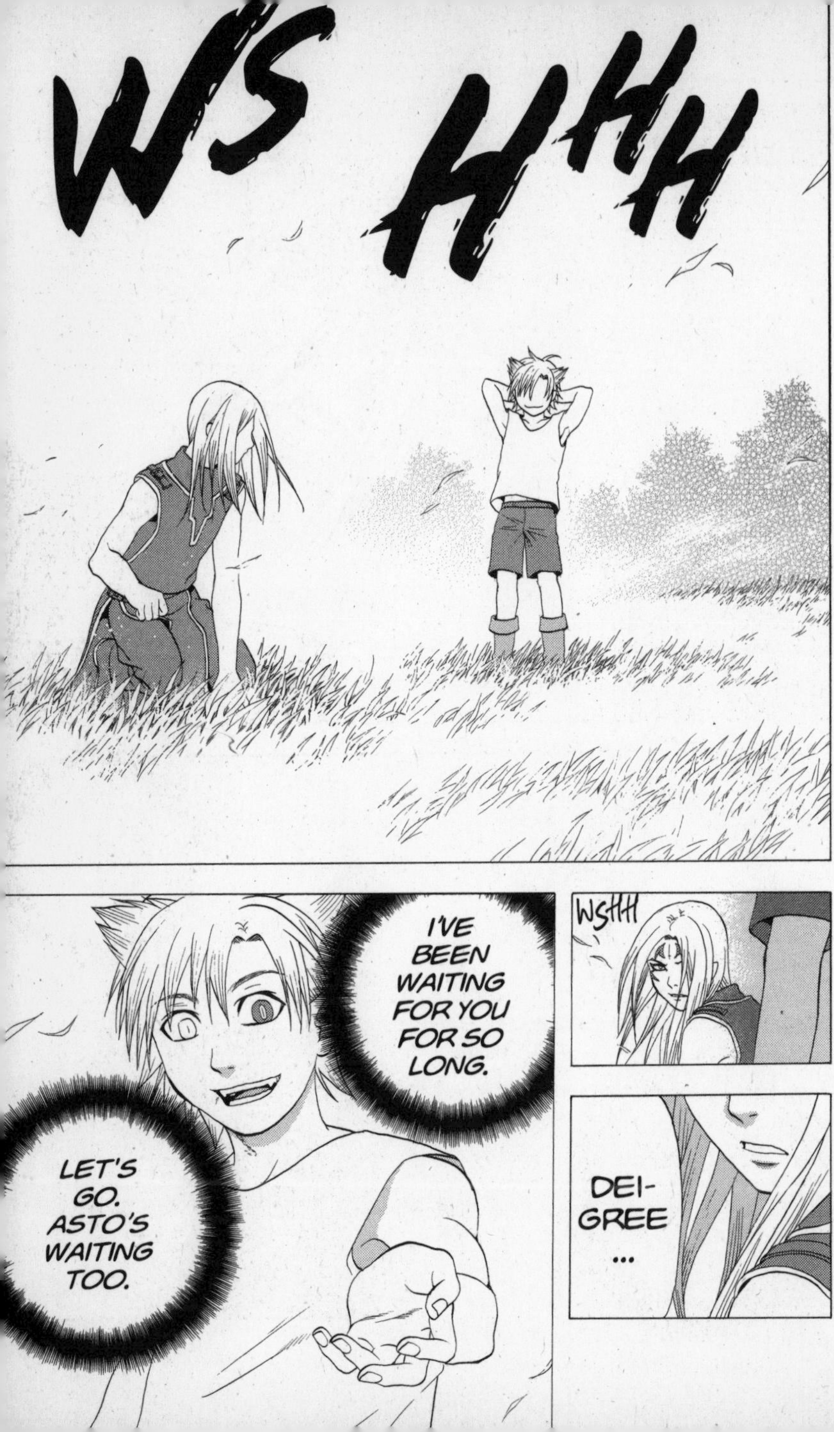
WSHHH
WSHHH
DEI-GREE...
I'VE BEEN WAITING FOR YOU FOR SO LONG.
LET'S GO. ASTO'S WAITING TOO.

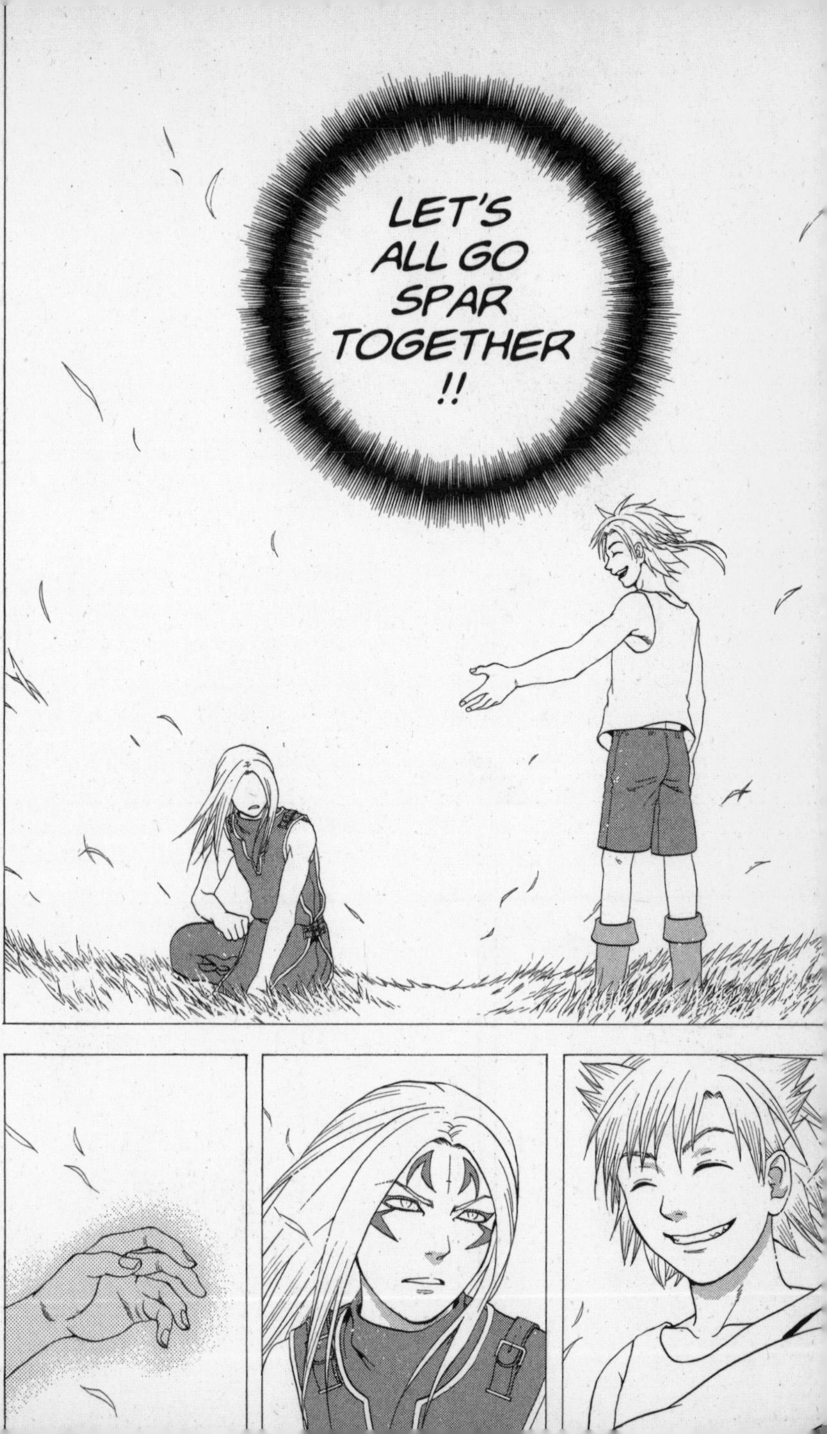
LET'S ALL GO SPAR TOGETHER !!

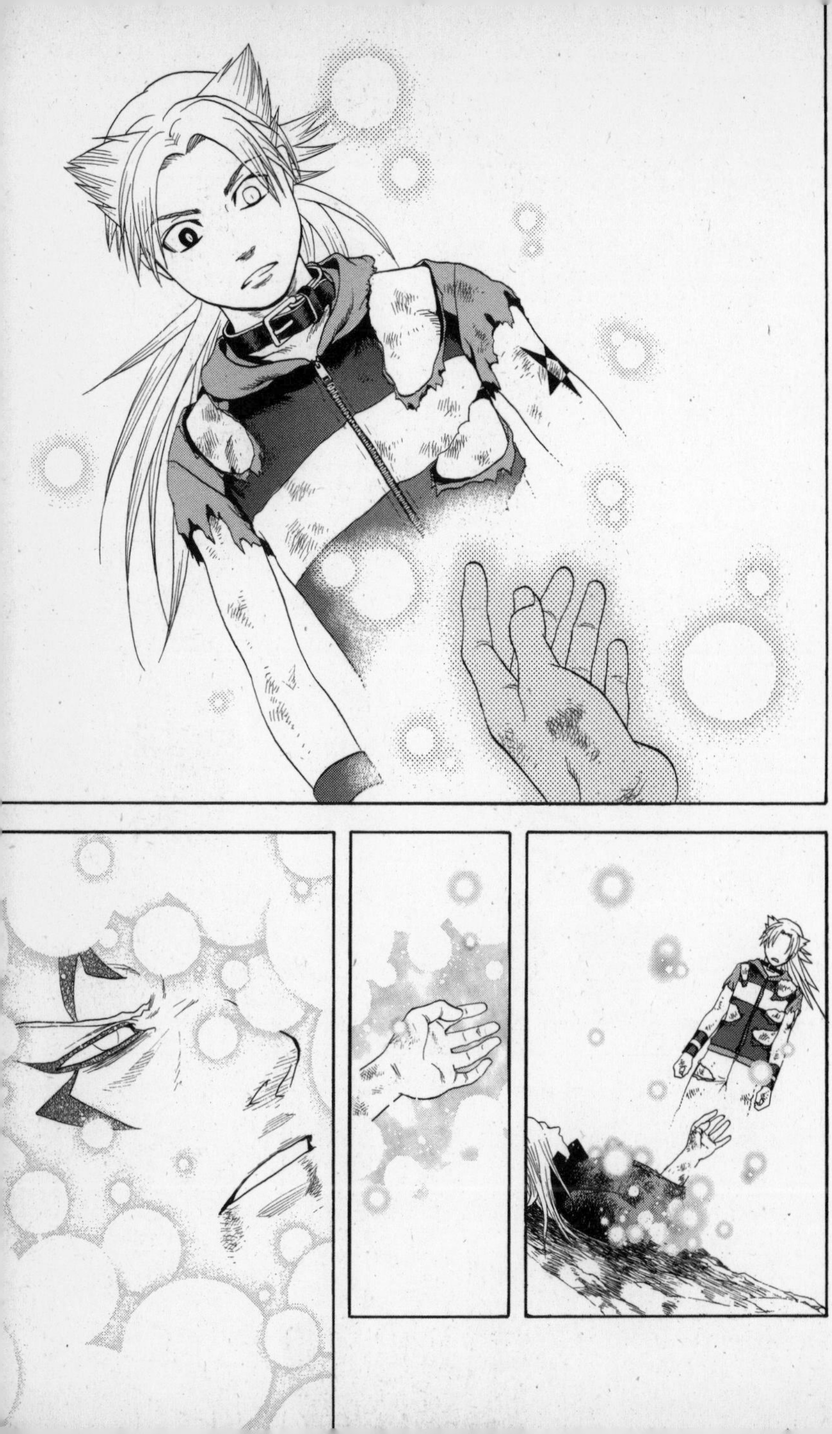

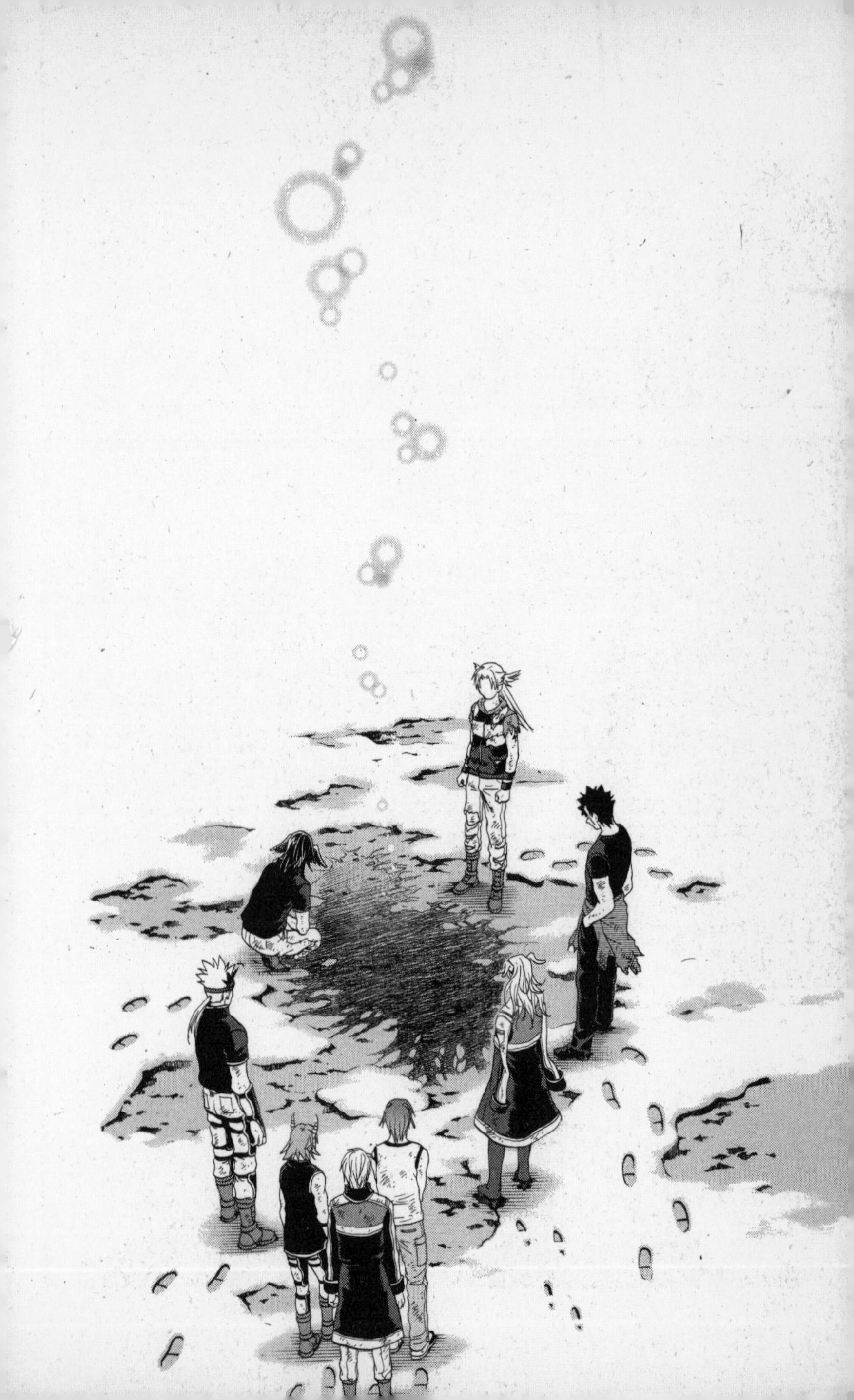

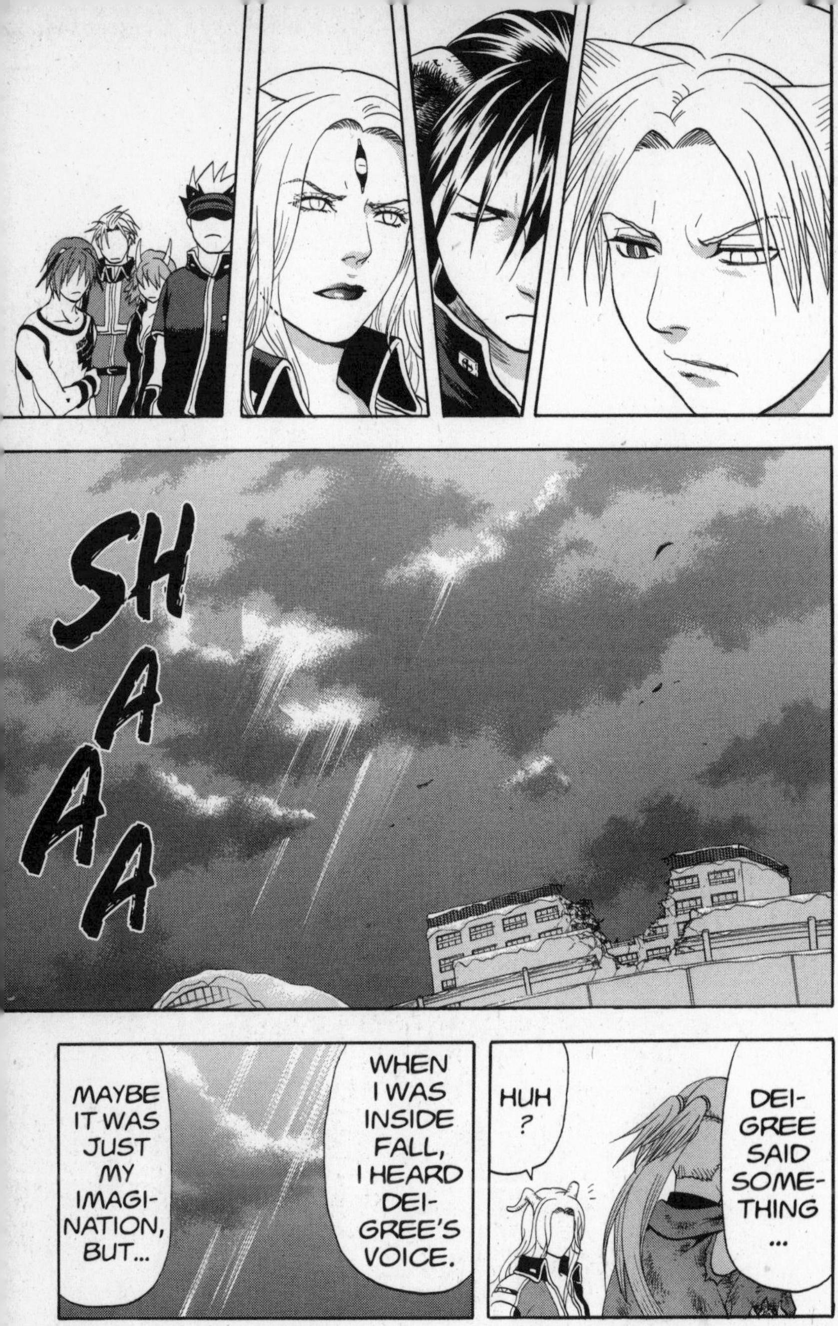
SHAAAA
DEI-GREE SAID SOME-THING ...
HUH ?
WHEN I WAS INSIDE FALL, I HEARD DEI-GREE'S VOICE.
MAYBE IT WAS JUST MY IMAGINATION, BUT...

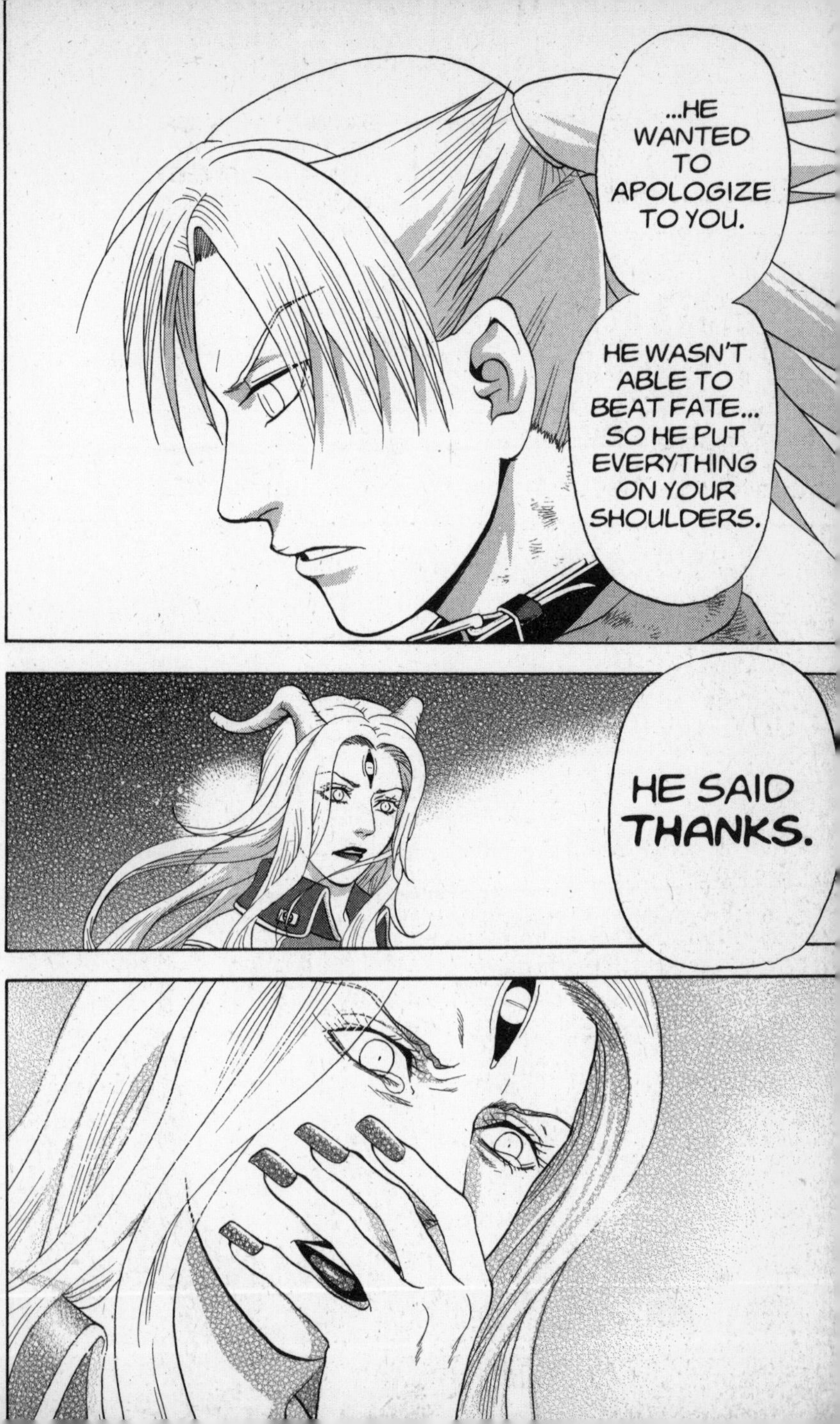
...HE WANTED TO APOLOGIZE TO YOU.
HE WASN'T ABLE TO BEAT FATE... SO HE PUT EVERYTHING ON YOUR SHOULDERS.
HE SAID **THANKS.**

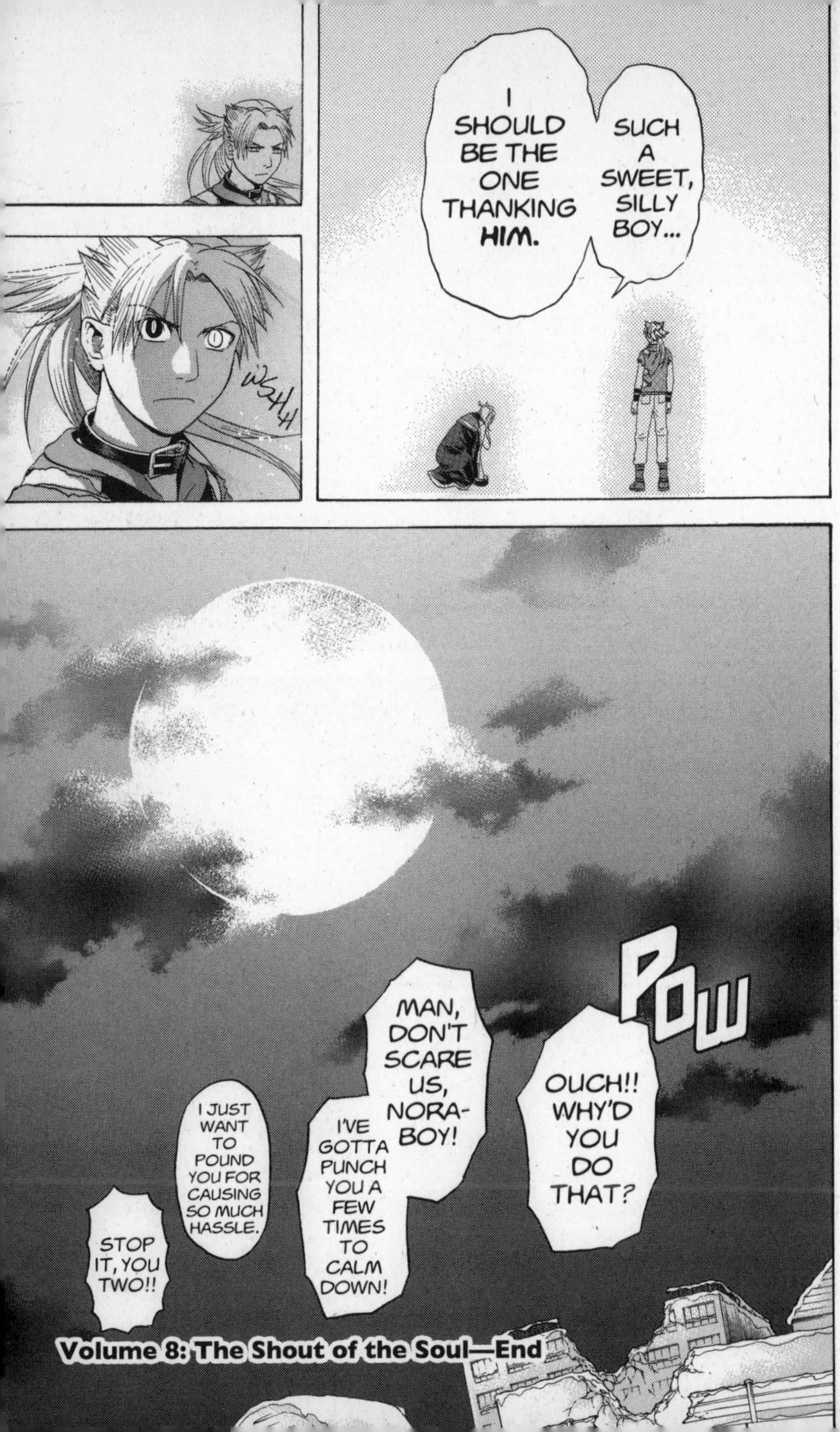
SUCH A SWEET, SILLY BOY...
I SHOULD BE THE ONE THANKING HIM.
WSHH
POW
OUCH!! WHY'D YOU DO THAT?
MAN, DON'T SCARE US, NORA-BOY!
I'VE GOTTA PUNCH YOU A FEW TIMES TO CALM DOWN!
I JUST WANT TO POUND YOU FOR CAUSING SO MUCH HASSLE.
STOP IT, YOU TWO!!
Volume 8: The Shout of the Soul—End

NORA MAIL BAG

FAN ART GUIDELINES

☆ IF YOU SEND IN FAN ART, PLEASE DRAW CLEARLY WITH BLACK INK. (PENCILS AND MECHANICAL PENCILS WILL NOT REPRODUCE.) BE SURE TO INCLUDE YOUR NAME AND ADDRESS. PEOPLE WHO DO NOT WANT THEIR FULL NAME PRINTED CAN USE A PEN NAME.

☆ WE CANNOT RETURN ANYTHING YOU SEND US. IF YOU WANT TO KEEP THE ORIGINAL, JUST SEND IN A COPY.

☆ ALL DRAWINGS BECOME THE PROPERTY OF *SHONEN JUMP*. HOWEVER, IF THEY ARE EVER REPRINTED WE WILL CONTACT THE APPLICANT AGAIN FOR CONSENT.

☆ SEND LETTERS AND FAN ART TO:

SHONEN JUMP
VIZ MEDIA, LLC
P.O. BOX 77010
SAN FRANCISCO, CA 94107

AND DON'T MISS THE CONCLUSION TO *NORA* IN VOLUME 9!

THE BUTTING-IN MASTER'S LONG NIGHT

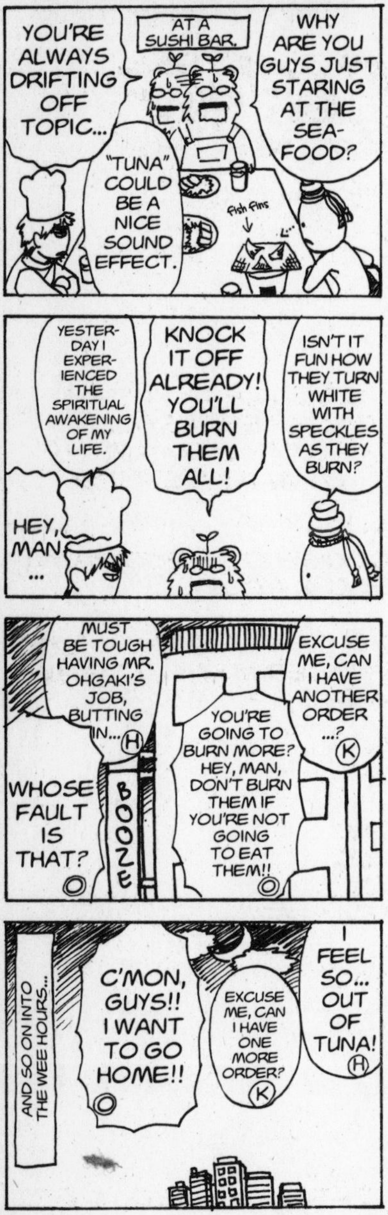
AT A SUSHI BAR.
WHY ARE YOU GUYS JUST STARING AT THE SEA-FOOD?
Fish Fins
"TUNA" COULD BE A NICE SOUND EFFECT.
YOU'RE ALWAYS DRIFTING OFF TOPIC...
ISN'T IT FUN HOW THEY TURN WHITE WITH SPECKLES AS THEY BURN?
KNOCK IT OFF ALREADY! YOU'LL BURN THEM ALL!
YESTER-DAY I EXPER-IENCED THE SPIRITUAL AWAKENING OF MY LIFE.
HEY, MAN ...
EXCUSE ME, CAN I HAVE ANOTHER ORDER ...?
YOU'RE GOING TO BURN MORE? HEY, MAN, DON'T BURN THEM IF YOU'RE NOT GOING TO EAT THEM!!
MUST BE TOUGH HAVING MR. OHGAKI'S JOB, BUTTING IN...
WHOSE FAULT IS THAT?
BOOZE
I FEEL SO... OUT OF TUNA!
EXCUSE ME, CAN I HAVE ONE MORE ORDER?
C'MON, GUYS!! I WANT TO GO HOME!!
AND SO ON INTO THE WEE HOURS...

STAFF PAGE

THE FIENDISH STAFF THAT WORKED ON VOLUME 8

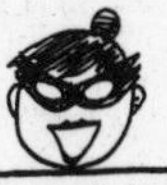

Empress Yoshinon

THE UNBEATABLE POISON QUEEN. HER VOCABULARY CONSISTS ENTIRELY OF SWEAR WORDS. SHE'S A SADIST—THE 21ST CENTURY KITTEN WITH A WHIP!

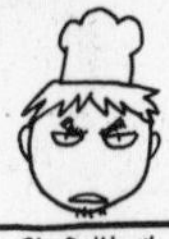

Chef Hitouji

BRILLIANT ILLUSTRATOR WHO PUTS HIS LIFE ON THE LINE FOR COOKING. HE'S TOTALLY ANAL-RETENTIVE ABOUT BOTH COOKING AND DRAWING. HE'S ALSO A SCAREDY-CAT WHO SPINS IN THE SHOWER SO NO ONE CAN SNEAK UP ON HIM.

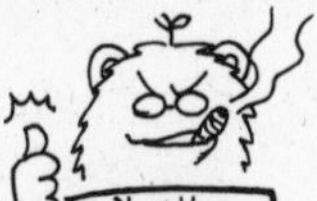

Ohga-king

THE MASTER OF BUTTING-IN, OFTEN COMPARED TO A CARTOON CHARACTER. HE'S ALSO A GOOD COOK. HE WANTED TO START WORKING OUT, BUT HIS FAVORITE PHRASE HAS BECOME, "I'LL DO IT STARTING TOMORROW!"

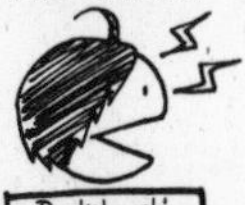

Dr. Kobayashi

THE KING OF 3-D DRAWING AND THE ARTIST WITH THE HANDS OF GOD. HE'S A DRAWING MACHINE WHO CAN'T STAND PRAISE.

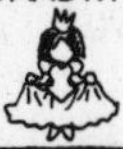

Princess Shibayan

DON'T LET HER SWEET FACE FOOL YOU: SHE'S A SCHEMING PATISSIER. DESPITE HER LOVELY SMILE, SHE'S OFTEN HEARD BITTERLY COMPLAINING IN THE BACKGROUND.

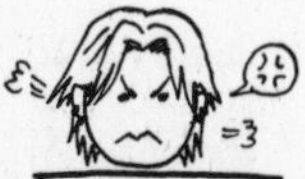

"Hirachi" Hirakawa

A DECENT GUY WHO JUST HAPPENS TO LOOK LIKE A HOODLUM. ORIGINALLY FROM HIROSHIMA. WHEN HE WALKED INTO A REAL ESTATE OFFICE, BEFORE HE COULD EVEN OPEN HIS MOUTH, HE WAS DRIVEN AWAY WITH SHOUTS OF, "NO! NO ROOMS AVAILABL

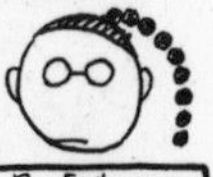

Ryu Fujiwara

A HONG KONG MOVIE FAN WHO'S TRYING TO GROW A CHINESE PIGTAIL. HE HAS A FANTASTIC BODY—THAT GETS BENT OUT OF SHAPE IF HE SLEEPS MORE THAN FIVE HOURS.

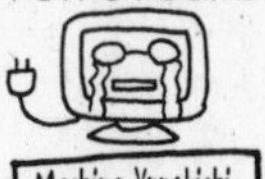

Machine Yunokichi

THE ONE WE RELY ON WHEN EVER WE NEED THE POWER HIS PC. BUT SOME OF US GE JEALOUS AND BERATE HIM: "DON'T THINK YOU'RE SO GR JUST BECAUSE YOU HAVE A YA FANCY-HAIRED FOUR EYE

AND THANKS FOR THE ADDITIONAL ASSISTANC O-BE, DELUSIONAL WEIRDO MONSTER☆, K-MURA MAN, S-SHIMA, F-I AND Y-NO!

AND THANKS FOR ALL OF THE HARD WORK, HIRACHI!!

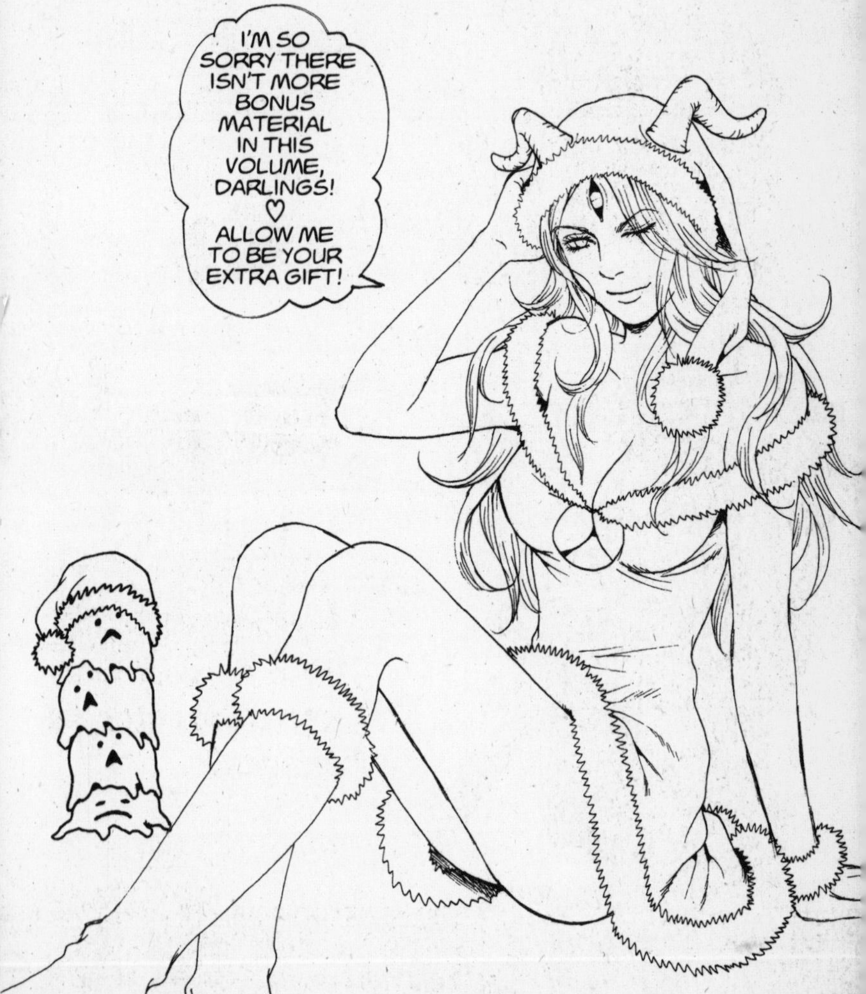
I'M SO SORRY THERE ISN'T MORE BONUS MATERIAL IN THIS VOLUME, DARLINGS! ♡ ALLOW ME TO BE YOUR EXTRA GIFT!

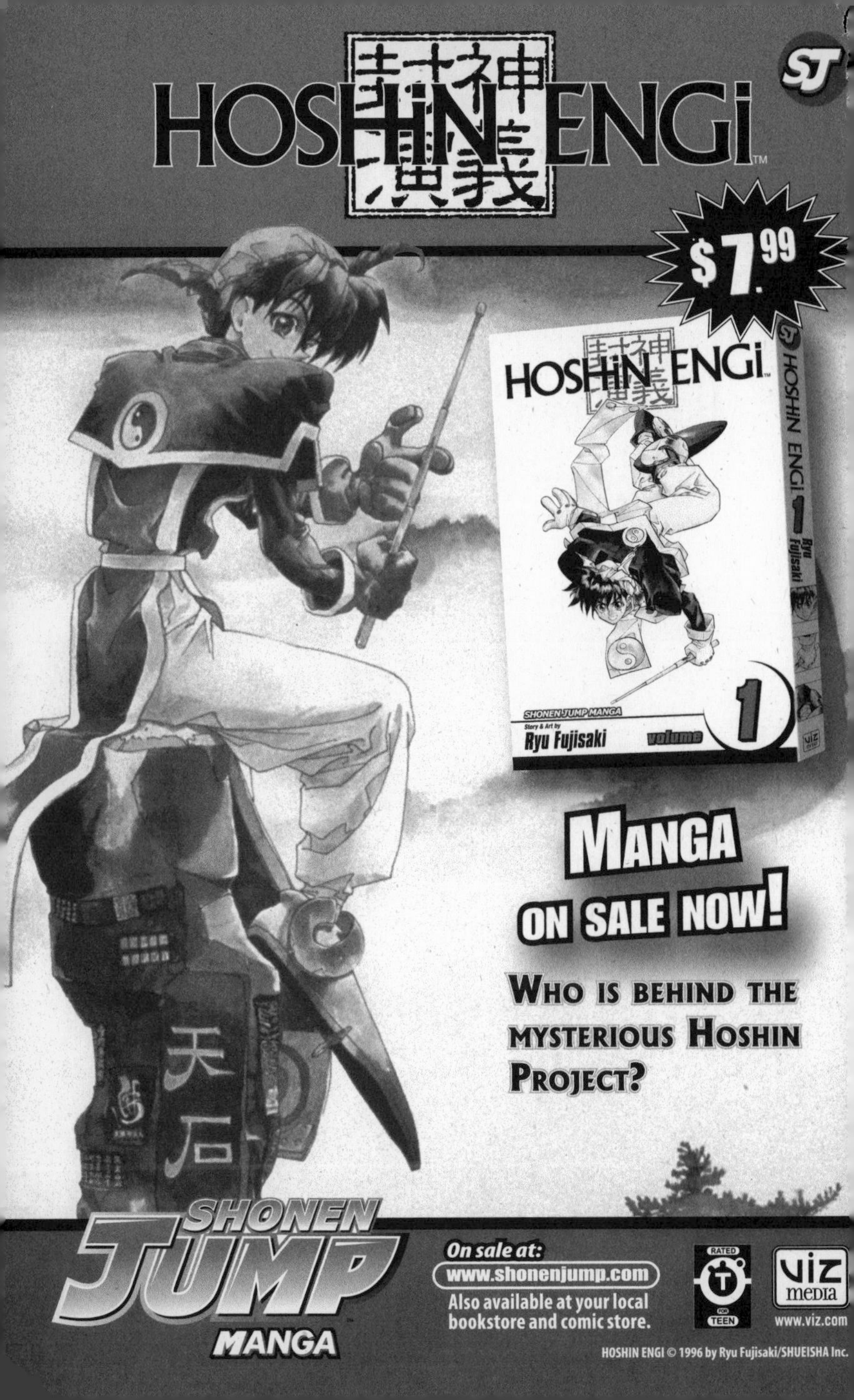
SJ
HOSHIN ENGI™
封神演義
$7.99
HOSHIN ENGI
SHONEN JUMP MANGA
Story & Art by
Ryu Fujisaki
volume 1
MANGA
ON SALE NOW!
WHO IS BEHIND THE
MYSTERIOUS HOSHIN
PROJECT?
SHONEN JUMP MANGA
On sale at:
www.shonenjump.com
Also available at your local
bookstore and comic store.
RATED T FOR TEEN
VIZ media
www.viz.com
HOSHIN ENGI © 1996 by Ryu Fujisaki/SHUEISHA Inc.